The Power and Pains of Polysemy: Maritime Trade, Averages, and Institutional Development in the Low Countries (15th–16th Centuries)

Brill's Studies in Maritime History

VOLUME 15

The titles published in this series are listed at *brill.com/bsmh*

The Power and Pains of Polysemy: Maritime Trade, Averages, and Institutional Development in the Low Countries (15th–16th Centuries)

By

Gijs Dreijer

BRILL

LEIDEN | BOSTON

This publication originates from a European Research Council (ERC) project, Grant Agreement 724544 (AveTransRisk), 2017–2022.

European Research Council
Established by the European Commission

Cover illustration: Schepen in de storm, Andries van Eertvelt (attributed to), 1600–1652.

Library of Congress Cataloging-in-Publication Data

Names: Dreijer, Gijs, 1992- author.
Title: The power and pains of polysemy : maritime trade, averages, and institutional development in the low countries (15th–16th centuries) / by Gijs Dreijer.
Description: Leiden ; Boston : Brill, [2023] | Series: Brill's studies in maritime history, 2405-4917 ; volume 15.
Identifiers: LCCN 2022058755 (print) | LCCN 2022058756 (ebook) | ISBN 9789004540347 (hardback) | ISBN 9789004540354 (ebook)
Subjects: LCSH: Average (Maritime law)—History. | Average (Maritime law)—Benelux countries—History—16th century.
Classification: LCC K1172 .D74 2023 (print) | LCC K1172 (ebook) | DDC 341.4/5—dc23/eng/20230103
LC record available at https://lccn.loc.gov/2022058755
LC ebook record available at https://lccn.loc.gov/2022058756

Typeface for the Latin, Greek, and Cyrillic scripts: "Brill". See and download: brill.com/brill-typeface.

ISSN 2405-4917
ISBN 978-90-04-54034-7 (hardback)
ISBN 978-90-04-54035-4 (e-book)

This book is printed on acid-free paper and produced in a sustainable manner.

Printed by Printforce, United Kingdom

Contents

Acknowledgements

This book is an adapted version of a dissertation defended at two universities (University of Exeter, UK and Vrije Universiteit Brussels, BE) in spring 2021. Compared to the original dissertation, the book has summarised the original first chapter in the introduction, as this was largely a literature review on the political-legal environment of the Low Countries. Moreover, the introduction and conclusion have been substantially revised for this publication, whilst the chapters themselves have largely remained as they were. For readability, I have substantially shortened footnotes in Chapters 3–6, omitting transcriptions of all the primary sourcework in the footnotes, except where the transcription was strictly necessary.

Since submitting the PhD, my insights have (inevitably) progressed further. For this, I would particularly like to thank my dissertation committee, consisting of Frederik Dhondt, Hester Schadee, Louis Sicking and Oscar Gelderblom, for the constructive discussion and feedback on the dissertation during the two defences. This has, without a doubt, further improved the original manuscript. The insights of the two anonymous peer reviewers offered useful feedback in terms of focus, sharpening up the overall argument. Presentations about (parts of) the manuscript, for example at the *Institute of Historical Research* in London, the *International Maritime History Association* conference in Porto an the *World Economic History Congress* in Paris, have also allowed me to incorporate new insights into this book.

In the acknowledgements of the dissertation, I already thanked at length those important in the development of the dissertation: my supervisors Maria Fusaro and Dave De ruysscher, all AveTransRisk members, and in particular Sabine Go, Marta García Garralón, Lewis Wade, Jake Dyble and Antonio Iodice, for making the PhD journey both more fun and more bearable. At the VUB, Marco in 't Veld and Pieter de Reu also deserve a special mention. Of course, I cannot go without thanking my old-and-new mentor Cátia Antunes, who has consistently supported me in the past twelve years. At Brill, I thank Gerlina Harlaftis, as the series editor of the *Studies in Maritime History*, and Alessandra Giliberto, as the editor in charge of handling my proposal, for the smooth and efficient process of turning the dissertation into a book.

I dedicate this book to Suzanne, for her unwavering support and love.

Gijs Dreijer
The Hague, The Netherlands
August 2022

Images, Tables, and Maps

Images

Tables

Maps

Abbreviations

Archives

BE-SAA	Felixarchief Antwerp (Municipal Archives of Antwerp)
BE-SAB	Stadsarchief Brugge (Municipal Archives of Bruges)
BE-RAA	Rijksarchief Antwerp (Antwerp State Archives)
BE-ARB	Rijksarchief België (Belgian State Archives)
BE-MPM	Museum Plantin-Moretus
NL-ZA	Zeeuws Archief Middelburg (Zeeland Archives)
NL-NEHA	Nederlands Economisch-Historisch Archief (Dutch Economic-Historical Archives)
IT-DAT	Fondazione Istituto Internazionale di Storia Economica "F. Datini"

Source Editions

Sneller & Unger, *Bronnen Frankrijk* (Vol. x) Sneller, Z.W. & Unger, W.S. (eds.), *Bronnen tot de geschiedenis van de handel met Frankrijk* (2 Vols.) (The Hague 1930–1942)

Smit, *Bronnen Engeland* Smit, H.J. (ed.), *Bronnen tot de geschiedenis van de handel met Engeland, Schotland en Ierland* (Vol. 2) (The Hague 1942–1950)

Unger, *Bronnen Middelburg* Unger, W.S. (ed.), *Bronnen tot de geschiedenis van Middelburg in den landsheerlijken tijd* (Vol. 3) (The Hague 1931)

Gilliodts-Van Severen, *Coutumes* (Vol. x) Gilliodts-Van Severen, L., *Coutumes des Pays en Comté de Flandre. Quartier de Bruges, Coutume de la Ville de Bruges* (2. Vols.) (Brussels 1874).

Gilliodts-Van Severen, *Espagne* Gilliodts-Van Severen, L., *Cartulaire de l'ancien consulat d'Espagne à Bruges: recueil de documents concernant le commerce maritime et intérieur, le droit des gens public et privé, et l'histoire économique de la Flandre* (Bruges 1901–1902)

Gilliodts-Van Severen, *Cartulaire* (Vol. x) Gilliodts-Van Severen, L., *Cartulaire de l'ancien Estaple de Bruges* (6 Vols.) (Bruges 1904–1909)

Gilliodts-Van Severen & Gaillard, *Inventaire* (Vol. x) Gilliodts-Van Severen, L. & Gaillard, E., *Inventaire des Chartes des archives de la ville de Bruges* (9 vols.) (Bruges 1871–1876).

Pardessus, *Collection* (Vol. x) Pardessus, J-M., *Collection de lois, maritimes antérieures au XVIIIe siècle* (Vols. II, IV & VI) (Paris 1828)

Spruit, *Corpus* Spruit, J.E. *et al* (eds.), *Corpus Iuris Civilis: tekst en vertaling* (vol. III) (The Hague 1996)

De Smidt, *Sententiën* De Smidt, J.T. *et al* (eds.), *Chronologische lijsten van de geëxtendeerde sententiën en procesbundels (dossiers) berustende in het archief van de Grote Raad van Mechelen* (6 Vols.) (Brussels 1988)

Desimoni & Belgrano, *Documenti* Desimoni, C. & Belgrano, L.T. (eds.), *Documenti riguardanti le relazione di Genova col Brabante, La Fiandra e la Borgogna: raccolti ed ordinati* (Genoa 1871)

De Longé, *Coutumes* (Vol. x) De Longé, G. (ed.), *Coutumes du Pays et Duché de Brabant. Quartier d'Anvers, Coutumes de la ville d'Anvers* (4 Vols.) (Brussels 1870–1874)

Strieder, *Notariatsarchiven* Strieder, J., *Aus Antwerpener Notariatsarchiven: Quellen zur deutschen Wirtschaftgeschichte des 16. Jahrhunderts* (Berlin 1930)

Braamcamp Freire, *Noticias* Braamcamp Freire, A., *Noticias da feitoria de Flandres precedidas dos brandies poetas do cancioneiro* (Lisbon 1920)

Drost, *Documents* (Vol. x) Drost, M.A. (ed.), *Documents pour server à l'histoire du commerce des Pays-Bas avec la France jusqu'à 1585* (2 Vols.) (The Hague 1983–1989)

CHAPTER 1

Introduction

1.1 General Average: A Long History from Rhodes to the *Ever Given*

On 23 March 2021, the *Ever Given* ran aground in the Suez Canal.[1] For six days, global trade came to a halt, as ships had to wait until the *Ever Given* was salvaged or take a detour around Africa to reach its destination. The salvage operation was broadcasted around the world (see image 1), as pictures showed small salvage boats trying to save the enormous *Ever Given*, with a capacity of roughly 20.000 TEU (Twenty-foot Equivalent Unit) one of the largest ships on earth. The blockage of the Suez Canal led to billions of euros of damages resulting from lengthy delays, and had repercussions for months as cargo was delayed and, in many cases, had to be disposed with as for example food had passed its due date, or items were already out of fashion by the time they arrived. Following the blockage, the Egyptian port authorities moreover seized the ship, making it impossible to sail further until the problem of compensation was solved. Only on 29 July, the *Ever Given* reached Rotterdam, its intended port of destination.[2]

On 1 April, shortly after the ship was salvaged but still remained in port in Egypt, the Japanese owner of the ship, *Shoe Kisen*, declared General Average. General Average (GA in short) is a procedure – well-known in maritime law since Roman times – that redistributes extraordinary, deliberate costs incurred to save the venture among those participating in it, for example in case of jettison, or, as in the example above, when salvage was necessary to continue the venture.[3] In the *Ever Given* case, the salvage costs were redistributed among all the parties involved, including those with only minor cargo interests on the ship. This meant that hundreds, if not thousands of stakeholders, were

1 The incident led to a wave of coverage. See e.g: 'Suez Canal: Fresh Efforts to Refloat Wedged Container Ship', *BBC*, available at https://www.bbc.com/news/world-middle-east-56550350 {Retrieved 20/12/2021}.

2 See: 'Ever Given, vrachtship dat wereldhandel ontregelde, arriveert in Rotterdam', *NRC*, available at https://www.nrc.nl/nieuws/2021/07/29/ever-given-vrachtschip-dat-wereldhandel-ontregelde-arriveert-in-rotterdam-a4052826 {Retrieved 20/12/2021}.

3 See for an overview of GA: R.H. Cornah & J. Reeder (eds.), *Lowndes and Rudolf: The Law of General Average and the York-Antwerp Rules* (14th edition) (London 2013). See also for a historical overview: J.A. Kruit, 'General Average – General Principle *plus* Varying Practical Application *equals* Uniformity?', *Journal of International Maritime Law*, 21 (2015), 190–202.

 | DOI:10.1163/9789004540354_002

IMAGE 1 Salvage operation of the *Ever Given*

suddenly liable for the salvage costs. It was therefore no surprise that experts predicted that the GA claim would take years to resolve: whilst the action was (eventually) successful and hence GA could in principle be applied, many insurers and other stakeholders already announced they would fight the GA declaration, claiming that the blockage was the fault of the ship crew or of the pilots steering the ship through the Suez Canal.

The *Ever Given* case clearly shows how an instrument drawn from ancient maritime law can still have a huge impact on present-day maritime issues. GA is an excellent example of an institution developed thousands of years ago still used today, even if many have called for its abolition in the meantime.[4] The *Ever Given* is not the only example of a modern GA claim, as was for example shown by the GA declaration following the fire on the *Maersk Honam* on 6 March 2018.[5] Only after lengthy legal proceedings was the GA declaration by the shipping company Maersk accepted by the insurers and other parties. At

4 Critical voices of GA include: K.S. Selmer, *The Survival of General Average: A Necessity or an Anachronism?* (Oslo 1958); P.K. Mukherjee, 'The Anachronism in Maritime Law that is General Average', *WMU Journal of Maritime Affairs*, 4, 2 (2005), 195–209. See for a history-informed defence: Kruit, 'General Average'.

5 'General Average Declared for Stricken Maersk Honam Vessel', *Lloyd's Loading List*, available at https://www.lloydsloadinglist.com/freight-directory/news/General-Average-declared-for-stricken-Maersk-Honam-vessel/71536.htm {Retrieved 18/03/2020}.

present, an internationally accepted maritime legal framework, the so-called York-Antwerp Rules (YAR), governs cases when GA is declared.[6]

Given that GA has existed for thousands of years, one might have expected that the *Ever Given* case could quickly be solved. However, many of the issues discussed in the *Ever Given* case were already points of discussion among parties in the maritime sector in Antiquity, the Middle Ages or the early modern period: the liability of insurers to pay for GA claims was for example a hotly debated topic in both sixteenth-century Castile and in the Low Countries, two important maritime regions in early modern Europe. In order to trace the historical roots of many of these developments, this book focuses on the development of GA and adjacent forms of so-called 'Averages' in the fifteenth and sixteenth-century Low Countries, at a time when economic expansion and concurrent legal and financial developments in risk management drove the expansion of major commercial cities like Bruges and Antwerp. The maritime sector was crucial for these two cities, offering an excellent laboratory to study the development of GA. GA was an important form of risk management in these centuries, but has often been neglected by scholars.

Take the following example: in 1548, the Castilian shipmaster Pedro Consalves Descalantes reached the coast of Bruges (present-day Belgium) with his ship *Madre Dyos*.[7] Descalantes and his crew members were on their way to Arnemuiden (present-day Zeeland, the Netherlands) and Sluis (also present-day Zeeland, but at the time part of the County of Flanders), to deliver Castilian merino wool to be sold in Bruges, one of the major commercial cities in the Low Countries.[8] However, as the ship encountered a storm just before

6 See for the various versions of the YAR: https://comitemaritime.org/work/york-antwerp-rules-yar/ {Retrieved 31/08/2020}. See section 2.4 for an analysis of historical reality and contemporary GA. See also for the settlement: 'High Costs expected after Maersk Honam Fire', *World Maritime News*, available at https://worldmaritimenews.com/archives/247260/high-costs-expected-after-maersk-honam-fire/ {Retrieved 25/03/2020}; 'More Holistic, Industry Wide Approach to Containers would be Welcomed: AP Muller-Maersk CTO', *Insurance Marine News*, available at https://insurancemarinenews.com/insurance-marine-news/more-holistic-industry-wide-approach-to-containers-would-be-welcomed-ap-moller-maersk-cto/ {Retrieved 30/10/2020}.

7 Stadsarchief Brugge (hereafter BE-SAB), Oud Archief, Spaans Consulaat, inv. 304, nr. V.A., *Libro de pleytos ordinarios*, fol. 52r–53r. The case is also transcribed in: L. Gilliodts-Van Severen, *Cartulaire de l'ancien consulat d'Espagne à Bruges: recueil de documents concernant le commerce maritime et intérieur, le droit des gens public et privé, et l'histoire économique de la Flandre* (Bruges 1901–1902) (hereafter: Gilliodts-Van Severen, *Espagne*), 339–341.

8 For the Castilian wool trade: C.R. Philips, 'Spanish Merchants and the Wool Trade in the Sixteenth Century', *The Sixteenth Century Journal*, 14, 3 (1983), 259–282; W.D. Philips jr., 'Merchants of the Fleece: Castilians in Bruges and the Wool Trade', in: P. Stabel, B. Blondé & A. Greve (eds.), *International Trade in the Low Countries (14th–16th Centuries): Merchants, Organisation, Infrastructure* (Leuven, 2000), 75–86.

sailing into port, Descalantes needed to cut masts and cables, which in turn necessitated the use of extraordinary pilotage ships to steer the *Madre Dyos* and its cargo safely into the port of Sluis. The ship voluntarily ran aground a sand bank called *De Zeven Torren* (an act called *strangen* in Dutch), while waiting for the pilots to arrive.[9] This act was successful, and ship and cargo therefore safely reached the port of Sluis. Descalantes subsequently requested the declaration of GA, which was possible when mast and cables were cut or when extraordinary pilotage was necessary.[10] Descalantes' request with the Bruges-based consuls of the Castilian *natio* (the organisational vehicles of foreign merchant communities[11]), who were in charge of administering GA procedure when only Castilians were involved in the County of Flanders, was resisted by the merchants involved in the venture. Represented by Pedro de Berastigny, the merchants argued that the costs for the cable and mast cutting were necessary to save ship and cargo, but that the pilotage costs were the result of negligence on behalf of Descalantes. Notwithstanding their protests, the Castilian consuls ruled in favour of Descalantes, citing the necessity of both acts to save ship and cargo, allowing the costs to be redistributed via GA.[12]

As this case suggests, the Castilians in the Low Countries regularly used GA, a risk management principle already found in Roman maritime law, to share risks when damage occurred. In addition, they actively worked to include new causes for GA under the instrument, for example extraordinary pilotage. Yet despite their frequent use of both GA and other Averages, the complexity of many cases involved and the interesting window that this provides onto early modern maritime trade has rarely been noted by historians. As the case of the *Ever Given* shows, cases of GA are already hard to solve in the present day, but in the late medieval and early modern period, similar issues after damage had occurred were even harder to resolve, because of the complex jurisdictional, legal, and political situation.[13] Add to this complex legal constellation

9 BE-SAB, *Libro de pleytos ordinarios*, fol. 52v.

10 See for an overview of GA: R.H. Cornah & J. Reeder (eds.), *Lowndes and Rudolf: The Law of General Average and the York-Antwerp Rules* (14th edition) (London 2013). See also for a historical overview: Kruit, 'General Average'.

11 See for an overview of the foreign merchant communities in the Low Countries: Blondé, O.C. Gelderblom & Stabel, 'Foreign Merchant Communities in Bruges, Antwerp and Amsterdam', in: D. Calabi & S.T. Christensen (eds.), *Cultural Exchange in Early Modern Europe. Volume 2: Cities and Cultural Exchange in Europe, 1400–1700* (Cambridge 2013), 154–174.

12 BE-SAB, *Libro de pleytos ordinarios*, fol. 53r.

13 See for the complex constellation of late medieval and early modern Europe: S.P. Donlan & D. Heirbaut, '"A patchwork of Accommodations": European Legal Hybridity and Jurisdictional Complexity – an Introduction', in: Donlan & Heirbaut (eds.), *The Laws'*

a growing number of interested parties in a maritime venture, for example the owner of the ship, the shipmaster, merchants and insurers, and one can imagine that dealing with risks, costs and damage in maritime ventures was not an easy task. At the dawn of the early modern period (late fifteenth–early sixteenth century), this was obviously even more difficult due to a lack of rapid communication, and those standardised legal agreements that govern maritime trade today. Attacks at sea and natural hazards were very real dangers which faced ship-owners. Notwithstanding these potential problems, maritime trade in Europe grew steadily between the tenth and eighteenth centuries, and presented Europeans with significant economic gains.[14] This process accelerated because of the so-called 'Commercial Revolution' of the thirteenth century, and the subsequent intensification of commercial ties across Europe has long intrigued historians.[15] Improvements in the maritime industry have figured prominently in the work of historians, as the efficiency of the shipping industry increased significantly between the fourteenth and the eighteenth centuries.[16] The shift from the 'travelling' to the 'sedentary' merchant slowly transformed them from traders into managers who also contributed to the

Many Bodies: Studies in Legal Hybridity and Jurisdictional Complexity, c. 1600–1900 (Berlin 2015), 9–34.

14 See for an excellent Europe-wide overview: P. Malanima, *Pre-Modern European Economy: One Thousand Years (10th–19th Centuries)* (Leiden/Boston 2009). See also: V.N. Bateman, *Markets and Growth in Early Modern Europe* (London 2012), 18–29.

15 See for the early 'Commercial Revolution': C. Wickham, *Framing the Early Middle Ages: Europe and the Mediterranean 400–800* (Oxford 2005); M. McCormick, *Origins of the European Economy: Communications and Commerce, A.D. 300–900* (Cambridge 2001). The term 'Commercial Revolution' originates from Robert Lopez: R.S. Lopez, *The Commercial Revolution of the Middle Ages, 950–1350* (Cambridge 1976). For an excellent historiographical overview of this debate, see: S.A. Reinert & R. Fredona, 'Merchants and the Origins of Capitalism', in: T. Da Silva Lopes, C. Lubinski & H. Tworek (eds.), *The Routledge Companion to Makers of Global Business* (London 2020), 171–188, there 175–177. See for a more general background: B.M.S. Campbell, *The Great Transition: Climate, Disease and Society in the Late-Medieval World* (Cambridge 2016).

16 J. Lucassen & R.W. Unger, 'Shipping, Productivity and Economic Growth', in: Unger (ed.), *Shipping and Economic Growth, 1350–1850* (Leiden/Boston 2011), 3–44; Unger, 'Ships and Shipping Technology', in: C. Jowitt, C. Lambert & S. Mentz (eds.), *The Routledge Companion to Marine and Maritime Worlds, 1400–1800* (London/New York 2020), 221–241; D.C. North, 'Sources of Productivity Change in Ocean Shipping, 1600–1850', *Journal of Political Economy*, 76, 5 (1968), 953–970. For a more critical perspective, see: R.R. Menard, 'Transport Costs and Long-Range Trade, 1300–1800: Was there a European "Transport Revolution" in the Early Modern Era?', in: J.D. Tracy (ed.), *The Political Economy of Merchant Empires: State Power and World Trade 1350–1750* (Cambridge 1991), 228–275.

increased demand for maritime trade, as overseas agents could handle trade in the port city of arrival.[17]

Indeed, technological improvements in shipbuilding and navigation made regular maritime trade between various regions in Europe possible, for example between Southern Europe (primarily the Iberian and Italian Peninsulas) and the Low Countries.[18] Ships became faster and bigger, while navigation instruments became more precise.[19] Correspondingly, operational changes in the position of the shipmaster, ship-owner(s) and merchant(s) had to be reflected in law.[20] These technological and operational changes of course did not mean that maritime trade should necessarily have increased in the late medieval and early modern period in Europe, as natural hazards and threats of attack at sea also made maritime trade a dangerous enterprise. As such, the economic, political and legal circumstances had to be favourable to merchants for them to even start trading via maritime routes and choose this over land transport, which was often slower and more expensive but potentially safer as well.[21]

To deal with all kinds of maritime hazards and risks, merchants used multiple techniques, for example convoys or cargo spreading.[22] Both maritime and economic historians have primarily pointed to the development of marine insurance as a risk management technique, marking it as an important

---

17 Reinert & Fredona, 'Merchants and the Origins of Capitalism', 171–174; F. Mauro, 'Merchant Communities, 1350–1750', in: Tracy (ed.), *The rise of Merchant Empires: Long-Distance Trade in the Early Modern World, 1350–1750* (Cambridge 1990), 255–286, especially 255–256.

18 E.S. Hunt & J.M. Murray, *A History of Business in Medieval Europe, 1200–1550* (Cambridge 1999), 174–176.

19 See for the Low Countries for example: Unger, 'Scheepsbouw en scheepsbouwers', in: G. Asaert, P.M. Bosscher, J.R. Bruijn, W.J. Hoboken, *et al* (eds.), *Maritieme Geschiedenis der Nederlanden* (Vol. 1) (Amsterdam 1976), 155–179.

20 See for a sketch of the major changes: Asaert, 'Scheepsbezit en havens', in: Ibidem, 180–205. In this book, I use shipmaster of commercial ships, as the term captain denoted the leader of a military vessel in the early modern period. See: https://humanities.exeter.ac.uk/history/research/centres/maritime/research/modernity/roles/ {Retrieved 11/09/2020}.

21 See Lucassen & Unger, 'Shipping, Productivity and Economic Growth'.

22 See for an overview: C.A. Davids, 'Zekerheidsregelingen in de scheepvaart en het landtransport, 1500–1800', in: J. Van Gerwen & M.H.D. Van Leeuwen (eds.), *Studies over zekerheidsarrangementen. Risico's, risicobestrijding en verzekeringen in Nederland vanaf de Middeleeuwen* (Amsterdam/The Hague 1998), 183–202; P. Mathias, 'Strategies for Reducing Risk by Entrepreneurs in the Early Modern Period', in: C. Lesger & L. Noordegraaf (eds.), *Entrepreneurs and Entrepreneurship in Early Modern Times: Merchants and Industrialists within the Orbit of the Dutch Staple Market* (The Hague 1995), 5–24, there 22–23; M. Kohn, 'Risk Instruments in the Medieval and Early Modern Economy', Dartmouth College Department of Economics Working Paper No 99-07, available at https://papers.ssrn.com/sol3/papers.cfm?abstract_id=151871.

innovation that enabled merchants to transfer 'uncertainty' into 'risk' by transferring the risk to a third party (i.e. the insurer).[23] Uncertainty, as this book defines it, is an *unanticipated*, possible and involuntary hazard;[24] risk is an *anticipated*, possible and involuntary hazard.[25] As risks can be anticipated, one can take measures to lower the possibility of the outcome, for example by protecting the ship against attacks or taking out insurance. In addition, costs will be defined as the *anticipated*, voluntary payments in exchange for services,[26] an important definition as merchants increasingly started to make a distinction between *risk* and *cost* management from the 1450s onwards. Insurance was indeed an important development to confront risk, but other instruments of maritime risk management with a much longer historical lineage played a major role as well. GA is such an instrument, dating back to Roman law.[27] It seeks to share and manage risk in maritime trade by redistributing extraordinary costs over involved parties in the case of voluntary damage.[28] The *Oxford Dictionary* defines GA as the

> apportionment of loss caused by intentional damage to ship (e.g. cutting away of masts or boats), or sacrifice of cargo and consequent loss of freight, or of expense incurred by putting into a port in distress, by acceptance of towage or other services, to secure the general safety of ship and cargo; in which case contribution is made by the owners (or insurers) of ship, cargo, and freight in proportion to the value of their respective interests.[29]

---

23 See, for a recent work on the subject: A.P. Leonard (ed.), *Marine Insurance: Origins and Institutions, 1300–1850* (Basingstoke 2015). An overview of early modern insurance in: P. Spufford, 'From Genoa to London: The Places of Insurance in Europe', in: Ibidem, 271–297. When referring to insurance, I refer to marine insurance.

24 See also definition #4 in the Oxford English Dictionary for a similar definition: https://www.oed.com/view/Entry/210212#eid17064071 {Retrieved 05/02/2021}.

25 See also definition #2 in the Oxford English Dictionary for a similar definition: https://www.oed.com/view/Entry/166306?rskey=t5t3bY&result=1&isAdvanced=false#eid {Retrieved 05/02/2021}.

26 See also definition #1.b in the Oxford English Dictionary for a similar definition: https://www.oed.com/view/Entry/42302?isAdvanced=false&result=3&rskey=R2ev64& {Retrieved 05/02/2021}.

27 Cornah & Reeder (eds.), *Lowndes and Rudolf*, 3–4.

28 M. Fusaro, 'Sharing Risks, on Averages and Why They Matter', in: Fusaro, A. Addobbati & L. Piccinno (eds.), *General Average and Risk Management in Medieval and Early Modern Europe* (forthcoming).

29 https://en.oxforddictionaries.com/definition/Average {retrieved 13/06/2018}.

GA is still used today, its rules governed by the *Comité Maritime International* under the York-Antwerp Rules, which were first codified in 1881 and have been regularly updated since then.[30] Apart from some general studies on its appearance in Roman and medieval maritime law, however, no academic studies have been dedicated to the development of the instrument after *c.*1450, whereas the early modern period witnessed significant new development in the instrument.[31] Various customary rules regarding contribution following jettison existed in both Europe and Asia, although these were primarily stated to be rules of thumb until the sixteenth century (e.g. 'jettison means average').[32] These rules were not yet actual abstract legal principles properly defined by lawyers, but rather 'guidelines' for merchants to solve the case when jettison occurred.[33] Although most present-day definitions talk about loss, this book will consistently use 'damage' rather than 'loss' for two reasons. First, damage can describe casualties arising to both cargo and ship, whereas loss primarily describes cargo losses or outright shipwreck. Second, losses imply that the situation was final and could not be resolved, which was often not the case: cargo could still be salvaged, for example, whereas ships could be repaired or abandoned to the insurer. For these reasons, the book will consistently use damage to describe both jettisoned cargo and damage to ships, only using loss in quotes and to describe actual, outright losses that could not be reversed (e.g.

30 See for the definition and short history: http://www.duhaime.org/LegalDictionary/Y/YorkAntwerpRules.aspx {retrieved 15/11/2017}.

31 See for dedicated studies on jettison in Roman law: J-J. Aubert, 'Dealing with the Abyss: The Nature and Purpose of the Rhodian Sea-law on Jettison (*Lex Rhodia De Iactu*, D 14.2) and the Making of Justinian's Digest', in: J.W. Cairns, & P.J. Du Plessis (eds.), *Beyond Dogmatics: Law and Society in the Roman World* (Edinburgh 2007), 157–172; E. Chevreau, 'La lex Rhodia de iactu: un exemple de la réception d'une institution étrangère dans le droit romain', *Legal History Review*, 73 (2005), 67–80. For GA in Hanseatic maritime law: G. Landwehr, *Die haverei in den mittelalterlichten deutschen Seerechtsquellen* (Hamburg 1985); Idem, 'Zur begriffsgeschichte der haverei vom 16. bis zum 18. Jahrhundert', in: E. Jayme *et al* (eds.), *Festschrift für Hubert Niederländer: zum siebzigsten Geburtstag am 10. Februar 1991* (Heidelberg 1991), 57–69; E. Frankot, *"Of Laws of Ships and Shipmen": Medieval Maritime Law and its Practice in Urban Northern Europe* (Edinburgh 2012). See for the Mediterranean: E.M. Férrandiz, 'Will the Circle be unbroken? Continuity and Change of the *Lex Rhodia*'s Jettison Principles in Roman and Medieval Mediterranean Rulings', *Al-Masaq: Journal of the Medieval Mediterranean*, 29, 1 (2017), 41–59; O.A. Constable, 'The Problem of Jettison in Medieval Mediterranean Maritime Law', *Journal of Medieval History*, 20, 3 (1994), 207–220.

32 Cornah & Reeder (eds.), *Lowndes and Rudolf*, 1–6. See also: D. De ruysscher, 'Maxims, Principles and Legal Change: Maritime Law in Merchant and Legal Culture (Low Countries, 16th Century)', *Zeitschrift der Savigny-Stiftung für Rechtsgeschichte. Germanistische Abteilung*, 138, 1 (2021), 260–275.

33 De ruysscher, 'Maxims, Principles and Legal Change'.

shipwreck). Furthermore, note that the English language makes a distinction between damage and damages, which is also used in this work: the singular denotes the harm done to someone or something (in our case for example a ship), the plural means "the sum of money claimed or adjudged to be paid in compensation for loss or injury sustained".[34]

Both legal and economic historians have either largely neglected the development of GA or treated it is an instrument that has been stable between its first ancient inception in the Greek 'Rhodian Law' and the current day. Of the latter group, some have used the existence of GA to support the supposed existence of an autonomous maritime law, the so-called *lex maritima*.[35] This has been reinforced by contemporary debates over the supposed outdatedness of GA, a frame unwittingly reinforced by those defending the instrument on historical grounds by pointing out the continuity of GA throughout history.[36] Although the principle has indeed existed for a long time, it is also clear that there have been numerous developments that do not support the idea that the instrument was perfectly stable throughout history. The history of GA for the early modern period is virtually unstudied, something the ERC-funded project *Average-Transaction Costs and Risk Management during the First Globalization (16th–18th centuries)* (in short: *AveTransRisk*) aims to change.[37] What emerged from this project is that there is no strict continuity in the application of GA throughout history, as societies constantly adapted the instrument to cover different needs, contradicting notions of a *lex maritima* and showing the variety of application throughout Europe.[38] To name but one example, many societies, including the sixteenth-century Low Countries, included costs to limit greater damage into GA, a significant deviation from the original principle which only included deliberate direct damage.[39] Not only did the application of GA change

34 See the definition in the *Oxford English Dictionary*: https://www.oed.com/view/Entry/47005?rskey=RZs3zv&result=1#eid {Retrieved 08/03/2021}.

35 An overview of the historiographical trends on GA in: Kruit, 'General Average'.

36 See e.g. Selmer, *The survival*; Mukherjee, 'The Anachronism'. For a defence: Kruit, 'General Average'.

37 See: https://humanities.exeter.ac.uk/history/research/centres/maritime/research/avetransrisk/ {Retrieved 01/05/2020}.

38 See for preliminary results: http://humanities.exeter.ac.uk/history/research/centres/maritime/research/avetransrisk/datasets/ {Retrieved 31/08/2020}.

39 As for example extraordinary pilotage was included in GA. In the Castilian New World trade, which always travelled in convoy, even individual shipwrecks were counted as GA when cargo was salvaged. See: M. García Garralón, 'The Nautical Republic of the *Carrera de Indias*: Commerce, Navigation, Fortuitous Mishaps, and *avería gruesa* in the Sixteenth Century', in: Fusaro, Addobbati & Piccinno (eds.), *General Average* (forthcoming). I thank Marta García Garralón for allowing early access to the draft.

during this period, but multiple varieties of Average were developed, for example to cover the foreseeable operational costs of a maritime venture. In the Low Countries Castilian and Biscayer merchants also introduced compulsory contributions to cover protection costs under the banner of Average, drawing from specifically 'Spanish' innovations that were the result of the complex organisational structure of maritime trade in Castile.[40]

This book fills this historiographical lacuna by studying the development of GA and other forms of Averages in the Low Countries during the fifteenth and sixteenth centuries, primarily in the major commercial cities of Bruges and Antwerp.[41] It uncovers how GA and other forms of Averages changed during this period in relation to the changing circumstances of maritime trade. Both the novelty of the topic and its complexity force us to be somewhat more descriptive than one would wish, but this is necessary to analyse its application fully. A study of the Low Countries highlights the significant changes in maritime risk management during this period vis-à-vis the changing role of GA. As merchants from all over Europe were active in the (southern part of the) Low Countries and actively tried to influence commercial institutions there, Bruges and Antwerp are an ideal laboratory to study the development of GA.[42] The book contributes to three major debates in economic and legal history. First, it studies the effect of GA and other Averages on transaction and protection costs in the framework of institutional formation and development; second, the book contributes to the study of maritime risk management; and third, it contributes to studies on the supposed existence of the *lex maritima*, for which GA has often been used as a *pars pro toto*.[43] In a nutshell, the book argues that the development of GA and other Averages shows a pattern of an operationally efficient combination of different institutions, notwithstanding the profound political, economic and social changes of the period in which the maritime sector was particularly crucial for all parties and stakeholders involved. It subsequently builds on this analysis to argue that without the broadening application of GA and the development of other forms of Average, the Low Countries' maritime economy would have suffered the adverse consequences of excessive

40 See for the so-called *Consulados*: R.S. Smith, *The Spanish Guild Merchant: A History of the Consulado, 1250–1700* (Durham, NC 1940).

41 The literature on Bruges and Antwerp is treated in section 1.5.

42 B.J.P. Van Bavel, 'History as a Laboratory to better Understand the Formation of Institutions', *Journal of Institutional Economics*, 11, 1 (2015), 69–91.

43 The focus inevitably means that other debates are only mentioned in passing or as background information, for example on the effectiveness of (foreign) merchant guilds, legal strategies of (foreign) merchants, conflict management and the facilitative roles of governmental layers. These debates will be introduced in section 1.2.

risk-taking by merchants, while leaving the bulk of the maritime sector without much of instruments to cover itself against risks.

1.2 Transaction Costs, Protection Costs, and Institutional Development

Studying the role of institutions in economic development, and acknowledging their importance, is now commonplace among (economic) historians. The economist Douglass North suggested the study of institutions which "are the humanly devised constraints that structure political, economic and social interactions. They consist of both informal constraints (sanctions, taboos, customs, traditions, and codes of conduct), and formal rules (constitutions, laws, property rights)".[44] Although many organisations are commonly termed 'institutions' in daily use, North warned that the two should remain separate from each other.[45] As such, GA is an institution, as it sets an extracontractual norm; whereas the foreign merchant guilds in the Low Countries (the so-called *nationes*), for example, were not institutions but rather organisational vehicles, although they did enforce norms and thus created and developed institutions to govern the behaviour of its members.[46] Some have tried to modify North's definition of institutions. Sheilagh Ogilvie, for example, stated that institutions are "the structures of rules and norms governing economic transactions".[47] These definitions roughly cover the same thing, but it is important to keep in mind that institutions can be both formal and informal.

Terminology here is important, as various kinds of institutions will be treated in this book. As both legal and economic historians have recognised, legal institutions are key for the possibility to solve conflicts without violence.[48] Much

44 North, 'Institutions', *The Journal of Economic Perspectives*, 5, 1 (1991), 97–112, there 97.

45 Ibidem, 100–101.

46 See for an overview of the foreign merchant communities in the Low Countries: Blondé, Gelderblom & Stabel, 'Foreign Merchant Communities'.

47 S. Ogilvie, '"Whatever is, is Right?" Economic Institutions in Pre-Industrial Europe', *Economic History Review*, 60, 4 (2007), 649–684, there 649–651.

48 As North already argued in: North, 'Law and Economics'. See also: Gelderblom, *Cities of Commerce*, 207; North & Thomas, *The Rise of the Western World*; Epstein, *Freedom and Growth. The Rise of States and Markets in Europe, 1300–1750* (London 2001); Idem, 'Constitutions, Liberties, and Growth in Pre-Modern Europe', in: M. Casson & A. Godley (eds.), *Cultural Factors in Economic Growth* (Heidelberg 2000), 152–181. See for a similar viewpoint: Bateman, *Markets and Growth*, 174. See for the Low Countries: Dumolyn & Lambert, 'Cities of Commerce, Cities of Constraints: International Trade, Government Institutions and the Law of Commerce in Later Medieval Bruges and the Burgundian state', *Tijdschrift voor Sociale en Economische Geschiedenis*, 11, 4 (2014), 89–102.

of the debate has focused on specific cases (e.g. the eleventh-century Maghribi traders or the Champagne Fairs[49]), but analysis of legal institutions in the Low Countries has not been absent from this debate.[50] So-called 'private-order' institutions denote those institutions that are self-enforcing without governmental backing, whilst in 'public-order' institutions (judicial) decisions are enforced by a governmental agency. In this framework, the term 'third-party enforcement' is often used, as governmental legal organisations were a third party when a dispute arose.[51] But note that third-party enforcement could also be private-order, as for example private arbitrators appointed by mutual agreement could solve disputes between merchants. Rather than seeing this as a strict dichotomy, it would be better to speak of a continuum of private-order and public-order solutions, as almost all solutions to resolve conflicts contained elements of both. In fifteenth-century Bruges, for example, arbitration was often mandated by the aldermen in mercantile disputes, but the exact applicable rules were left to the arbitrators.[52]

49 For the Maghribi traders: Greif, 'Reputations and Coalitions in Medieval Trade: Evidence on the Maghribi Traders', *The Journal of Economic History*, 44, 4 (1989), 857–882; Idem, 'Contract Enforceability and Economic Institutions in Early Trade: The Maghribi traders' Coalition', *The American Economic Review*, 83, 2 (1993), 525–548; 'Impersonal Exchange without Impartial Law: The Community Responsibility System', *Chicago Journal of International Law*, 139 (2004), 109–138; 'The Maghribi Traders: A Reappraisal?', *The Economic History Review*, 65, 2 (2012), 445–469; Idem, *Institutions and the Path to the Modern Economy: Lessons from Medieval Trade* (Cambridge 2006), 58–90; J. Edwards & Ogilvie, 'Contract Enforcement, Institutions, and Social Capital: The Maghribi Traders Reappraised', *The Economic History Review*, 65, 2 (2012), 421–444; J.L. Goldberg, 'Choosing and Enforcing Business Relationships in Eleventh-Century Mediterranean: Reassessing the Maghribi Traders', *Past & Present*, 216, 1 (2012), 3–40. Other work on reputations and institutional development is for example: Y. González de Lara, 'The Secret of Venetian Success: A Public-Order, Reputation-Based Institution', *European Review of Economic History*, 12 (2008), 247–285; Van Doosselaere, *Commercial Agreements*, 11. For the Champagne Fairs: Milgrom, North & Weingast, 'The Role of Institutions'; Edwards & Ogilvie, 'What Lessons for Economic Development can we Draw from the Champagne Fairs?', *Explorations in Economic History*, 49 (2012), 131–148.

50 See e.g. Puttevils, *Merchants and Trading*; Gelderblom, *Cities of Commerce*.

51 See for example: Go, 'The Amsterdam Chamber'.

52 See for example: Gilliodts-Van Severen, *Espagne*, 73–75, 95–97 & 137–139. See also: N. Fieremans, '"In the Hope to have Judged a Good Sentence as Merchants": Arbitration as a Litigation Strategy in Late Medieval Bruges', *Tijdschrift voor Rechtsgeschiedenis*, 89, 3–4 (2021), 439–480. See also for comparative cases: S.E. Sachs, 'Conflict Resolution at a Medieval English Fair', in: Cordes & Dauchy (eds.), *Eine Grenze in Bewegung. Öffentliche und private Justiz im Handels- und Seerecht* (Munich 2013), 19–38. An excellent overview can be found in: Cordes & Höhn, 'Extra-Legal and Legal Conflict Management', 515–518.

Furthermore, there is the distinction between 'generalised' and 'particularised' institutions: generalised institutions are open to everyone (e.g. the Antwerp municipal court), but particularised institutions are only accessible to certain groups (e.g. guilds).[53] Closely related to generalised institutions is the concept of the open-access institutions, denoting institutions accessible for everyone. The two things are related and often went hand-in-hand, although institutions could in principle be open access but also be enforced by particularised institutions. There is, by and large, an agreement that 'generalised' institutions are preferable for economic development, but the usefulness of their 'particularised' counterparts is not yet a settled matter in the literature.[54] For the Low Countries, there is also much debate over the various types of legal institutions that could be found, most importantly on the question of which institutional level most efficiently facilitated mercantile and maritime conflict resolution. Oscar Gelderblom has argued that the municipal levels, for example Bruges, Antwerp and Amsterdam were best placed to offer speedy conflict resolution to merchants.[55] Jan Dumolyn and Bart Lambert by contrast argued that Gelderblom understated the role central courts played in conflict resolution, particularly for conflicts that stretched across borders of regions or states or concerned privileges in the Low Countries more broadly.[56] Chapters 4 and 6

53 Ogilvie & Carus, 'Institutions and Economic Growth', 428–436.

54 Ogilvie, *Institutions and European trade: Merchant Guilds, 1000–1800* (Cambridge 2011); Idem, *The European Guilds: An Economic Analysis* (Princeton 2019); Idem & Carus, 'Institutions and Economic Growth', 428–436; R. Grafe & Gelderblom, 'The Rise and Fall of Merchant Guilds: Re-Thinking the Comparative Study of Commercial Institutions in Premodern Europe', *Journal of Interdisciplinary History*, 40, 4 (2010), 477–511; Lucassen & T. De Moor (eds.), *The Return of the Guilds* (Cambridge 2008). For the Low Countries: B. De Munck, P. Lourens & Lucassen, 'The Establishment and Distribution of Craft Guilds in the Low Countries 1000–1800', in: M. Prak *et al.* (eds), *Craft Guilds in the Early Modern Low Countries: Work, Power and Representation* (Aldershot 2006), 32–73.

55 Gelderblom, *Cities of Commerce*, especially 102–140. A similar view can be found in: Stabel, 'Economic Development, Urbanization and Political Organisation in the Late Medieval Low Countries', in: P. Bernholz, M.E. Streit & R. Vaubel (eds.), *Political Competition, Innovation and Growth: A Historical Analysis* (Berlin/Heidelberg 1998), 183–204; Blockmans, 'Voracious States and Obstructing Cities: An Aspect of State Formation in Preindustrial Europe', *Theory and Society*, 18, (1989), 733–755; Idem, 'The Low Countries in the Middle Ages', in: R. Bonney (ed.), *The Rise of the Fiscal State in Europe, c. 1200–1815* (Oxford 1999), 281–308. In a comparative perspective, others have also pointed to the examples of Bruges, Antwerp and Ghent. See for example: J. Bradford DeLong & A. Shliefer, 'Princes and Merchants: European City Growth before the Industrial Revolution', *Journal of Law and Economics*, 36, 3 (1993), 671–702, there 677; G.W. Cox, 'Political Institutions, Economic Liberty, and the Great Divergence', *Journal of Economic History*, 77, 3 (2017), 724–755, there 732.

56 Dumolyn & Lambert, 'Cities of Commerce, Cities of Constraints'.

tackle this question on the basis of original source analysis, arguing that until the 1530s the central courts indeed played an important role in conflict resolution: from the 1540s onwards, Antwerp consolidated mercantile and maritime jurisdiction.[57]

For North and others associated with the school of 'New Institutional Economics', good institutions promote economic growth by reducing so-called 'transaction costs'.[58] Transaction costs are all the costs that are associated with participating in a market. Transaction costs are usually divided into three categories: information costs (e.g. surveying the market), bargaining costs (e.g. drawing contracts) and enforcement costs (e.g. the costs of enforcing contracts). Legal institutions are a key element in North's view, as they can offer low enforcement and bargaining costs when properly devised.[59] Lower transaction costs from a proper institutional-legal design can be managed, for example when courts offered speedy and impartial judgements. It is often difficult to measure transaction costs, even with available quantitative sources. The direct 'costs' of participating in a market, such as entry fees for a guild, are measurable, in principle, but by contrast, information costs are hard to pin down.[60] As a result, discussions on transaction costs are primarily theoretical. Sources in the Low Countries do not allow for a quantitative assessment of GA, and even where the sources offer quantitative information, sources cannot properly measure all the effects of GA on transaction costs. What can be done, however, is assess the impact of GA and other Averages in a theoretical way on transaction costs such as bargaining and enforcement costs.

Another well-known conundrum in economic history is the issue of protection costs. The economic historian Frederic Lane proposed that part of the explanation for Venetian success was its ability to shift so-called protection costs to

57 See also: De ruysscher, *"Naer het Romeinsch recht"*.

58 O.E. Williamson, 'The Economics of Organization: The Transaction Costs Approach', *American Journal of Sociology*, 87, 3 (1981), 549–577; Idem, 'Transaction-Cost Economics: The Governance of Contractual Relations', *Journal of Law and Economics*, 22 (1979), 233–262; R.H. Coase, 'The Nature of the Firm', *Economia*, 16, 4 (1937), 386–405. See for Douglass North's idea: North, *Transaction Costs, Institutions, and Economic Performance*, International Center for Economic Growth Occasional Paper Series, nr. 30 (San Francisco 1992).

59 North, 'Law and Economics in Historical Perspective', in: F. Cafaggi, A. Nicita & U. Pagano (eds.), *Legal Orderings and Economic Institutions* (London 2007), 46–53, there 47.

60 J. Maucourant, 'New Institutional Economics and History', *Journal of Economic Issues*, 46, 1 (2012), 193–208; see also Q. Van Doosselaere, *Commercial Agreements and Social Dynamics in Medieval Genoa* (Cambridge 2009), 6–7. Most discussions are therefore theoretical, see e.g.: North, 'Transaction Costs in History', *Journal of European Economic History*, 14, 3 (1985), 557–576; Idem, 'Law and Economics'.

the state in the trade with the Levant.[61] This, for example, meant guarding its ships against violence. However, by paying for those costs, the Venetian state also allowed Venetian merchants to defend its monopolistic trade in the Levant. The profits flowing from the monopolistic trade is what Lane called 'protection rents'. Other examples of organisations and states successfully incorporating protection costs (thus creating protection rents) were the Dutch East India Company (*Vereenigde Oostindische Compagnie*, VOC) and the Portuguese *Estado da Índia* in Asia.[62] On the other hand, Lane also pointed out that other (state or non-state) entities could raise protection costs for enemies and hence diminish protection rents.[63] In short, Lane saw violence and profit as intimately connected.[64]

Lane noted the Castilian efforts to provide convoy ships and artillery for the New World trade, but stopped short of providing a full analysis of the case.[65] In Castile, the efforts to provide protection rents for the merchants of the various *Consulados* (the monopolistic merchant guilds running the trade, for example with Flanders[66]) were intimately connected to Average, as their names all included a nod to 'Averages' (*avería* in Castilian). Several non-contractual compulsory contributions, paid in advance, were levied by the *Consulados* and the Spanish *nationes* in the Low Countries to cover protection costs (artillery and convoy ships) for its trading fleet, among other expenses. Spanish historiography has paid particular attention to the New World trade and the so-called *avería*, although the theory of protection costs and protection rents has not been explicitly used in this regard.[67] This clearly shows the numerous meanings of Average in the sixteenth century, as these compulsory contributions were not necessarily intrinsically linked to GA in any sense (see Chapter 6). The next chapter analyses all varieties of Average and introduces the concept of polysemy, the fact that the same word can have multiple meanings, as key to understand the different applications of Averages in the Low Countries.[68]

---

61 F.C. Lane, *Profits from Power: Readings in Protection Costs and Violence-Controlling Enterprises* (New York 1979), 13 & 25–26.

62 Ibidem, 15–20; N. Steensgaard, 'The Dutch East India Company as an Institutional Innovation', in: M. Aymard (ed.), *Dutch Capitalism and World Capitalism* (Cambridge 1982), 235–257.

63 Lane, *Profits from Power*, 13.

64 Ibidem, 50–65.

65 Ibidem, 37 & 44.

66 See for an overview: Smith, *The Spanish Guild Merchant*.

67 G. Céspedes del Castillo, 'La Avería en el Comercio de Indias', *Anuario de Estudios Americanos*, 2 (1945), 515–698; M.L. Talavan, 'La avería en el tráfico marítimo-mercantil indiano: notas para su studio (siglos XVI–XVIII)', *Revista Complutense de Historia de América*, 24 (1998), 113–145. See also: R.P. Fagel, *De Hispano-Vlaamse wereld: de contacten tussen Spanjaarden en Nederlanders 1496–1555* (Nijmegen 1996), 135–162.

68 These varieties are introduced in detail in the first chapter.

Both transaction and protection costs are useful analytical tools when analysing GA and other Averages in the sixteenth-century Low Countries. The Spanish varieties for example raised protection costs, but not necessarily transaction costs.[69] The goal was to minimise the risk of damage, thus in theory lowering transaction costs, diminishing the need to take out insurance and prevent disputes afterwards. Yet equalling the two types of 'costs' obscures the important conceptual differences between them. Most importantly, transaction costs are often analysed on the level of 'the economy' or 'the market'.[70] This means that institutions and their effects on transaction costs are studied on the aggregate level, as they are supposed to have similar effects on those participating in 'the market'. Although these costs were of course very real, they were also more abstract costs. In contrast, protection costs had a direct monetary impact. When protection costs rose, transaction costs may well have risen as well, due to higher risk and/or uncertainty, but a relatively small increase in protection costs should have had no significant influence on the ability of a group of merchants to participate in the market. In the Castilian case, for example, the *Consulado* and the *natio* were instrumental in lowering transaction costs, as they lowered information costs (by bringing together information and knowledge[71]) and enforcement costs (by negotiating an internal jurisdiction, making conflict resolution speedy and cheap), whilst on the other hand actual protection costs rose to protect trade.[72] Chapter 6 analyses this contradictory situation in greater detail.

The concurring and competing effects on transaction and protection is exactly what makes the study of GA so fascinating, for it offers a historical case study in the complexity of institutions and institutional formation. This book therefore takes issue with the singular focus on 'good' institutions as lowering transaction costs, as the historical record on GA shows it could have both positive and negative effects, depending on the circumstances. Moreover, criticising compulsory contributions as institutions which potentially raised transaction costs ignores their significant role in minimising moral hazard (defined as the "the lack of incentive to avoid risk where there is protection

69 Fagel, *De Hispano-Vlaamse wereld*, 484.

70 See e.g.: North, 'Transaction Costs in History'.

71 Although this should not be taken too far. Good business after all depends largely on having access to unique information. Even within a *natio*, information therefore differed among the members, as all were engaged in their own trade. See for the importance of information: F. Trivellato, *The Familiarity of Strangers: The Sephardic Diaspora, Livorno, and Cross-Cultural Trade in the Early Modern Period* (New Haven 2014), 153–193.

72 Lane, *Profits from Power*, 12–22.

against its consequences, e.g. by insurance"[73]) from insurance, as well as its ability to incorporate protection costs.[74] Although the analytical tools of New Institutional Economics (e.g. transaction costs) are definitely useful for historical analysis, a singular focus on 'efficiency' (i.e. "the rational allocation of resources for economic purposes"[75]) obscures historical reality, as efficiency was never a goal for merchants in the sixteenth-century Low Countries. For the government, meanwhile, the goal was rather to make the management of the economy into an acceptable moral endeavour, respecting the peculiar legal status of all actors involved.[76] Hence the focus of many contemporary jurists was on the concept of equity as well, into which discussions on GA fitted well thanks to its equitable nature.

The role of institutions often figures in debates on the economic development of Europe, for example discussions of the so-called 'Great Divergence' or the European 'Little Divergence'.[77] Many authors have taken up the argument that institutions are the most important factor in economic development, most famously in the work of Daron Acemoglu and James Robinson on the relationship between 'inclusive' institutions and economic growth, primarily on the Anglo-American world.[78] Criticism is however also commonplace when examining the institutional approach, for example because North's acceptance of culture and ideology as a key point can lead to an "idealist or cultural

73 See the definition in the *Oxford English Dictionary*: https://www.oed.com/view/Entry/122086?redirectedFrom=moral+hazard#eid36035063 {Retrieved 21/01/2021}.

74 Ibidem. For moral hazard in insurance contracts: C.A. Heimer, *Reactive Risk and Rational Action: Managing Moral Hazard in Insurance Contracts* (Berkeley, CA 1985), 123–125.

75 Definition taken from: https://www.britannica.com/topic/efficiency-economics-and-organizational-analysis {Retrieved 22/01/2021}.

76 See for a general idea of the 'moral economy': C. Muldrew, *The Economy of Obligation: The Culture of Credit and Social Relations in Early Modern England* (Basingstoke 1998). For a plea to reconnect cultural and economic approaches: Trivellato, 'Economic and Business History as Cultural History: Pitfalls and Possibilities', *I Tatti Studies in the Italian Renaissance*, 22, 2 (2019), 403–410.

77 See for an overview: P.H.H. Vries, *Escaping Poverty: The Origins of Modern Economic Growth* (Vienna 2013); North & R.P. Thomas, *The Rise of the Western World: A New Economic History* (Cambridge 1973); A.M. De Pleijt & J.L. Van Zanden, 'Accounting for the "Little Divergence": What Drove Growth in Pre-Industrial Europe?', *European Review of Economic History*, 20, 4 (2016), 387–416. An excellent recent article on the Great Divergence is: V. Court, 'A Reassessment of the Great Divergence Debate: Towards a Reconciliation of Apparently Distinct Determinants', *European Review of Economic History* (2019), 1–42.

78 D. Acemoglu & J.A. Robinson, *Why Nations Fail: The Origins of Power, Prosperity and Poverty* (London 2013).

deadlock".[79] Other critics have advanced that it is especially hard to measure transaction costs in a concrete manner in historical situations, a point that is also true for GA, meaning effects on transaction costs have to be assessed in a qualitative manner.[80] Other approaches critical of the institutionalist framework for example point to the role of individuals ('agents') who both worked within and outside established institutional frameworks to create new business opportunities.[81] Finally, criticism has been levelled at the fact that institutions focus too much on continuity rather than *dis*contuity.[82]

Deirdre McCloskey, one of the main criticasters of the New Institutional Economics, in particular has argued against the idea of path dependency, a concept commonly invoked in the New Institutional Economics.[83] Path dependency broadly denotes the idea that 'history matters', but in more expansive definitions means that historical choices constrain the future decisions of actors in society as the set of choices is narrowed.[84] According to North, path dependency is "a way to narrow conceptually the choice set and link decisions making through time".[85] Path dependency has for example been invoked by North to explain the economic rise of Britain.[86] Yet the theory of path dependence also has its limits in explaining historical development, particularly as it

79 See also: K. Basu, E. Jones & E. Schlicht, 'The Growth and Decay of Custom: The Role of the New Institutional Economics in Economic History', *Explorations in Economic History*, 24 (1987), 1–21; Maucourant, 'New Institutional Economics', there 193 for the quote.

80 Maucourant, 'New Institutional Economics'; see also Van Doosselaere, *Commercial Agreements*, 6–7.

81 See for example: C.A.P. Antunes & A. Polonia (eds.), *Beyond Empires: Global, Self-Organizing, Cross-Imperial Networks, 1500–1800* (Leiden 2016). This trend has to date primarily focused on the role of agents in an (inter-)imperial setting, for example in the chartered companies.

82 D.N. McCloskey, 'The Great Enrichment: A Humanistic and Social Scientific Account', *Scandinavian Economic History Review*, 64, 1 (2016), 6–18. A critique in: A. Greif & J. Mokyr, 'Institutions and Economic History: A Critique of Professor McCloskey', *Journal of Institutional Economics*, 12, 1 (2016), 29–41. See for long-term institutional perspectives: North & Thomas, *The Rise of the Western World*, 146–156. See also for a similar argument: Van Zanden, *The Long Road to the Industrial Revolution: The European economy in a Global Perspective, 1000–1800* (Leiden/Boston 2009), especially 233–266.

83 See for theoretical work: A. Bennett & C. Elman, 'Complex Causal Relations and Case Study Methods: The Example of Path Dependence', *Political Analysis*, 14, 3 (2006), 250–267. For a critical discussion: A. Kay, 'A Critique of the Use of Path Dependency in Policy Studies', *Public Administration*, 83, 3 (2005), 553–571. For its uses in an economic-historical setting: North, *Institutions, Institutional Change and Economic Performance* (Cambridge 1990), 92–104, especially 98–99.

84 Kay, 'A Critique', 553–554.

85 North, *Institutions*, 98.

86 Idem, 'Law and Economics', 49–50.

is quite good at explaining continuity but not so much at explaining *dis*continuity.[87] This is a fair point (and path dependency on its own can rarely if ever explain economic outcomes), yet one useful part of theories of path dependency, as also emphasised by North, is that *constraints* matter in the development of institutions.[88] And indeed, while path dependency does not explain the development of GA on its own, this book shows that the choices of various governmental and private actors were constrained in tense negotiations with the other parties on the subject. As no party was powerful enough to push through its will in the Low Countries' maritime sector, negotiations were ways at the order of the day and therefore *constraints* were common for all actors, with clear consequences for future actors as well.[89] What we observe in the development of GA is not necessarily the long-term effects of the constraints, but rather where the constraints originated.

Notwithstanding criticism on the institutionalist school, this book will still employ an analysis largely based on their toolkit for four reasons, even if it does not accept all the premises of the New Institutional Economics. First, this enables comparisons between different geographical regions, since merchants dealt with transaction costs almost everywhere.[90] Second, the institutional approach allows for a long-term, evolutionary analysis, which is apt in the case of GA.[91] Third, it allows us to integrate legal-historical and economic-historical approaches, as North already advocated.[92] Fourth and finally, on a more practical note, the (primarily legal) sources permit an in-depth institutional analysis

87 Key, 'A Critique', 554. Other criticisms include the lack of a clear normative focus, or the fact that path dependency does not include the distributive effects of institutions. See: Ibidem. See also: Ogilvie, '"Whatever is, is Right?"', 656–657.

88 North, *Institutions*, 98–99. See also: Bennet & Elman, 'Complex Causal Relationships', 256–259.

89 As also shown in insurance negotiations: De ruysscher & J. Puttevils, 'The Art of Compromise: Legislative Deliberations on Marine Insurance Institutions in Antwerp (c. 1550–c. 1570)', *BMGN-Low Countries Historical Review* 130, 3 (2015), 25–49.

90 North, 'Law and economics', 48–50.

91 See: Puttevils, 'Waarom deden sommige handelssteden het zo goed? Een overzicht van het historisch onderzoek naar handel en instituties in Nederlandse en Europese steden, 1300–1800', *Stadsgeschiedenis*, 10, 1 (2015), 74–95.

92 North, 'Law and Economics'; also R. Harris, 'The Encounters of Economic History and Legal History', *Law and History Review*, 21, 2 (2003), 297–346; Idem, 'The Uses of History in Law and Economics', *Theoretical Inquiries in Law*, 4, 2 (2003), 659–696; Idem, 'Legal Scholars, Economists, and the Interdisciplinary Study of Institutions', *Cornell Law Review*, 96 (2011), 789–810.

but hardly leave a basis for other approaches such as the network-and-agent approach, which depends on the study of individuals and their actions.[93]

How to analyse institutions is still subject of debate, as many have found the overarching focus on efficiency insufficient to explain economic success and failure. Following this critique, this book uses alternative approaches from mainstream institutional literature, in particular drawing on the work of Sheilagh Ogilvie. Ogilvie argued that most economists and economic historians view institutions that come into being as efficient, simply because their mere existence in an economically successful society proves the efficiency of these institutions.[94] Simply because Antwerp was an economically successful city does not mean *per se* that its institutions were efficient, as other factors could play a role as well (e.g. geography, or simply luck). A distributional or conflictual view of institutions fits the pre-modern study of institutions better. In the words of Ogilvie,

> [...] institutions affect not just the efficiency of an economy but also how its resources are distributed; that is institutions affect both the size of the total economic pie and who gets how big a slice. [...] Which institution (or set of institutions) results from this conflict will be affected not just by its efficiency but by its distributional implications for the most powerful individuals and groups.[95]

Therefore, she argues for an approach that "incorporates the distributional activities of institutions into its analysis without assuming such activities to be efficient, [which] can explain many facts about pre-modern institutions that 'efficiency' views cannot".[96] Indeed, using modern eyes to study pre-modern institutions (e.g. through the lens of 'efficiency') is misleading, as the concept of efficiency is *an sich* modern, and was not on the mind of the early modern merchant or lawmaker. Among the advantages of Ogilvie's approach is that it explicitly takes stock of the social, cultural or political reasons behind the emergence and existence of institutions.[97] Moreover, this approach emphasises the

93 For the Low Countries, the institutionalist approach has in any case offered fruitful results, see: Gelderblom, *Cities of Commerce – The Institutional Foundations of International Trade in the Low Countries, 1250–1650* (Princeton 2013); Puttevils, *Merchants and Trading in the Sixteenth Century: The Golden Age of Antwerp* (London 2015).

94 Ogilvie, "'Whatever is, is Right?'", 651–658.

95 Ibidem, 662.

96 Ibidem, 663.

97 Ibidem, 662–665. A similar view in: Acemoglu, S. Johnson & Robinson, 'Institutions as the Fundamental Cause of Long-Run Growth', in: P. Aghion & S.N. Durlauf (eds.), *Handbook of Economic Growth* (Amsterdam/Paris 2005) (Vol. 1), 385–472, there 410–417.

interplay between different institutions: institutions never existed on their own, but were part of a larger institutional framework and changes in a particular institution had effects on the equilibrium in which it existed.[98] This book therefore aims to incorporate power and economic interests into the institutionalist framework, offering an alternative, more complete analysis of institutional development.

For the study of GA and other Averages, this conceptualisation is especially fruitful for five reasons. First, the development of GA in legal practice and formal law was the result of protracted negotiations between various powerful parties (e.g. the central government and the Castilian *natio*), emphasising the effects of political and judicial power (but also the constraints that all actors faced[99]), as every scrap of jurisdiction was the object of a fierce power struggle which also had repercussions for the wider maritime sector.[100] Second, GA belies the idea that all institutions were necessarily efficient, for it had ambivalent effects on transaction costs as it could in theory both raise and lower those costs.[101] Third, GA and other Averages often served multiple goals, even if this was not the initial goal of the institution: managing protection costs was for example a form of cost management, but also lowered moral hazard related to the employment of insurance as those insured were obliged to contribute to mutual protection efforts, and lowered the risk of actual damage in the third place.[102] Fourth, we cannot understand the development of GA without taking into account the wider institutional framework, for example developments in marine insurance.[103] Finally, neither 'efficiency', 'cultural' or 'accidental' approaches to institutions can on their own explain the development of GA in the sixteenth-century Low Countries, whereas the distributional approach allows for a combination of factors to explain its development. The complex interplay between the various factors (legal, social, political, economic) also

98 Ibidem, 681. This was for example the case, in the maritime sector, with insurance and GA, whose governance systems mutually influenced the other. See section 4.2.

99 North, *Institutions*, 98–99. See also: Bennet & Elman, 'Complex Causal Relationships', 256–259.

100 See e.g. for the jurisdictions of the Southern European *nationes* in Antwerp, who had jurisdiction over internal maritime cases: J.A. Goris, *Étude sur les colonies marchandes méridionales (Portugais, Espagnols, Italiens) à Anvers de 1488 à 1567* (Louvain 1925) (hereafter: Goris, *Étude*), 36; De ruysscher, *"Naer het Romeinsch recht alsmede den stiel mercantiel". Handel en recht in de Antwerpse rechtbank (16e–17e eeuw)* (Kortrijk 2009), 119–121.

101 This depended largely on the enforcement mechanism, see below.

102 Heimer, *Reactive Risk and Rational Action*, 123–125.

103 Ogilvie & A.W. Carus, 'Institutions and Economic Growth in Historical Perspective', in: Aghion & Durlauf (eds.), *Handbook of Economic Growth* (Amsterdam/Paris 2014) (Vol. 2A), 403–513, there 461. See also section 4.2.

offers a nuanced take on institutional formation and development that does not simplify historical complexities.

GA was not *necessarily* efficient, as it could both raise and lower transaction costs, depending on the enforcement mechanism; the basic principle could be found in all kind of societies, including in the Middle East and China, casting doubt on cultural explanations;[104] and nor was the institution 'accidental', for the institution was consciously incorporated in legal compilations since Roman times surviving until the present day. Whilst this book uses Ogilvie's conceptualisation, it does not deny that GA could, in principle, have efficient characteristics. As Ogilvie herself also notes, the distributive approach to institutional development does not *per se* exclude the possibility of efficiency, but argues that the efficiency and distributive implications of institutions simply cannot be separated.[105] Moreover, she does not exclude the possibility of path dependency in institutional development, but argues that present models often do not allow for 'institutional externalities' that can explain potential disruptions to the path.[106] For these reasons, this book will employ Ogilvie's distributional view of institutions.

1.3 Maritime Trade and Risk Management

Whereas GA has rarely merited proper attention in the study of maritime risk management, marine insurance has been given abundant attention by economists and historians. Carl Reatz for example already published a volume on the history of European insurance in 1870.[107] The economists Frank Knight and Douglass North subsequently incorporated insurance into their theoretical economic frameworks, famously portraying insurance as an important institutional development underpinning the expansion of European trade between the twelfth and eighteenth centuries.[108] According to Knight,

104 For the Middle East: H.S. Khalilieh, *Islamic Maritime Law: An Introduction* (Leiden/Boston 1998), 87–91. For China: A. Reid, 'The Hybrid Maritime Actors of Southeast Asia', in: C. Buchet & G. Le Bouëdec (eds.), *The Sea in History – the Early Modern World* (London 2017), 112–122, there 118.

105 Ogilvie, '"Whatever is, is Right?"', 665–668.

106 Ibidem, 667.

107 C.F. Reatz, *Geschichte des Europäischen Seeversicherungsrecht* (Leipzig 1870).

108 North, *Institutions*, 126–127; Idem, 'Law and Economics', 49; Idem, 'Institutions, Transaction costs, and the Rise of Merchant Empires', in: Tracy (ed.), *The Political Economy of Merchant empires*, 22–40, there 28–29; F.H. Knight, *Risk, Uncertainty, and Profit* (Boston/New York 1921), 247–253; A.C. Williams & R.M. Heins, *Risk Management and Insurance* (New York 1964), 240–258, especially 240–241.

insurance was an example of an "innovation that transformed uncertainty into risk".[109] North followed this claim, arguing that merchants were able to make an adequate assessment of the risks involved with maritime trade and were able to anticipate these risks, for example by insuring the cargo.[110] According to North, this institutional development facilitated the commercial expansion of European trade, alongside other important inventions such as to banking, the Bill of Exchange (BoE), and new partnership forms such as the *commenda*.[111] The elegance of insurance lay in the ability merchants could *transfer* risk to a third party before the venture (*ex ante*) in exchange for a small part of the insured sum (the premium), as opposed to GA which *shared* risks *ex post*.[112] Since the work of scholars like Reatz, Knight, Violet Barbour, and Florence Edler-De Roover, the development of (marine) insurance has therefore figured as a major object of study for economic and legal historians as one of the factors that made commercial (maritime) expansion possible.[113] For Bruges and Antwerp its historical development is also well-studied.[114]

Notwithstanding its advantages, the fact that insurance also allowed for speculative behaviour means it has serious drawbacks in studying transaction costs in a historical setting.[115] The development of financial markets at early

109 Knight, *Risk, Uncertainty, and Profit*, 247–253; North, *Institutions*, 126–127.

110 North, *Institutions*, 126–127.

111 Ibidem. For the commercial expansion, see: McCormick, *Origins of the European Economy*; Spufford, *Profits and Power: The Merchant in Medieval Europe* (London 2006). For a general overview: Reinert & Fredona, 'Merchants and the Origins of Capitalism'; Hunt & Murray, *A History of Business*. For a general perspective on financial innovation in the pre-modern economy: Spufford, *From Antwerp to London. The Decline of Financial Centres in Europe*. Ortelius Lecture NIAS 4 (Wassenaar 2005). More specifically for the Low Countries, see: R. De Roover, *Money, Banking and Credit in Mediaeval Bruges* (Cambridge MA 1948); E. Aerts, 'Wisselruiterij in de Lage Landen. De wisselbrief op de Brugse geldmarkt tijdens de late middeleeuwen', in: G. Le Clercq (ed.) *Ter Beurze: Geschiedenis van de Aandelenhandel in België, 1300–1900* (Bruges/Antwerp 1992), 32–47; Idem, 'Geld en krediet: Brugge als financieel centrum', in: V. Vermeersch (ed.), *Brugge en Europa* (Antwerp 1992), 56–71; Idem, 'Italian Presence in the Late Medieval Bruges Stock Market', in: L. Brunori, S. Dauchy, O. Descamps & X. Prévost (eds.), *Le droit face à l'économie sans travail: l'approche internationale* (Vol. 2), 169–221; H. Van der Wee, 'Sporen van disconto te Antwerpen tijdens de 16e eeuw', *Bijdragen voor de Geschiedenis der Nederlanden*, 10 (1956), 68–128.

112 J.P. Van Niekerk, *The Development of the Principles of Insurance Law in the Netherlands from 1500 to 1800* (2 vols.) (Hilversum 1998), 713–808.

113 Reatz, *Geschichte*; V. Barbour, 'Marine Risks and Insurance in the Seventeenth Century', *Journal of Economic and Business History*, 1, 4 (1928–1929), 561–596; F. Edler-De Roover, 'Early Examples of Marine Insurance', *Journal of Economic History*, 5, 2 (1945), 172–200; Knight, *Risk, Uncertainty and Profit*, 247–253.

114 See section 4.2 for extensive references and a historiographical appraisal.

115 See: North, 'Transaction Costs in History'.

stock exchanges in Bruges and Antwerp in the fourteenth to sixteenth centuries and Amsterdam in the seventeenth century coincided with the coming-of-age of insurance, both for speculative and risk management purposes.[116] On these stock exchanges (so-called 'bourses'), insurance policies could be traded to third parties or used as a collateral for loans.[117] As a result, insurance was subject to quick change over time, as it not only adapted to the needs of merchants trying to insure their maritime ventures, but also to the particular needs of the developing financial markets in north-western Europe. Herman van der Wee has for example pointed out that in Antwerp, until the 1550s insurance was largely a speculative tool rather than an instrument of risk management, indicating it was still used under circumstances of uncertainty rather than under circumstances of risk.[118] This was largely the case until the emergence of actuaries and the rise of statistical analysis in the seventeenth century.[119] The Habsburg central government also disliked insurance on the basis of the speculation argument, and moreover argued that insurance in itself did not offer proper protection against attacks at sea.[120]

GA, on the other hand, does not have this problem as an analytical object, as its very nature does not allow for speculation.[121] GA's application changed more gradually than insurance. When examining the legal and economic

116 Aerts, 'Wisselruiterij'; J. Materné, '"Schoon ende bequaem tot versamelinge der cooplieden". Antwerpens beurswereld tijdens de gouden zestiende eeuw', in: Le Clercq (ed.), *Ter Beurze*, 51–85.

117 This developed mainly on the Amsterdam stock market. See: L.O. Petram, *The World's First Stock Exchange* (New York 2014).

118 Van der Wee, *The Growth of the Antwerp Market and the European economy, Fourteenth-Sixteenth centuries* (3 vols.) (Vol. 2) (The Hague 1963), 327–328. See also: De ruysscher, 'Antwerp 1490–1590: Insurance and Speculation', in: Leonard (ed.), *Marine Insurance*, 79–105, there 96.

119 There are signs that this development had already taken place during the late sixteenth century, for example as the Castilian Antwerp-based insurer Juan Henriquez for example already incorporated losses in a rudimentary mathematical way. See: G. Ceccarelli, 'The Price for Risk-Taking: Marine Insurance and Probability Calculus in the Late Middle Ages', *Electronic Journal for History of Probability and Statistics*, 3, 1 (2007), 1–26; Puttevils & M. Deloof, 'Marketing and Pricing Risk in Marine Insurance in Sixteenth-Century Antwerp', *The Journal of Economic History*, 77, 3 (2017) 796–837. A similar argument has been made for the Venetian insurance market: A. Tenenti, *Naufrages, corsairs et assurances maritimes à Venise: 1592–1609* (Paris 1959).

120 L.H.J. Sicking, *Neptune and the Netherlands: State, Economy, and War at Sea in the Renaissance* (Leiden/Boston 2004), 247–253.

121 As argued in: G. Felloni, 'Una Fonte Inesplorata per la Storia dell'economia Marittima in Etá Moderna: I Calco di Avaria', in: J. Schneider (ed.), *Wirtschaftskräfte und Wirtschaftwege: Festschrift für Herman Kellenbenz, vol 2: Wirtschaftkräfte in der Europaischen Expansion*, 37–57.

underpinnings of the long European maritime and mercantile expansion of the medieval and early modern period, GA therefore has an analytical edge over insurance. Other varieties of Averages did not allow for speculation either, as cost management varieties did not contain 'to bearer' clauses meaning that, in contrast to insurance, the contract could not be sold to a third party.[122] Parties in maritime ventures therefore established new techniques for *risk* management, the *anticipated*, possible and involuntary hazards (GA and insurance), and for *cost* management, the *anticipated*, voluntary payments in exchange for services which underpinned all maritime ventures (e.g. Contractual Average). This distinction is crucial to understand the development of the various Averages in the Low Countries, as parties in the maritime sector clearly did not only think about risks, but also about operational aspects and its relation to risk.

Risk management was an increasingly complex business during the fifteenth and sixteenth centuries and older tools such as GA were widely used and adapted to cover various kinds of risk.[123] Merchants always used a combination of tools, for example GA and other Averages, insurance and even bottomry, all at the same time.[124] Older tools such as cargo spreading and the joint ownership of ships (the so-called *partenrederij* in Dutch) were still widely used as well.[125] Following Edwin Hunt and James Murray's argument that innovations in business techniques were almost always incremental, this book thus challenges the idea that institutions are simply disposable.[126] Risk management techniques were adapted and improved to face new challenges, rather than replaced.[127]

---

122 De ruysscher, 'Antwerp 1490–1590', 92; Van der Wee, *The Growth* (Vol. 2), 327–329.

123 Hunt & Murray, *A History of Business*, 60–63 & 174–176; Van der Wee, *The Growth* (Vol. 2), 327–329; Sicking, 'A Wider Spread of Risk: A Key to Understanding Holland's Domination of Eastward and Westward Seafaring from the Low Countries in the Sixteenth Century', in: H. Brand & L. Müller (eds.), *The Dynamics of Economic Culture in the North Sea- and Baltic region* (Hilversum 2007), 122–135.

124 Van Niekerk, *The Development*, 16–88, offers an excellent overview of insurance and other tools of maritime risk management such as bottomry and GA. See for an older but useful study of the historical development of bottomry loans: B. Matthias, *Das Foenum Nauticum und die Geschichtliche Entwicklung der Bodmerei* (Würzburg 1881).

125 Asaert, 'Scheepsbezit en havens', 181–182 & 199–201; W. Brulez, *De firma Della Faille en de internationale handel van Vlaamse firma's in de zestiende eeuw* (Brussels 1959), 157–159. See for the *partenrederij*: J.M. De Jongh, *Tussen* societas *en* universitas: *de beursvennootschap en haar aandeelhouders in historisch perspectief* (Alphen aan de Rijn 2014), 14–17.

126 Hunt & Murray, *A History of Business*, 178–179 & 249.

127 North, *Institutions*, 92–105.

GA was widely used by merchants for five interconnected reasons.[128] First, GA offered *ex post* risk management and covered a wide variety of maritime risks by sharing (i.e. the compensation) in an equitable way.[129] Second, GA did not require an upfront payment. This made it useful for some parties who had no upfront capital to spare (e.g. the shipmaster) and might therefore have been preferred by many in the interest community. Costs for both ordinary and extraordinary pilotage were for example primarily shared via GA and cost management varieties of Averages, although nothing in theory prohibited insurers from providing insurance for pilotage costs.[130] Third, GA provided the certainty of a closed interest community, minimising enforcement costs as damages were shared by a small group of people who had often signed a freight contract, influencing the distribution of risk.[131] Fourth, some costs or damage simply could not be insured, for example damage to artillery, due to the prohibition by the central government.[132] Indeed, uninsurable costs were increasingly folded under GA over the course of the sixteenth century. Fifth, insurance was, according to Van der Wee, largely a speculative instrument until the early 1550s as Southern European merchants underwrote policies to make money by speculating on the safe return of a vessel, sometimes even when ships had already left Antwerp.[133] The fact that it was often classified under wagering provides more evidence that many lawmakers viewed insurance with suspicion, even if merchants in reality saw it as a useful risk management tool.[134] These reasons indicate that institutions were not simply disposable but adapted to cover new risks and challenges. What it also shows, however, is that GA did not simply exist 'next to insurance', but that it existed as a proper risk management

128 See also: G.P. Dreijer, 'Maritime Averages and the Complexity of Risk Management in Sixteenth-Century Anwerp', *Tijdschrift voor Sociale en Economische Geschiedenis / Low Countries Journal of Social and Economic History*, 17, 1 (2020), 31–54.

129 Van Niekerk, *The Development*, 61–62 & 77.

130 See for example the overview of policies in: H.L.V. De Groote, *De zeeassurantie te Antwerpen en te Brugge in de zestiende eeuw* (Antwerp 1975), 96–125. None of the policies mention (extra)ordinary pilotage.

131 Van Niekerk, *The Development*, 74–76.

132 Sicking, *Neptune and the Netherlands*, 249–253. Shipping (or 'hull') insurance was not prohibited, although in comments on a draft of the 1550 *Ordonnance* merchants argued for this. See: Idem, 'Los grupos de intereses marítimos de la Península Ibérica en la ciudad de Amberes: la gestión de riesgos y la navigación en el siglo XVI', in: J.A.S. Telechea, M. Bochaca & A.A. Andrade (eds.), *Gentes de mar en la ciudad Atlántica medieval* (Logroño 2012), 167–199, there 197.

133 De ruysscher, 'Antwerp 1490–1590', 96; Van der Wee, *The Growth* (Vol. 2), 365.

134 Van Niekerk, *The Development*, 89–194.

tool on its own, offering a distinct form of *ex post* risk management.[135] Insurers could even be held liable to pay GA claims under certain circumstances, diminishing the moral hazard that resulted from insurance and protecting the interest community (i.e. all the interests of the venture, for example ship and cargo) that underlay the venture, although this also may have raised transaction costs as insurers could have become warier of underwriting.[136]

The steady fall of insurance premiums in the Low Countries and other places in Europe during the early modern period hints to the fact that the insurance market did become more 'efficient' during the sixteenth century.[137] However, this does not fully explain the endurance of the complexity of risk management in the early modern period. To combat the moral hazard arising from insurance (e.g. by not putting enough effort into protection of the ship), the liability for mutual protection costs such as convoy ships and artillery were forcibly shared under the Spanish compulsory contributions.[138] Besides GA and the Iberian innovations, merchants themselves also developed varieties of Averages to respond to the complexities of risk management. Following Knight's dictum that insurance was an innovation which turned uncertainty into risk, this development can also be observed in the development of Averages, for example by developing cost management varieties of Averages.[139] Different actions of pilotage, for example, were subsequently categorised as GA or under cost management varieties depending on their circumstances and necessity. Again, this is in line with the analysis that new tools and techniques were often adapted and improved to face new challenges in a

135 The view that GA still exists 'next to insurance' is common in contemporary debate, but as this book shows, it simply does not hold for the sixteenth century. See for example: Selmer, *The Survival*, and section 2.4.

136 Van Niekerk, *The Development*, 76–80. For moral hazard in marine insurance: Heimer, *Reactive Risk and Rational Action*, 123–125.

137 See for the efficiency of the sixteenth-century Antwerp insurance market: Puttevils & Deloof, 'Marketing and Pricing Risk'. See for the general efficiency of European insurance markets: F.C. Spooner, *Risk at Sea: Amsterdam Insurance and Maritime Europe, 1766–1780* (Cambridge 1983), 248; C. Kingston, 'Governance and Institutional Change in Marine Insurance, 1350–1850', *European Review of Economic History*, 18, 1 (2013), 1–18. The NWO-funded international project led by dr. Sabine Go (VU Amsterdam) will shed further light on the efficiency of insurance markets in early modern Europe. See: http://riskybusinessdb.nl/ {Retrieved 24/04/2020}. The fall of insurance premiums was however not a Europe-wide phenomenon necessarily, as the cases of Livorno and Venice show. See: Addobbati, 'Italy 1500–1800: Cooperation and Competition', in: Leonard (ed.), *Marine Insurance*, 47–78, there 66–71.

138 As Knight already noted: Knight, *Risk, Uncertainty, and Profit*, 251. See also: Heimer, *Reactive Risk and Rational Action*, 28–48 & 123–125.

139 Knight, *Risk, Uncertainty and Profit*, 247–253; Dreijer, 'Maritime Averages'.

new business environment.[140] Moreover, this clarified liability for both risks and cost management. Operational costs were, for example, incorporated into freight contracts, as they were relatively predictable and could thus be classified as foreseeable.[141] This provided additional legal security and predictable costs for all parties engaged in the venture.

1.4 General Average and the *lex maritima*

Besides the previous two economic-historical contributions, the third contribution of the book has a more legal-historical angle. GA has regularly been used as evidence of the existence of an autonomous maritime law across late medieval and early modern Europe, the so-called *lex maritima*. As the principle behind GA existed since Antiquity and comparable solutions could be found inside and outside Europe, GA has often been used as a *pars pro toto* for maritime law at large.[142] Questions around *lex maritima* follow in the footsteps of the debate on *lex mercatoria*, a supposedly transnational, autonomous law applied in most parts of medieval Europe by merchants and merchant-judges to offer speedy proceedings.[143] This debate has deep roots in Anglo-American

140 Hunt & Murray, *A History of Business*, 178–179 & 249. Similar processes can be detected in the application of sea loans and bottomry loans, which were still widely used in the eighteenth century. Roman-Dutch law also treated the subject at length, indicating its enduring influence. See: Van Niekerk, *The Development*, 16–53.

141 As per Knight: Knight, *Risk, Uncertainty and Profit*, 247–253.

142 The literature on *lex maritima* is voluminous. See, *inter alia*: W. Tetley, 'The General Maritime Law – the Lex Maritima', *Syracuse Journal of International Law & Commerce*, 20 (1994), 105–146; G.W. Paulsen, 'Historical Overview of the Development of Uniformity in International Maritime Law', *Tulane Law Review*, 57 (1982–2983), 1065–1091; A. Cordes, 'Lex Maritima? Local, Regional and Universal Maritime law in the Middle Ages', in: W.P. Blockmans, M.M. Krom & J.J. Wubs-Mrowewicz (eds.), *The Routledge Handbook of Maritime Trade around Europe 1300–1600* (Abingdon/New York 2017), 69–85; Frankot, 'Medieval Maritime Law from Oléron to Wisby: Jurisdictions in the law of the sea', in: J. Pan-Montojo & F. Pedersen (eds.), *Communities in European History: Representations, Jurisdictions, Conflicts* (Pisa 2007), 151–172; Idem, '*Die Ehrbaren Hanse-Städte See-Recht*: Diversity and Unity in Hanseatic Maritime Law', in: J.J. Wubs-Mrozewicz & S. Jenks (eds.), *The Hanse in Medieval and Early Modern Europe* (Leiden 2013), 109–128.; Idem, "*Of Laws of Ships*"; J.W. Shephard, 'The Rôles d'Oléron: A Lex Mercatoria of the Sea?', in: V. Piergiovanni (ed.), *From Lex Mercatoria to Commercial Law* (Berlin 2005), 207–253; Kruit, 'General Average'; W. Senior, 'The History of Maritime Law', *The Mariner's Mirror*, 38, 4 (1952), 260–275.

143 Supporters of *lex mercatoria* include: L.E. Trakman, 'The Evolution of the Law Merchant: Our Commercial Heritage', *Journal of Maritime Law and Commerce*, 24, 1 (1980), 1–21; B.L. Benson, 'The Spontaneous Evolution of Commercial Law', *Southern Economic Journal*,

academia, often underpinned by a strong libertarian belief by scholars on the self-regulatory ability of merchants and commercial law. Gerald Malynes popularised this idea in a 1629 publication, arguing that the *lex mercatoria* was well-known across Europe in merchant circles, standing apart from state-backed law such as English common law.[144] Thorough archival work by (legal) historians has however resolutely shown that the idea of a late medieval *lex mercatoria* is a fantasy.[145] Emily Kadens, a particularly vocal critic of the *lex mercatoria*, has argued that there is no historical evidence, as laws were mainly derived from customs that could not easily be transferred to other

---

55, 3 (1989), 644–661; H.J. Berman, *Law and Revolution: The Formation of the Western Legal Tradition* (Cambridge, MA 1983); P.R. Milgrom, North & B.R. Weingast, 'The Role of Institutions in the Revival of Trade: The Law Merchant, Private Judges, and the Champagne Fairs', *Economics and Politics*, 2, 1 (1990), 1–23; C. Wasserstein Fassberg, 'Lex Mercatoria – Hoist with its own Petard', *Chicago Journal of International Law*, 139 (2004), 67–82; R.A. Epstein, 'Reflections on the Historical Origins of Economic Structure of the Law Merchant', *Chicago Journal of International Law*, 139 (2004), 1–20; Leonard, 'London 1426–1601: Marine Insurance and the Law Merchant', in: Leonard (ed.), *Marine Insurance*, 151–178; Brunori, 'History of Business Law: A European History?', *Glossae. European Journal of Legal History* 15 (2018), 62–79; A. Dixit, *Lawlessness and Rconomics: Alternative Modes of Governance* (Princeton 2007).

144 G. Malynes, *Consuetudo, vel, Lex Mercatoria: or, the Ancient Law-Merchant. In three parts, according to the Essentials of Traffick. Necessary for Statesmen, Judges, Magistrates, Temporal and Civil Lawyers, Mint-men, Merchants, Mariners, and all other Negotiating in an Parts of the World* (London 1629/1686). See for an in-depth analysis: De ruysscher, 'Conceptualising *lex mercatoria*: Malynes, Schmitthoff and Goldman Compared', *Maastricht Journal for European and Comparative Law*, 27, 4 (2020), 465–483.

145 Cordes, 'The Search for a Medieval *Lex mercatoria*', in: Piergiovanni (ed.), *From Lex Mercatoria to Commercial Law*, 53–67; De ruysscher, 'La Lex Mercatoria Contextualiseé: Tracer son Parcours Intellectuel', *The Legal History Review*, 90, 4 (2012), 499–515; Idem, 'Law Merchant in the Mould. The Transfer and Transformation of Commercial Practices into Antwerp Customary Law (16th–17th centuries)', in: V. Duss, N. Linder, K. Kastl, C. Börner, F. Hirt & F. Züsli (eds.), *Rechtstransfer in der Geschichte – Legal Transfer in History* (Munich 2006), 433–445; N. Foster, 'Foundation Myth as Legal Formant: The Medieval Law Merchant and the New *Lex Mercatoria, Forum Historiae Iuris*', available at https://forhistiur.de/legacy/zitat/0503foster.htm {Retrieved 14/05/2020}; C. Donahue jr., 'Medieval and Early Modern Lex Mercatoria: An Attempt at the Probatio Diabolica', *Chicago Journal of International Law*, 139 (2004), 21–37; O. Volckart & A. Mangels, 'Are the Roots of the Modern Lex Mercatoria really Medieval?', *Southern Economic Journal*, 65, 3 (1999), 427–450; E. Kadens, 'The Myth of the Customary Law Merchant', *Texas Law Review*, 90 (2012), 1153–1206; Idem, 'Order within Law, Variety within Custom: The Character of the Medieval Law Merchant', *Chicago Journal of International Law*, 139 (2004), 39–65; Idem, 'The Medieval Law Merchant: The Tyranny of a Construct', *Journal of Legal Analysis*, 7, 2 (2015), 251–289; J.H. Baker, 'The Law Merchant and the Common Law before 1700', *The Cambridge Law Journal*, 38, 2 (1979), 295–322.

places.[146] Moreover, there was no strong need for a *lex mercatoria*, since brokers and middlemen were often able to overcome the problems associated with the variety of customs.[147] As Kadens noted, it was not the *lex mercatoria* but "rather *iura mercatorum*, the laws of merchants: bundles of public privileges and private practices, public statutes and private customs" which existed.[148] These *iura mercatorum* (note the plural) existed in merchant circles in medieval and early modern Europe based on general principles, but application was neither autonomous nor uniform, for states or municipalities set their own rules and procedures.[149] This gave merchants a certain common background, but practical application was different everywhere as different laws co-existed and overlapped.[150] An extent of legal pluralism was therefore a fact of life in medieval and early modern Europe.[151]

As Albrecht Cordes has noted, the *lex maritima* should function as a 'key witness' for the *lex mercatoria*, because its sources are more tangible and thus should provide documentary evidence.[152] Supporters of the idea of the *lex maritima* argue that a general (private) maritime law existed in late medieval Europe, based on compilations of medieval maritime law, supposedly with a common basis in Roman maritime law.[153] An early argument for the existence of a general maritime law came from the German scholar Levin Goldschmidt, who argued that certain 'legal circles' (*Rechtskreise* in German) existed in medieval Europe (e.g. a Mediterranean and a northern European one). Goldschmidt

146 Kadens, 'The Myth', 1153.

147 Ibidem. This has also been observed for Bruges: J.A. Van Houtte, 'Makelaars en waarden te Brugge van de 13e tot de 16e eeuw', *Bijdragen voor de Geschiedenis der Nederlanden*, 5 (1950), 1–30 & 177–197; B. Verbist, *Traditie of innovatie? Wouter Ameyde, een makelaar in het laatmiddeleeuwse Brugge* (Unpublished PhD thesis, University of Antwerp 2014); Greve, 'Brokerage and Trade in Medieval Bruges: Regulation and Reality', in: Stabel, Blondé & Greve (eds.), *International Trade in the Low Countries*, 37–44.

148 Idem, 'Order within law', 42.

149 C. Petit, 'Handelsrecht und Rechtsgeschichte', *Zeitschrift der Savigny-Stiftung für Rechtsgeschichte: Germanistische Abteilung*, 136, 1 (2019), 306–337.

150 See also: Kruit, 'General Average', 201–202.

151 On legal pluralism: W. Twining, 'Normative and Legal Pluralism: A Global Perspective', *Duke Journal of Comparative and International Law*, 20 (2010), 473–517. For a historical perspective: Cordes & P. Höhn, 'Extra-Legal and Legal Conflict Management among Long-Distance Traders (1250–1650)', in: H. Pihlajamäki, M.D. Dubber & M. Godfrey (eds.), *The Oxford Handbook of European Legal History* (Oxford 2018), 509–528.

152 Cordes, 'Lex Maritima?', 70–71.

153 An early effort to describe maritime law can be found in: L. Goldschmidt, *Universalgeschichte des Handelsrechts: Erste Lieferung* (Stuttgart 1891), 335–354. See also: Tetley, 'The general maritime law'. For a critical perspective: Cordes, 'Lex Maritima?'; Kruit, 'General Average'. See for an excellent general introduction: R.J. Blakemore, 'Law and the Sea', in: Jowitt, Lambert & Mentz (eds.), *The Routledge Companion*, 388–425, especially 389–394.

argued that all these 'circles' had a common basis in Roman maritime law.[154] Since maritime trade was (and is) almost by definition international, it should not be a surprise that compilations setting out basic principles for maritime trade were drawn up to regulate maritime affairs throughout Europe, as indeed happened between the twelfth and fourteenth centuries. Three collections are believed by many scholars to have played an important role in the governance of maritime affairs: the *Rôles d'Oléron* governing the Atlantic zone in Europe (primarily Atlantic France, England and parts of the Low Countries), the *Consolat del Mar* in the Mediterranean area (Mediterranean France, the Iberian Peninsula and Italy) and the Wisby Laws in the North Sea area (primarily the Hanseatic cities).[155] Although these compilations were indeed important, many other local compilations existed, such as the compilations dealing with maritime law of several Italian city-states.[156]

Some scholars of maritime history have implicitly used Goldschmidt's conceptualisation, especially as the diffusion of these medieval compilations of maritime law more or less correspond to the *Rechtskreise* proposed by Goldschmidt.[157] GA has in this regard often acted as a *pars pro toto* for maritime law at large. Harold Berman for example has argued that the three compilations, alongside the *lex rhodia de iactu*, were incorporated into the

154 Goldschmidt, *Universalgeschichte des Handelsrechts*, 335–337, page 344 for GA.

155 All three the collections have been studied extensively in various languages. See for the *Rôles d'Oléron*: T. Kiesselbach, 'Der Ursprung der rôles d'Oléron und des Seerechts von Damme', *Hansische Geschichtblätter*, 12 (1906), 1–60; K-F. Krieger, *Ursprung und Wurzeln der Rôles d'Oléron* (Cologne/Vienna 1970); T.J. Runyan, 'The Rolls of Oleron and the Admiralty Court in Fourteenth Century England', *American Journal of Legal History*, 19 (1975), 95–111; R. Ward, *The World of the Medieval Shipmaster: Law, Business and the Sea c. 1350–c. 1450* (Cambridge 2009); Shephard, 'The *Rôles d'Oléron*'. See for the *Consolat del Mar*: Constable, 'The Problem of Jettison'; Krieger, 'Die Entwicklung des Seerechts im Mittelmeerraum von der Antinke bis zum Consolat de Mar', *German Yearbook of International Law*, 16 (1973), 179–208. See for the Wisby Laws: Frankot, 'Medieval Maritime Law'; Idem, '*Die Ehrbaren Hanse-Städte See-Recht*'; M.T. Goudsmit, *Geschiedenis van het Nederlandsche zeerecht* (The Hague 1882), 142–193; C. Jahnke, 'The Maritime Law of the Baltic Sea', in: M. Balard (ed.), *The Sea in History. The medieval world* (Woodbridge 2017), 574–582; Idem, 'Hansisches und anderes Seerecht', in: Cordes (ed.), *Hansisches und hansestadtliches Recht* (Trier 2008), 41–68; Landwehr, 'Das Seerecht im Ostseeraum vom Mittelalter zum Ausgang des 18. Jahrhunderts', in: J. Eckert, *Geschichte und perspektiven des Rechts im Ostseeraum: erster Rechthistorikertag im Ostseeraum: 8–12 März 2000* (Berlin 2002), 275–303; Idem, *Das Seerecht der Hanse (1365–1614): vom Schiffordungsrecht zum Seehandelsrecht* (Hamburg 2003).

156 As both Pisa and Amalfi for example already published collections in the twelfth century. See: Blakemore, 'Law and the Sea', 389.

157 This is especially clear in: Tetley, 'The General Maritime Law'.

broader *lex mercatoria*.[158] William Tetley, one of the most vocal supporters of the idea of a *lex maritima*, drew a straight line from the Roman and medieval compilations to current-day maritime law to prove that it has been autonomous and harmonised in Europe since Antiquity.[159] A scholar of contemporary maritime law, Andreas Maurer, has moreover argued that the medieval *lex maritima* could provide the blueprint for a new *lex maritima*.[160] Opponents of the *lex maritima*, such as Cordes and Edda Frankot, have in contrast pointed to the differences in the application in legal practice in many areas in maritime laws throughout Europe, for example in the areas of jettison, salvage and shipwreck.[161] Different regions and cities often chose different solutions to similar problems, which was often based on local needs or customs. Other comparative studies have also confirmed this, as the *Consolat del Mar* and *Rôles d'Oléron* for example differed on many issues including GA.[162] Laws and regulations on GA were never strictly uniform, neither in Europe nor in the Low Countries. As Jolien Kruit noted, one cannot speak of an autonomous and uniform law of GA, neither in historical terms nor in present-day maritime law.[163] As a result, present consensus among historians has firmly swung towards the idea that no *lex maritima* existed.[164]

Against this background, the development of GA in the Low Countries becomes an extremely poignant case study, as merchants from all over Europe were present in the Low Countries, and therefore this region can be seen as a laboratory to investigate these issues in depth. The abundance of material from both formal law and legal practice offers decisive proof that, in the jurisdictionally complex and legal-pluralistic environment of the Low Countries, a *lex maritima* did not exist. Chapters 2 and 4 refute the idea of the existence of a *lex maritima* in greater detail, pointing out that whilst transnational principles

---

158 Berman, *Law and Revolution*, 340 & 355. This is similar to William Tetley, although the latter makes this more explicit. See: Tetley, 'The General Maritime Law', 108–109.

159 Tetley, 'The General Maritime Law', 109–115 & 133–144.

160 A. Maurer, *Lex Maritima: Grundzüge eines transnationalen Seehandelsrechts* (Tübingen 2012), 7–11.

161 Cordes, 'Lex Maritima?', 80–82; Frankot, "*Of Laws of Ships*", 199.

162 As is for example clear from: J. Schweitzer, *Schiffer und Schiffsmann in den Rôles d'Oléron und im Llibre del Consolat de Mar: ein Vergleich zweier mittelalterlicher Seerechtsquellen* (Frankfurt am Main/New York 2007), 181–191.

163 Kruit, 'General Average', 202.

164 Although contemporary lawyers have not taken much note: Cordes, 'Conflicts in 13th-Century Maritime Law: A Comparison between Five European ports', *Oxford University Comparative Law Forum* 2 (2020), https://ouclf.law.ox.ac.uk/conflicts-in-13th-century-maritime-law-a-comparison-between-five-european-ports/ {Retrieved 19/10/2020}, there before note 1.

such as deliberate damage for the common benefit existed, local customs always determined the practical application of GA.[165] On many issues, sources in the Low Countries agreed, but differences existed particularly between Habsburg legislation and Antwerp municipal law, not to speak of the customs of the foreign merchants that were applied in consular courts. Although the problem is largely a legal-historical problem, the evidence also shows how legal change and institutional development interacted, and which constraints were present.

1.5 Introducing the Low Countries' Maritime Economy

Besides the fact that the Low Countries offer an excellent case study for the questions at hand, there are more reasons for choosing to study the region. For north-western Europe, the case of the Low Countries offers plenty of source material, especially when it comes to legal practice.[166] For the fifteenth and sixteenth centuries, a case study of GA in north-western Europe is virtually impossible save for Bruges and Antwerp, as other commercial cities (e.g. Amsterdam and London) do not offer much material on GA until the late sixteenth or early seventeenth century. Moreover, developments from Bruges and Antwerp offered a blueprint for GA legislation in those cities (often following the insurance framework).[167] The case study presented here is therefore not only of interest to scholars of the southern part of the Low Countries, but also for those interested in examining maritime risk management institutions in cities like early modern Amsterdam, London or Hamburg.

165 In line with: Frankot, "*Of Laws of Ships*".

166 Edda Frankot includes cases of legal practice in her work, but for the fifteenth century such cases remain rather limited. See: Frankot, "*Of Laws of Ships*".

167 Although GA and insurance legislation was rarely copied one-on-one, there is strong evidence that Habsburg legislation, Antwerp municipal law and the 1569 *Hordenanzas* of the Castilian *natio* were influential in Amsterdam and London. See for Amsterdam: Gelderblom, *Cities of Commerce*, 134; J.P. Vergouwen, *De geschiedenis der makelaardij in assurantiën hier te lande tot 1813* (The Hague 1945), 22–27; S.C.P.J. Go, 'The Amsterdam Chamber of Insurance and Average: A New Phase in Formal Contract Enforcement (Late Sixteenth and Seventeenth Centuries)', *Enterprise & Society*, 14, 3 (2013), 511–543, there 524–525. See also for financial law: De ruysscher, 'Antwerp Commercial Legislation in Amsterdam in the 17th Century: Legal Transplant or Jumping Board?', *Tijdschrift voor Rechtgeschiedenis*, 77 (2009), 459–479. See for the influence of the *Hordenanzas* in London: G. Rossi, *Insurance in Elizabethan England: The London Code* (Cambridge 2016), 20 & 148–158. In London, only drafts for sixteenth-century GA legislation are known.

IMAGE 2 Pauwels van Overbeke, map of Antwerp (1568)

It should come as no surprise that the Low Countries, and more specifically its southern part, offer an excellent focus for a study concerned with maritime trade, as Flanders and Brabant were already important economic regions in high and late medieval Europe thanks to their thriving trade in wool and cloth, and also due to three further important advantages.[168] First, the region was

168 J.L. Abu-Lughod, *Before European Hegemony: The World System A.D. 1250–1350* (Oxford 1989), 78–100; Lopez, *The Commercial Revolution*, 112–118 & 136–139. See for early trading links across Europe: H. Van Werveke, '"Hansa" in Vlaanderen en aangrenzende gebieden', *Handelingen van het Genootschap voor Geschiedenis*, 90, 1–2 (1953), 5–42; Idem, *Brugge en Antwerpen, acht eeuwen Vlaamse handel* (Ghent 1941), 12–18; C. Wijffels, 'De Vlaamse Hanze van Londen op het einde van de XIIIe eeuw', *Handelingen van het Genootschap voor Geschiedenis*, 97, 1 (1960), 5–30; De Roover, 'La balance commerciale entre les Pays-Bas et l'Italie au quinzième siècle', *Revue belge de philologie et d'histoire*, 37, 2 (1959), 374–386; Stabel, Puttevils & J. Dumolyn, 'Production, Markets and Socio-Economic Structures I: c. 1100–c. 1320', in A. Brown & Dumolyn (eds.), *Medieval Bruges, c. 850–c. 1550* (Cambridge 2018), 86–123, there 88–103; Stabel, Puttevils, B. Lambert, Murray & G. Dupont, 'Production Markets and Socio-Economic Structures II: c. 1320–c. 1500', in: Ibidem, 196–267, there 200–205; Stabel, 'Marketing Cloth in the Low Countries: Manufacturers, Brokers and Merchants (14th–16th centuries)', in: Stabel, Blondé & Greve (eds.), *International Trade in the Low Countries*, 15–36; J. Van Gerven, 'Antwerpen in de veertiende eeuw. Kleine stad zonder toekomst of opkomend handelscentrum?', *Revue belge de philologie et d'histoire*, 76, 4 (1998), 907–938, especially 924–928.

already relatively urbanized in the High Middle Ages;[169] second, it had extensive maritime connections via the estuary systems in the Zwin and Scheldt area, as well as good river and overland connections and transport facilities to important hinterland cities such as Cologne;[170] and third, it possessed a highly developed textile proto-industry.[171] After the decline of the Champagne Fairs in the fourteenth century, Bruges became a natural trading place for foreign traders, including Italian and Spanish merchants who circumvented France owing to improvements in maritime transport technology, whilst Hanseatic merchants had already received staple rights (the place where foreign merchants paid all taxes and tolls[172]) for their wool trade in the thirteenth century.[173] Antwerp, together with the Zeeland ports Middelburg, Flushing and Veere, and

---

169 Abu-Lughod, *Before European Hegemony*, 78–100; A. Verhulst, 'An Aspect of the Question of Continuity between Antiquity and Middle Ages: The Origin of the Flemish Cities between the North Sea and the Scheldt', *Journal of Medieval History*, 3 (1977), 175–206, there 202.

170 Dumolyn & W. Leloup, 'The Zwin Estuary: A Medieval Portuary Network', in: Telechea, B.A. Bolumburu & Bochaca (eds.), *Las Sociedades Portuarias de la Europa Atlántica en la Edad Media* (Logroño 2016), 197–212; J. Parmentier, 'Een maritiem-economische schets van de deltahavens, 1400–1800', in: M. Ebben & S. Groenveld (eds.), *De Scheldedelta als verbinding en scheiding tussen Noord en Zuid, 1500–1800* (Maastricht 2007), 11–26, there 12–15.

171 J.H. Munro, 'Hanseatic Commerce in Textiles from the Low Countries and England during the Later Middle Ages: Changing Trends in Textiles, Markets, Prices, and Values, 1290–1570', in: M. Heckman & J. Röhrkasten (eds.), *Von Nowgorod bis London: studien zu Handel, Wirtschaft und Gesellschaft in mittelalterlichten Europa: Festschfit für Stuart Jenks zum 60. Geburtstag* (Berlin 2008), 97–182, there 97–102. See also: Idem, 'Patterns of Trade, Money, and Credit', in: Brady, Oberman & Tracy (eds.), *Handbook of European History*, 147–195, there 155–157; Idem, 'The Origin of the English "New Draperies": The Resurrection of an Old Flemish Industry, 1270–1570', in: N.B. Harte (ed.), *The New Draperies in the Low Countries and England, 1300–1800* (Oxford 1997), 35–128, there 45–48 & 64–65. Antwerp's initially successful cloth industry declined, as rural centres made better quality products, mostly supplied by Iberian merchants who brought the high-quality Merino wool to Bruges.

172 R.F.G.M. Zijlmans, *Troebele betrekkingen. Grens, scheepvaart- en waterstaatskwesties in de Nederlanden tot 1800* (Hilversum 2017), 267–272. F. Doeleman, 'Le tonlieu Zélandais et le privilège de Zierikzee', *Revue belge de phililogie et d'histoire*, 62, 4 (1984), 682–688; Idem, 'Zeggenschap op de Honte', *Tijdschrift voor Rechtsgeschiedenis*, 43 (1975), 23–43; L.T. Maes, 'Twee arresten van de Grote Raad van Mechelen over de Tol van Iersekeroord', *Acta Juridica* (1977), 167–188; Goris, *Étude*, 175–178.

173 Ibidem, 51–77 & 87–88. See for an economic analysis: S.R. Epstein, 'Regional Fairs, Institutional Innovation, and Economic Growth in Late Medieval Europe', *Economic History Review*, 47, 3 (1994), 459–482; Hunt & Murray, *A History of Business*, 174–176; W. Paravicini, 'Brugge en Duitsland', in: Vermeersch (ed.), *Brugge en Europa*, 98–127, there 103.

the Brabantian town Bergen-op-Zoom, also functioned as an effective maritime gateway system for (regional) trade between the thirteenth and fifteenth centuries, organising annual well-visited fairs.[174] In the estuaries of the Scheldt and the Zwin rivers, well-integrated maritime economic systems developed, with port towns in Zeeland, such as Arnemuiden, specialising in short-route maritime transport.[175] Southern German and English merchants already regularly visited Antwerp in the thirteenth and fourteenth centuries, creating a major regional market focusing on the cloth trade during this period, before the Antwerp cloth trade lost ground to rural draperies.[176] Offering legal security, privileges such as consular jurisdictions and a relative openness to financial innovations was an important pull factor for many foreign *nationes*.[177]

The economic boom of Bruges and Antwerp has produced a significant number of studies on the economic characteristics of both cities. The literature on the rise and economic flowering of Bruges and Antwerp is extensive. James Murray has called Bruges the "cradle of capitalism", whereas Fernand Braudel called Antwerp "the true capital {…} of the Atlantic", indicating the attention historians have given to both cities.[178] Scholarly work on Bruges and Antwerp

174 W. Scheltjens, *Dutch Deltas: Emergence, Functions and Structure of the Low Countries' Maritime Transport System, ca. 1300–1850* (Leiden/Boston 2015), 31–33; Y. Kortlever, 'De jaarmarkten van Bergen op Zoom', in: M. Van Gelder & E. Mijers (eds.), *Internationale handelsnetwerken en culturele contacten in de vroegmoderne Nederlanden* (Maastricht 2009), 9–26. See for Zeeland in the fifteenth century: Z.W. Sneller, *Walcheren in de vijftiende eeuw* (Utrecht 1916). See also for the sixteenth century: V. Enthoven, *Zeeland en de opkomst van de Republiek: handel en strijd in de Scheldedelta, c. 1550–1621* (Leiden 1996).

175 Scheltjens, *Dutch Deltas*, 31–33, 46 & 54; Idem, 'Het ontstaan van een geïntegreerde maritieme transportruimte in de Lage Landen, ca. 1300–1800', *Revue belge de philologie et d'histoire*, 92, 2 (2014), 293–363, there 306. See also: W.S. Unger, 'Middelburg als handelsstad (XIIIe tot XVIe eeuw)', *Archief van het Zeeuws Genootschap*, 1, 3 (1935), 1–176.

176 Van Gerven, 'Antwerpen in de veertiende eeuw', 924–928 & 931. See also footnote 158.

177 Gelderblom, *Cities of Commerce*, 19–41.

178 Murray, *Bruges, Cradle of Capitalism, 1280–1390* (Cambridge 2005); F. Braudel, *The Mediterranean and the Mediterranean World in the Age of Philips II* (London 1992), 480. See also for cultural importance: J. De Rock, Puttevils & Stabel, 'Handelsnetwerken, stedelijke ruimte en culturele omgeving in het 16e-eeuwse Antwerpen', in: Van Gelder & Mijers (eds.), *Internationale handelsnetwerken*, 27–42; Gelderblom & J. Jonker, 'The Low Countries', in: L. Neal & J.G. Williamson (eds.), *The Cambridge History of Capitalism* (Vol. 1) (Cambridge 2014), 314–356, there 333–335; M. Limberger, '"No Town in the World provides More Advantages": Economies of Agglomeration and the Golden Age of Antwerp', in: P. O'Brien, D. Keene, M.C. 't Hart & Van der Wee (eds.), *Urban Achievement in Early Modern Europe: Golden Ages in Antwerp, Amsterdam and London* (Cambridge 2001), 39–62. See for the Flemish urban network: Stabel, *Dwarfs among Giants: The Flemish Urban Network in the Later Middle Ages* (Leuven 1997).

has mainly focused around four issues: the long-term trends in trade;[179] the relationship between Bruges' 'fall' and Antwerp's 'rise';[180] the role of foreign and local merchants;[181] and the institutional underpinnings of the economic success.[182] Here we will very shortly summarise the first three debates as basic background knowledge. Bruges was primarily dependent upon wool[183] and

179 Especially Wilfrid Brulez and Herman van der Wee have been particularly important. See for example: Brulez, 'Le commerce international des Pays-Bas au XVIe siècle: Essai d'appréciation quantitative', *Revue belge de philology et d'histoire*, 46, 4 (1968), 1205–1221; Idem 'De handelsbalans der Nederlanden in het midden van de 16e eeuw', *Bijdragen voor de Geschiedenis der Nederlanden*, 21, 1 (1966–1967), 278–310; Idem, 'Antwerpens bloeitijd', *Bijdragen voor de Geschiedenis der Nederlanden*, 19 (1965), 151–161; Idem, 'Anvers de 1585 à 1650', *Vierteljahrschrift für Sozial- und Wirtschaftgeschichte*, 54, 1 (1967), 75–99; Idem, 'De handel', in: R. Couvreur, *Antwerpen in de zestiende eeuw* (Antwerp 1975), 109–142; Van der Wee, *The Growth*. Recent work is: Puttevils, *Merchants and Trading*. A more general European overview in: Munro, 'Patterns of Trade, Money, and Credit'.

180 Early works are: R. Häpke, *Brügges Entwicklung zum mittelalterlichen Weltmarkt* (Berlin 1908); Van Werveke, *Brugge en Antwerpen*, 95–117; E. Gottschalk, 'Het verval van Brugge als wereldmarkt', *Tijdschrift voor Geschiedenis*, 66 (1953), 1–26; Van Houtte, 'Bruges et Anvers, marchés "nationaux" ou "internationaux" du XIVe au XVIe siècle', *Revue du Nord*, 34, 134 (1952), 89–108; Idem, 'The Rise and Decline of the Market of Bruges', *The Economic History Review*, 19, 1 (1966), 29–47; Idem, 'La genèse du grand marché international d'Anvers à la fin du Moyen-Âge', *Revue belge de philologie et d'histoire*, 19 (1940), 87–126. The standard work dealing with this question is: Brulez, 'Brugge en Antwerpen in de 15e en 16e eeuw: een tegenstelling?', *Tijdschrift voor Geschiedenis*, 83 (1970), 15–37. A recent work is: Puttevils, Stabel & Verbist, 'Een eenduidig pad van modernisering van het handelsverkeer: van het liberale Brugge naar het gereguleerde Antwerpen?', in: Blondé (ed.), *Overheid en economie: geschiedenissen van een spanningsveld* (Antwerp 2014), 39–54.

181 General introductions to the foreign merchants in Bruges and Antwerp in: A. Vandewalle, 'De vreemde naties in Brugge', in: Idem (ed.), *Hanzekooplui en Medicibankiers: Brugge, wisselmarkt van Europese culturen* (Oostkamp 2002), 27–42; Stabel, 'Kooplieden in de stad', in: Vandewalle (ed.), *Hanzekooplui en Medicibankiers*, 85–96; J. Maréchal, 'Le depart de Bruges des marchands étrangers (XVe et XVIe siècle)', *Handelingen voor het Gemootschap 'Société d'Émulation' te Brugge*, 88 (2005), 26–74; Blondé, Gelderblom & Stabel, 'Foreign Merchant Communities'; D.J. Harreld, 'The Individual Merchant and the Trading Nation in Sixteenth-Century Antwerp', in: C. Parker & J.H. Bentley (eds.), *Between the Middle Ages and Modernity: Individual and Community in the Early Modern World* (Lanham 2007), 271–284. Older works emphasising the foreign merchants are: For example: Pirenne, *Historique de Belgique* (7 vols, vol. 3) (Brussels 1902–1932), 267–282; Van Werveke, *Brugge en Antwerpen*, 127. For more recent work: Brulez, *De Firma Della Faille*; Puttevils, *Merchants and Trading*, 167–170; Puttevils, Stabel & Verbist, 'Een eenduidig pad van modernisering', 44–50. See also: Van der Wee, *The Growth* (Vol. 2), 321–323.

182 Major works are: Gelderblom, *Cities of Commerce*; Puttevils, *Merchants and Trading*; Brown & Dumolyn (eds.), *Medieval Bruges*.

183 Philips jr., 'Merchants of the Fleece', 76; Philips, 'Spanish Merchants and the Wool Trade', 274.

cloth,[184] first English[185] and Hanseatic[186] and later Spanish,[187] and remained a major wool market even after most foreign merchants moved to Antwerp

---

184 Murray, *Cradle of Capitalism*, 259–299. See for an overview of the cloth trade: Stabel, 'Marketing Cloth'.

185 Munro, 'Bruges and the Abortive Staple in English Cloth: An Incident in the Shift of Commerce from Bruges to Antwerp the Late Fifteenth Fentury', *Revue belge de philology et d'histoire*, 44, 4 (1966), 1137–1159; Idem, 'The Origin of the English "New Draperies"'.

186 See for the Hanseatic trade in the Low Countries: J. Denucé, *De Hanze en de Antwerpsche handelscompagnieën op de Oostzeelanden* (Antwerp/The Hague 1938); Murray, 'The Well-Grounded Error: Bruges as *Hansestadt*', in: Wubs-Mrozewicz & Jenks (eds.), *The Hanse*, 181–190. A more general overview can be found in: M. Burkhardt, '*Kontors* and Outpost', in: Harreld, (ed.) *A Companion to the Hanseatic League* (Leiden/Boston 2015), 127–161; Munro, 'Hanseatic Commerce in Textiles', 97–98; Idem, 'Bruges and the Abortive Staple', 1151–1153; Stabel, 'Bruges and the German Hanse: Brokering European Commerce', in: L. François & A.K. Isaacs (eds.), *The Sea in European History* (Pisa 2001), 35–56; U. Kypta, 'Von Brügge nach Antwerpen. Institutionen statt Organisation', in: R. Hammel-Kiesow & S. Selzer (eds.), *Hansischer Handel im Strukturwandel vom 15. Zum 16. Jahrhundert* (Trier 2016), 161–181; U.C. Ewert & Selzer, *Institutions of Hanseatic Trade: Studies on the Political Economy of a Medieval Network Organisation* (Frankfurt 2016), 82–85.

187 For the Castilian and Biscayer communities: Philips jr., 'Merchants of the Fleece'; Idem, 'Local Integration and Long-Distance Ties: The Castilian Community in Sixteenth-Century Bruges', *The Sixteenth Century Journal*, 17, 1 (1986), 33–49; Idem, 'Spain's Northern Shipping Industry in the XVIth century', *Journal of European Economic History*, 17, 2 (1988), 267–301, there 270–276; Philips, 'Spanish Merchants and the Wool Trade'; Philips jr & Philips, 'Spanish Wool and Dutch Rebels: The Middelburg Incident of 1574', *The American Historical Review*, 82, 2 (1977), 312–330; Maréchal, 'La colonie espagnole de Bruges du XIVe au XVIe siècle', *Revue du Nord*, 35, 137 (1953), 5–40; H. Casado Alonso, 'Brugge, centrum van uitwisseling met Spanje', in: Vandewalle (ed.), *Hanzekooplui en Medicibankiers* 51–57; Idem, 'La nation en le quartier des Castillians de Bruges (XVe et XVIe siècles)', *Handelingen van het Genootschap voor Geschiedenis*, 133, 1–3 (1996), 61–77; Idem, 'La colonie des marchands Castilllans de Bruges au milieu du XVe siècle', *Publications du centre Europeén d'études Bourguignonnes*, 51 (2011), 233–251; P. Chaunu, 'Seville et la "Belgique" (1555–1648)', *Revue du Nord*, 42, 166 (1960), 259–292; J-M. Yante, 'Le commerce espagnol dans les Pays-Bas (XVe–XVIe siècles)', *Publications du Centre Européen d'Etudes Bourguignonnes*, 51 (2011), 217–232; Vandewalle, 'El Consulado de Burgos en los Países Bajos', *Actas del V Centenario del Consulado de Burgos* (Vol. 1) (Burgos 1994), 283–300; Idem, 'Brugge en het Iberisch schiereiland', in: Vermeersch (ed.), *Brugge en Europa*, 158–181; J.D. González Arce, 'La Universidad de mercaderes de Burgos y el consulado castellano en Brujas durante el siglo XV', *En el Espãna Medieval*, 33 (2010), 161–202; Fagel, *De Hispano-Vlaamse wereld*; For the Catalan community: P.D. Bielsa, 'El Consulado Catalán de Brujas (1330–1488)', in: C.O. Gros (ed.), *Aragón en la Edad Media. XIV–XV. Homenaje a la profesora Carmen Orcástegui Gros* (Zaragoza 1999), 375–390; D. De Boer, 'Joan Fogassot and "los fets de Flandes". A Forgotten Episode of the Catalan Mercantile Connections with Flanders in 1460–1461', in: P.C.M. Hoppenbrouwers, A. Janse & R. Stein (eds.), *Power and Persuasion: Essays on the Art of State Building in Honour of W.P. Blockmans* (Turnhout 2010), 243–272.

in the late fifteenth century.[188] In sixteenth-century Antwerp, the commodity chain of Portuguese spices and sugar, English cloth and German silver drove trade.[189] Although early twentieth-century authors blamed either the silting

188 A general introduction to Bruges' economic system: Van Houtte, *De geschiedenis van Brugge* (Tielt/Bussum 1982), 431–435; Blockmans, 'Brugge als Europees handelscentrum', in: Vermeersch (ed.), *Brugge en Europa*, 40–55; M. Ryckaert, 'Brugge als Europese haven', in: Vermeersch (ed.), *Brugge en Europa*, 26–39. For the English trade in Bruges: Brulez, 'Engels laken in Vlaanderen in de 14e en 15e eeuw', *Handelingen van het Genootschap voor Geschiedenis*, 108, 1–2 (1971), 5–25; P. Carson, 'Brugge en de Britse eilanden', in: Vermeersch (ed.), *Brugge en Europa*, 128–145; Munro, 'Bruges and the Abortive Staple'; D. Nicholas, 'The English Trade at Bruges in the Last Years of Edward III', *Journal of Medieval History*, 5 (1979), 23–61. See for the French trade: Lambert, '"Marchands parfois, marins plus souvent": le commerce Breton à Bruges au quinzième siècle', in: J.A.S. Telechia, B.A. Bolumburu & Sicking (eds.), *Diplomacia y comercio en la Europa atlantíca medieval* (Logroño 2015), 147–160; J. Paviot, 'Brugge en Frankrijk', in: Vandewalle (ed.), *Hanzekooplui en Medicibankiers*, 43–44; Blockmans, 'Brugge en Frankrijk', in: Vermeersch (ed.), *Brugge en Europa*, 206–223. For the French trade in Antwerp: E. Coornaert, *Les Francais et le commerce international a Anvers: fin du XVe–XVIe siècle* (2 vols.).

189 Van der Wee, *The Growth* (vol. 2), 123–136. For Antwerp's fifteenth-century trade: H. Soly, 'De aluinhandel in de Nederlanden in de 16e eeuw', *Revue belge de philologie et d'histoire* 52, 4 (1974), 800–857, there 800–803; Van Gerven, 'Antwerpen in de veertiende eeuw', 930–932. For the English trade in Antwerp: O.C. De Smedt, *De Engelse natie te Antwerpen (1496–1582)* (2 vols.) (Antwerp 1951–1954) (vol. 1), 43–50; Munro, 'English "Backwardness" and Financial Innovations in Commerce with the Low Countries, 14th to 16th Centuries', in: Stabel, Blondé & Greve (eds.), *International Trade in the Low Countries*, 122–144; I. Blanchard, *The International Economy in the 'Age of Discoveries', 1470–1570: Antwerp and the English Merchants' World* (Stuttgart 2009); R. Davis, 'The Rise of Antwerp and its English Connection', in: D.C. Coleman & A.J. John (eds.), *Trade, Government, and Economy in Pre-Industrial England: Essays presented to FJ Fisher* (London 1976), 2–20. For the Southern German merchants in Antwerp: J.L. Bolton & F. Guidi Bruscoli, 'When did Antwerp Replace Bruges as the Commercial and Financial Centre of North-Western Europe? The Evidence of the Borromei Ledger for 1438', *Economic History Review*, 61, 2 (2008), 360–379; Harreld, *High Germans in the Low Countries: German Merchants and Commerce in Golden Age Antwerp* (Leiden/Boston 2004); Idem, 'Atlantic Sugar and Antwerp's Trade with Germany in the Sixteenth Century', *Journal of Early Modern History*, 7, 1 (2003), 148–163; Idem, 'German Merchants and their Trade in Sixteenth-Century Antwerp', in: Stabel, Blondé & Greve (eds.), *International Trade in the Low Countries*, 169–192; Paravicini, 'Brugge en Duitsland'. See for the Portuguese: Van Houtte, 'Portugal en de Brugse handel tijdens de middeleeuwen', in: E. Stols & J. Everaert (eds.), *Vlaanderen en Portugal: op de golfslag van twee culturen* (Antwerp 1991), 33–52; Paviot, 'Brugge en Portugal', in: Vandewalle (ed.), *Hanzekooplui en Medicibankiers*, 45–50; Idem, 'Les Portugais à Bruges', in: Stabel, Blondé & Greve (eds.), *International trade in the Low Countries*, 55–74; H. Pohl, *Die Portugiesen in Antwerp (1567–1648): zur Geschichte einer minderheit* (Wiesbaden 1977); Idem, 'De Portugezen in Antwerpen', in: Stols & Everaert (eds.), *Vlaanderen en Portugal*, 53–80. For other links from Antwerp: Denucé, *Afrika in de XVIde eeuw en de*

of the Zwin or the political fall-out of the Flemish Revolt (1482–1492) for the economic shift from Bruges to Antwerp during the late fifteenth century, more recent research has shown that the shift was more gradual,[190] as Antwerp was already a significant economic powerhouse during the fifteenth century; Bruges remained one until at least the 1540s in regard to financial instruments and the wool trade.[191] Wilfrid Brulez has therefore proposed that the two cities should be seen as complementary in the highly specialised economy of the Low Countries.[192] Over the course of the sixteenth century, local merchants slowly but gradually took over the active trade in Antwerp as they moved from

---

handel van Antwerpen (Antwerp 1937); P. Jeannin, 'Anvers et la Baltique au XVIe siècle', *Revue du Nord*, 37, 146 (1955), 93–114. Other economic links of both Bruges and Antwerp: Parmentier, 'Brugge en Scandinavië', in: Vermeersch (ed.), *Brugge en Europa*, 146–157; N. Geirnaert, 'Brugge en de Noordelijke Nederlanden', in: Vermeersch (ed.), *Brugge en Europa*, 72–97; M. Van Tielhof, *De Hollandse graanhandel, 1470–1570: koren op de Amsterdamse molen* (The Hague 1995).

190 Bolton & Guidi Bruscoli, 'When did Antwerp Replace Bruges', 361–365; J. Haemers & Stabel, 'From Bruges to Antwerp. International Commercial Firms and Government's Credit in the Late 15th and Early 16th century', in: C.S. Ayan & B.J.G. García (eds.), *Banca, crédito y capital. La monarquía Hispánica y los antiguos Países Bajos (1505–1700)* (Seville 2006), 21–37; Munro, 'Bruges and the Abortive Staple', 1143.

191 Lambert, 'Steep Fall or Gradual Decline? International Trade in Sixteenth-Century Bruges', in: J. Oberste & S. Ehrich (eds.), *Italien als Vorbild? Ökonomische und kulturelle Verflechtungen europäischer Metropolen am Vorabend der 'ersten Globalisierung' (1300–1600)* (Regensburg 2019), 167–176; L. Vandamme *et al*, 'Bruges in the Sixteenth Century: A "Return to Normalcy"', in: Brown & Dumolyn (eds.), *Medieval Bruges*, 445–484.

192 Brulez, 'Brugge en Antwerpen', 16–17. See for the specialisation: Van der Wee, 'De economie als factor bij het begin van de opstand in de Zuidelijke Nederlanden', *Bijdragen en Mededelingen van het Historisch Genootschap*, 83 (1969), 15–32; Idem, 'De handelsbetrekkingen tussen Antwerpen en de noordelijke Nederlanden tijdens de 14e, 15e en 16e eeuw', *Bijdragen voor de Geschiedenis der Nederlanden*, 20 (1966), 267–285; Van Houtte, 'Het Nederlandse marktgebied in de vijftiende eeuw: eenheid en differenciëring', *Bijdragen en Mededelingen van het Historisch Genootschap*, 70 (1956), 11–30; Van Zanden, 'Holland en de Zuidelijke Nederlanden in de periode 1500–1570: divergerende ontwikkelingen of voortgaande economische integratie', in: Aerts, B. Henau, B. Janssens & R. Van Uytven (eds.), *Studia historica oeconomica. Liber Amicorum Herman van der Wee* (Louvain 1993), 357–368; Blockmans, 'The Economic Expansion of Holland and Zeeland in the Fourteenth-Sixteenth Centuries', in: Ibidem, 41–58; Brulez, 'Brugge en Antwerpen', 21; Asaert, 'Gasten uit Brugge: nieuwe gegevens over Bruggelingen op de Antwerpse markt in de vijftiende eeuw', in Wijffels (ed.), *Album Carlos Wijffels* (Brussels 1987), 23–41. Visitors from Holland were also coming to Antwerp: Idem, 'Hollandse bezoekers in de haven van Antwerpen voor 1585', *Neerlandia*, 89, 3 (1985), 103–114.

brokerage to trade,[193] with most Southern European merchants resorting to financial services such as banking and insurance.[194] This was also the case in

193 Similar to the situation in Bruges: Greve, 'Brokerage and Trade'; Idem, 'Hoteliers en Hanzekooplieden in Brugge in de 14de en 15de eeuw', in: Vandewalle (ed.), *Hanzekooplui en Medicibankiers*, 99–104; Idem, 'Brügger Hosteliers und hansische Kaufleute: ein Netzwerk vorteilhafter Handelsbeziehungen oder programmierte Interessenkonflikte?', in: N. Jörn, Paravicini & H. Wernicke (eds.), *Hansekaufleute in Brügge. Teil 4, Beitragen der Internationalen Tagung in Brügge April 1996* (Frankfurt 2000), 151–161. An older text is: Van Houtte, 'Makelaars en waarden'. See for a case study of Wouter Ameyde, one of the most famous brokers in Bruges: Verbist, *Traditie of innovatie?* Moreover, many Flemish merchants established overseas trading colonies: Brulez, 'De diaspora der Antwerpse kooplui op het einde van de 16e eeuw', *Bijdragen voor de Geschiedenis der Nederlanden*, 15 (1960), 279–306. See for the Iberian Peninsula: A. Crespo Solana, 'Diasporas and the Integration of "Merchant Colonies": Flemish and Dutch Networks in Early Modern Spain', *Le verger – Bouquet*, 5 (2014), 1–21; E. Crailsheim, *The Spanish Connection: French and Flemish Merchant Networks in Seville (1570–1650)* (Cologne 2016), there 182–228; J. Everaert, 'A Trail of Trials: A "Flemish" Merchant Community in Sixteenth-Century Valladolid and Medina del Campo', *Tijdschrift voor Sociale en Economische Geschiedenis*, 14, 1 (2017), 5–35; Fagel, *De Hispano-Vlaamse wereld*, 209–280; Stols, *De Spaanse Brabanders, of de handelsbetrekkingen der Zuidelijke Nederlanden met de Iberische wereld, 1598–1648* (Brussels 1971); Idem, 'Les marchands flamands dans la Péninsule Ibérique à la fin du seizième siècle et pendant la première moitié du dix-septième siècle', in: H. Kellenbenz (ed.), *Fremde Kaufleute auf der Iberischen halbinsel* (Cologne 1970), 226–238. See for the Italian Peninsula: Van Gelder, *Trading places: The Netherlandish Merchants in Early Modern Venice* (Leiden/Boston 2009); Geirnaert, 'Brugge en Italië', in: Vermeersch (ed.), *Brugge en Europa*, 182–205.

194 Puttevils, *Merchants and Trading*, 176–177. See for the Italian trade and other activities: W.B. Watson, 'The Structure of the Florentine Galley Trade with Flanders and England in the Fifteenth Century', *Revue belge de philologie et d'histoire*, 39, 4 (1961), 1073–1091 & 40, 2 (1962), 317–347; P. Subacchi, 'Italians in Antwerp in the Second Half of the Sixteenth Century', in: Soly & K.L. Thijs (eds.), *Minderheden in Westeuropese steden (16e–20e eeuw)* (Brussels 1995), 73–90; Idem, 'The Italian Community in 16th-century Antwerp', in: J. Veeckman, S. Jennings, C. Dumortier, D. Whitehouse & F. Verhaeghe (eds.), *Majolica and Glass. From Italy to Antwerp and Beyond. The Transfer of Technology in the 16th–Early 17th century* (Antwerp 2002), 23–38; Stabel, 'Venice and the Low Countries: Commercial Contacts and Intellectual Inspirations', in: B. Aikema & B.L. Brown (eds.), *Renaissance Venice and the North: Crosscurrents in the Time of Bellini, Dürer and Titian* (New York 2000), 30–43; Idem, 'Italian Merchants and the Fairs in the Low Countries (12th–16th centuries)', in: P. Lanaro (ed.), *La pratica dello scambio: Sistemi di fiere, Mercanti e città in Europa (1400–1700)* (Venice 2003), 131–159; Idem, 'De gewenste vreemdeling', *Jaarboek voor Middeleeuwse geschiedenis*, 4 (2001), 189–221; Yante, 'Commerce et marchands italiens dans les Pays-Bas (XIVe–XVIe siècles)', *Publications du Centre Européen d'Etudes Bourguignonnes*, 49 (2009), 87–99; De Roover, 'La balance commerciale'; G. Petti Balbi, 'Brugge, haven van de Italianen', in: Vandewalle (ed.), *Hanzekooplui en Medicibankiers*, 58–64; Blockmans, 'Financiers

the maritime sector, as shipmasters from the Low Countries largely started dominating shipping during the sixteenth century.[195]

As GA was firmly entrenched in the maritime world, this section primarily focuses on the characteristics of maritime organisation and the maritime economy in the Low Countries. The trade of Bruges was largely based on maritime routes and the associated infrastructure, with foreign merchants transporting cargo to Bruges' ante-ports and subsequently piloting goods via riverine transport to Bruges.[196] For a city largely dependent on maritime trade, the maritime organisation of the city is surprisingly understudied, although a recent project on the towns in the Zwin area has offered new information on the role of the ante-ports.[197] These towns (Damme, Hoeke, Monnikenreede and Mude) were established in the High Middle Ages and were fairly prosperous on their

Italiens et Flamands aux XIII–XIVe siècle', in: S.A., *Aspetti della vita economia medievale. Atti del convegno di Studi nel X anniversario della morta Federigo Melis* (Florence 1985), 192–214; Denucé, *Italiaansche koopmansgeslachten te Antwerpen in de XVIe–XVIIIe eeuwen* (Mechlin/Amsterdam 1934); Geirnaert, 'Brugge en Italië'; Lambert, '"Se fist riche par draps de soye": The Intertwinement of Italian Financial Interests and Luxury Trade at the Burgundian Court (1384–1481)', in: Lambert & K.A. Wilson (eds.), *Europe's Rich Fabric: The Consumption, Commercialisation, and Production of Luxury Textiles in Italy, the Low Countries and Neighbouring Territories (Fourteenth–Sixteenth Centuries)* (Abingdon 2016), 91–106; Idem, 'Making Size Matter Less: Italian Firms and Merchant Guilds in Late Medieval Bruges', in: De ruysscher, Cordes, Dauchy & Pihlajamäki (eds.), *The Company in Law and Practice: Did Size Matter?* (Leiden/Boston 2017), 34–48; Idem, *The City, the Duke and their Banker: The Rapondi Family and the Formation of the Burgundian State (1384–1430)* (Turnhout 2006). See for the development of financial markets in Bruges and Antwerp: Aerts, 'Geld en krediet'; Idem, 'Wisselruiterij'; Le Clercq, 'In Brugge is er een plein ... Brugge als financiële markt in de 14e–15e eeuw', in: Ibidem (ed.), *Ter Beurze*, 15–32; Murray, 'Handels- en financiële technieken', in: Vandewalle (ed.), *Hanzekooplui en Medicibankiers*, 107–111; Materné, '"Schoon ende bequaem"'. A general assessment of Bruges' commercial infrastructure: Murray, *Bruges, Cradle of Capitalism*; Idem, 'Of Nodes and Networks: Bruges and the Infrastructure of Trade in Fourteenth-Century Europe', in: Stabel, Blondé & Greve (eds.), *International Trade in the Low Countries*, 1–14.

195 See Asaert, 'Onder de vlag met de hand' (Unpublished book, Antwerp, 2019) (2 Vols.), 1–17.

196 R. Degryse, 'Brugge en de pilotage van de Spaanse vloot in het Zwin in de XVIde eeuw', *Handelingen voor het Genootschap voor Geschiedenis*, 67, 1–2 (1980), 105–178 & 67, 3–4 (1980), 227–288. See also: Dumolyn & Leloup, 'The Zwin Estuary'.

197 See for example: Stabel *et al*, 'Production, Markets and Socio-Economic structures II', 199–218, which contains a lot of information on trade flows but nothing on the maritime organisation of transport. New work is: Dumolyn & Leloup, 'The Zwin Estuary'; W. De Clercq, K. Dombrecht, Dumolyn, Leloup & J. Trachet, 'Monnikerede: The Rise and Decline of a Medieval Port Community in the Zwin Estuary', *Medieval Low Countries, an Annual Review*, 7 (2020), 97–130; K. Dillen, 'A Paradox of Maritime Access. Origins and Consequences of Subaltern Relations in a Medieval Portuary System in Flanders: The Case of Hoeke', *International Journal of Maritime History*, 30, 3 (2018), 405–421.

own until roughly the mid-fourteenth century, offering staples themselves and an active maritime sector, for example by offering transport facilities.[198] Bruges gradually established judicial control over those port towns from 1352 onwards, a development which increased in speed after the Bruges Revolt of 1436–1438 when these towns largely lost their privileges.[199] The case of Sluis, another ante-port closest to the sea, was different, as the town neglected the privileges of Bruges and the other ante-ports, actively offering its own pilotage services.[200] The city supported the Burgundian dukes during the 1436–1438 Revolt and was therefore rewarded with additional privileges, but the Zwin area's economic prospects declined after the shift to Antwerp. In 1566, Bruges even bought Sluis, but to little avail as the Dutch Revolt soon turned the Zwin area into a battle ground.[201]

Most foreign merchant communities organised their own transport rather than rely on local transport facilities, except for compulsory pilotage on the Zwin river.[202] Both the skippers' guilds of Sluis and Bruges were allowed to pilot ships on the Zwin in their own jurisdictional area, but from the late fifteenth century onwards most foreign merchants sailed to a natural port in Zeeland, for example Arnemuiden or Middelburg rather than one of the ante-ports of Bruges as the Zwin silted up.[203] The Castilian and Biscayer *nationes*, responsible for a significant part of maritime transport to the Low Countries, even appointed a representative (the comptroller-general or *controlador*) in Arnemuiden to structure their trade and levy applicable duties and compulsory contributions.[204]

We are slightly better informed on Antwerp's maritime economy. As Van der Wee has noted, until the 1530s, Antwerp's trade was largely riverine-based, for example with Cologne or the triangular trade with France and Zeeland.[205] Yet only a few studies exist for Antwerp's maritime structure in the fifteenth

198 Dumolyn & Leloup, 'The Zwin Estuary', 209.

199 Ibidem, 208–211; Dumolyn, *De Brugse opstand van 1436–1438* (Kortrijk-Heule 1997).

200 Ibidem, 208.

201 Ibidem, 212.

202 Degryse, 'Brugge en de pilotage'. See also: Philips jr., 'Spain's Northern Shipping Industry'.

203 Ibidem, 107–110. Degryse however warns that the Castilians still used the Zwin as well, as the agreements with the Bruges skippers' guild attests. See Chapter 5 for more information. See also: Sicking, 'Le paradoxe de l'accès: le rôle des avant-ports dans les anciens Pays-Bas à la fin du Moyen Âge et au début de l'époque moderne (approche comparative générale)', in: Bochaca & J-L. Sarrazin (eds.), *Ports et littoraux de l'Europe atlantique: transformations naturelles et aménagements humains* (*XIV*ᵉ*–XVI*ᵉ *siècles*) (Rennes 2007), 227–255, there 231–235.

204 Fagel, *De Hispano-Vlaamse wereld*, 138–139 & 484.

205 Van der Wee, *The Growth* (Vol. 2), 326–328: Coornaert, *Les francais*.

and sixteenth century, and many of them are unpublished as well.[206] From the scant evidence it appears that the Antwerp skippers' guild was largely a monopolistic organisation when it came to maritime transport from and to Antwerp, although skippers from elsewhere were allowed to sail between their home city and Antwerp.[207] As pilotage remained a pillar of maritime transport, the Zeeland maritime transport services became even more important, benefiting from the highly specialised economic ecosystem of the four seaborne provinces of the Low Countries (Flanders, Brabant, Holland and Zeeland).[208] As a result, the Antwerp skippers' guild was dependent on pilotage on the Scheldt river for income, as most foreign merchants preferred their own ships for seaborne transport.

Until the mid-sixteenth century, ship ownership in Antwerp was sometimes spread over multiple merchants and masters (the so-called *partenrederij*), although this was a more widespread development in Holland than in Flanders or Brabant.[209] Although some large firms, such as the famous Della Faille firm, owned ships themselves, most merchants rented ships for one venture.[210] According to Brulez, this may be the result of the fact that there were so many investment opportunities in sixteenth-century Antwerp that investment in ship-owning was unattractive compared to other, less risky but more profitable investment, in notable contrast to seventeenth-century Amsterdam.[211] Yet under the influence of Antwerp's booming maritime economy, shipmasters were often able to become ship-owners as well towards the mid-sixteenth century, renting out the ship and his service to merchants.[212] In any case shipmasters rarely acted as merchants as well, indicating specialisation.[213] Until the mid-sixteenth century, regulation on maritime law was virtually non-existent,

---

206 Asaert, *De Antwerpse scheepvaart in de XVe eeuw (1394–1480)* (Brussels 1973); Idem, 'Scheepsbezit en havens'. See also for the sixteenth century: M. Cassiers, *Bijdrage tot de geschiedenis van de Antwerpse scheepvaart en scheepvaartbeweging in het midden van de 16e eeuw (1555–1558)* (Unpublished MA thesis, Ghent University, 1978); Asaert, 'Onder de vlag'.

207 Cassiers, *Bijdrage*, 98–102; Asaert, 'Onder de vlag' (Vol. 2), 423.

208 Brulez, 'De handel', 111. See also: Idem, 'De scheepvaartwinst in de nieuwe tijden', *Tijdschrift voor Geschiedenis*, 92, 1 (1979), 1–19.

209 Asaert, 'Scheepsbezit en havens', 181–182; Idem, 'Onder de vlag' (Vol. 1), 66, shows that at the end of the fifteenth century 37% of Antwerp shipmasters participated in a *partenrederij*.

210 Brulez, *De firma Della Faille*, 157–159; Asaert, 'Scheepsbezit en havens', 199–201; Idem, 'Onder de vlag' (Vol. 2), 493.

211 Idem, 'De handel', 111–112.

212 Asaert, 'Onder de vlag' (Vol. 2), 26 & 65.

213 De ruysscher, 'Maxims, Principles and Legal Change', 271. See also: Asaert, 'Hollandse bezoekers', 111–112; Idem, 'Onder de vlag' (Vol. 1), 368.

indicating that Antwerp's maritime sector may have been relatively underdeveloped compared to what one would expect for an economy which was dependent to a significant extent on overseas trade.[214] Yet this changed in the second half of the sixteenth century.[215] For example, in the 1550 *Ordonnance* promulgated by Charles V, both the charter-party and the bill of lading (*cognossement*) became obligatory before a venture sailed out of port.[216] From the late 1540s onwards, the negotiations over (control of) the maritime sector intensified, of which GA was an important part, as Chapter 3 shows.

1.6 State Formation, Jurisdictional Complexity, and Legal Sources[217]

Before moving on to the actual analysis of the Averages in the Low Countries, some words are necessary about the political and legal background, in particular focusing on state formation and the fiscal-naval state, as well as introducing the jurisdictions and sources of law which play a major role in Chapters 3 to 6. The story of state formation in the Low Countries essentially revolves around the four main seaborne provinces of Flanders, Brabant, Holland and Zeeland, and the focus will therefore be on these provinces.[218] The efforts by the central administration to build a state primarily focused on these four provinces, with the other (more peripheral) provinces less affected by the processes of state formation. Over the course of the fifteenth and sixteenth centuries, the Low Countries developed from a patchwork of semi-independent political entities to a unified state, first under the Burgundians (Philip the Bold (1384–1404), John the Fearless (1404–1419), Philip the Good (1419–1467), Charles the Bold (1467–1477) and Mary of Burgundy (1477–1482)) and from 1482 onwards under the Habsburg rulers. Despite revolts over the Habsburg

214 Cassiers, *Bijdrage*, 50–70.

215 See Chapter 3.

216 Asaert, 'Scheepsbezit en havens', 201; Idem, 'Onder de vlag' (Vol. 1), 447–452.

217 For this section I draw primarily on the following works: Stein, *Magnanimous Dukes and Rising States: The Unification of the Burgundian Netherlands, 1380–1480* (Oxford 2007); Blockmans, *Metropolen aan de Noordzee: De geschiedenis van Nederland, 1100–1560* (Amsterdam 2010), 346–407 & 449–531; Idem & W. Prevenier, *The Promised Lands: The Low Countries under Burgundian rule* (Pennsylvania 1999), 35–20; H.G. Koeningsberger, *Monarchies, States Generals and Parliaments: The Netherlands in the Fifteenth and Sixteenth Centuries* (Cambridge 2001).

218 Blockmans, *Metropolen aan de Noordzee*, 649–651; Sicking, *Neptune and the Netherlands*, 5–8. Stein, *Magnanimous Dukes*, 13–14; J-M. Cauchies & H. De Schepper, 'Legal Tools of the Public Power in the Netherlands, 1200–1600', in: A. Padoa-Schioppa (ed.), *Legislation and Justice* (Oxford 1997), 229–268, there 263–265.

IMAGE 3 Map of the Low Countries around 1350

takeover by the Flemish cities, the Low Countries were incorporated into the Habsburg composite monarchy which also included Spain, Austria and parts of the Holy Roman Empire and southern Italy.[219]

Under Maximilian's successors, particularly Charles v, the Low Countries were eventually united under Habsburg leadership after Charles (re-)conquered Guelders in 1543.[220] Charles v delegated leadership to his family members for lengthy periods, for example Margareta of Austria (1506–1515 & 1517–1530, officially from 1522 onwards) and Maria of Hungary (1531–1555), as so-called *landvoogden* (governor or vice-roy).[221] Charles' son, Philip II, also left daily policy matters to the *landvoogden*, but was faced with the advancing Reformation in the Low Countries and other problems, including unpopular tax increases.[222] Under the reign of Charles v, a tenuous balance was found through lengthy negotiations with individual provinces, cities and the nobility.[223] Under

219 See for the Flemish Revolt: Haemers, *De strijd om het regentschap*; Blockmans, 'Autocratie ou polyarchie? La lutte pour le pouvoir politique en Flandre de 1482 à 1492', *Bulletin de la Commission royale d'Histoire*, 140 (1974), 257–368. See for a more general history of revolts and rebellion in fifteenth-century Flanders: Dumolyn, 'The Legal Repression of Revolts in Late Medieval Flanders', *Legal History Review*, 68, 4 (2000), 479–521; Idem & Haemers, 'Patterns of Urban Rebellion in medieval Flanders', *Journal of Medieval History*, 31, 4 (2005), 369–393. For Maximilian's support of Antwerp: Blockmans, *Metropolen aan de Noordzee*, 555–556. See for the composite monarchy: Elliot, 'A Europe of Composite Monarchies', 50–51. Elliott took this concept from the work of Koeningsberger. See: H.G. Koeningsberger, '"*Dominium Regale*" or "*Dominium Politicum et Regale*": Monarchies and Parliaments in Earl Modern Europe', Inaugural lecture, University of London King's College, 25th February 1975. See for an account of state formation in Castile and the broader Iberian Peninsula: B. Yun-Casalilla, *Iberian World Empires and the Globalization of Europe 1415–1668* (Singapore 2019), especially 10–50 & 156–162. The Habsburgs relied on Burgundian titles for a long time, see: L. Duerloo, 'The Utility of an Empty Title. The Habsburgs as Dukes of Burgundy', *Dutch Crossing*, 43, 1 (2019), 63–77; H. Pirenne, 'The Formation and Constitution of the Burgundian State (Fifteenth and Sixteenth Centuries)', *The American Historical Review*, 14, 3 (1909), 477–502, there 478.

220 The bibliography about Charles v is enormous. A recent analytical synthesis: G. Parker, *Emperor: A New Life of Charles v* (New Haven 2019). See for Philip II: Idem, *Imprudent King: A New Life of Philip II* (New Haven/London 2014).

221 Blockmans, *Metropolen aan de Noordzee*, 594. A good overview of the reign of Mary of Hungary is: L.V.G. Gorter-Van Royen, *Maria van Hongarije regentes der Nederlanden. Een politieke analyse op basis van haar regenschapsordonnanties en haar correspondentie met Karel v* (Hilversum 1995), especially 129–195.

222 See for the proposed wealth tax: F.H.M. Grapperhaus, *Alva en de tiende penning* (Zutphen 1982). See for the Reformation in Antwerp and the *Bloedraad*: G. Marnef, *Antwerpen in de tijd van de Reformatie. Ondergronds protestantisme in een handelsmetropool 1550–1577* (Amsterdam/Antwerp 1996), there 149–202.

223 Koeningsberger, *Monarchies, States Generals and Parliaments*, 140–145.

IMAGE 4 The Habsburg Low Countries in 1555, with years of conquest/acquisition

Philip II, who advanced a system of intense centralisation, tensions came to the forefront, with the four core provinces spearheading the charge against him and leading to the Dutch Revolt and the break-up of the Low Countries.[224]

As part of the exercise of power, both the Burgundians and the Habsburgs employed various initiatives to advance state formation and the development of the so-called fiscal-military state (or, when applied to the maritime world, the fiscal-naval state) to their benefit.[225] Among other things, jurisdiction, legislation and taxation were important factors of state formation, as the Burgundian and Habsburg sovereigns established several organisations (e.g. new courts or audit chambers[226]) to centralise state tasks in Brussels, often

---

224 Blockmans, *Metropolen aan de Noordzee*, 624. A most interesting overview of the relations between Philip II and Antwerp can be found in: G.E. Wells, *Antwerp and the Government of Philip II: 1555–1567* (Unpublished PhD thesis, Cornell University, 1982). This is also a heavily debated topic, that will not be considered here. Important works on the subject are: Gelderblom, *Zuid-Nederlandse kooplieden en de opkomst van de Amsterdamse stapelmarkt (1578–1630)* (Hilversum 2000); Lesger, *The Rise of the Amsterdam Market and Information Exchange: Merchants, Commercial Expansion and Change in the Spatial Economy of the Low Countries* (Farnham 2006).

225 The classic book on late medieval and early modern state formation is: C. Tilly, *Coercion, Capital, and European States: AD 990–1992* (Cambridge MA 1992). For the military-fiscal state: J. Glete, *War and the State in Early Modern Europe: Spain, the Dutch Republic and Sweden as Fiscal-Military States, 1500–1660* (London 2006). See for an overview of European state formation in the late medieval era: Blockmans, 'Voracious States and Obstructing Cities'. See also for an overview of late medieval and early modern Europe: J.H. Elliott, 'A Europe of Composite Monarchies', *Past & Present*, 137 (1992), 48–71. A distinction, made by Hugo de Schepper, can be made between centralization and state formation. The former denotes to the idea that rulers created institutions and organisations for the purpose of centralising a certain task, whereas state formation refers to a broader development, describing a more cultural process of state-building. See: De Schepper, 'Staatsgezag en macht in de Nederlanden: verworvenheden en beperkingen in het Bourgondisch-Habsburgse systeem', in: J. Geurts & De Schepper (eds.), *Staatsvorming onder Bourgondiërs en Habsburgers: theorie en praktijk* (Maastricht 2006), 13–49, there 21–28. An English version can be found in: Idem, 'The Burgundian-Habsburg Netherlands', in: T.A. Brady, H.A. Oberman & Tracy (eds.), *Handbook of European History in the Later Middle Ages, Renaissance and Reformation, 1400–1600* (Leiden/Boston 1994), 499–533, there 506–511.

226 For example the Great Council of Mechlin. See: J. Van Rompaey, 'Het onstaan van de Grote Raad onder Filips de Goede', Koninklijke Zuidnederlandse Maatschappij voor Taal- en Letterkunde en Geschiedenis. Handelingen, 25 (1971), 297–310; Idem, *De Grote Raad van de hertogen van Boergondië en het Parlement van Mechelen* (Brussels 1973), 18–28. Its first *Ordonnance* is printed in: Idem, 'Hofraad en Grote Raad in de hofordonnantie van 1 januari 1469', in: Asaert *et al* (eds.), *Recht en instellingen in de oude Nederlanden tijdens de Middeleeuwen en de nieuwe tijd: Liber Amicorum Jan Buntinx* (Leuven 1981), 303–324. See also: J. Gilissen, 'De Grote Raad van Mechelen. Historisch overzicht', *Belgisch bulletin*

inspired by the establishment of similar organisations in the various provinces during the fifteenth century.[227] Here, we will focus on jurisdiction and legislation, as they were of primary importance for the development of GA in the Low Countries.

As was common across Europe in the medieval and early modern period, the Low Countries were characterised by a jurisdictionally complex legal landscape (Table 1).[228] Various courts, backed by various powerful factions, scrambled for jurisdictional space.[229] In practice, most citizens, merchants and shipmasters chose the local municipal court as the place for first instance proceeding: in general, only high-profile cases, such as those between cities and regions, or very specific exceptions ended up before the central courts.[230] Table 1 summarises the existing courts in the Low Countries, and the extent of their jurisdictions. Yet as multiple courts competed, conflicts were inevitable. This led to so-called forum shopping, whereby litigants tried to steer a dispute towards the courts they saw as most favourable to their interests.[231]

Table 2 summarises the privileges of foreign merchant communities (the so-called *nationes*), who as part of their privileges often received their own

van de internationale unie der magistraten, 20 (1970), 2–22. For the lawyers staffing the court: H. De Ridder-Symoens, 'De universitaire vorming van de Brabantse stadsmagistraat en stadsfunktionarissen – Leuven en Antwerpen, 1430–1580', *Studia Historica Gandensia*, 208 (1977), 21–125. See also: S.A., *The University of Louvain 1425–1975* (Louvain 1975), there 27–33 for the general history & 107–121 & 134–135 for the history of the Law Faculties.

227 See for Flanders for example: Dumolyn, *Staatsvorming en vorstelijke ambtenaren in het graafschap Vlaanderen (1419–1477)* (Antwerp & Apeldoorn 2003); Idem, *De Raad van Vlaanderen de Rekenkamer van Rijsel: gewestelijke overheidsinstellingen als instrumenten van de centralisatie (1419–1477)* (Brussels 2002). See for a more general overview: Stein, *Magnanimous Dukes*, 152–225.

228 Cordes & Höhn, 'Extra-Legal and Legal Conflict Management'; Donlan & Heirbaut, '"A Patchwork of Accommodations"'.

229 This was of course a pan-European phenomenon at the time: Ibidem & Blockmans, 'Voracious States and Obstructing Cities'.

230 See e.g.: Wijffels, 'Taxation and Litigation: Dutch Cities as Litigants in Late Fifteenth-Century Tax-Cases', in: M. Ascheri *et al* (eds.), *"Ins Wasser geworfen und Ozeane durchquert": Festschrift für Knut Wolfgang Nörr* (Cologne 2003), 1075–1097; Idem, 'Zeeuwse steden voor de Grote Raad', *Pro Memorie*, 4, 2 (2002), 266–293. See for an example of intermunicipal conflict: Sicking, 'De zaak Draeck: Antwerpen tegenover Zierikzee. Een interstedelijk conflict tijdens de Vlaamse opstand', in: P. Delsalle, G. Docquier, A. Marchandisse & B. Schnerb (eds.), *Pour la singuliere affection qu'avons a luy. Etudes bourguignonnes offertes à Jean-Marie Cauchies* (Turnhout 2017), 406–417.

231 See for an overview of strategies at multiple levels: Wubs-Mrozewicz, 'Conflict Management and Interdisciplinary History', *Tijdschrift voor Sociale en Economische Geschiedenis*, 15, 1 (2018), 89–107.

consular jurisdiction to hear intra-*natio* cases.[232] In general, most first-instance cases between merchants were heard before the municipal courts of Bruges and Antwerp, with more complex cases going to regional superior or central courts (see Chapters 4 and 6 for more detailed analysis).[233] Over the course

232 See for an overview of the foreign merchant communities in the Low Countries: Blondé, Gelderblom & Stabel, 'Foreign Merchant Communities'. See for the Spanish *nationes*: Casado Alonso, 'La nation'; Maréchal, 'La colonie espagnole'; Idem, 'Le depart'; Vandewalle, 'De vreemde naties in Brugge'; Idem, 'Brugge en het Iberisch schiereiland', in: Vermeersch (ed.), *Brugge en Europa*, 158–181; Fagel, 'Spanish Merchants in the Low Countries: Stabilitas Loci or Peregrinatio?', in: Stabel, Blondé & Greve (eds.), *International Trade in the Low Countries*, 87–103; Idem, *De Hispano-Vlaamse wereld*; Goris, *Étude*, 55–70; González Arce, 'La Universidad'; Yante, 'Le commerce espagnol'; J. Finot, *Étude historique sur les relations commerciales entre la Flandre & L'Espagne au Moyen Age* (Paris 1899) (hereafter: Finot, *Étude de Espagne*); Gilliodts-Van Severen & E. Gaillard, *Inventaire des Chartes des archives de la ville de Bruges* (9 vols.) (Bruges 1871–1876) (Vol. 2) (hereafter: Gilliodts-Van Severen & Gaillard, *Inventaire*), 132. See for the various Italian *nationes*: Goris, *Étude*, 70–80; Stabel, 'Italian Merchants and the Fairs'; Idem, 'De gewenste vreemdeling'; Subacchi, 'Italians in Antwerp'; Idem, 'The Italian Community'; De Roover, 'La communauté des marchands Lucquois à Bruges de 1377 à 1404', *Handelingen van het Genootschap voor Geschiedenis*, 86, 1 (1949), 23–89; Geirnaert, 'Brugge en Italië'; J. Braekevelt, 'Entre profit et dommage: presence et privileges de la nation Génoise à Bruges sous les Ducs de Bourgogne (1384–1477)', *Publications du Centre Européen d'Études Bourguignonnes*, 49 (2009), 117–129; Yante, 'Commerce et marchands italiens'; L. Maggiore, *De Italiaanse kolonie te Antwerpen (1598–1648)* (Unpublished MA thesis, Leuven University 1998); Finot, *Étude historique sur les relations commerciales entre la Flandre et la Républicque de Gênes au Moyen Age* (Paris 1906) (hereafter: Finot, *Étude de Gênes*). Notably the Southern Germans and French chose different solutions by not opting for a *natio*: Harreld, 'The Individual Merchant and the Trading Nation', 276–277; Coornaert, *Les Français* (Vol. 2), 131–134; R. Ehrenberg, *Das Zeitalter der Fugger: Geldkapital und Creditverkehr im 16. Jahrhunderts* (Jena 1896).

233 Verhulst, 'An Aspect of the Question of Continuity', specifically 202; Idem, *The Rise of Cities in North-West Europe* (Cambridge 1999), 75–79 & 88–95 & 98–102. For a wider European perspective: Pirenne, *Les villes du Moyen Âge: essai d'histoire économique et sociale* (Brussels 1927), 149–185. For Antwerp: C. Laenens, *Geschiedenis van het Antwerps gerecht* (Antwerp 1953), 28 & 264–268. See for its civil jurisdiction: Ibidem, 256–299, especially 299 for the jurisdiction over foreign merchants. See also: Puttevils, *Merchants and Trading*, 140. See for the Council of Flanders: J. Buntinx, 'De Raad van Vlaanderen', in: S.A., *Consilium Magnum 1473–1973: herdenking van de 500e verjaardag van de oprichting van het Parlement en Grote Raad van Mechelen* (Brussels 1988), 187–198; J. Monballyu, 'Van appellation ende reformatien: de ontwikkeling van het hoger beroep bij de Audientie, de Camere van den Rade en de Raad van Vlaanderen (ca. 1379–ca. 1550)', *Tijdschrift voor Rechtsgeschiedenis*, 61 (1993), 237–275; H. Verhaest, 'De gedwongen tenuitvoerlegging van vonnissen en acten in de rechtspraak van de Raad van Vlaanderen (1430–1520)', in: A.A. Wijffels (ed.), *Miscellanea Consilii Magna (III)* (Amsterdam 1988), 295–324. For the Council of Brabant: P.L. Nève, 'Hoe "soeverein" was de Raad van Brabant?', in: E.J.M.F.C. Broers, B.C.M. Jacobs, & Lesaffer (eds.), *Ius Brabanticum, Ius Commune, Ius Gentium: opstellen aangeboden aan prof. Mr. J.P.A. Coopmans ter gelegenheid van zijn*

of the fifteenth and sixteenth centuries, the central courts established by the Burgundians and Habsburgs eventually consolidated power as superior courts,[234] assuming jurisdiction over a wide range of cases including (*ratione materiae*) maritime transport (and thus Averages).[235] Notably, Brabant remained outside of the purview of the most important court, the Great Council,[236] as the province called upon the 1349 'Golden Bull' (*bulla aurea*) which included the so-called *Ius de non Evocando et de non Appellando*, a

tachtigste verjaardag (Nijmegen 2006), 9–20; E. Puts, 'Raad van Brabant', in: Van Uytven, C. Bruneel, H. Coppens & B. Augustyn (eds.), *De gewestelijke en lokale overheidsinstellingen in Brabant en Mechelen tot 1795* (Brussels 2000), 147–171; P. Godding, 'Une justice parallèle? L'arbitrage au Conseil de Brabant (15e siècle)', in: Wijffels (ed.) *Miscellanea Consilii Magna* (*III*), 123–142; Idem, *Le Conseil de Brabant: sous le règne de Philippe le Bon (1430–1467)* (Brussels 1999). For the privileged status of foreign merchants: C.H. Van Rhee, *Litigation and Legislation: Civil Procedure at First Instance in the Great Council for the Netherlands in Malines (1522–1559)* (Brussels 1997), 42. See also for the procedural questions: C.L. Verkerk, 'Evocatie in de Landen van Herwaarts-over tussen 1470 en 1540 (avec résumé)', in: S.A., *Consilium Magnum*, 419–447, there 432–445.

234 Van Rhee, 'Continental European Superior Courts and Procedure in Civil Actions (11th–19th Centuries)', in: O. Moreteau, A. Masferrer & K.A. Modéer (eds.), *Comparative Legal History* (Cheltenham/Northampton MA 2019), 318–340, there 324–325. The book follows Van Rhee's terminology, using superior, for the reason that the Great Council was indeed never supreme in any sense, neither in terms of jurisdiction nor in terms of competence. For the Parliament, see: Maes, *Het Parlement en de Grote Raad*, 69–72.

235 Van Rompaey, *De Grote Raad*, 19–23; Van Rhee, *Litigation and Legislation*, 35–41.

236 There were various precedecessors to the Great Council. See e.g. the Parliament of Paris, which had jurisdictional claims until the early sixteenth century over parts of Flanders, see: Dauchy, *De processen in beroep uit Vlaanderen bij het Parlement van Parijs (1320–1521): een rechtshistorisch onderzoek naar de wording van de staat en soevereiniteit in de Bourgondisch-Habsburgse periode* (Brussels 1995), 9–14 & 100–208 for a more in-depth analysis. See also: Stein, *Magnanimous Dukes*, 179–180; Braekevelt, *Une prince de justice. Vorstelijke wetgeving, soevereiniteit en staatsvorming in het graafschap Vlaanderen tijdens de regering van Filips de Goede (1419–1467)* (Unpublished PhD thesis, Ghent University, 2013), 81–462. As this was Charles V himself from 1519 onwards, the claims were silently dropped. The Parliament in Mechlin, active 1473–1477: Maes, *Het Parlement en de Grote Raad van Mechelen, 1473–1797* (Mechlin 2009), 69–72; Idem & G. Dogaer, 'De oudst bekende tekst van de stichtingsakte van het Parlement van Mechelen (1473)', *Handelingen van de Koninklijke Kring voor Oudheidkunde, Letteren en Kunst van Mechelen*, 71 (1972), 41–60. For the *Groot Privilege*: Blockmans, 'De "constitutionele" betekenis van de privilegiën van Maria van Bourgondië (1477)', in: Blockmans (ed.), *Het algemene en de gewestelijke privilegiën van Maria van Bourgondië voor de Nederlanden* (Kortrijk-Heule 1985), 473–494. For the consequences in Flanders, see: Idem, 'Breuk of continuïteit? De Vlaamse privilegiën van 1477 in het licht van het staatsvormingsproces', in: Ibidem, 97–144. For Brabant, see: Van Uytven, '1477 in Brabant', in: Ibidem, 253–372. The tensions before Mary's death are described in: Haemers, *For the Common Good. State Power and Urban Revolts in the Reign of Mary of Burgundy (1477–1482)* (Turnhout 2009). For the States General: Blockmans, *Metropolen aan de Noordzee*, 475–476. For its development: Stein, *Magnanimous Dukes*, 53–78.

privilege confirmed again by Charles V in 1512.[237] Next to the Great Council, the Secret Council also held some jurisdictional power, which can be seen in Table 1 and which will be analysed further in Chapter 6.[238] A final jurisdictional layer was that of the Admiralty, the organisation in charge of the naval defence of the Low Countries, based in Veere, Zeeland, which heard cases of Prize Law and maritime labour law.[239]

237 Nève, 'Hoe soeverein', 11–17; De Schepper & Cauchies, 'Legal Tools', 232–233. Literally: 'right of non-evocation and non-appeal'. See for its genesis: U. Eisenhardt, 'Entstehung und bedeutung der kaiserlichen privilegia de non appellando', in: S.A., *Consilium Magnum*, 319–341.

238 De Schepper, 'De Grote Raad van Mechelen, hoogste rechtscollege in de Nederlanden?', *Bijdragen en Mededelingen voor de Geschiedenis der Nederlanden*, 93, 3 (1978), 389–411. Before this work, it was generally assumed that the Great Council was the highest court in the Low Countries. See for example: J.T. De Smidt & A.H. Huussen jr., 'De Grote Raad van Mechelen als hoogste rechtscollege in de Nederlanden', *Tijdschrift Holland*, 2, 4/5 (1970), 89–107. M. Baelde, *De collaterale raden onder Karel V en Philips II (1531–1578): bijdrage tot de geschiedenis van de centrale instellingen in de zestiende eeuw* (Brussels 1965), 44–45.

239 Paviot, *La politique navale des Ducs de Bourgogne 1384–1482* (Lille 1995), 328–329; Degryse, 'De admiraals en de eigen marine van de Bourgondische hertogen', *Mededelingen van de Marine Academie*, 17 (1965), 139–225; C.G. Roelofsen, 'L'amirauté à Veere, considérée dans ses attributions judiciaires (XVe–XVIe siècles)', *Publications du Centre Européen d'Etudes Bourguignonnes*, 24 (1984), 67–80; Sicking, *Neptune and the Netherlands*; Idem, 'Prijsrechtspraak in de Nederlanden: de Admiraliteiten van Veere, Duinkerke en Gent, 1488–1568', in: Heirbaut & D. Lambrecht (eds.), *Van oud en nieuw recht: handelingen van het XVde Belgisch-Nederlandse rechtshistorisch congres, Universiteit Gent, 16 en 17 april 1998* (Antwerp 1999), 69–84; Degryse, 'De admiraals', 156–157. See for the legal history of Letters of Marque: N.A.M. Rodger, 'The Law and Language of Private Naval Warfare', *Mariner's Mirror*, 100, 1 (2014), 5–16. See for the Prize Law processes at the Admiralty in Veere (mostly mid-sixteenth century): Zeeuws Archief (hereafter NL-ZA), Admiraliteit van Veere, inv. 243, nrs. 16–47; also in NL-ZA, Vierschaar Veere (hereafter RAZE), inv. 341, nrs. 1–33. See for the processes at the Admiralty in Brussels (post-1592): BE-ARB, Admiraliteitsarchief, inv. T094, nrs. 952–953, 959, 961 & 963–966; Sicking & Van Rhee, 'Procedure en proceskosten. De afhandeling van een prijszaak volgens de Romano-Canonieke procedure voor de Admiraliteit en de Grote Raad van Mechelen tijdens de Engels-Schotse Oorlog van 1547', *Tijdschrift voor Rechtsgeschiedenis*, 71 (2003), 337–357; Idem, 'Prize Law, Procedure and Politics. The Settlement of a Prize Case before the Admiralty Court and the Great Council of the Netherlands (1554–1555)', in: H. Dondorp, M. Schermaier & B. Sirks (eds.), *De rebus divinis et humanis. Essays in Honour of Jan Hallebeek* (Göttingen 2019), 302–322; Van Rhee, *Litigation and legislation*, 42; Wijffels, 'Justitia in Commerciis: Public Governance and Commercial Litigation before the Great Council of Mechlin in the late fifteenth and early sixteenth century', in: Pihlajamäki, Cordes, Dauchy & De ruysscher (eds.), *Understanding the Sources*, 32–54, there 48–49; Idem, 'Business Relations between Merchants in Sixteenth-Century Belgian Practice-Orientated Civil Law Literature', in: Piergiovanni (ed.), *From Lex Mercatoria to Commercial Law*, 255–290.

TABLE 1 Jurisdictional layers in the Low Countries (fifteenth–sixteenth century)

Level	For Whom?	Competence
Consular	Foreign merchants organised in *nationes*	Contract litigation between merchants of the same *natio*
Municipal	Citizens and (foreign) merchants of the city	First instance court for almost everything, often appeal court for consular jurisdiction
Regional	(Wealthy) Citizens of the regions, foreign merchants sometimes as privileged litigants	Appeals court to municipal courts, first instance cases for disputes between municipalities
Central (Great Council)	Citizens of the Low Countries, foreign merchants privileged litigants	Appeals courts to either municipal or regional court: first instance court for privileged litigants, also jurisdiction *ratione materiae* over various cases
Central (Secret Council)	Privileged litigants (i.e nobility)	Petitions possible to complain about decisions made by Great Council (1500 onwards); first instance court for privileged litigants
Admiralty	Litigants under limited jurisdiction	Prize Law, criminal law on ships, wages in maritime cases

TABLE 2 *Nationes* in the Low Countries (thirteenth–sixteenth centuries)

Natio	First Privileges in Bruges	First Privileges in Antwerp
Castilian	1343	–
Biscayers	1447	–
Aragonese-Catalan	1389	1528
Andalusian	1505	– (1510 in Middelburg)
Navarese	1556	–
Lombards	1281	1415
Lucchese	1377	1549
Genoese	1414	1501
Florentine	1379	1510

TABLE 2 *Nationes* in the Low Countries (thirteenth–sixteenth centuries) (*cont.*)

Natio	First Privileges in Bruges	First Privileges in Antwerp
Portuguese	1411	1511
Venetian	1358	–
English	1275	1305
Hanseatic	1212	1315
'Greeks' (Constantinople)	–	1582

SOURCES: GORIS, *ÉTUDE*, 23–80; DE SMEDT, *DE ENGELSE NATIE*, 43–50; MUNRO, 'BRUGES AND THE ABORTIVE STAPLE', 102; IDEM, 'HANSEATIC COMMERCE', 97–98; MARÉCHAL, 'LA COLONIE ESPAGNE', 7–11; FAGEL, 'SPAANSE KOOPLIEDEN IN MIDDELBURG', 22–23; STABEL, 'DE GEWENSTE VREEMDELING', 192–209; DE ROOVER, 'LA COMMUNAUTÉ DES MARCHANDS LUCQUOIS', 23–89; BRAEKEVELT, 'ENTRE PROFIT ET DOMMAGE', 117–119; BLOCKMANS, 'FINANCIERS ITALIENS ET FLAMANDS', 193–197; BE-SAA, PRIVILEGIEKAMER, GRIEKSE NATIE (NATIE VAN CONSTANTINOPEL), INV. PK1080.

IMAGE 5 The Great Council of Mechlin under Charles the Bold

As the jurisdictional situation in the Low Countries was complex, this was by extension also the case for the sources of law. Following the idea of *iura mercatorum* (see section 1.4), we can distinguish between various sources. When looking at the development of GA in the sixteenth-century Low Countries, four general categories can be distinguished: first, customs and customary law; second, Roman law and *Ius Commune*; third, princely legislation, and fourth,

(Antwerp) municipal law.[240] All these sources will be analysed in greater detail in Chapter 3: here it suffices to shortly define these sources. Customs were the originally unwritten sources of law governing (economic) life: medieval lawyers distinguished between two types of customs: general customs, which were known and accepted by everybody and could in principle overrule other sources of law (such as *Ius Commune*, see below), and particular customs, which were only valid in a limited time or space.[241] Emily Kadens has, with some justification, described the gradual attempts to get a grip on customs by municipal or central authorities as 'the colonisation of custom', as in the age of state formation, local communities were increasingly forced to write down their (formerly) unwritten customs, a process that can be observed throughout Europe.[242] Next to customs, the role of *Ius Commune*, the collection of Roman law-inspired legal scholarship, was very important, although scholars nowadays emphasise the interaction between *Ius Commune* and other sources of law, rather than present the early modern period as a triumph of *Ius Commune*.[243] For the case of Antwerp, presented in Chapters 3 and 4, it is clear that there was very much a process of acculturation (i.e. mutual influence), as jurists slowly

---

240 Very specific sources of law, such as the medieval compilations of maritime law or the 1569 *Hordenanzas* of the Castilian *natio*, are treated in Chapter 3.

241 B.C.M. Jacobs, '*Ius Patrium* en *Ius Commune*: twee zijden van een medaille', *Pro Memorie*, 19, 1 (2017), 22–46, there 39–44; Lesaffer, *European Legal History: A Cultural and Political Perspective* (Cambridge 2009), 269–270.

242 Kadens, 'Convergence and the Colonisation of Custom in Pre-Modern Europe', in: Moreteau, Masferrer & Modéer (eds.), *Comparative Legal History*, 167–185, there 168.

243 Examples include: B.H.D. Hermesdorf, *Römisches Recht in den Niederlanden* (Varese 1968), 8–160; Van Caenegem, *Le droit Romaine en Belgique* (Varese 1966), 9–65; Van Caenegem, 'Ouvrages de droit Romain dans les catalogues des anciens Pays-Bas Méridionaux', *Tijdschrift voor Rechtsgeschiedenis*, 28 (1960), 297–347 & 403–438, there 297; Gilissen, 'À propos de la réception du droit romain dans les provinces méridionales des pays de par-deçà aux XVIe et XVIIe siècle', *Revue du Nord*, 40, 158 (1958), 259–271, there 259–260; Idem, *Introduction historique au droit*, 327–332; Idem, 'Romeins recht en inheems gewoonterecht', 125–126. Sceptical takes in: Nève, 'Ius Commune oftewel "gemeen recht": traduttore traditore?', in: O.E. Tellegen-Couperus, Nève & J.W. Tellegen (eds), *Tertium Datur. Drie opstellen aangeboden aan Prof. Mr. J.A. Ankum* (Tilburg 1995), 3–58; Idem, '(Europäisches) ius commune und (nationales) gemeines Recht: Verwechslung von Begriffen?', in: G. Köbler & H. Nehlsen (eds.), *Wirkungen europäischer Rechtskultur. Festschrift für Karl Kroeschell zum 70. Geburtstag* (Munich 1997), 871–884; D.J. Osler, 'The Myth of European Legal History', *Rechtshistorisches Journal*, 16 (1997), 393–410. But see also for a more modern perspective: T. Herzog, *A Short History of European Law: The Last Two and a Half Millennia* (Cambridge, MA 2018), 152–164; Lesaffer, *European Legal History*, 269–275; Padoa-Schioppa, *A History of Law in Europe: From the Early Middle Ages to the Twentieth Century* (Cambridge 2007), 204–205.

but steadily incorporated elements of *Ius Commune*, for example on contract law, into Antwerp municipal law, particularly inspired by the Italian tradition of the *mos italicus*.[244] Merchants generally seem to have accepted jurists incorporating new techniques and instruments (e.g. insurance) into an existing legal framework, since it offered them legal security.[245]

From the mid-fifteenth century onwards, the wish for greater judicial control by the Burgundians also translated into increased legislative activity, the third source of law. Both Charles v and Philip ii actively issued *Ordonnances* to regulate subjects ranging from commerce to criminal law.[246] A significant part of them concerned maritime and naval affairs (see Table 3), which will be analysed in Chapter 3.[247]

---

244 Lesaffer, *European Legal History*, 372. See for an example of the sixteenth-century Antwerp jurist Leonard Lessius: Decock, 'In Defense of Commercial Capitalism: Lessius, Partnerships and the *Contractus Trinus*', in: B. Van Hofstraeten & Decock (eds.), *Companies and Company Law in Late Medieval and Early Modern Europe* (Leuven / Paris / Bristol, CT 2016), 55–90. For *mos italicus*: Wijffels, '*Mos Italicus* in der Antwaltspraxis des Grossen Rates zu Mecheln und des Hofes von Holland (ca. 1460–1580)', in: De Schepper (ed.), *Höchste Gerichtsbarkeit im spätmittelalter und der frühen Neuzeit* (Amsterdam 1985), 105–123; Van Hofstraeten, *Juridisch humanisme en costumiere acculturatie: Inhouds- en vormbepalende factoren van de Antwerpse* Consuetudines Compilatae (1608) *en het* Gelderse Land- en Stadrecht (1620) *van het Roermondse Overkwartier* (Maastricht 2008).

245 Lesaffer, *European Legal History*, 381; Gelderblom, *Cities of Commerce*, 135–139; De ruysscher, "*Naer het Romeinsch recht*", 371–372; Idem, 'L'acculturation juridique des coutumes commerciales à Anvers. L'exemple de la letter de change (xvie–xviie siècle)', in: B. Coppein, F. Stevens & Waelkens (eds.), *Modernisme, tradition et acculturation juridique* (Brussels 2011), 151–160. See also for a more general overview: J. Hilaire, 'Reflexions sur l'heritage romain dans le droit du commerce au Moyen-Age', *Tijdschrift voor Rechtsgeschiedenis*, 70, 3 (2002), 212–228.

246 Cauchies, "*Es plantar un mundo nuevo*", 125–131.

247 See e.g. for the 1550, 1551 and 1563 *Ordonnances*: Sicking, *Neptune and the Netherlands*, 242–280; Idem, 'Stratégies de réduction de risque dans le transport maritime des Pays-Bas au xvie siècle', in: S. Cavaciocchi (ed.), *Ricchezza del mare – ricchezza dal mare, secc. xiii–xviii: atti della Trentasettesima settimana di studi, 11–15 Aprile 2005* (2 vol.) (Florence 2006), 795–808; Idem, 'A Wider Spread of Risk'; Idem, 'Les marchands espagnols et portugais aux Pays-Bas et la navigation à l'époque de Charles Quint: gestion des risques et législation', *Publications du Centre Européen d'Etudes Bourguignonnes*, 51 (2011), 253–274; Idem, 'Los grupos de intereses'; S.M. Coronas González, 'Carlos v, asegurador: una propuesta original de los comerciales de Amberes (1551)', in: A. Iglesia Ferreirós & A. Sanchez-Lauro (eds.), *Centralismo y autonomismo en los siglos xvi–xvii. Homenaje al Profesor Jesús Lalinde Abadía* (Barcelona 1989), 121–130. For the 1569–1571 insurance *Ordonnances*: Reatz, 'Ordonnances du duc d'Albe sur les assurances maritimes de 1569, 1570, 1571, avec un précis de l'histoire du droit d'assurance maritime dans les Pays-Bas', *Compte-rendu des séances de la commission royale d'histoire*, Deuxième Série, 5 (1878), 41–118 ; Puttevils & De ruysscher, 'The Art of Compromise'.

TABLE 3 *Ordonnances* on maritime law in the Low Countries (fifteenth–sixteenth centuries)

Year	Subject	Issued by
1458	Marine insurance	Philip the Good
1488	Admiralty	Maximilian of Austria
1537	Marine insurance	Charles V
1540	Admiralty	Charles V
1550	Navigation	Charles V
1551	Navigation, marine insurance & GA	Charles V
1563	Navigation, marine insurance & GA	Philip II
1569	Marine insurance	Philip II/Duke of Alva
1570	Marine insurance	Philip II/Duke of Alva
1571	Marine insurance	Philip II/Duke of Alva
1579	Navigation	Philip II
1590	Admiralty	Philip II

SOURCE: DE GROOTE, *DE ZEEASSURANTIE* 28–31.

Among the many *Ordonnances* promulgated by the Habsburg rulers, a 1531 *Ordonnance* compelling all towns and cities to compile their local customs (so-called 'homologation') also spurred legal development in Antwerp.[248] After various initial fifteenth-century compilations,[249] four versions of the so-called *Costuymen* ('customs') were compiled published in Antwerp: those of 1548 (*Consuetudines Antiquissimae*), 1570 (*Consuetudines In Antiquis*), 1582 (*Consuetudines Impressae*) and 1608 (*Consuetudines Compilatae*).[250] Particularly the latter two are considered by legal historians as landmarks for their

248 See for literature on the *Costuymen*; M. Gotzen, 'De costumiere bronnen voor de studie van het Oud-Antwerpsch burgerlijk recht', *Rechtkundig tijdschrift voor België*, 39 (1949), 3–16, 105–124 & 191–208; Idem, 'Het Oud-Antwerps burgerlijk procesrecht volgens de Costumiere Redacties van de 16e–17e eeuw', *Rechtskundig tijdschrift voor België*, 41 (1951), 292–315 & 424–468; Van Hofstraeten, *Juridisch humanisme*; De ruysscher, "*Naer het Romeinsch recht*".

249 De ruysscher, "*Naer het Romeinsch recht*", 47–48; Idem, *De ontwikkeling van het Antwerpse privaatrecht in de eerste helft van de zestiende eeuw: uitgave van het Gulden Boeck (ca. 1510–ca. 1537), (ontwerpen van) ordonnanties (1496–ca. 1546), een rechtsboek (ca. 1541–ca. 1545) en proeven van hoofdstukken van de costuymen van 1548* (Brussels 2014), 76–80; Gotzen, 'De costumiere bronnen', 8–9; Gilissen, *Introduction Historique au droit* (Brussels 1979), 282–288.

250 Gotzen, 'De costumiere bronnen', 10–16 & 105–124.

high level of legal sophistication and incorporation of legal scholarship.[251] The 1608 *Compilatae* covered more than 200 articles dealing with GA and 300 with insurance, making it a vital resource to study the development of maritime risk management in sixteenth-century Antwerp. The *Compilatae* for example incorporated rules on insurance and GA from the 1569 *Hordenanzas*, a compilation of insurance customs drawn up by the Castilian *natio* in Antwerp.[252] Moreover, the so-called *enquête par turbe*, a procedure designed to write down customs by interviewing experts, also gave merchants the option of influencing both what custom consisted of and how it was recorded.[253]

1.7 Sources, Approach and Structure of the Book

This book combines approaches from maritime, economic and legal history to study the development of GA and other Averages in the Low Countries during the fifteenth and sixteenth centuries. Whereas economic and legal history are of course separate disciplines, recently they have started to communicate more, following the interaction between lawyers and economists in the so-called Law and Economics movement.[254] Ron Harris has listed some *desiderata* for the interaction between legal and economic history, especially in moving away from the strictly economic approach to law (for economists) or the strictly legal approach to economics without focusing on the wider institutions (for lawyers).[255] Whereas legal historians can sometimes ignore developments that

---

251 See for example: Ibidem; Gotzen, 'De costumiere bronnen', 3–16, 105–124 & 191–208; Idem, 'Het Oud-Antwerps burgerlijk procesrecht volgens de Costumiere Redacties van de 16e–17e eeuw', *Rechtskundig tijdschrift voor België*, 41 (1951), 292–315 & 424–468.

252 Van Hofstraeten, 'Recording Customs in Early Modern Antwerp, a Commercial Metropolis', *Zeitschrift des Max-Planck-Instituts für europäische Rechtsgeschichte*, 24 (2016), 288–301, there 292–293.

253 See for its origins: L. Waelkens, 'Origine de l'enquete par turbe', *Tijdschrift voor Rechtsgeschiedenis*, 53, 3–4 (1985) 337–346. See also: De ruysscher, *"Naer het Romeinsch recht"*, 94–95; Gelderblom, *Cities of Commerce*, 135–139.

254 For its use in history: North, 'Law and Economics'. An excellent methodological approach in: A. Fleming, 'Legal History as Economic History', in: Pihlajamäki, Dubber & Godfrey (eds.), *The Oxford Handbook of European Legal History*, 207–220. A classic although outdated work in the field is: R.A. Posner, *Economic Analysis of Law* (New York 2007).

255 Harris, 'The Encounters'; Idem, 'The Uses of History'; Idem, *Going the Distance: Eurasian Trade and the Rise of the Business Corporation, 1400–1700* (Princeton NJ 2020), 7–11. Some lawyers have however opted for an efficiency approach to Low Countries legal history, e.g.: M.F. Van Dijck, 'Towards an Economic Interpretation of Justice? Conflict Settlement, Social Control and Civil Society in Urban Brabant and Mechelen during the Late Middle Ages and the Early Modern Period', in: M. Van der Heijden, E. Van Nederveen Meerkerk &

are not strictly legal, and hence see institutions too narrowly, economic historians' analysis of legal developments is often disappointing as well. Law is too often seen as static, while economic historians see norms as dynamic, a distinction that is rather unhelpful for they are extensions of each other and fundamentally intertwined.[256]

Notwithstanding these major issues, recent work on the history of mercantile and maritime law has presented some excellent examples of fruitful collaborations and mutual insights.[257] This book aims to follow this approach, of course in the context of the maritime world of the Low Countries. A combination of the methodological approaches from economic and legal history offers historians a more nuanced picture to analyse the past, especially when it comes to the legal framework of maritime trade. As for analytical tools, the book will primarily work through the concepts of transaction and protection costs, concepts taken from economic history. As noted above, however, whilst its tools are useful, this book will also point out problems with the theories of the New Institutional Economics (NIE) when applied to complex historical situations. The centrality of legal-historical analysis will furthermore signal defects in the NIE's analysis of legal development, as their theories focus almost solely on legal institutions that lower transaction costs, whereas the persistence of GA and other Averages shows the more ambivalent effects of (legal) institutions, which could be beneficial but not strictly economically efficient.

Another important point to make is that this book views 'law' as historians would: hence, this book follows 'external' legal history, focusing on its interaction with mercantile and legal practice, rather than 'internal' legal history, focusing on specific doctrinal questions. The book also follows Maria Fusaro's idea that law is a 'supremely social construct', taking this idea to analyse the development of mercantile and maritime law.[258] In short, this book takes a

---

G. Vermeesch (eds.), *Serving the Urban Community: The Rise of Public Facilities in the Low Countries* (Amsterdam 2009), 62–88.

256 For a similar argument: Fleming, 'Legal History as economic history'. See also: Twining, 'Normative and Legal Pluralism'.

257 See for example the excellent volumes in the history of commercial law in the Brill Studies of Private Law: De ruysscher, Cordes, Dauchy & Pihlajamäki (eds.), *The Company in Law and Practice*; Pihlajamäki, Cordes, Dauchy & De ruysscher (eds.), *Understanding the Sources of Early Modern and Modern Commercial Law: Courts, Statutes, Contracts, and Legal Scholarship* (Leiden/Boston 2018); S. Gialdroni, Cordes, Dauchy, De ruysscher & Pihlajamäki (eds.), *Migrating Words, Migrating Merchants, Migrating Law: Trading Routes and the Development of Commercial Law* (Leiden/Boston 2019).

258 Fusaro, '"Migrating Seamen, Migrating Laws"? An Historiographical Genealogy of Seamen's Employment and States' Jurisdiction in the Early Modern Mediterranean', in: Gialdroni, Cordes, Dauchy, De ruysscher & Pihlajamäki (eds.), *Migrating Words*, 54–83,

'law in history' approach, emphasising its interplay with other social, economic and political factors.[259] This also fits with Ogilvie's approach to institutions.[260]

Meanwhile, maritime history plays its fair share in providing much of the background knowledge to this study, although methodologically this book primarily relies on legal-institutional analysis following the availability of sources.[261] Maritime history has long foregone abstract institutional analysis, something that has started to change, also because it has sought to employ to use approaches from other disciplines, such as global, economic and legal history, an interdisciplinarity that is also very fitting for this book.[262] Whilst this book does not offer a full analysis of the Low Countries' maritime sector, it emphasises the interplay of institutions for maritime trade (e.g. of GA and insurance) and the importance of the maritime sector for governmental (e.g. central government and Antwerp) and governance (e.g. private actors) layers in the wider political, legal and economic setting.[263]

This book primarily draws on legal sources, for these are the main sources providing information on GA and other varieties of Averages in the Low Countries. Part 1 studies the development of GA 'proper', focusing primarily on its role in risk management. Chapter 2 first provides a guide to further reading, as the history of Averages is both linguistically and legally so complex that many issues must be clarified before studying the actual sources. To explain this, it therefore draws on the concept of polysemy, the fact that the same word

---

there 66–67. See for a similar view: L.M. Friedman, *The Legal System: A Social Science Perspective* (New York 1987).

259 See: R.C.H. Lesaffer, 'Law and History', in: B. Van Klink & S. Taekema, *Law in Method: Interdisciplinary Research into Law* (Tübingen 2011), 133–154, there 136. Lesaffer also distinguishes 'history in law' (i.e. the lawyers' approach to history) and 'history of law' (the legal historians' approach to history, emphasising the history of law as an autonomous object of study).

260 Ogilvie, '"Whatever is, is Right?"'.

261 See for example for an overview of sources of maritime law in the medieval period: P.J.A. Clavareau, 'Les sources du droit maritime du Moyen Age', *Tijdschrift voor Rechtsgeschiedenis*, 18 (1950), 385–412.

262 Fusaro, 'Maritime History as Global History? The Methodological Challenges and a Future Research Agenda', in: Fusaro & Polónia (eds.), *Maritime History as Global History* (St. John's Newfoundland 2010), 267–282, there 267–269. See also: Van Zanden, 'The "Revolt of the Early Modernists" and the "First Modern Economy": An Assessment', *The Economic History Review*, 55, 4 (2002), 619–641, there 623–624, for the role of maritime trade in economic development.

263 Ibidem, 275 & 278–281. See also: Lucassen & Unger, 'Shipping, Productivity and Economic Growth'; North, 'Sources of Productivity Change'. For sixteenth-century Antwerp: Brulez, 'De scheepvaartwinst'. For the Low Countries more generally: Van Zanden & Van Tielhof, 'Roots of Growth and Productivity Change in Dutch Shipping Industry, 1500–1800', *Explorations in Economic History*, 46 (2009), 389–403.

can have multiple meanings. Chapter 3 draws on 'formal' sources of law, such as compilations of medieval maritime law, Antwerp municipal law, Habsburg princely legislation and mercantile custom, attacking the supposed existence of the *lex maritima*. Chapter 4 focuses on the interaction between formal and legal practice, drawing on court cases from Bruges, Antwerp, Zeeland and the Great Council and on notarial records from Antwerp. Given the importance of Castilian legislation and the Castilian *natio* in Bruges on the development of GA, the records of the Castilian consular court between 1546 and 1561 are also studied. This chapter highlights the important role of mercantile innovations and legal practice in influencing and codifying formal law, following Lawrence Friedman's theory of legal change.[264] Part 2 studies other varieties of Averages, shifting the view to *cost* (as opposed to *risk*) management, techniques. Chapter 5 draws on similar sources as Chapter 4 but focuses on contractual cost management varieties of Averages. Chapter 6 studies the Spanish compulsory contributions by drawing on privileges of the *nationes* and court cases from Bruges, Antwerp and the Great Council, showing the connection between Averages and protection costs. A conclusion follows, returning to the main themes of the book.

Two types of sources have been left out deliberately. First, given that there are almost complete source editions by Louis Gilliodts-Van Severen for the Bruges municipal court and the fact that the Antwerp municipal court rarely heard GA case before 1550, it is unlikely that many court cases could be found in the records of the Bruges municipal court for the fifteenth century.[265] Hence I have not gone through these voluminous (microfilm) records. Second, I have omitted the records of the Councils of Brabant and Flanders, the superior courts of the two provinces. These records are, in contrast to the Great Council, either unavailable for the early sixteenth century or the records do not have a proper inventory. Because it is likely that these courts rarely heard disputes on GA, as well as the fact that most foreign merchants went straight to the Great Council for important cases on the *avería de nación*, the focus here is on the Great Council archives.

---

264 Friedman, *The Legal System*.

265 Although the source editions of Louis Gilliodts-Van Severen are fairly complete, they are not always reliable. In most cases, I have thus checked underlying archival documents and noted where I discovered discrepancies.

PART 1

The Development of General Average and Risk Management

CHAPTER 2

The Power and Pains of Polysemy

2.1 Introduction: The Polysemic Meanings of Averages

Researching the history of 'Averages' in the late medieval and early modern period is, to recycle Johan van Niekerk's words on the history of insurance law, a "completist's nightmare".[1] Both from a legal-historical and quantitative viewpoint, a significant number of sources across Europe have survived, meaning a comparative effort takes much work.[2] Besides developments in the use and application of GA itself to manage risk, various other tools were developed to manage the operational costs or protection costs of a venture shared under the name 'Average'. In the Southern Low Countries, this was especially common and as a result, Part 2 of this book deals with the varieties of Averages for *cost* management. This chapter introduces all varieties in detail, to clarify the complex linguistic, economic and political meanings of the terms. It will show both the sheer complexity (the 'pains of polysemy'), but also argue that the various applications offered various advantages for merchants (the 'power of polysemy'). Of particular complexity was the Spanish (more specifically Castilian and Biscayer) case, where multiple Averages existed to cover a wide array of costs, for example protection costs, or the ordinary costs of the *natio*.[3] Polysemy, "the fact of having several meanings; the possession of multiple meanings, senses, or connotations" was omnipresent in sixteenth-century Averages.[4] The same word – *averij*, in Dutch, or *avería* in Castilian – did not necessarily indicate an intrinsic connection with GA 'proper'; and nor was its application and/or rationale similar. This polysemic aspect of Averages is key to understand the various applications in the Southern Low Countries and the distinction between risk and cost management.

1 Van Niekerk, *The Development*, xxix. I thank Maria Fusaro for suggesting the title of this chapter.

2 Even within the AveTransRisk project, not everything can be studied. For example, the German territories and Eastern Europe have been left out of the project, as is the Portuguese case. See: http://humanities.exeter.ac.uk/history/research/centres/maritime/research/ave transrisk/ {Retrieved 15/10/2020}.

3 I thank Marta García Garralón for helping me with the Spanish side of the project.

4 The definition of polysemy comes from the *Oxford English Dictionary*: https://www.oed.com /view/Entry/147370?redirectedFrom=polysemy#eid {Retrieved 21/01/2021}.

 | DOI:10.1163/9789004540354_003

This chapter therefore serves as an introduction to the varieties of Averages and their conceptual differences. It can be read in two ways: either as an executive summary of the research or as a guide to the later discussion in chapters 3–6.[5] It is important to note that it is very difficult to understand what follows without reading this chapter as a step-by-step guide, as the linguistic, polysemic elements of the various Averages cause substantial confusion. All these varieties were widely used in the Low Countries, but even during the sixteenth century there was sometimes a substantial lack of clarity over the application of the instruments. The polysemic nature of Averages therefore had effects on both transaction and protection costs, which we will explore in greater detail in Chapters 3–6.

2.2 Etymological Origins of GA

The principle behind General Average (GA) has ancient origins, going back to the *lex rhodia* quoted in Justinian's Digest.[6] Its linguistic origin is still the subject of debate.[7] In contemporary English usage, 'average' means the 'mathematical mean', although the first use as such only originates in the eighteenth century, as before it had polysemous meaning including contribution and damage.[8] In other languages, such as Dutch, French and German, the two words do not suffer from the same confusing similarity. *Averij*, in Dutch meant (and still denotes) either contribution or damage to cargo or ship, although in contemporary common usage it can mean any type of damage.[9] In the standard legal practice work on the present-day General Average rules, the editors argue that the *Constitutum Usus* of Pisa (*c.*1160) has a vague mention of 'average' as it included 'havere', indicating all the property of the ship, but also claim that the first express definition comes from the sixteenth-century *Guidon de*

5 Or, of course, as both.

6 See Chapter 3 for an analysis of the principle of GA in classical Roman law.

7 An excellent summary of the linguistic question can be found: Addobbati, 'Principles and Inferences of General Average: Statutory and Contractual Loss Allowances from the *Lex Rhodia* to the Early Modern Mediterranean', in: Fusaro, Addobbati & Piccinno (eds.), *General Average* (forthcoming).

8 Addobbati, 'Principles and Inferences'; S. Schaffer, 'Newtonian Calculations', Unpublished paper presented Genoa 18-05-2019.

9 As is the case in many other languages, for example German (*Haverei*) or Italian (*avaria*).

la Mer (dating roughly from the 1550s, and probably published around 1585).[10] This is not true, as both the 1538 Burgos *Ordonnance* (in Castile) and the 1551 *Ordonnance* of Charles V (in the Low Countries) already contained the term, the latter even providing a full definition.[11]

According to Andrea Addobbati, two serious options are still viable to explain the origin of the word 'average': first, the Arabic word '*awārīya*', meaning damaged cargo.[12] This is a common reference, and the present author has also used this reference in a previous publication.[13] Addobbati however argues that it is more likely that the word has Byzantine origins, although there is also substantial disagreement over which word would then be the exact predecessor. Most Roman and Byzantine legal compilations used the term 'contribution', adding to the confusion on the origins of the term.[14] As both Islamic and Byzantine legal compilations (eighth to tenth centuries) included jettison and mast cutting, it is therefore hard to be sure about the actual origins.[15] As the principle included the idea of deliberate damage and subsequent contributions by all in the interest community, both meanings – damage and contribution – could be valid in principle, although Averages were always about contributions in one way or the other.[16] In the Low Countries, the meaning of average was also always polysemic – in the case of risk management the contribution was to reimburse the person having incurred damage, and in the case of cost management the contribution was to common operational costs.[17] The goals of these contributions were therefore simply different, only linked by the same name.

10 Cornah & Reeder (eds.), *Lowndes and Rudolf*, 6–7. Yet the term 'varea' was already used in 1063 in the Statute of Trani. See : A. Lefebvre d'Ovidio, 'La contribuzione alle avarie comuni', *Rivista di Diritto della Navigazione*, 1 (1935), 36–140, there 71. I thank Maria Fusaro for this reference. See for the reference in the *Constitutum Usus*: J-M. Pardessus, *Collection de lois, maritimes antérieures au XVIIIe siècle* (6 vols., Paris 1828–1845) (Vol. 4) (hereafter: Pardessus, *Collection*), 581.

11 See sections 3.2.3 & 3.2.4.

12 For example in: Khalilieh, *Islamic Maritime Law*, 87–91. Other references to the supposed Arabic origin include: Céspedes del Castillo, 'La Avería', 518.

13 Dreijer, 'Maritime Averages'.

14 Addobbati, 'Principles and Inferences'.

15 For an overview of jettison in Islamic law and a discussion of its meaning see: Khalilieh, 'Rules and Practices of General Average in the Islamic Mediterranean on the Eve of the Emergence of the Italian Communes', in: Fusaro, Addobbati & Piccinno (eds.), *General Average*, forthcoming.

16 Addobbati, 'Principles and Inferences'.

17 Ibidem.

2.3 The Principle of GA Explained

The principle of risk-sharing via deliberate acts of jettison or mast-cutting was already known in legal sources of late antiquity, such as the sixth-century Justinian's Digest, the tenth-century *Basilica* of the Eastern Byzantine Empire and even in eighth- and ninth-century Islamic law.[18] GA was a principle built on equity, meaning that it was considered fair for all stakeholders to contribute when damage was incurred, to save the venture. Underlying the principle was the idea that all in a venture were engaged in a closed interest community (also 'danger community', *Gefahrengemeinschaft* or *communio periculis*).[19] The interest community denotes the "specific community of loss and risk that existed between the various interests on the same ship, engaged in the same common venture".[20] An interest community was sealed by concluding freight contracts, but this was more common practice than a prerequisite for the existence of the interest community *per se*. The basis of GA thus did not lie in an explicit contract, but rather in the fact that the venture legally resembled a (tacit) partnership structure.[21] The obligation to pay for GA lay in the fact that everyone involved in the venture took part in this tacit maritime partnership (*societas et communio tacita*), although this was a much-discussed issue by lawyers.[22] In the seventeenth-century Dutch Republic, insurers or merchants sometimes put clauses 'free of average' (*vrij van averij*) in freight contracts or insurance policies, aiming to escape the logic of the interest community.[23]

In classical Roman law in Antiquity, the GA contribution was shared among the participants in the interest community (including the persons whose cargo

---

18 Kruit, 'General Average', 192–194; W. Ashburner, *The Rhodian Sea-Law* (Oxford 1909), ccli–cclxxxv; Khalilieh, *Islamic Maritime Law*, 87–104.

19 Johan van Niekerk uses the term 'risk community', but to avoid confusion I have chosen the word 'interest community'. This concerns all the interests in the venture, including the ship and cargo. The term 'risk community' could be particularly confusing when talking about cost management in the risk community, which is the subject of Part two of the book.

20 Van Niekerk, *The Development*, 61–62. See also the Glossary of the AveTransRisk project: https://humanities.exeter.ac.uk/history/research/centres/maritime/research/avetransrisk/glossary/ {Retrieved 30/06/2020}. At the time of writing, this was still work in progress.

21 Ibidem, 74–76.

22 Ibidem, 76.

23 Ibidem, 1035–1037. This was also allowed in the 1608 *Compilatae* of Antwerp, but it does not appear to have been customary in sixteenth-century Antwerp. Only one court case from Zeeland concerned this: see section 5.2.3 for this singular case. Insurers still occasionally opt out of Averages, either GA or PA.

or ship were damaged).[24] A merchant entrusted the master with his cargo, promising to make a rateable compensation to cover damage when GA was declared.[25] The fact that merchants increasingly stayed onshore meant that much of the decision-making on a ship was delegated to the shipmaster, a development that can clearly be observed in legal sources in the Low Countries in the sixteenth century (Chapter 3). The shipmaster was given greater freedom to act in times of danger at sea, but liability was also sharpened in legal sources to prevent fraud.[26] In the Low Countries, the shipmaster himself also contributed, either via a share of his freight or after valuing the ship on which basis the contribution was determined.[27] After a jettison had occurred, generally speaking the procedure went as follows. A shipmaster applied for GA when he reached the first port after the incident. Subsequently, public authorities would appoint a panel of experienced merchants and/or shipmasters to survey the damage and hear testimonies, deciding whether the act had been necessary to (successfully) save the venture. In some places, public authorities delegated the work to private actors to adjudicate the case, for example in early sixteenth-century Antwerp, where minimal public oversight existed until the 1550s.[28] In such cases, an arbitration panel was appointed by mutual agreement among the parties, for example some trusted merchants or a notary. They would subsequently calculate the total damage, for example valuing the jettisoned cargo or the cut mast. How the value of the cargo was calculated depended on local customs. Cargo could for example be valued according to market value or cost value.[29]

A merchant whose cargo was lost or damaged incurred the loss or damage on behalf of the other participants in the venture.[30] The other participants then paid a *pro rata* reimbursement to the person who had suffered the damage. Average adjusters took the value of the damage (the so-called 'active mass') and divided this as a percentage of the contributory value ('passive mass') to

---

24 Ashburner, *The Rhodian Sea-Law*, ccliv–cclv.

25 Cornah & Reeder (eds.), *Lowndes and Rudolf*, 4–5.

26 See for a general overview of the position of the shipmaster and his liability: Rossi, 'The Liability of the Shipmaster'.

27 Van Niekerk, *The Development*, 72–73: Frankot, "*Of Laws of Ships*", 39–43.

28 See for the GA procedure in Antwerp Chapter 4.

29 See for example the different solutions in Hanseatic towns: Frankot, "*Of Laws of Ships*", 36–39. See also section 3.2.2.

30 A more detailed explanation of GA can be found here: http://humanities-research.exeter.ac.uk/avetransrisk/Average/example/ {Retrieved 20/07/2020}.

determine the share of the contribution for each participant.[31] An important principle in Roman-Dutch maritime law, made explicit by the Dutch lawyer Taco van Glins, was that a merchant would not have to pay 'more to the sea than he had entrusted to the same sea', meaning that a merchant could never pay more than the value of the cargo he put into the venture.[32] This was why a merchant whose cargo was jettisoned was reimbursed by the other participants in the venture, except for his share of the venture. If a merchant for example had 1/8 of the cargo on the ship, he also had to contribute 1/8 of the value of the cargo lost. In this simplified example, those whose cargo was not lost contributed 7/8 of the value of the damage, whereas the merchant whose cargo was lost had to bear the remaining 1/8 damage. When there was damage to a ship, for example when a shipmaster cut the mast, the contribution would be paid to the person who owned the ship, in the medieval period often the master himself.[33]

In the late medieval and early modern period, a more advanced system took hold as ship ownership was either joint (the so-called *partenrederij*) or large ship-owners hired shipmasters for individual ventures.[34] As ships got bigger, the volume of cargo transported rose as well.[35] When the cargo of multiple merchants was jettisoned, the complexity of the calculations rose accordingly. Another complicating factor was that by the mid-sixteenth century insurers could be held liable for GA payments in two ways.[36] First, the insurer was liable to pay the remainder of the damage to insured cargo when a merchant was reimbursed by other merchants after an act of GA (e.g. paying the remaining 1/8 damage in the example above); and second, when a merchant had to make a contribution based on the value of his cargo to someone else's damage and his own cargo was insured.[37] According to Van Niekerk, this was a widely accepted premise in Roman-Dutch law to ensure that no one could opt out of the interest

---

31 This is clearly visible in the database of the AveTransRisk project. See: http://humanities-research.exeter.ac.uk/avetransrisk {Retrieved 05/05/2020}. See also: Go, 'GA Adjustments in Amsterdam: Reinforcing Authority through Transparency and Accountability (Late Sixteenth–Early Seventeenth Century)', in: Fusaro, Addobbati & Piccinno (eds.), *General Average*, forthcoming. I thank Sabine Go for allowing me early access to her essay.

32 Goudsmit, *Geschiedenis*, 236–237; T. Van Glins, *Aenmerckingen Ende Bedenckingen over Zee-Rechten, uyt het Placcaet van Konick Philips* (Amsterdam 1665), 62–65.

33 Ward, *The World of the Medieval Shipmaster*, 64–67 & 95–97.

34 Ibidem, 51–63; Asaert, *De Antwerpse scheepvaart*, 146–158. See also: Go, 'GA adjustments'. See for the legal background to the *partenrederij*: De Jongh, *Tussen* societas *en* universitas, 14–17.

35 Lucassen & Unger, 'Shipping, Productivity and Economic Growth', 23.

36 Van Niekerk, *The Development*, 76–80.

37 Ibidem, 78–80.

community.[38] In sixteenth-century Antwerp this principle was accepted from the late 1540s onwards.[39] Given the expanding set of rules on GA and increasing complexity of calculations, it may be no surprise that specialised Average adjusters appeared on the scene.[40] Even today, Average adjustment is so complex that specialised Average adjusters are charged with making those calculations, reflecting the historical legacy of the maritime sector.[41]

2.4 Contemporary GA and Historical Reality

As already noted in the introduction, GA has largely been neglected in the (economic- and legal-)historical literature, in notable contrast to insurance. For the few scholars working on contemporary GA, history has nevertheless proved a common point of reference, steadily pointing out its existence since Antiquity.[42] Notwithstanding the lack of attention, GA is interesting for historians for four reasons: first, the risk-sharing element of GA has existed from Roman times until the present day, offering an excellent opportunity for a long-term history of (dis)continuity; second, it can illuminate gaps in the largely a-historical literature on the supposed *lex maritima*; third, it functions as an excellent object of comparative research, given its existence across Eurasia; and fourth, the increased use of insurance also necessitated clarifying the role of GA in insurance contracts, an issue still relevant today.[43]

For those who argue for the existence of a *lex maritima*, GA serves as an example of remarkable continuity throughout history.[44] In contrast, Edda Frankot and Albrecht Cordes have pointed out the manifold differences in the application of GA throughout Europe in the late medieval and early modern period.[45] Jolien Kruit, writing on the history of GA in the context of the debate on the *lex maritima* in the present day, has also argued that

---

38 Ibidem, 77. The 1608 *Compilatae* of Antwerp allowed insurers to opt out, the so-called *vrij van averij* contracts. See section 3.2.5.

39 See section 4.4.1.

40 De Groote, *De zeeassurantie*, 143–146. See also section 4.2.

41 See for example: Kruit, *General Average, Legal Basis and Applicable Law: The Overrated Significance of the York-Antwerp Rules* (Zutphen 2017).

42 See for example: Mukherjee, 'Essentials of General Average: A Synoptic Overview of an Ancient Maritime Law', *WMU Journal of Maritime Affairs*, 6, 1 (2007), 21–36.

43 See: Dreijer, 'Maritime Averages'; Van Niekerk, *The Development*, 76–80.

44 See for example: Tetley, 'The General Maritime Law'; Paulsen, 'Historical Overview'. A more nuanced view of the development of GA: Mukherjee, 'Essentials of General Average', 24–26.

45 Cordes, 'Lex Maritima?', 80–82; Frankot, *"Of Laws of Ships"*, 199.

> An analysis of the various historic regimes shows that they all incorporated the concept that expenditure and sacrifices made for the common safety of the parties interested in the maritime adventure were to be paid by (some of) the parties who had benefited therefrom. The analysis also makes it clear that each period of time and geographic area had its own regulations and application of the general average principle with specific features. [...] There has never been an overall uniform regulation in place. Even today, the YAR have not created a uniform application of the concept of general average.[46]

The application of GA in the Low Countries was by no means strictly uniform, as jurisdictional complexity and legal pluralism were facts of life. Notwithstanding these differences, parties were able to create workable solutions within this framework. As Kruit's quote makes clear, this is still the case today. The York-Antwerp Rules, first codified in 1890 and regularly updated since then under the auspices of the *Comité Maritime International* (CMI, the international association of maritime lawyers) regulate General Average worldwide, the last time being in 2016.[47] In practice, however, older versions of the YAR are still used (especially those of 1994), as not every country has ratified the new version of YAR.[48] Whilst the CMI strives to achieve uniformity in maritime law, it has no enforcement mechanism at its disposal. Although progress has been made, uniformity is still a long way off.[49] As Kruit argues, the YAR are therefore overrated, as parties to the contract (the interest community) are free to choose which YAR they use (or, in theory, are even allowed not to use them at all).[50] Moreover, for inland shipping several other legal agreements exist, such as the 'Rhine Rules Antwerp-Rotterdam' and the 1990 'Danube Rules on General

---

46 Kruit, 'General Average', 202.

47 The first YAR version had various predecessors, as discussions had already started in 1860 in Glasgow. In 1864, the first so-called York Rules were established. After the 1877 Antwerp conference, the amended rules were named the York-Antwerp Rules. Only with the 1890 update of the YAR was international recognition attained, however. See: Selmer, *The Survival*, 54–55; Cornah & Reeder (eds.), *Lowndes and Rudolf*, 44–52.

48 See for the current YAR and those back to 1994: https://comitemaritime.org/work/york-antwerp-rules-yar/ {Retrieved 30/06/2020}. See also: Kruit, 'General Average', 201–202; Idem, *General Average*, 32–37 & 67; Cornah & Reeder (eds.), *Lowndes and Rudolf*, 58–64. For the background to the 2004 changes: Cornah, 'The Road to Vancouver – the Development of the York-Antwerp Rules', *Journal of International Maritime Law*, 10 (2004), 155–166.

49 Kruit, 'General Average', 202.

50 Ibidem, 200–201. Marc De Decker also points to the differences in legal incorporation, as for example Switzerland have simply adopted the YAR, whilst Belgium and Germany have a legal provision to regulate GA. M. De Decker, *Europees internationaal rivierenrecht* (Antwerp & Apeldoorn 2015), 1214–1215.

Average'.[51] Interestingly, the fact that the CMI regulates the YAR means that GA is presently largely a private-order institution.[52] This may partly explain the wish of present-day maritime lawyers to characterise the history of GA as a private-order solution, although the extant historical evidence firmly shows that GA was for a long time grounded in public-order institutions.[53]

Contemporary scholarly debate about GA primarily centres on its future (or lack thereof). Both Knut Selmer and Proshanto Mukherjee have for example called for its abolition, calling it obsolete as technological development limits the need to share compensation.[54] Neither of them question the usefulness of GA for the period until roughly 1800, but they state that presently both the complexity and length of GA procedures, combined with developments in marine techniques and insurance, make the instrument obsolete. Yet despite repeated calls for its abolition, GA has withstood the test of time. Part of the call for the abolition of GA follows from the (mistaken) idea that there was a lack of innovation and development in the use of GA throughout history. Perhaps unwittingly, some defenders of the instrument have also incorporated this frame, pointing to the relative stability of the instrument throughout the ages.[55] Yet what this book and the *AveTransRisk* project clearly shows, is that the applications of GA and other Averages were manifold in the early modern period.

Discussions over GA were primarily jurisdictional rather than existential in the period under study, as in who should manage them, and what should be included in GA.[56] Over time, other damage besides jettison were added as legitimate for inclusion in GA, such as costs to prevent greater damage or shipwreck, voluntarily running aground, shying away from the strict principle of deliberate damage; and the relationship with insurers was clarified in formal sources of law. This coincided with major improvements in shipping technology, also impacting labour relations, as shipmasters more often became simple agents/employees rather than part ship-owners.[57] In short, the present

51 De Decker, *Europees internationaal rivierenrecht*, 1214–1215.

52 Kruit, *General Average*, 54–64.

53 See for example section 4.2 for evidence on the Southern Low Countries.

54 Selmer, *The Survival*; Mukherjee, 'The Anachronism'.

55 Kruit, 'General Average', 202. Her argument is nevertheless rather nuanced, as she also notes the development of costs to prevent greater damage as a major development in the history of GA. Yet the existence of many varieties of Averages rarely figure in the literature, except for the Spanish case. Some have also noted the 'backward' development of GA, for example in The Netherlands. See: Go, 'Governance of General Average in the Netherlands in the Nineteenth Century: A Backward Development?', in: P. Hellwege & Rossi (eds.), *Maritime Risk Management: Essays on the History of Marine Insurance, General Average and Sea Loan* (Berlin 2021), 247–264.

56 Or part of discussions on 'political economy', if one will.

57 See: Asaert, 'Scheepsbezit en havens'.

discussion does not bear much usefulness for the historical study of GA, as the instrument was clearly important for the interested parties in the maritime sector and was never in question.

2.5 Averages in the Sixteenth-Century Low Countries

Let us start the inquiry into sixteenth-century Averages with some basic definitions (Table 4). Some varieties, such as GA, PA and SA, were clearly defined in formal sources of law, for example in princely legislation (1551 *Ordonnance*) and Antwerp municipal law (1608 *Compilatae*). In contrast, Contractual Average can only be studied through notarial records and a small number of court cases: for the Spanish varieties, a scattered source corpus exists around the *Consulados*, including both formal sources of law (privileges, legislation) and court cases. Besides definitions, Table 4 also distinguishes the various Averages on the basis of three categories: first, *risk* versus *cost* management, second *ex ante* versus *ex post*, and third *contractual* versus *non-contractual*.

TABLE 4 Definitions of varieties of Averages

Variety	Risk/cost management	Ex ante/ ex post	Contractual/ non-contractual	Definition	Source
General average	Risk	*Ex post*	Non-contractual	Deliberate damage for the common benefit, shared by all in the interest community	1551 *Ordonnance*; Van Niekerk, *The development*, 63
Particular average	Risk	*Ex post*	Non-contractual	Accidental damage, borne by the particular interest involved	1608 *Compilatae*; Van Niekerk, *The development*, 63–64
Small/ common average	Cost	*Ex ante*	Contractual	Ordinary operational costs of the venture (e.g. pilotage)	1551 *Ordonnance*; Van Niekerk, *The development*, 63

TABLE 4 definitions of varieties of Averages (*cont.*)

Variety	Risk/cost management	Ex ante/ ex post	Contractual/ non-contractual	Definition	Source
Contractual average	Cost	*Ex ante*	Contractual	Division of payment of Averages (SA & PA) in freight contract	Van Niekerk, *The development*, 64–65
Avería de nación	Cost	*Ex ante*	Non-contractual	Annual membership fee of the *natio*, partly used for maritime protection costs (artillery & convoy ships). **False friends:** *massaria* (Genoese) & *direito da nação* (Portuguese)	Gilliodts-Van Severen, *Espagne*, 595–596; Goris, *Étude*, 171–172; Guiard y Laurrauri, *Historia*, 86
Avería(s)	Cost	*Ex ante*	Non-contractual	Compulsory contribution for protection costs on the Castile-Low Countries route, probably levied from 1553 onwards.	Fagel, *De Hispano-Vlaamse wereld*, 419; Basas Fernández, *El Consulado*, 168–171; Céspedes del Castillo, 'La avería', 524; Talavan, 'La avería', 133 & 142; García Garralón, 'The Nautical Republic', 10–11

SOURCES: SEE TABLE.

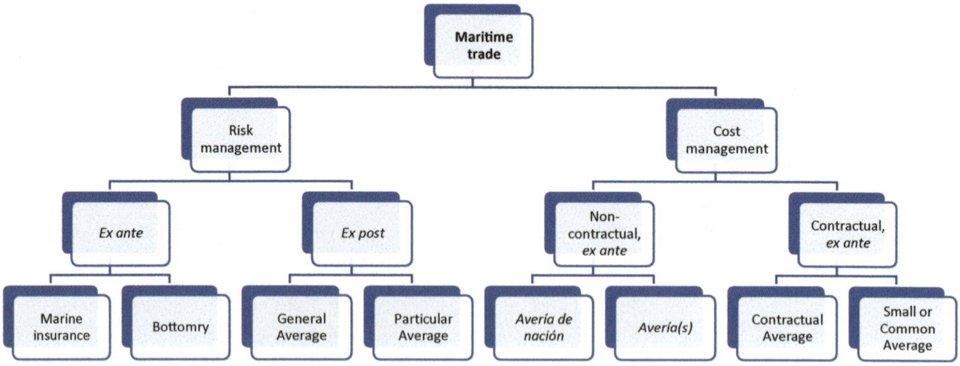

FIGURE 1 Varieties of Averages in the Southern Low Countries (fifteenth–sixteenth centuries)

Next to the definitions presented in Table 4, Figure 1 shows a visual categorisation of the various Averages. We will run through all these Averages here, based on the two major categories of risk and cost management. First, there was *risk* management, having defined *risk* in the introduction as an anticipated, possible and involuntary hazard. Merchants could (besides the more basic measures such as cargo spreading) manage risks both before and after a voyage. Before the voyage (*ex ante*), one could of course transfer the risk of damaged or lost cargo to an insurer by paying a premium, or in earlier times take out a bottomry loan.[58] When damage occurred at sea with or without insurance, *ex post* risk management came into force. When the damage was deliberate and for the common benefit, GA could be declared: as we have seen above, the costs for the damage were then shared by all in the risk community. Otherwise, for example when cargo was simply lost due to bad weather (in a so-called 'Act of God'[59]), Particular Average (PA) would apply. PA signified the accidental damage that was borne by the particular interest involved (e.g. the merchant in case of cargo). Both PA and GA could also be covered by insurers.[60]

The second category was *cost* management. Remember that we have defined *cost* in the introduction as the *anticipated*, voluntary payments in exchange for services. In this definition, we therefore also denote costs as foreseeable and relatively predictable. For example, on the river Zwin, pilotage was

58 Van Niekerk, *The Development*, 713–808 for the premium.

59 According to Black's Law Dictionary, an Act of God is "a natural event that causes loss. No human force is used and the event cannot be controlled". See: https://thelawdictionary.org/act-of-god/ {Retrieved 17/07/2020}.

60 Van Niekerk, *The Development*, 76–80.

compulsory because of the monopolies of the various skippers' guilds (e.g. Bruges and Sluis[61]): if (foreign) merchants wanted to sell their cargo in Bruges, one had to accept these costs. Ordinary (i.e. foreseeable) pilotage thus exemplifies how Averages were related to *cost* management: operational costs were first simply paid under the banner of 'Average' and from the 1520s onwards under the name *averij-commune* (Small or Common Average, SA).[62] The operational costs included not only pilotage, but also customs, port duties or whatever foreseeable costs the interest community wanted to include. In the Low Countries, these costs were often shared among the interest community in a freight contract, making them *contractual* obligations. Merchants therefore promised to pay for these operational costs *ex ante*, although payment happened only upon safe arrival along with the freight due (often called 'freight and Average'), as the costs could fluctuate depending on circumstances. In sixteenth-century Antwerp, Contractual Average (CA) built on these developments, often also including protection costs or PA costs in freight contracts via the same formula.[63]

These forms of cost management were primarily local variations. Castilian and Biscayer merchants in the Low Countries also developed cost management structures under the flag of the *nationes*. Those Averages were levied by the merchant guilds controlling the trade to and from the Low Countries from the late fifteenth century onwards: the Burgos *Consulado* for the Castilians and the Bilbao *Consulado* for the Biscayers.[64] Their satellite organisations in the Low Countries were the *nationes*.[65] Section 2.7.3 sketches the relations between these organisations in greater detail, but here it is enough to know that the *Consulados*, and by extension the related *nationes*, were allowed to levy so-called 'consular Averages' (*echar las averías*).[66] The *nationes* also had jurisdiction over GA cases within their community, but these consular Averages were different as they were used to cover all kinds of expenses that the *Consulado* or *natio* incurred. In theory, these consular Averages were related to the fact that the *Consulados* and *nationes* were responsible for outfitting the trading fleets. Yet in the case of the Bilbao *Consulado* and the Biscayer *natio*, the consular Averages soon encompassed a wide range of expenses.[67]

61 See for example: Dumolyn & Leloup, 'The Zwin Estuary', 208–211.

62 De ruysscher, 'Maxims, Principles and Legal Change'.

63 See: Dreijer, 'Maritime Averages', 46–49.

64 See Smith, *The Spanish Guild Merchant*.

65 See: Maréchal, 'La colonie espagnole', particularly 8–11.

66 Smith, *The Spanish Guild Merchant*, 86–90.

67 T. Guiard y Laurrauri, *Historia del Consulado y Casa de Contractación de Bilbao y del comercio de la ville* (Vol. 1) (Bilbao 1913), 86.

Most importantly, members of the Castilian *natio* in Bruges paid an annual, compulsory contribution based on the value of imports and exports of cargo (1% in this case) under the banner of the consular Averages.[68] Crucially, this covered protection costs such as artillery and convoy ships: as they were paid from a compulsory contribution which had already been collected, these were *ex ante* cost management structures. Yet they were non-contractual (as opposed to the local cost management varieties), as the obligation did not originate in the freight contract but rather in membership of a merchant guild. The book will primarily focus on the use of consular Averages by the Castilian *natio* in Bruges, and to a lesser extent on the Biscayer *natio* (Chapter 6). The Castilian *natio*, by virtue of its privileges, was allowed to levy compulsory contributions for the common expenses of the *natio* (e.g. political representation costs, legal fees and devotional expenses[69]) under the banner of the consular Averages. This was common, as the Genoese (under the name *massaria*) and the Portuguese (under the name *direito da nação*) were also allowed to levy a compulsory contribution for common expenses. The Castilian and Biscayer *nationes* called their compulsory contribution the *avería de nación*, clearly connecting it to (consular) Averages. One of the main differences between the *avería de nación* and the other compulsory contributions of the Southern European *nationes* was the protection costs element, on which legal practice also focused to a large extent. Following the promulgation of the 1551 *Ordonnance*, the Castilians had to comply with new protection costs measures and established a separate compulsory contribution to meet these new demands, the so-called *avería*(*s*) of 2.5%.[70]

68 Gilliodts-Van Severen, *Cartulaire de l'ancien Estaple de Bruges* (6 vols.) (Bruges 1904–1909) (hereafter: Gilliodts-Van Severen, *Cartulaire*) (Vol. 1), nr. 469 (pp. 394–396); Goris, *Étude*, 77; Finot, *Étude de Gênes*, 202.

69 These are just the main examples. Pilotage costs were included in Bilbao, among many other expenses. See: Guiard y Laurrauri, *Historia*, 339. For the Seville *Consulado*, see Céspedes del Castillo, 'La Avería', 518–519.

70 Fagel, *De Hispano-Vlaamse wereld*, 419–422. This was similar to the *avería* established by the Seville *Consulado*, but I will denote it as *avería*(*s*) as it was written both with and without the s at the end: moreover, this allows us to distinguish the Seville *avería* for protection costs from the compulsory contribution for the Low Countries trade protection costs. To make things even more confusing, the Seville *Consulado* also established the so-called *avería de excedo* or *avería gruesa*, which specifically denoted the contribution for the costs associated with having to stay for the winter in La Habana (present-day Cuba) following unforeseen circumstances (e.g. weather conditions or the threat of attacks at sea). See: García Garralón, 'The Nautical Republic', 10–11.

2.6 Risk Management

2.6.1 *General Average*

Acts like jettison were already included in medieval compilations such as the *Rôles d'Oléron* and a Dutch translation, the so-called *Vonnisse van Damme* (see Chapter 3).[71] In those older collections, reasons for a contribution from the interest community were jettison and mast cutting, offering rules of thumb rather than actual legal principles.[72] This idea appears to never have been questioned, although the details of the actual procedures provide different answers to some common questions: how should the cargo be valued? Who should contribute and how? What was the operational procedure in case of jettison? Although we observe a growing harmonisation in the sixteenth century, even within the Low Countries rules always differed on details, which was the logical outcome of the jurisdictionally complex and legal-pluralistic nature of the Low Countries.[73] Expenses to prevent (greater) damage were incorporated into GA, for example extraordinary pilotage in time of peril was allowed for the first time in the Amsterdam *Ordonnantie* of the early fifteenth century. Moreover, the insurability of GA led to significant changes in legal strategies and the use of GA.[74] This probably developed in Castile and then spread throughout Europe to preserve the interest community, including the Low Countries.[75] The 1551 *Ordonnance* was the first source of law in the Low Countries to define GA, moving from rules of thumb to an actual legal principle.[76]

2.6.2 *Particular Average*

Particular Average (PA) was first defined in the 1608 Antwerp *Compilatae*.[77] PA denotes damage that fell onto a specific interest. When a ship was damaged in a storm, for example, the cutting of the mast was not deliberate damage and had to be borne by the ship-owner. From the perspective of GA, PA can also be framed as those damages that cannot be shared within the interest community. PA still exists today next to GA. The legal definition of PA was of particular

---

71 This was the main text known in the Low Countries, although both Hanseatic maritime laws and various compilations in the Mediterranean also included this. See: Blakemore, 'Law and the Sea', 389–394.

72 De ruysscher, 'Maxims, Principles and Legal Change'.

73 See Chapter 3 for an in-depth analysis.

74 Van Niekerk, *The Development*, 76–80. See also section 4.4.2.

75 See for example: Rossi, *Insurance in Elizabethan England*, 137–139: K. Nehlsen-Van Stryk, *Die venezianische Seeversicherung in 15. Jahrhundert* (Ebelsbach am Main 1986), 165–180.

76 Kruit, *General Average*, 27; De ruysscher, 'Maxims, Principles and Legal Change'.

77 See section 3.2.5 & 4.3.4.

importance to insurers, as they could be held liable to contribute to GA damage as well as common damage (i.e. PA), but of course the actual monetary contribution significantly differed. As Charles MacArthur stated in 1893

> A general average differs from a particular average in its nature and incidence. The former is a partial loss, voluntarily incurred for safety, and made good proportionately by all parties concerned in the adventure; the latter is a partial loss, fortuitously caused by a maritime peril, and which has to be borne by the party upon whom it falls.[78]

Thus, declaring either GA or PA was important as it clearly demarcated the contribution of the insurer. This is still the case today: PA damage is fully borne by the insurer unless negligence can be shown, whereas GA damage requires only a partial contribution from the insurer on the basis of the value of the cargo or ship.[79]

2.7 Cost Management

2.7.1 *Contractual Cost Management Varieties: SA, CA, and* flete y averías

Besides GA, the 1551 *Ordonnance* defined Small or Common Average (SA).[80] SA was, in short, the operational costs to run the ship: for example, ordinary pilotage, port duties and custom costs. These costs were often paid by merchants together with the freight upon arrival, but contractualised before the voyage to provide legal certainty to all parties. The expression *averij-commune* for SA was used for the first time in the 1520s in the Low Countries.[81] That did not mean, however, that ordinary costs were not paid before this time. These were usually part of the freight, and denoted as 'freight and Average' (*vracht ende averij*) in freight contracts. This distinction between freight and average was already made in the fifteenth century. As the freight was fixed as a fee per unit, only the operational costs could vary. In freight contracts, the distinction was therefore made to make sure that only the Averages could vary. Of course, these costs were relatively foreseeable, but gave the master the necessary flexibility to make a necessary stop or incur other operational expenses. The polysemic

78 Quoted in: Mukherjee, 'Essentials of General Average', 23.

79 Insurers are often unwilling to pay for GA compensation, even today. See: Ibidem, 27.

80 See Section 3.3.3 for the references.

81 De ruysscher, 'Maxims, Principles and Legal Change'. The expression *avería común* was also already commonly used in the various Spanish privileges for the *Consulados* of the 1530s to the 1550s. See Chapter 3.

meaning of Averages was clear as well, as the contribution was made towards costs rather than to reimburse damage for the common benefit.[82]

In sixteenth-century Antwerp, both SA and protection costs (e.g. artillery) were often incorporated in freight contracts, a form that we call Contractual Average.[83] Cost management varieties were also common among Castilian merchants, for example as they used Contractual Average in Antwerp.[84] One specific cost management variety however stood out: the so-called *flete y averías* (literally 'freight and Average'), which members of the Castilian *natio* paid for ordinary pilotage in the Zwin and other operational costs upon arrival in the Low Countries.[85] The crucial difference between the local cost management varieties was that the *natio* administered payment through the *controlador* based in Zeeland.[86] The advantage for parties in the interest community lay in the fact that the *natio* subsequently used its bargaining power to negotiate lower fees for the compulsory pilotage in the Zwin, leading to low(er) predictable costs for the members of the *natio*.[87] Otherwise, the *flete y averías* was similar to the local cost management varieties and therefore different from the consular Averages, as it was a *contractual* form of Average for an individual trading voyage between the Iberian Peninsula and the Low Countries, based on a freight contract between master and merchant (yet under the supervision of *Consulado* and *natio*).[88] *Averías*, in this meaning, simply denoted the fluctuating element of the operational costs and therefore cannot be classified as a separate form of Average: Teófilo Guiard y Laurrauri has for example published three *cartas de flete y averías* drawn from the archives of the Bilbao *Consulado*, which all stated that masters paid 'the ship's bottom with pitch, "mangas, chapas y claos"',[89] payment of the harbour pilot, payment of shallops, navigating the ship on the riverbank, and other ordinary Averages and customary Averages' from the *flete y averías*.[90] In short, this covered all kinds of common operational costs but could include other costs as well.

82 Addobbati, 'Principles and Inferences'.
83 See: Dreijer, 'Maritime Averages': Van Niekerk, *The Development*, 64–65.
84 Goris, *Étude*, 173.
85 Fagel, *De Hispano-Vlaamse wereld*, 129–138 & 484.
86 See for the structure of the Consulate: Maréchal, 'La colonie espagnole', 28–29. See also: Fagel, *De Hispano-Vlaamse wereld*, 129–138 & 484.
87 See section 5.3.2.
88 Fagel, *De Hispano-Vlaamse wereld*, 129–138.
89 There are two explanations for the meaning of 'claos' in the 'mangas, chapas y claos': one refers to the size of the vessel(s), the other to the necessities of the *maestre* (shipmaster). I thank Carla Rahn Phillips and Marta García Garralón for the constructive discussion on this subject.
90 Ibidem. I thank Marta García Garralón for the translation.

2.7.2 *Consulados*, nationes *and the Non-Contractual 'Spanish' Consular Averages*

The Spanish so-called consular Averages form the most challenging part of research into sixteenth-century Averages. As multiple scholars working on the Spanish case have remarked, the polysemic aspect of the consular Averages is bewildering to modern eyes, particularly as they have no logical connection to GA.[91] The development of compulsory contributions[92] under the privileges of the consular Averages can be understood only by taking stock of the complex administrative structure that governed Spanish maritime trade. In the Castile-Low Countries trade, the *Consulados* were the most important organisations. The *Consulados* were monopolistic merchant guilds tasked with the organisation and transport to sell wool in Flanders, but it also had significant jurisdictional powers over its members.[93] The Burgos *Consulado* received royal privileges in 1494, followed in 1512 by the Bilbao *Consulado* after repeated complaints by the Biscayer merchants that their trade with Flanders was inhibited by the monopoly of the Burgos *Consulado*.[94]

A significant part of the disputes was over who had the competence to collect the consular Averages (so-called *echar las averías*), leading to the 1496 *Prágmatica* issued by the Castilian King Ferdinand V which established a protocol for the levying of those Averages.[95] The *echar las averías* was the overarching term for the privilege of levying the consular Averages (and therefore did not denote the separate jurisdictional privilege over GA). The consular Averages were all the Averages levied by the *Consulados*, or their satellite organisations the *nationes*, to cover expenses related to the organisation.[96] Needless to say, this was a major privilege for the *Consulados*. As one of the main tasks of the *Consulados* was to organise maritime transport for trading purposes, many costs were by necessity 'maritime'. Yet soon the expenses covered by the consular Averages of the Bilbao *Consulado* included charitable costs, church maintenance costs, rescue of kidnapped seafarers, getting poor people out of jail, dressing beggars, rescuing sailors from shipwrecks or from

---

91 See Talavan, 'La Avería'; Céspedes del Castillo, 'La Avería'.

92 These were after all contributions that members of the *Consulado* or *natio* could not avoid paying. Moreover, this term is preferred to tax, particularly as the *natio* was dependent upon both the *Consulado* at home and the local sovereign to levy the compulsory contribution, taking away the state element necessarily linked to taxation.

93 As defined by Ogilvie: Ogilvie, *Institutions and European Trade*, 19–40.

94 Smith, *The Spanish Guild Merchant*, 67–90.

95 Guiard y Laurrauri, *Historia*, 86.

96 See e.g.: Ibidem, 68–84; M. Basas Fernández, *El Consulado de Burgos en el Siglo XVI* (Madrid 1963), 129–154.

attacks by corsairs and pirates, distribution of alms to the poor, maintenance expenses of the house in Bruges, payment of employees, road and port repairs, and (maritime) protection costs, to name but a few.[97]

These disputes between the various *Consulados* did not only play out in the Iberian Peninsula, but also in the Low Countries where their 'daughter' organisations, the *nationes*, existed. Castilian merchants received privileges in Flanders in 1343, with more extensive privileges following throughout the next centuries.[98] Until the mid-fifteenth century, Biscayer merchants trading with the Low Countries formally fell under the Castilian *natio*. In 1447, they negotiated their own privileges.[99] Despite Castilian protests, further developments meant that from 1494 onwards, Iberian merchants in the Low Countries were divided into three formal *nationes*: Castilian, Biscayer and Catalan-Aragonese.[100] In 1500, the Andalusian *natio* also received privileges in Antwerp, before moving to Middelburg (Zeeland) in 1505.[101] The Navarrese *natio* received privileges in 1530, renewed in 1556.[102] It is important that all were allowed to levy a compulsory contribution, but only the Castilians and Biscayers used it for maritime protection costs. Tensions between Castilians and Biscayers continued both in Castile and in the Low Countries, although on occasion they also litigated together in the Low Countries to protect their mutual interests abroad, emphasising the opportunistic nature of merchants trading abroad.[103]

Similar to the *Consulados*, the Castilian and Biscayer *nationes* in the Low Countries levied consular Averages. The most important one (and for a long time the only one) was the so-called *avería de nación* (also known as *dinero de nación*, or in French *denier de nation*), an annual contribution to the *natio* for common costs based on a percentage of the imports and exports of the members. All members of the *natio* paid this contribution, regardless of

97 Guiard y Laurrauri, *Historia*, 86.

98 Gilliodts-Van Severen, *Espagne*, 8–12.

99 Ibidem, 31.

100 The standard text on the Spanish *nationes* is: Maréchal, 'La colonie espagnole', especially 7–10. See also: Idem, 'Le depart'; Casado Alonso, 'La colonie', 233–251; Idem, 'La *nation*', 61–77.

101 Fagel, 'Spaanse kooplieden in Middelburg vóór de Opstand: succesvolle integratie met behoud van eigen identiteit', in: 't Hart, Lucassen & H. Schmal, *Nieuwe Nederlanders. Vestiging van migranten door de eeuwen heen* (Amsterdam 1996), 21–33, there 22–23.

102 Gilliodts-Van Severen, *Espagne*, 242–245 & 370–371.

103 This is further analysed in: Dreijer, 'Identity, Conflict and Commercial Law: Legal Strategies of Castilian Merchants in the Low Countries (Fifteenth–Sixteenth Centuries)', in: De ruysscher *et al* (eds.), *Commerce, Citizenship and Identity in Legal History* (Leiden & Boston 2021), 118–138. See also: Cordes & Höhn, 'Extra-Legal and Legal Conflict Management'.

shipping interests.[104] Annual, compulsory contributions to cover ordinary costs were characteristic of the Southern European *nationes* in the Low Countries. English Merchant Adventurers for example levied an initial membership fee, but not an annual contribution to cover the ordinary expenses of the *natio*.[105] Although the Southern European compulsory contributions all appeared to have a similar basis, a close reading of the privileges and contextualisation shows that there were differences between the 'Spanish' variant which was clearly connected to protection costs, and the compulsory contributions of the Portuguese and Italian *nationes*, which were not, and simply covered the ordinary expenses and costs of the *natio* (see below).[106] Following from the privilege to levy consular average, the Burgos *Consulado* and the Castilian *natio* in Bruges also established the so-called *avería(s)* around 1553, a compulsory contribution of 2.5% of imports and exports to cover the rising protection costs following the 1551 *Ordonnance*, stipulating obligatory convoy ships and artillery.[107] Both were non-contractual obligations to contribute to protection costs provided by the *natio*: in the terminology of the New Institutional Economics, the *nationes* provided club goods (i.e. an artificially scarce item, in this case protection such as convoy ships and artillery[108]) for its members.

2.7.3 *False Friends and Polysemy: The* **droit d'avarie** *and the* **nationes**

According to Louis Gilliodts-Van Severen, all Southern European *nationes* were allowed to levy a membership fee in the form of a compulsory contribution on its members, known as either the *droit d'avarie* ('right of average') or the *denier de nation* ('money of the nation').[109] The Castilian and Biscayer *nationes* called the privilege either the *avería de nación* or the *dinero de nación*, although the former was more common. The Portuguese called the privilege to levy an annual contribution the *direito da nação* ('right of the nation'), whilst various Italian *nationes* (Genoese, Florentines, Lucchese) called it *massaria*.[110]

104 Gilliodts-Van Severen, *Espagne*, 595–596.

105 De Smedt, *De Engelse natie* (Vol. 2), 30–31.

106 In contrast to what most scholars have assumed. See for example: Gilliodts-Van Severen, *Espagne*, 595–596; Goris, *Étude*, 171–173; Guiard y Laurrauri, *Historia*, 86.

107 Fagel, *De Hispano-Vlaamse wereld*, 419. This was similar to the *avería* levied for protection costs in the Seville *Consulado*: see section 6.2 & García Garralón, 'The Nautical Republic', 10–11.

108 Definition from: https://en.wiktionary.org/wiki/club_good {Retrieved 27/01/2020}.

109 Gilliodts-Van Severen, *Espagne*, 595–596. See also: Goris, *Étude*, 173–174; Guiard y Laurrauri, *Historia*, 86.

110 Adding to the substantial linguistic complexity, the *massaria* could mean different things. See for the *massaria* in Alexandra, Famagusta and Crimea: Petti Balbi, 'La

The latter two do not contain a reference to 'Average' in their name, but still Gilliodts-Van Severen and other authors put all these contributions on equal footing.[111] Yet both the *direito da nação* and the *massaria* were never used for purposes other than the ordinary expenses of the *natio*, such as devotional expenses, wages of the consuls and legal fees.[112] The Spanish *nationes* of course also used the *avería de nación* for such costs. In that sense, the 'deeper' purpose of these compulsory contributions was rather similar. Yet crucially, as Chapter 6 argues, they also used their compulsory contribution to cover maritime protection costs, such as convoy ships and artillery.[113] In contrast, the only maritime costs the Genoese and Portuguese could cover were salvage costs.[114] The question whether the Castilians and Biscayers could request foreign merchants to pay for the *avería de nación* when using Castilian or Biscayer ships for transport purpose, and therefore contribute to the protection costs, became the major question during the late fifteenth and early sixteenth century, leading to a flurry of lawsuits which will be studied in Chapter 6. This had a significant impact on both transaction costs (e.g. enforcement costs for the Spanish *nationes*) and protection costs (for both the Spaniards and the Genoese).

---

massaria genovese di Allesandria d'Eggito nel Quattrocentro', *Studia Storici*, 38, 2 (1997), 339–353; Balard, 'The Greeks of Crimea under Genoese rule in the XIVth and XVth centuries', *Dumbarton Oaks Papers*, 49 (1995), 23–32, there 24; Idem, 'La *Massaria* génoise de Famagouste', in: A.D. Beihammer, M.G. Parani & C.D. Schabel (eds.), *Diplomatics in the Eastern Mediterranean 1000–1500: aspects of cross-cultural communication* (Leiden/Boston 2008), 235–250. Both in Caffa (Crimea) and Famagusta (Cyprus) the *massaria* denoted the register of income of the Genoese colony there. In eleventh-century Alexandria, it was rather a contribution to build a church. In the text, the *massaria* will denote the compulsory contribution of the *natio* in Bruges and Antwerp, but readers should beware that the problem of 'polysemy' also exists in the Genoese case. Compare the Venetian case, which also levied compulsory contributions: U. Signori, 'Reti consolari veneziane nell'Impero ottomano del Seicento', in: A. Gallia, L. Pinzarrone & G. Scaglione (eds.), *Isole e frontiere nel Mediterraneo moderno e contemporaneo* (Palermo 2017), 19–34; Idem, *Venezia e Smirne tra sei e settecento. Istituzioni, commerci e communitá mercantile* (Unpublished PhD thesis, University of Padova 2014).

111 Gilliodts-Van Severen, *Espagne*, 595–596.

112 Martyn, 'De Portugese natie in Antwerpen: drie eeuwen kwaliteitsbewaking van privileges en gewoonterecht', in: G.P. Van Nifterik, J. De Vries & M. De Wilde (eds.), *De achterkant van Minerva: opstellen aangeboden aan prof. Kees Cappon ter gelegenheid van zijn afscheid aan de Universiteit van Amsterdam* (Amsterdam 2019), 74–87, there 80; Pohl, *Die Portugiesen*, 54; R. Van Answaarden, *Les Portugais devant le Grand Conseil des Pays-Bas (1460–1580)* (Paris 1991), 208–209.

113 Gilliodts-Van Severen, *Espagne*, 595–596.

114 Ibidem; Finot, *Étude de Gênes*, 206–207; Pohl, *Die Portugiesen*, 54.

2.7.4 *The* avería(s)

Following the increased threat of piracy and the promulgation of the 1550 and 1551 *Ordonnances* (see section 3.2.3), the *avería de nación* was probably no longer adequate to cover all the protection costs of the new measures. Whilst the Castilians frustrated efforts for state-backed convoy systems and central taxation to pay for these measures,[115] it nevertheless appears that the Burgos *Consulado* and Castilian *natio* internally did actually act to meet these demands by establishing the *avería(s)*, a development only picked up by a few authors.[116] *Avería(s)*, as we understand it here, was a contribution for protection costs, primarily artillery and convoy ships.[117] Manuel Basas Fernández mentions that this was also levied in Bruges to pay for the protection costs of the Castile-Low Countries route, but does not mention a temporal limitation or particular details.[118] According to Raymond Fagel, around 1553 a new form of *avería(s)* of 2.5% of the imports and exports was established within the *natio* to meet the new demands for protection costs including artillery and convoy ships, but this is the sole reference in the context of the Low Countries.[119] Fagel suggests, but does not make explicit, that this new *avería(s)* was established as the 'normal', because the *avería de nación* could not provide enough money to meet the new demands.[120] Archival material on the *avería(s)* levied for the Low Countries is extremely limited, making it hard to assess the impact of the instrument.[121]

2.8 Conclusion

Polysemy was at the heart of the development of Averages in the sixteenth century. The simple term 'Average' could mean at least three separate types of contributions: a contribution to reimburse a deliberate damage for the common benefit (GA); a contribution to common operational costs (e.g. in SA); and a contribution to the expenses of the Castilian and Biscayer *nationes* (the

115 Sicking, *Neptune and the Netherlands*, 253–260; see also Fagel, *De Hispano-Vlaamse wereld*, 413–422.

116 Céspedes del Castillo, 'La Avería', 524; Talavan, 'La avería', 133 & 142; García Garralón, 'The Nautical Republic', 10–11; Basas Fernández, *El Consulado*, 168–171; E. Vila Vilar, *El Consulado de Sevilla de Mercaderes a Indias. Un Órgano de Poder* (Seville 2016), 89; Idem, 'Algunas consideraciones sobre la creación del Consulado de Sevilla', in: S.A. (ed.), *Congreso de Historia del Descrubrimiento (1492–1556): Actas* (Vol. 4) (Madrid 1992), 53–66, there 55–56.

117 Fagel, *De Hispano-Vlaamse wereld*, 419–422.

118 Basas Fernández, *El Consulado*, 168–171.

119 Fagel, *De Hispano-Vlaamse wereld*, 419.

120 Ibidem. See also: Sicking, *Neptune and the Netherlands*, 247–260.

121 In notable contrast to the *avería* for the New World trade. See footnote 116 of this chapter.

so-called consular Averages, partly based on the privileges of the 'mother' *Consulados*). Whereas rules-of-thumb on jettison had existed since Roman times, the other two sorts of Averages developed during the fifteenth and sixteenth centuries. The polysemic aspect is at the same time extremely complex (the 'pain' of polysemy) and crucial to understand the development of Averages, as merchants sought to cover new risks and costs arising in an increasingly complex world where the maritime sector played a crucial role for transport purposes (the 'power' of polysemy).[122]

This chapter has argued that the various Averages should be categorised under either *risk* management or *cost* management. Under the first fell GA and PA, as they *ex post* covered the anticipated but involuntary hazards that could befall a venture at sea. The second category first contained contractual varieties, such as SA, CA and *flete y averías*, covering foreseeable costs such as ordinary pilotage. This offered legal security to all in the interest community, thereby lowering enforcement costs and offering the necessary flexibility to the shipmaster following the distinction between freight and average, as the latter could fluctuate when necessary. The second subcategory of the cost management varieties were the 'Spanish' consular Averages. They covered a wide variety of expenses and costs of the *Consulado* or *natio* but were particularly important in covering protection costs for the Castile-Low Countries trade, setting it apart from the other Southern European compulsory contributions. This had significant effects on both transaction and protection costs.

Having now laid down the basis for the further analysis of the Averages, why does this matter in the first place? Let us return to the three major debates we have introduced in the introductory part. First, the sheer complexity of Averages (again) shows that a *lex maritima* was a fantasy for sixteenth-century Europe, as many local varieties existed next to the variations in applications of GA itself. Second, it shows that maritime risk management was a complex business in the sixteenth century, but that historians should also seriously consider cost management structures besides risk management 'proper'. Moreover, it shows that these institutions often address multiple problems:[123] the Spanish compulsory contributions for example offered a system of cost management for protection costs, but these protection efforts in turn *also* lowered risk. Third, it shows that Averages had profound effects on both transaction and

122 Lucassen & Unger, 'Shipping, Productivity and Economic growth'; North, 'Sources of Productivity Change'.

123 Following Ogilvie, '"Whatever is, is Right?"'.

protection costs, having profound distributive effects.[124] For example, the power of the Castilian *natio* to compel their members to contribute to protection costs but also to offer club goods impacted the distribution of protection rents. In other cases, for example in the case of risk management, a relatively efficient operational combination of insurance and GA was developed, allowing merchants both to transfer risk *ex ante* and share risk *ex post*.

124 Ibidem, 662–665.

CHAPTER 3

General Average in Formal Sources of Law

3.1 Introduction

This chapter focuses on the development of the formal sources of law dealing with GA in the Low Countries during the fifteenth and sixteenth centuries. Contrary to the scholarly attention given to the development of insurance,[1] there has not been an overview of the development of GA in the Low Countries. The principle behind GA was broadly agreed upon by the various interested parties in the Low Countries during the fifteenth and sixteenth centuries, but it was noted that particularities and application varied greatly across regions and jurisdictions.[2] Even if rules of thumb existed both in Roman law and in various compilations of medieval maritime law based on local legal customs, in the Low Countries GA (*groote avarye*) was properly defined only in the 1551 *Ordonnance* of Charles V, and subsequently extensively regulated in the 1563 *Ordonnance* of Philip II, the latter analysed by Quintin Weytsen in his *Tractaet van Avarien*. Both princely legislation and Antwerp municipal law were of particular importance to define the instrument in legal terms, moving from the 'rules-of-thumb' approach found in the medieval compilations to general legal principles, offering greater legal security.[3]

Despite the fact that the various parties interested in the maritime sector at the time held differing normative positions on both GA and insurance, the chapter will show that the development of GA was largely evolutionary rather than revolutionary and therefore offered continuity. Through long negotiations, workable rules were established on GA during the sixteenth century. Whilst it would be too far-reaching to speak of 'path dependency', we can see that in these negotiations *constraints* played a major role, as no party in the maritime sector was able to push through all its wishes. As a result of the negotiations, some uninsurable expenses were folded under GA. In short, we can see the contours of a certain equilibrium arise between the various tools of risk management by studying the formal sources of law. The operational aspects of

1 Goris, *Étude*, 170–174; De ruysscher, 'Belgium: Marine Insurance', in: Hellwege (ed.), *Comparative History of Insurance Law in Europe. A Research Agenda* (Berlin 2018), 110–132, there 113–115.

2 Frankot, "*Of Laws of Ships*"; Kruit, 'General Average', 201–202.

3 De ruysscher, 'Maxims, Principles and Legal Change'.

 | DOI:10.1163/9789004540354_004

risk management in the Low Countries therefore became a relatively efficient set of institutions, even if, in addition, we can clearly observe that certain parties were also able to influence the distributional effects of GA.[4] Part of these efforts was a constant search for legal authority by jurists and lawmakers to justify their normative position(s) on maritime law and GA, for example by referring to Roman law or the 'usages and customs of the sea'.[5] Chapter 4 will subsequently show that legal practice often preceded formal law.[6]

Four major developments can be identified in the Laws of General Average in the (Southern) Low Countries between roughly 1350 and the 1608 *Compilatae*.[7] First, the freedom of action of the shipmaster was broadened to perform an act of GA, but his liability also became stricter when damage could have been prevented;[8] second, new causes for GA were allowed besides jettison and mast cutting, for example uninsurable costs such as the expenses for wounded men fighting pirates and privateers, as well as those incurred to prevent greater damage, such as extraordinary pilotage; third, lawyers gradually started to distinguish between various forms of Averages, such as General, Small or Common and Particular Average (*averij-grosse*, *averij-commune* and *averij-simpel*), offering general principles rather than solely 'rules of thumb', thereby enhancing legal security;[9] and fourth, Castilian normative practice inspired the formal liability of insurers for GA claims, as the interest community had to be protected to diminish moral hazard.[10]

---

4 Ogilvie, '"Whatever is, is Right?"', 667.

5 As Randall Lesaffer has noted, Roman law was not necessarily the ultimate authority (*Auctoritas*) any more during the sixteenth century. However, many jurists still studied Roman law as an important source of law and drew inspiration from this, something that can be observed in maritime law as well. This process is called *Emulatio*, whereby Roman law still played an inspirational role in crafting the practice of contemporary law. See: Lesaffer, *European Legal History*, 366–367; for *Auctoritas*: 283–284.

6 As is also emphasised in the theory of legal change of: Friedman, *The Legal System*.

7 And which, as noted in the introduction, serves as the end point of this research.

8 A development which can be observed in other places in Europe as well: Rossi, 'The Liability of the Shipmaster'.

9 Before the 1550s, no strict distinction was made between the various forms of Average. GA existed, while most other costs were grouped under Common Average, which was basically everything that was not GA. This included the running costs of the ship, but also some costs included as PA later, such as ordinary pilotage. PA was only defined as such in the 1608 *Compilatae*, since it was of special importance when deciding on insurance pay-outs. See: Van Niekerk, *The development*, 64–65; De ruysscher, 'Maxims, Principles and Legal Change'.

10 Van Niekerk, *The Development*, 76–80. Whilst the Castilians codified this principle in the *Hordenanzas*, this principle was also known in various Italian city-states. See section 3.2.4 for an inquiry.

The chapter, following the debate described in the introduction, will show that the idea of a *lex maritima* did not exist in the sixteenth-century Low Countries. But rather than simply attack this idea, the chapter will argue that principles such as the deliberate damage for the common benefit were commonly known throughout Europe during this time, but application strongly differed according to region.[11] As both Albrecht Cordes and Edda Frankot have shown, different solutions to similar problems were the hallmark of late medieval trade.[12] In the Low Countries, all governmental and private actors accepted the rationale for GA, but there was no agreement over its application besides some procedural rules, leading to lengthy negotiations over the application within the legal-pluralistic setting of the Southern Low Countries. Yet under the *iura mercatorum* the new rules did offer legal security, particularly as the more abstract rules found in princely legislation enabled jurists to incorporate GA into existing legal frameworks.[13]

Section 3.2 analyses the principle of GA in Roman law and its incorporation into various compilations of medieval maritime law, before moving on to investigate sixteenth-century sources of law, those being princely legislation, the *Hordenanzas* of the Castilian *natio* and Antwerp municipal law. The subsequent section 3.3 analyses the (legal) boundaries between GA, shipwreck and salvage, as the three were connected and separate at the same time, impacting the development of GA in connection to the other institutions. Moreover, this section deals with the vexed issue of ship collisions, which was a topic discussed at length by both Roman-Dutch jurists and in the courts in the Low Countries. Section 3.4 is a close reading of Quintin Weytsen's treatise, the major doctrinal source on GA in the Low Countries, before the chapter comes to a close. Three caveats are necessary upfront. First, as the distinction between 'public' and 'private' law is a distinctly nineteenth-century one, this chapter necessarily has to deal with both aspects as, for example, the 1551 *Ordonnance* dealt with both issues.[14] The second caveat concerns terminology surrounding piracy and privateering. There was a significant difference between the two, as pirates were, legally speaking, looting criminals, whereas privateers were those operating under a Letter of Marque (e.g. from the Admiralty), allowing them to legally reprise actions of war or aggression against subjects of other

---

11 A similar point is made by both Frankot and Cordes: Cordes, 'Lex Maritima?', 80–82; Frankot, *"Of Laws of Ships"*, 199.

12 Ibidem. See also: Cordes, 'Conflicts in 13th-Century Maritime Law'.

13 De ruysscher, 'Maxims, Principles and Legal Change'; Kadens, 'Order within Law', 42.

14 This is not particularly surprising as the distinction is a nineteenth-century one, resulting from the codification movement. The distinction is therefore highly anachronistic.

states.[15] Yet in the primary sources, the difference is not always fully clear, as the 1551 *Ordonnance*, for example, spoke of 'enemies and sea-rovers' (*vyanden ende zeerovers*). Therefore, this chapter and the following ones will make the distinction between pirates and privateers where this is clear, but when a legal text is unclear what is meant, will speak of 'piracy'. The third caveat is that GA was, in principle, limited to maritime (i.e. oceanic) affairs, and thus not applicable to riverine law until the late nineteenth century.[16] Pilotage however concerned both ocean and river navigation and was regulated in formal sources of law, making it an essential element in the analysis of GA.

3.2 GA in Sources of Formal Law

3.2.1 *GA in Roman Law and the Basilica (Sixth–Tenth Centuries)*

The principle behind GA was first written down in sixth-century Roman law. Digest 14.2 of Justinian's compilation under the title *De lege rhodia de iactu* ('on the Rhodian law of jettison') in D.14.2.1, attributed to the third century Roman jurist Julius Paulus.[17] This concerned jettison and stated that

> It is provided by the Lex Rhodia that if merchandise is thrown overboard for the purpose of lightening a ship, the loss is made good by the assessment of all which is made for the benefit of all.[18]

It makes a reference to the Greek *lex rhodia de iactu* (which has not survived, indicating the rule was even older). This clause did not (yet) mention the strict necessity of the damage as a prerequisite for contribution. Julius Paulus also argued that accidental damage did not require a contribution.[19] Although jettison was the most commonly cited example, ransom paid to pirates to save

15 See: Rodger, 'The Law and Language'; Sicking, 'The Pirate and the Admiral: Europeanisation and globalisation of Maritime Conflict Management', *Journal of the History of International Law*, 20 (2018), 429–470. Moreover, the definition depended on the various parties, for example as one party could designate someone a pirate whereas the person sailed with a Letter of Marque, depending on political and legal circumstances.

16 De Decker, *Europees internationaal rivierenrecht*, 1210–1213.

17 The edition used for this research is: J.E. Spruit *et al* (eds.), *Corpus Iuris Civilis: tekst en vertaling (vol. III, Digesten 11–24)* (The Hague 1996) (hereafter: Spruit, *Corpus*), D.14.2.1. An analysis is provided in: Ashburner, *The Rhodian Sea-Law*, ccli–cclxxxv.

18 See the footnote above for the original Latin. The English translation is taken from: http://www.duhaime.org/LawMuseum/LawArticle-383/Lex-Rhodia-The-Ancient-Ancestor-of-Maritime-Law-800--BC.aspx {Retrieved 03/10/2019}.

19 Spruit *et al* (eds.), *Corpus*, D.14.2.2, D.14.2.2.1 & D.14.2.4.

the venture, mast cutting to avert common danger and actions to lighten ships to prevent further damage were also cited as a cause for contribution by other jurists.[20] Hence costs made to prevent (greater) damage were also incorporated in some of the legal opinions of the Roman jurists. Salvaged cargo contributed to the calculation, but owners of salvaged cargo could not receive any form of compensation. If merchants had already paid the contribution before the cargo was salvaged, they could ask for their contribution back.[21] The jurist Hermogenianus noted that the contribution had to be done in an equitable way, absolving those who had lost their cargo from additional contributions.[22] The sacrifice, in Roman law, was thus strongly linked to the idea of averting a common danger to ship or cargo. An enslaved person transported as cargo to be sold at the destination who jumped overboard could, according to this logic, not be cause for a contribution.[23] The idea of risk-sharing therefore had its roots in classical Roman law, because it was considered fair for all the parties involved that they would have to share the costs (*aequitas*).[24] According to Emmanuelle Chevreau, Roman law already made a distinction between GA and Small or Common Average (SA), but this seems highly unlikely and anachronistic.[25] GA was understood as an equitable tool to share actual damage. Merchants largely remained outside the Roman legal framework of *locatio conductio* (the Roman contract of letting and hiring), with GA an entirely alien rule to standard contract law.[26]

The *Basilica*, a compilation originating in the Byzantine Empire around 900, largely adopted the rules of the Digest in a simplified manner.[27] The *Basilica* however also added a section called the Rhodian Sea Law (not to be confused with the *lex rhodia de iactu*), offering a wider interpretation of what could be a cause for contribution and moving away from the principle of a communal

20 Ibidem, D.14.2.2.3 & D.14.2.3.

21 Ibidem, D.14.2.2.7.

22 Ibidem, D.14.2.5.

23 Ibidem, D.14.2.2.5.

24 This is the concept of *aequitas*. See for an analysis in the framework of GA: Ashhburner, *The Rhodian Sea-Law*, cclv–cclvi.

25 Chevreau, 'La lex Rhodia de iactu', 76. Although it is unlikely that the operational costs were already conceived as an 'Average', there may of course have been a way to share those costs.

26 An oppositional view of this is found in: Aubert, 'Dealing with the Abyss'. Aubert argues that the rules on GA were incorporated into the framework of *location conductio*, but it appears that the rules on GA were largely separate from contract law provisions. I thank Guido Rossi (University of Edinburgh) for helping me with these paragraphs.

27 Ashhburner, *The Rhodian Sea-Law*, cclv–cclvi.

danger.[28] The main focus was still on jettison. Chapter 9 for example stated that the master had to receive agreement from the merchants on the ship before jettisoning cargo and that personal cargo (i.e. of the seaman, master, etc.) had to contribute a limited amount to the overall contribution. Enslaved people jettisoned to lighten the ship were valued as a fixed cost, so that the value of an enslaved person did not have to be calculated afterwards.[29] There may also have been a special form of Average beyond GA, as the *Basilica* included contributions after wide-ranging examples such as shipwreck not caused by the fault of the master and seamen, theft by pirates, unintentional damage caused by water or fires after a storm, or the unintentional collision of two ships.[30] These were of course all non-deliberate damage, but did then also fall under a separate category: GA remained limited to deliberate damage to ship or cargo, for example jettison.

Jettison was indeed the most commonly cited example for a contribution by all engaged in the venture, a development that can be observed outside Roman law as well. Islamic jurists from the eighth and ninth centuries were also concerned with the jettison of enslaved people.[31] In medieval China, jettison and subsequent damage-sharing was also known as a legal principle.[32] In the Eastern Adriatic, jettison was a topic of contention in both formal law and legal practice.[33] Mediterranean compilations of maritime law, such as the eleventh-century Ancona maritime statutes and the twelfth-century *Constitutum Usus* of Pisa also mentioned jettison and subsequent risk-sharing.[34] Throughout the medieval period, the 'problem of jettison' remained a major issue for jurists, leading to what Olivia Remie Constable has called 'an insoluble problem', as questions abounded over the exact application (e.g. value of

28 Ibidem, cclvii.

29 Ibidem, clviii.

30 N. Bogojevic-Gluscevic, 'The Law and Practice of Average in Medieval Towns of the Eastern Adriatic', *Journal of Maritime Law & Commerce*, 36, 1 (2005), 21–60, there 28.

31 Khalilieh, *Islamic Maritime Law*, 87–104. The main issue in Islamic maritime law was whether enslaved people could be jettisoned, something that is not often mentioned in the Western literature. One English case from 1804, however, became notorious when enslaved persons were jettisoned in a storm. See: I. Baucom, *Specters of the Atlantic: Finance, Capital, Slavery and the Philosophy of History* (Durham/London 2005).

32 Reid, 'The Hybrid Maritime Actors', 118.

33 Bogojevic-Gluscevic, 'The Law and Practice', 25–26.

34 An excellent overview of Italian maritime laws in: Krieger, 'Die Entwicklung', 185–193. See for jettison specifically: Constable, 'The Problem of Jettison', 215–217. The *Constitutum Usus* distinguished between *iactus cum concordia* and *iactus sine concordia*, forcing the master to liaise with the merchants on board unless their ship was in imminent danger, in which case jettison was allowed without their agreement (*sine concordia*). See: Ashburner, *Rhodian Sea-Law*, cclxix–cclxx.

the cargo or the contribution of the shipmaster).[35] This already shows that the existence of a *lex maritima*, even within one of the 'legal circles'[36] (in this case the Mediterranean), cannot have existed.

3.2.2 *Compilations of Medieval Maritime Law in Europe (Thirteenth–Sixteenth Centuries)*

Risk-sharing techniques were subsequently incorporated into various compilations of medieval maritime laws. Practicalities, however, strongly differed between regions. In Edda Frankot's study on these developments in high medieval north-western Europe, jettison, shipwreck and salvage figure as important examples.[37] She studied both the normative legal framework and the legal practice in the towns of Kampen, Aberdeen, Reval (current-day Riga), Lübeck and Danzig, concluding that the collections of maritime law (such as the *Rôles d'Oléron* and the Wisby Laws) contained basic rules of thumb on maritime trade. These examples were however always complemented with local bylaws and customs. Differences for example existed on the valuation of cargo and ship, the procedure to follow in case of jettison and exactly which objects should contribute.[38] In legal practice, municipal courts often provided ample room to accommodate customs from other cities or regions, for example when foreign masters applied for GA. They moreover communicated with courts in other cities to check which customs were valid.[39]

Frankot therefore concluded that the *lex maritima* did not exist in late medieval northern Europe, since both the procedural framework and legal practice on the principle differed across Europe. Albrecht Cordes, also reviewing the evidence for northern Europe, has pointed to the fact that two different models existed for GA contributions: a northern one, which excluded the shipmaster from making a contribution, and a southern one which included him doing so.[40] During the fourteenth century, the southern principle 'triumphed' in the Hanseatic area, but this did not mean that there was a harmonised rule as there were still discussions over how much he should contribute, and how (e.g. via his freight or via the value of the ship when he was part- or

35 Constable, 'The Problem of Jettison', 220.

36 As per Goldschmidt, *Universalgeschichte des Handelsrecht.*

37 Frankot, *"Of Laws of Ships"*, 27–52.

38 Ibidem, 31–46.

39 Ibidem, 164–165. This was also common during the sixteenth century. See: Wubs-Mrozewicz & Wijffels, 'Diplomacy and Advocacy: The Case of the *King of Denmark v. Dutch Skippers* before the Danzig City Council (1564–1567)', *Tijdschrift voor Rechtsgeschiedenis*, 84 (2016), 1–53.

40 Cordes, 'Lex Maritima?', 76.

full-owner).[41] The southern principle would, eventually, be incorporated in most legal sources in the Low Countries. This differed from most Mediterranean rules. Julia Schweitzer, comparing the *Rôles d'Oléron* and the *Consolat del Mar* in a wider sense, also pointed to the differences between the two collections, for example on labour issues.[42]

Hanseatic maritime laws were, alongside Mediterranean compilations, among the most developed in the High Middle Ages. The German-language literature reflects this with multiple studies which touch on GA.[43] Both the cities of Lübeck and Hamburg commonly incorporated the principle of deliberate damage for the common benefit into municipal law, primarily in case of jettison.[44] The *Schiffersordnung* of 1591, promulgated in Lübeck, was among the most influential and was also translated in various European languages.[45] Although most collections dealt primarily with jettison, the 1591 *Schifferordnung* also stipulated that GA could be declared when pirates or privateers attacked the ship and a seaman was injured fighting them.[46] In the Bruges *Kontor* of the *Hanse*, the so-called *Waterrecht* was created, combining the Amsterdam *Ordonnantie* and the *Vonnisse van Damme* (see below).[47] The *Waterrecht* also contained several articles of older *Schifferordnungs*.[48] Also called the *Flandrischer Copiar*, it was used by Hanseatic merchants in Bruges and formed the basis for the Wisby Laws, commonly cited as the most

41 Ibidem: see also Landwehr, *Die Haverei*, 50–57.

42 Schweitzer, *Schiffer und Schiffsmann*, 181–191 for jettison.

43 The most important work is: Landwehr, *Die Haverei*. See also: Idem, 'Zur begriffsgeschichte', 57–69; Idem, 'Prinzipien der Risikotragung beim Seefrachtvertrag. Rechtverhältnisse bei Haverei und Schiffbruch in der Nord- und Ostseeschifffahrt vom 13. Bis zum 17. Jahrhundert', in: Köbler & Nehlsen (eds.), *Wirkungen europäischer Rechtskultur*, 595–615.

44 Idem, 'Seerecht im Hanseraum im 15. Jahrhundert: die Hanzerezesse, die Vonnesse von Damme und die Ordinancie der Zuidersee im Flandrischen Copiar Nr.9', in: Jahnke (eds.), *Seerecht im Hanseraum des 15. Jahrhunderts. Edition und Kommentar zur Flandrischen Copiar Nr. 9* (Lübeck 2003), 95–117, there 96–97 &115–117. Lübeck for example published compilations in 1240 and 1299, Hamburg around 1250 and 1306. The Hanseatic *Diets* also published so-called *Schifferordnungs* containing rules on jettison in 1434, 1441, 1447, 1482, 1530, 1542 and 1572.

45 Ibidem, 116. See for a seventeenth-century English translation: G. Miège, *The Ancient Sea-Laws of Oleron, Wisby and the Hanse-Towns still in Force* (London 1686).

46 Ibidem. The text can be found in: Pardessus, *Collection* (Vol. 1), 507–527, there Title XXXVI. This clause was similar to the 1551 and 1563 Low Countries *Ordonnances*.

47 The manuscript was published in: Jahnke (eds.), *Seerecht im Hanseraum*, 7–94.

48 Landwehr, 'Seerecht im Hanseraum', 115–117.

influential compilation in the Low Countries.[49] In this way, Hanseatic maritime law was an important influence in the Low Countries.

Besides Hanseatic maritime law, Mediterranean maritime laws were of course also well-developed. An early reference to jettison and mast cutting for example can already be found in the *Código de las Partidas* of Alfonso X (1266).[50] The *Consolat del Mar*, probably the most influential compilation, originated in the area of Catalonia-Aragon. A first complete version was printed in Barcelona in 1502, but the collection was compiled from multiple sources, including princely legislation and older compilations. The two most important parts were the 1407 Valencian customs which formed the initial core, and the (much larger) 1435 Barcelona maritime customs.[51] Even if some of the Valencian chapters touched on contribution after accidents, nothing was specifically mentioned on jettison.[52] The Barcelonan customs, in contrast, did discuss this.[53] Most rules were fairly standard and dealt with issues such as the valuation of cargo and jettison procedure.[54] In the *Consolat*, both bad weather and fear of pirates or privateers could be a reason to jettison cargo, marking a wider acceptance of jettison.[55] Whereas in older Mediterranean compilations (such as the eleventh-century *Constitutum Usus* of Pisa and the twelfth-century *Tabula de Amalfi*) the masters' contribution was still an unclarified subject,[56] the *Consolat* forced the master to contribute and share in the damages, although he was allowed to choose how, an important distinction from Low Countries formal law. A master had two options. The preferred way was to contribute via the value of the ship, with the master not requiring freight money for the lost cargo. Another option was to contribute via the freight, which a master would receive in full and from which he would subsequently pay the contribution.[57]

49 Ibidem.

50 See Pardessus, *Collection* (Vol. 6), 16–57, there 45–47 for jettison and other actions leading to contribution.

51 Krieger, 'Die Entwicklung', 206–208.

52 The edition of the *Consolat del Mar*, with an English translation, used here can be found in: T. Twiss (ed.), *The Black Book of Admiralty* (Vol. 3) (Cambridge 2013), 50–658. The relevant Valencian laws are Chapters xix–xxi.

53 Ibidem. The relevant Barcelona Chapters are l–liv, lxvi–lxvii, ccv & ccli. Chapters xix–xxi for example concerned the contribution and reimbursement by the master when cargo were spoilt due to his negligence.

54 For example Chapters lii, liv & lxiv.

55 *Consolat del Mar*, Chapter LI.

56 Constable, 'The Problem of Jettison', 217.

57 *Consolat del Mar*, Chapter LIII.

Given the presence of foreign merchants from various parts of Europe, it may have been the case that some of these collections were known in commercial cities such as Bruges by the late fifteenth century.[58] The *Rôles d'Oléron* were however the most influential collection in the Low Countries. The *Rôles* were initially compiled in the form of judgements to provide twenty-six standard rules for the wine trade in the Bordeaux area during the thirteenth century, although the exact date of origin is still subject of debate.[59] The *Rôles* were translated (*inter alia*) into English and published, with a number of changes, as the *Black Book of Admiralty*.[60] In the original version of the *Rôles*, articles 8 and 9 dealt with jettison and mast cutting, clearly limiting itself to direct deliberate damage as a cause for contribution.[61] In both cases, when a shipmaster acted in good faith, merchants were obliged to repay their share of the damage to the shipmaster, which was calculated 'over ship and cargo'. Article 8 on jettison stated that the shipmaster always had to consult with the merchants on board the ship, or if there were none, the master had to consult with the crew, who would later have to swear an oath that the jettison was necessary. The contribution by the shipmaster was calculated either according to the damage done to the ship and cargo or according to the freight money paid, and he could choose between these two. In most collections in the Low Countries, this choice was to be made by merchants rather than the master, whereas Iberian maritime law stuck with the master.[62] Shipmasters themselves preferred this, as merchants could try to inflate the value of a ship to raise the relative contribution of the master.[63] Seamen on board were allowed to have one chest with them which would not be included, as long as they made their best effort to save the ship.[64] Article 9 dealt with mast and rope cutting and stated that this was only allowed in times of great danger, for example in case of lightningstrike.

58 Kiesselbach, 'Der Ursprung', 1–3; A. Telting, *Die alt-Niederländischen Seerechte* (The Hague 1907). Already in the early fourteenth century, the *Vonnisse van Damme* were incorporated in the privilege books of the city of Bruges. See: BE-SAB, Oud Archief, Bijlage 1, nr. 22, *Purpurenboek* (*14e eeuw–1540*), fol. 3r–5v.

59 The debate over when the *Rôles* were written down, and where this happened, is a major topic in the literature. Nowadays, it is accepted that the *Rôles* were written down in France around 1220. The best introduction to the subject is: Krieger, *Ursprung und Wurzeln*.

60 Runyan, 'The Rolls of Oleron', 96–97. In the *Black Book of Admiralty*, an extra rule was added which stated that the cargo had to be value according to market value. This can be found in: Pardessus, *Collection* (Vol. 1), 346, Art. 35.

61 The following edition of the *Rôles* is taken from: Kiesselbach, 'Der Ursprung', 44–60. *Rôles d'Oléron*, Arts. 8 & 9.

62 See for example section 3.2.4 for the Castilian examples.

63 De ruysscher, 'Maxims, Principles and Legal Change'.

64 *Rôles d'Oleron*, Art. 8.

Merchants had to reimburse the master for the damage incurred immediately after the voyage. If the merchants did not have enough money, they had to sell or pawn the cargo and pay the master from this income, even if they wished to pursue legal action.[65] The rules in the *Rôles* were thus quite advantageous to the master. Clearly, the *Rôles* contained rules of thumb ('deliberate jettison and mast cutting lead to Average') instead of general legal principles about GA.[66]

Already in the fourteenth century, a translation of the *Rôles* under the name of *Vonnisse van Damme* (named after the port town in the Zwin estuary) was incorporated into the municipal privilege books of Bruges.[67] Yet multiple versions of the collection existed and other translations of the *Rôles* were adapted at various times in various places in the Low Countries.[68] One version has for example been found in Amsterdam, another sixteenth-century copy in Zeeland which was known as the *Rechten van Westcappelle*.[69] The translations were largely similar to the original of the *Rôles*, except that Article 8 of the *Vonnisse* made mention of Sluis, another port town in the Zwin estuary.[70] In the *Rechten van Westcappelle*, a third article was added stating that a master could hire pilots when a ship ran aground in case of imminent danger (so-called *strangen*), adding an expense to prevent greater damage.[71] Moreover, the article stipulated that the master and two senior crew members should make the decision if no merchants were on board.

To what extent the *Vonnisse* were used in Bruges is hard to test given the dispersed nature of the municipal archive, but it is clear that they were known since at least the mid-fourteenth century in Flanders and were also used in

65 *Rôles d'Oléron*, Art. 9. This was similar to the so-called *namptissement* in Antwerp insurance law.

66 De ruysscher, 'Maxims, Principles and Legal Change'.

67 Kiesselbach, 'Der Ursprung', 1–3; BE-SAB, *Purpurenboek*, fol. 3r–5v. See for a description of the Zwin Estuary: Dumolyn & Leloup, 'The Zwin Estuary'.

68 A transcription of the *Vonnisse van Damme*, also used here, can be found in: C.A. Den Tex, 'Oud-Nederlandsch zeerecht: kritische bewerking van den tekst der Vlaamse Zeeregten', *Bijdragen tot rechtsgeleerdheid en wetgeving*, 5 (1830), 33–62. See for the two texts compared: Kiesselbach, 'Der Ursprung', 44–60. Dirk Van den Auweele has however pointed to the differences between the various translations. See: D. Van den Auweele, 'Zeerecht', in: Asaert *et al*, *Maritieme Geschiedenis der Nederlanden* (Vol. 1), 220–226, there 221–223; Idem, 'Het Brugse zeerecht, schakel in een supranationaal geheel', in: Vermeersch (ed.), *Brugge en de zee: van Bryggia tot Zeebrugge* (Antwerp 1982), 145–155, there 147–150.

69 Den Tex, 'Oud-Nederlandsch zeerecht', 33–36; Van den Auweele, 'Zeerecht', 223; Idem, 'Het Brugse zeerecht', 148; A. Korthals Altes, *Ons oudste zeerecht* (Zwolle 1976), 3–13.

70 *Vonnisse van Damme* Arts. 8 & 9.

71 Korthals Altes, *Ons oudste zeerecht*, 20.

the Bruges municipal court.[72] The *Vonnisse* was not the only compilation in existence in the Low Countries. Two other compilations were the so-called *Ordonnantie* (*c.*1400–1413), of which versions were found in Amsterdam and Stavoren (Friesland),[73] and the *Gulden Boeck*, a compilation of maritime laws of the Hanseatic town of Kampen (*c.*1430).[74] Like most compilations on maritime laws, both primarily dealt with issues of what would nowadays be called labour law. The *Ordonnantie* regulated the trade of Amsterdam and nearby maritime towns in the Zuiderzee area.[75] On jettison and mast and/or rope cutting the *Ordonnantie* was similar to the *Rôles*.[76] It added three more rules: first, the so-called *lotegelt*, which was money paid for a pilgrimage made to thank God for a safe voyage;[77] second, employing lighter ships when the ship could not reach a port by itself;[78] and third, extraordinary pilotage (similar to the *Rechten van Westcappelle*).[79] The *Ordonnantie* was hence the first local text to clearly incorporate costs to prevent greater damage such as extraordinary pilotage, shying away from the strict principle of deliberate damage in case of jettison or mast cutting.

The Kampen town laws are an often overlooked yet important source for the study of GA in the Low Countries. Kampen, a Hanseatic town east of the Zuiderzee, was a transit port for the Hanseatic merchants sailing to Holland. The aldermen compiled a collection, called *Dat Boek van Rechte,* in the early fourteenth century. This collection was amended during the fifteenth century and republished as the *Gulden Boeck*.[80] The *Gulden Boeck* stated that the *lotegelt* was a contribution to make for a pilgrimage (after *lot*, fate or destiny).[81] Although money for the pilgrimage was only collected after the voyage arrived safely, the promise was made when a ship encountered a heavy storm. The

72 See section 3.3.2 for proof.

73 Frankot, 'De "Ordinancie van Staveren" en het Hanzeatisch zeerecht', *It beaken*, 77, 1–2 (2015), 1–23.

74 Ibidem; Idem, *"Of Laws of Ships"*, 27–52.

75 Landwehr, 'Seerecht im Hanseraum', 106–108. Indeed, the collection was probably drawn up to regulate maritime transport in the *Zuiderzee* area, and as such examples have been found in Amsterdam, Enkhuizen and Staveren, towns that took part in this local trade. A transcription, also used here, can be found in: Den Tex, 'Oud-Nederlandsch zeerecht: kritische bewerking van den tekst der Amsterdamse Ordonnantie', *Bijdragen tot rechtsgeleerdheid en wetgeving*, 5 (1830), 170–208.

76 *Ordonnantie* Amsterdam, Art. 5.

77 Ibidem.

78 Ibidem, Art. 19.

79 Ibidem, Art. 20.

80 Frankot, *"Of Laws of Ships"*, 89.

81 Ibidem, 32.

crew hoped to avoid disaster and prevent greater damage by praying to God.[82] This article was subsequently also included in the *Ordonnantie*.

The *Gulden Boeck* followed established practice in many regards (e.g. including expenses to limit greater damage), but also offered new solutions. One article for example concerned jettison and proposed a relatively novel solution to the problem of freight and the contribution of the master. The *Rôles* stipulated that the master only had to contribute in case of damage, and hence not when the cargo was salvaged. In principle, this meant the GA contribution was cancelled but no normative sources provide an explanation of how this worked in practice. In contrast, the *Gulden Boeck* proposed that freight had to be paid for the transport of both salvaged and jettisoned cargo. Although the master still had to contribute via either freight and ship, this meant that the master could not be punished for jettisoning cargo.[83] Other rules were similar to those in the *Ordonnantie*, for example on the contribution of the seamen, mast cutting and lighter ships.[84] As opposed to the *Ordonnantie*, the Kampen town laws did not contain the clause that seamen could have one free chest on board.[85] The liability of the shipmaster was more clearly defined in the *Gulden Boeck*. If a master overloaded his ship, there could be no contribution in any circumstance.[86] One remarkable clause should also be mentioned: when a ship was arrested in a foreign port and a ransom had to be paid, these costs could be shared among the participants.[87] When cargo still reached its destination port, merchants had the choice to either abandon the cargo or contribute. When cargo was lost as a result of a pirate or privateer attack, the merchants did not have to contribute.[88] The *Gulden Boeck* mentioned that rules on contribution could be different in other ports, a clear recognition of legal pluralism.[89] The *Gulden Boeck* indeed differed from the laws of other Hanseatic cities such as Lübeck and Hamburg, whose laws only included jettison as a cause for contribution.[90]

The *Vonnisse* and the Amsterdam *Ordonnantie* were, during the fifteenth century, combined and incorporated into the Hanseatic *Waterrecht*.[91] Hanseatic merchants in Bruges combined these rules with some stipulations from various

82 Goudsmit, *Geschiedenis*, 121–123. See also: Frankot, "*Of Laws of Ships*", 31–32.

83 Frankot, '*Die Ehrbaren Hanse-Städte See-Recht*', 114–115; Goudsmit, *Geschiedenis*, 306–307.

84 Goudsmit, *Geschiedenis*, 307–309.

85 Ibidem.

86 Ibidem.

87 Ibidem, 308.

88 Ibidem.

89 Ibidem, 307–308: "*Wanneer sie comen tandern havenen in andern lande dar nemen si dat recht alse daer zedelic ende woentlic is*".

90 Ibidem.

91 Frankot, "*Of Laws of Ships*", 21–22.

Hanzerezesse, resulting from the meetings of the Hanseatic towns.[92] In later versions, twelve articles from Lübeck municipal law were added rather than the various *Hanzerezesse*, forming the so-called Wisby Laws. This collection was named after the town of Visby (present-day Sweden), where a first version was most likely printed.[93] In the Lübeck articles, only one article concerned jettison, stating cargo had to be valued according to market prices at the destination.[94] The Wisby Laws became the most influential compilation of maritime laws in the Low Countries during the sixteenth century, although some of its rules contradicted each other, for example on how cargo should be valued.[95] Some early modern Dutch jurists, such as Adriaen Verwer, suggested that the Wisby Laws were the customary maritime laws of the Low Countries.[96] Even if this was a dubious claim, it was widely accepted in contemporary sources.[97] Notwithstanding their influence, the Wisby Laws were essentially a compilation of older rules, offering a (perhaps useful) synthesis but no new rules. Frankot's research has subsequently also shown that the hypothesis that the Wisby Laws were the 'law of the land' across Europe cannot be held up, as few cities used the Wisby Laws as their main blueprint.[98]

3.2.3 *Princely Legislation (Sixteenth Century)*

This section discusses legislation issued by the Habsburg sovereigns Charles V and Philip II. It is largely limited to the 1550, 1551 and 1563 *Ordonnances*, of which the latter two dealt with GA. The *Ordonnances* of Charles V (in 1550 and 1551) and Philip II (in 1563) were of great importance for the maritime economy since they provided the most far-reaching measures on the matter. The increase in privateer attacks were partly the result and partly the motivation of Charles V's Habsburg-Valois War of 1551–1559 against the French. The 1550 and 1551 *Ordonnances* were aimed specifically at navigation to the West, as Scottish and French privateers threatened the maritime route between the

92 Landwehr, 'Seerecht im Hanseraum', 100–105.

93 Frankot, "*Of Laws of Ships*", 22–24.

94 *Waterrecht*, Lübeck Laws, Caput 134.

95 Van den Auweele, 'Zeerecht', 223; Idem, 'Het Brugse zeerecht', 151.

96 A. Verwer, *Nederlants See-Rechten: Avaryen en Bodemereyen Begrepen in de Gemeene Costuimen vander See; de Placcaten van Keiser Karel den Vijfden 1551 en Koning Filips den II 1563 't Tractaet van Mr Quintyn Weitsen van de Nederlantsche Avaryen* (Amsterdam 1711), fol. 2–4. See for Verwer: Hermesdorf, 'Adriaen Verwer (1655–1717) en de Ordonnance de la Marine', *Rotterdams Jaarboekje*, 7, 5 (1967), 227–261.

97 Especially for the 1551 *Ordonnance* also referred to the Wisby Laws as the 'customs of the sea'.

98 Frankot, "*Of Laws of Ships*", 108–109.

IMAGE 6 Titian, portrait of Emperor Charles v seated (1548)

Low Countries and the Iberian Peninsula.[99] Following medieval practice, the *Ordonnances* stipulated a number of practical measures to limit damage.[100] The *Ordonnances* therefore largely offered continuity, but following tense negotiations the *Ordonnances* did also offer some new rules, particularly on the subject of privateering and piracy. Moreover, princely legislation was instrumental in *defining* GA and moving beyond the rules of thumb found in the medieval compilations.[101]

Starting work in 1549, Charles V and one of his main advisors, Cornelis de Schepper, proposed obligatory taxation on cargo transported to and from the Iberian Peninsula to pay for protection measures, such as artillery and convoy costs.[102] They also proposed to curb the use of insurance and bottomry loans, two instruments for risk management seen by the central government as harmful for trade because of their speculative elements.[103] The government had two principal objections to the use of insurance: that it was used for speculation rather than for managing risk in maritime trade; and that it did not in itself offer proper protection against privateer attacks.[104] The Habsburg administration played a double role in the matter, for it actively stimulated privateering by means of Letters of Marque themselves, but also pursued far-reaching and costly measures to protect merchant ships against privateers from Scotland, England or France.[105] The proposal to limit the use of insurance led to heavy protests by both foreign and local merchants in Bruges and Antwerp, as well as the skippers' guild in Holland. The 1550 *Ordonnance* forced them to reckon with higher protection costs, while simultaneously not being allowed to transfer those costs and the associated risks to a third party by means of insurance. In practice, they largely ignored the contents of the *Ordonnances*.[106] Skippers from Holland, meanwhile, had long preferred techniques such as cargo spreading and joint ship ownership (the *partenrederij*), and were able to offer

99 Although the *Ordonnance* also applied to all eastward trading from 1557 onwards. See: Sicking, *Neptune and the Netherlands*, 280–286. An excellent introduction into the differences between piracy and privateering is: Rodger, 'The Law and Language'.

100 The 1551 *Ordonnance* can be found in: J. Lameere (ed.), *Recueil des ordonnances des Pays-Bas. Deuxième série, 1506–1700* (Vol. 6) (Brussels 1922), 163–177.

101 De ruysscher, 'Maxims, Principles and Legal Change'.

102 Sicking, *Neptune and the Netherlands*, 251–252.

103 Ibidem, 249–250.

104 Ibidem, 242–280; De ruysscher & Puttevils, 'The Art of Compromise', 25–49; De Groote, *De zeeassurantie*, 33–44; Gelderblom, *Cities of Commerce*, 190–196.

105 Idem, 'State and Non-State Violence at Sea: Privateering in the Habsburg Netherlands', in: D.J. Starkey & M. Hahn-Pedersen (eds.), *Bridging Troubled Waters. Conflict and Co-Operation in the North Sea Region since 1550* (Esbjerg 2005), 31–43, there 33–37.

106 Idem, *Neptune and the Netherlands*, 252–256.

extremely low freight rates due to rigorous cost-cutting.[107] However they also had to make significant adjustments to their ships before sailing to the Iberian Peninsula, such as installing additional artillery, incurring higher costs than those already using protection measures (e.g. the Castilians). As they were willing to take more risk than merchants in Antwerp, these protection cost-raising measures significantly impacted their competitiveness in a negative way.[108]

The 1550 *Ordonnance* was published but, in practice, had limited effect.[109] Work soon began on a second *Ordonnance* that included further-reaching measures. Iberian merchants were still exempted from the 1550 *Ordonnance*, but the proposals in the 1551 *Ordonnance* would also apply to them.[110] To enlist support for the *Ordonnance*, a draft of the 1551 *Ordonnance* was sent out to various stakeholders, including skipper guilds in Holland and Antwerp, the local merchant communities in Bruges and Antwerp, and the Castilian and Portuguese *nationes* in Bruges and Antwerp.[111] In the archives of the Brussels Admiralty, drafts of the 1551 *Ordonnance* survive with comments from the Castilians, whereas the Antwerp municipal archives contain the draft accompanied by commentaries by the Portuguese.[112] These documents constitute a unique insight into the viewpoints of these Iberian merchants on the matters at hand. According to the proposal for the 1551 *Ordonnance*, the costs for the obligatory measures set were to be borne by the merchants themselves through a tax, without financial aid offered by the central government in Brussels.[113] Especially for large ships, protection costs would rise in such a situation, and this hit the Iberian merchants disproportionally.[114] Merchants would also pay a significant amount for extra artillery and convoy ships, costs that were also uninsurable under the very same proposals. Moreover, the existing financial instruments of the Castilian *natio* were not sufficient to cover these costs.[115]

---

107 Idem, 'A Wider Spread of Risk', 126–132.

108 Ibidem.

109 Idem, *Neptune and the Netherlands*, 247–253.

110 Ibidem, 251.

111 Idem, 'A Wider Spread of Risk', 125–126.

112 BE-ARB, Admiraliteitsarchief, nr. 106; BE-SAA, Privilegiekamer, Handel en Scheepvaart, *Verzameling 'Raeckt den Handel'*, 1551–1572 Toerusting van Schepen, inv. PK#1021.

113 Sicking, *Neptune and the Netherlands*, 263–264. For the costs of the 1552 convoys, the Habsburg government for example only wanted to pay 1/3 of the costs. Additionally, the government instituted a so-called 'fiftieth penny' (i.e. a 2% tax) on all imports and exports.

114 Ibidem, 270.

115 Protection costs were levied via the *avería de nación*, but the rise in costs was not sufficient to be covered by this instrument. Therefore, they had to establish the *avería(s)*. See: Fagel, *De Hispano-Vlaamse wereld*, 419–422 & Chapter 6.

The discussion between the central government and the various stakeholders boiled down to the question of who should bear the costs for the protection of commercial vessels between the Low Countries and the Iberian Peninsula.[116] The Castilians and Portuguese argued against these measures by employing two arguments. First, that protection costs carried by merchants were too high and threatened the viability of profitable trade on this route; and second, that individual measures such as insurance and GA were more effective in countering the threats of Scottish and French privateering.[117] After all, they argued, premiums reflected risk and if merchants were willing to take it, it was not something the central government should worry about.[118] Iberian merchants moreover argued that the Habsburg government should provide basic security, and that the remaining risks should be borne and countered by individual merchants, for example by taking out insurance.[119] They advocated a solution that put responsibility for the merchant's vessels firmly with the individual merchant or merchant communities, with the central government providing basic safety measures and conducting diplomacy to limit the threat of privateering. The central government, in contrast, argued for regulated commercial traffic in which safety was guaranteed by the proposed system of obligatory convoys and better protection efforts including heavy artillery. The Iberian merchants in the end negotiated lower taxation, although the obligatory convoy ships and artillery were included in the final *Ordonnances*.[120] The actual enforcement of the measures was subsequently effectively sabotaged by Castilian merchants in the Low Countries.[121] As Chapter 6 shows, Castilians nevertheless developed a compulsory contribution, the *avería(s)*, to meet these new demands. Charles and Philip promulgated the measures in Castile as well, thereby necessitating both the Burgos *Consulado* and the Castilian *natio* in the Low Countries to act, despite their initial protests.[122]

Charles had promised that the 1551 *Ordonnance* would also contain regulations on issues of 'private' maritime law. In the 1551 *Ordonnance*, there was indeed an appendix dealing with this (the contents of which were not sent to the maritime interest groups beforehand). This was the first time the central government actively regulated what we would nowadays consider 'private'

116 Sicking, *Neptune and the Netherlands*, 263–264.

117 BE-ARB, Admiraliteitsarchief, nr. 106 (23/10/1549 & 1563); BE-SAA, nr. PK#1021 (23/02/1551).

118 Ibidem. See also: De Groote, *De zeeassurantie*, 148–151.

119 BE-ARB, Admiraliteitsarchief, nr. 106 (23/10/1549).

120 Sicking, *Neptune and the Netherlands*, 255–270.

121 Ibidem, 267–273.

122 Fagel, *De Hispano-Vlaamse wereld*, 413–422, especially 419–422.

maritime law (of course with the notable exception of insurance).[123] This part has been virtually neglected in the literature, as most authors focused on the contents of the first part of the *Ordonnance*.[124] The 1551 *Ordonnance* was the first time GA (*groote avarye*) was described as such in formal legislation, making princely legislation a key turning point in the transfer from the rules-of-thumb-approach to actual legal principles.[125]

Article 41 defined GA, and this was also the first time in the Low Countries that an actual distinction was made between GA and other forms of Averages.[126] It included both deliberate damage and costs to prevent (greater) damage, continuing the customary practices found in the Amsterdam *Ordonnantie* and other compilations. Offering a definition, the *Ordonnance* stated that all damage suffered for the common beneficiary of the ship were to be shared over the ship and cargo after 'old customs of the sea' ('*nae ouder gewoonten van der zee*').[127] Even if this was still a very general description of GA, it enshrined this principle in princely legislation for the first time. Besides GA, the 1551 *Ordonnance* introduced the principle of Small or Common Average (SA) (*gemeyne avarye*) into princely legislation. The rules in Articles 42 and 43 stated that the master had to take all the necessary precautions to keep the cargo safely, but if there were extraordinary costs flowing from repairing the ship, they could be shared as SA: yet when the cargo was damaged by the masters' fault, the master would have to reimburse the merchant(s) for his negligent behaviour.[128] In their comments on the *Ordonnance*, Iberian merchants had pushed for a broad scope of GA that also included involuntary damage caused by pirates and privateers.[129] Their lobbying succeeded in one respect, as the costs related to dead or wounded seamen after fighting off pirates or privateers were accepted as GA costs in the *Ordonnance*.[130] In Article 28, the *Ordonnance* stated that costs resulting from fighting those attackers should be brought under GA, for example when a seaman was wounded or had died. The damage was to be shared over 'ship and cargo' (*schepe ende goeden*).[131]

123 De Groote, *De zeeassurantie*, 28 & 33–34; Sicking, *Neptune and the Netherlands*, 249.

124 See for the most important literature, often dealing with the public law element: Sicking, *Neptune and the Netherlands*, 242–280; J. Craeybeckx, 'De organisatie en de konvooiering van de koopvaardijvloot op het einde van de regering van Karel V', *Bijdragen tot de Geschiedenis der Nederlanden* (1949), 179–208.

125 Kruit, 'General Average', 198–199.

126 Ibidem.

127 1551 *Ordonnance*, Art. 41. See also: De ruysscher, 'Maxims, Principles and Legal Change'.

128 Ibidem, Arts. 42 & 43.

129 BE-ARB, Admiraliteitsarchief, nr. 106 (23/10/1549 & 1563); BE-SAA, nr. PK#1021 (23/02/1551).

130 1551 *Ordonnance*, Art. 28. Subsequently, the 1563 *Ordonnance* also included a similar rule.

131 Ibidem.

Of course the Castilians (and Portuguese) preferred to share damage or losses caused by privateer attacks to be covered by insurance, but given the central government's adamant opposition a compromise was found by sharing part of the costs under GA. As none of the parties was powerful enough to push through its solution (a clear example of constraints), uninsurable costs were therefore folded under GA, broadening its application.[132] Whilst this is not hard evidence of path dependency, we can observe the effects of the constraints in the negotiations for all parties.[133] Clearly, the bargaining power of the Castilians was significant, as their demands were partly incorporated, whereas for example those of the Holland skippers' guilds were largely neglected.[134] Whilst the goal may not have been to include the costs for fighting off privateers or pirates under GA for ever, these clauses were subsequently included in other princely legislation and the Antwerp *Compilatae* (see below). GA was part of a larger policy package of the central government, emphasising the interplay between various institutions (in this case in the maritime sector).[135]

In 1563, Philip II issued a follow-up to Charles' *Ordonnances*. It was aimed at all aspects of maritime law, including both insurance and GA. The introduction remarked that the 1550 and 1551 *Ordonnances* were still valid, but that new developments had forced additional measures, including the continuing use of speculative insurance by merchants.[136] The chapter of the *Ordonnance* stipulating a standard insurance policy has received much attention in the literature,[137] but the *Ordonnance* also contained a full chapter dedicated to GA.[138] The 1563 *Ordonnance* was the first to systematically describe in which cases GA could be declared in the Low Countries and was hence a major legal milestone, also inspiring Weytsen's treatise. In the wake of the long negotiations over insurance,[139] Philip II apparently also felt the need to spell out the rules on GA, as well as on ship collisions and maritime labour issues, offering a relatively complete set of rules on maritime laws. As a result, princely legislation was a (perhaps unwitting) major catalyst in the legal development of GA, as it both offered a definition (in the 1551 *Ordonnance*) and extensive rules and procedures (in the 1563 *Ordonnance*), offering legal security to those in

132 Van Niekerk, *The Development*, 60–80.

133 North, *Institutions*, 98–99. See also: Bennet & Elman, 'Complex Causal Relationships', 256–259.

134 Sicking, 'A Wider Spread of Risk', 126–127 & 130–132.

135 Ogilvie, '"Whatever is, is Right?"', 681.

136 The 1563 *Ordonnance* can be found in: Pardessus, *Collection* (Vol. 4), 64–102.

137 Ibidem, 93–95 for the standard insurance policy. See for the literature: De ruysscher, 'Antwerp 1490–1590', 94–95; Reatz, 'Ordonnances', 66–74.

138 1563 *Ordonnance*, Title IV.

139 For example: De ruysscher, 'Antwerp 1490–1590', 93–95; Idem & Puttevils, 'The Art of Compromise'.

the interest community. Most of the rules were practical or procedural rules, but some betrayed the influence of principles of Roman law, especially when it came to the ownership rights of those whose cargo were salvaged. No new effort was made to define the principles of GA and PA, since this was already in the 1551 *Ordonnance*. Therefore the 1563 *Ordonnance* again primarily contained rules of thumb, although more sophisticated rules drawn from Roman law were also included. Beyond the Low Countries, it was a major influence on the general development of maritime laws; the *Guidon de la Mer*, a compilation of maritime customs codified in sixteenth-century Rouen, made multiple references to this *Ordonnance*.[140]

The legal position of the shipmaster was clearly one of the major issues in the 1563 *Ordonnance*, where we can observe a double-edged development. The liability of the shipmaster in case of negligent or fraudulent behaviour became stricter, but the rules also provided the master with more discretionary power to act when the venture was in peril.[141] Some of these rules were drawn from medieval compilations, for example on the discretion of the shipmaster to jettison cargo when no merchants were on board, or in case of negligence when a ship was overloaded.[142] Rules like these were common to ensure that a shipmaster did not engage in negligent behaviour or outright fraud (so-called barratry).[143] Other rules were new but largely followed in the same vein, for example as the *Ordonnance* started by reminding shipmaster and crew to take good care of all the cargo on board, and not to be negligent.[144] Article 3 stipulated that if a ship was damaged, the master should repair the ship as soon as possible.[145] Article 11 stipulated that before starting a voyage, the master had to invite all crew members and ask for advice on whether the ship was

140 See: E. Cleirac, *Us et coutumes de la mer, divisées en trois parties. I: de la navigation. II: du commerce naval & contracts maritimes. III: de la jurisdiction de la marine. Avec un traicté des termes des marine & reglemens de la nauigation des fleuves & rivieres* (Bordeaux 1647). See also: Trivellato, 'Usages and Customs of the Sea: Ettiene Cleirac and the Making of Maritime Law in Seventeenth-Century France', *Tijdschrift voor Rechtsgeschiedenis*, 84, 1–2 (2016), 193–224.

141 This was a general European phenomenon. See: Rossi, 'The Liability of the Shipmaster'.

142 1563 *Ordonnance*, Arts. 4 & 8.

143 An overview of barratry in early modern law can be found in: Rossi, 'The Barratry of the Shipmaster in Early Modern Law: Polysemy and *mos Italicus*', *Tijdschrift voor Rechtsgeschiedenis*, 87 (2019), 65–85, there especially 79–84. See for legal practice: Idem, 'The Barratry of the Shipmaster in Early Modern Law: The Approach of Italian and English Law Courts', *Tijdschrift voor Rechtsgeschiedenis*, 87, 4 (2019), 504–574. From now on, I will refer to the articles by number (I) or (II), (I) corresponding to 'polysemy and *mos italicus*' and (II) to 'the approach of Italian and English law courts'.

144 1563 *Ordonnance*, Art. 1.

145 Ibidem, Art. 3.

IMAGE 7 Titian, portrait of Philip II in armour (1550s)

seaworthy, similar to rules from the 1551 *Ordonnance*.[146] More than half of the crew members involved in the venture had to agree. Without such an agreement, the master or the shipowner would have to pay for any damage which ensued.[147]

Two clauses continued a further explanation to rules already found in the 1551 *Ordonnance*. Article 2 for example stipulated that not only the costs for seamen killed in a fight with pirates or privateers could be brought into GA, but also the costs of their funeral and the remainder of their wages (to be paid to the widow).[148] Article 9 built on the distinction between GA and SA, stating on pilotage that if the shipmaster failed to hire pilots to sail into a port safely, he could be held liable to pay for the damage to either ship or cargo, depending on the damage that had ensued.[149] Only if the costs of ordinary pilotage exceeded six pounds *Grooten Vlaams*, the costs could be brought into GA.[150] This is an interesting clause because it implies that large SA claims could become GA claims, although this stipulation is not found in other sources. This may be drawn from the idea that pilotage costs prevented greater or further damage. The distinction between GA and SA was further described in article 10, stating that masters were allowed to hire lighter ships when a ship had run aground in a storm, and the risk of a shipwreck was real, following established practice.[151] If a ship, however, had run aground in a river or port that was not deep enough to sail through, 2/3 of the costs would be borne by the master, and 1/3 contributed by the cargo of the merchants as SA (see also section 3.4 on Weytsen).[152] If such an effort failed, all costs had to be deducted from the master's freight.[153] The rationale behind this clause was that a master should be knowledgeable: if lighter ships were necessary this was a failure by the master. If cargo was transferred to the lighter ship and would still be lost (e.g. because of bad weather), the costs could nevertheless be brought into GA.[154]

The 1563 *Ordonnance* contained three main causes to allow GA: jettison (*werpen*), mast and/or rope cutting (*kerven*), and voluntarily running aground

146 Ibidem, Art. 11.

147 Ibidem.

148 Ibidem, Art. 2. Some Castilians already used life insurance, but this technique was not common among those in the Low Countries maritime sector: Casado Alonso, 'Insuring Life, Insuring Debt: Life Insurance in Sixteenth-Century Spain', *Pedralbes*, 40, 2 (2020), 75–95, specifically 81–82 for life insurance in Antwerp.

149 Ibidem, Art. 9.

150 Ibidem.

151 Ibidem, Article 10.

152 Ibidem.

153 Ibidem.

154 Ibidem.

(*strangen*), the latter being when a heavy storm took a ship by surprise.[155] The third reason was new in the Southern Low Countries, although the rule was already in some compilations of maritime law from Southern Europe.[156] The *Ordonnance* also stated that the calculations had to be made by neutral experts.[157] Rules on contribution followed the *Ordonnantie*, giving merchants the choice of how the master should contribute.[158] More procedural rules were included. Article 5 stated that the heaviest but cheapest cargo had to be thrown overboard first.[159] Article 7 discussed money that was carried on board, which according to the *Ordonnance* should be estimated according to its intrinsic value.[160] This clause may sound rather vague, but its goal appears to have been to reassure merchants and investors that the Spanish Crown would not devalue their coin, despite the 1557 and 1560 bankruptcies of the Habsburg state.[161] Valuable cargo, including jewels, gold, and silver would instead always contribute in GA, even if kept 'close to the body'.[162]

Finally, articles 12 and 13 dealt with jettisoned cargo that was salvaged.[163] Seamen were obliged to do their utmost best to salvage cargo, and if they were

155 Ibidem, Art. 6.

156 Cordes, 'Conflicts in 13th-Century Maritime Law', after note 42.

157 1563 *Ordonnance*, Title IV, Art. 6.

158 Ibidem.

159 Ibidem, Art. 5.

160 Ibidem, Art. 7: "*Ende indien onder de voorseyde goeden eenich ghemunt ghelt is, zal gheestimeert worden naer zyne inwendighe ofte intrynsicque weerde ende valeur, welverstaende dat al t'ghene dat yemant an syn lyf heeft ende men ordinairlick is draghende* (*uuyt ghesundert baghen, juwelen, ghesteenten, gout ende zilver*) *in gheen avarye noch contributie en sal commen*". This was the common way to evaluate money.

161 I thank Maria Fusaro and Guido Rossi for clarifying this point. The recurring bankruptcies of the Habsburg Crown led to fears among creditors of the devaluation of the currency, but in fact the Spanish state never devalued its currency despite Spain's relative decline during the sixteenth to eighteenth centuries. This clause was hence a way to promote the use of the Spanish currency, for other currencies were less stable and would thus be valued higher than their extrinsic value. Debasing the currency was a much-discussed subject among lawyers, for the subject was intimately connected to the monarchs' position of power. The Great Debasement of Henry VIII was the most important example. The literature on debasement is enormous but see for some references to the subject in the Low Countries: Edler-De Roover, 'The Effects of the Financial Measures of Charles V on the Commerce of Antwerp, 1539–42', *Revue belge de philologie et d'histoire*, 16, 3–4 (1937), 665–673; L-F. Li, 'Information Asymmetry and the Speed of Adjustment: Debasements in the Mid-Sixteenth Century', *Economic History Review*, 68, 4 (2015), 1203–1225; Van der Wee, *The Growth* (Vol. 2), 146–150, 200–204 & 240–243. See for Castile and Philip II: M. Drelichman & H-J. Voth, *Lending to the Borrower from Hell: Debt, Taxes and Default in the Age of Philip II* (Princeton 2014).

162 1563 *Ordonnance*, Title IV, Art. 7.

163 Ibidem, Arts. 12 & 13.

successful, the master could be held liable to pay the seamen an additional sum of money, taken from the freight that had to be paid by the owner of the cargo.[164] This was a form of so-called *negotiorum gestio* (*zaakwaarneming* in Dutch), a principle of Roman law which recognised spontaneous actions on behalf of someone else without the latter's prior consent.[165] Article 13 dealt with fraud regarding salvage, which was also based upon a principle of Roman law stating that an owner could always reclaim his cargo, even if they were found and subsequently kept by someone else.[166] If a seaman kept the cargo for himself after having salvaged cargo, by the same principle he would be punished by hanging.[167]

Both the 1551 and the 1563 *Ordonnance* were milestones for the development of GA. Notable in these two *Ordonnances* were the definitions of GA and SA, the addition of a number of concrete causes and the increasingly strict liability of shipmaster and crew. The latter was balanced by a greater ability to act when danger loomed, reflecting the increasing specialisation of the maritime sector during the fifteenth and sixteenth century.[168] Most rules from the *Ordonnantie* and the Wisby Laws were incorporated in the Habsburg *Ordonnances* and were only slightly modified or elaborated upon, largely offering continuity. The 1563 *Ordonnance* provided parties involved in maritime ventures with procedural rules to follow as well.[169] For GA a *modus vivendi* was found between the various foreign merchant communities and the central government, also given the success of the Iberian merchants lobbying for incorporating GA costs associated with attacks at sea into the 1551 and 1563 *Ordonnances*. This also entrenched the co-existing nature of the two institutions of GA and insurance, progressively offering both *ex ante* and *ex post* risk management for merchants. Given the constraints set by the central government over the use of insurance, GA became the preferred compromise to cover uninsurable risks.

3.2.4 *The* Hordenanzas *and the Insurability of* GA *(1569)*

Besides lobbying, the Castilian merchants in Bruges also published their own collection of insurance customs in response to the 1551 and 1563 *Ordonnances*,

164 Ibidem, Art. 12.

165 This was also recognised in the Basilica: Ashburner, *The Rhodian Sea-Law*, ccxxxxix. Thanks to Dave De ruysscher for helping me with this section.

166 1563 *Ordonnance*, Title IV, Art. 13. See for the principle: Ashburner, *The Rhodian Sea-Law*, cclxxxviii.

167 Ibidem.

168 Lucassen & Unger, 'Shipping, Productivity and Economic Growth', 5–6; Asaert, 'Onder de vlag'.

169 De ruysscher, 'Maxims, Principles and Legal Change'.

the so-called *Hordenanzas* of 1569 which was published in print, both in Castilian and in French in order to be widely accessible.[170] The Castilians presented the *Hordenanzas* as following the customs of the stock exchanges of Antwerp and London at the time, the two main insurance centres of the mid-sixteenth century in north-western Europe.[171] Charles Verlinden, who published editions of both the Castilian and French versions of the *Hordenanzas*, accepted this contemporary interpretation, but this has been challenged by other authors such as Guido Rossi, Henry de Groote and Santa Coronas González.[172] Rossi pointed to the strong similarities with the 1538 Burgos and 1556 Seville *Ordonnances*, which were issued by Charles v and Philip ii as instructions for the *Consulados* based in those cities.[173] De Groote meanwhile pointed to the fact that the *Hordenanzas* was sparsely referred to in actual insurance policies or in the princely insurance *Ordonnances* of 1569–1571.[174] The insistence on the supposed customary nature of the *Hordenanzas* and its rules regarding maritime laws was more likely a way to boost the legitimacy of the collection.

The *Hordenanzas* is also a suitable path for studying GA, since it brings together mercantile customs, Castilian princely legislation and a case of legal transplants in a legal-historical setting together in one text.[175] It set out the most important Castilian customs regarding insurance and dealt with the entanglement of insurance with GA. This focused chiefly on jettison,[176] and is the first explicit (normative) mention of the interaction of the two tools outside of legal practice. This could take two forms. Insurers were liable for the remaining damage to insured cargo after a GA declaration; and were also liable when the value of insured cargo was used to determine the contribution

---

170 See for a more detailed analysis: Dreijer, 'Identity, Conflict and Commercial Law'.

171 Rossi, *Insurance in Elizabethan England*, 148–157.

172 The original text can be found in: BE-SAB, Spaans Consulaat, nr. III.A.2, *Libro de las ordenanças*. Transcriptions in: C. Verlinden, 'Código de seguros marítimos según la costumbre de Amberes: promulgado por le Consulado Español de Brujas en 1569', in: *Sección Española del Instituto de Investigaciones Históricas* (Buenos Aires 1947), 146–193; Idem, 'Code d'assurances maritimes selons la coutume d'Anvers, promulgué par le consulat espangol de Bruges en 1569', *Handelingen van de Koninklijke Commissie voor de Uitgave der oude wetten en verordeningen van België*, 16 (1950), 38–142. But see: De Groote, *De zeeassurantie*, 52–58; Rossi, *Insurance in Elizabethan England*, 148–157; Coronas González, 'La Ordenenza de seguros maritimos del Consulado de la Nacion de España en Brujas', *Anuario de Historia del Derecho español*, 54 (1984), 385–407.

173 Rossi, *Insurance in Elizabethan England*, 151–153.

174 De Groote, *De zeeassurantie*, 52–58.

175 See for an overview of the theoretical origins of legal transplants and its uses: M.M. Siems, *Comparative Law* (Cambridge 2018), 232–261.

176 1569 *Hordenanzas*, Title x, Art. 6.

of a merchant to a GA declaration.[177] This had profound implications for the parties in an insurance agreement, as insurers were now liable for more losses than they would be under a 'pure' insurance contract. From the viewpoint of Averages, both PA and GA had to be covered by insurers.

This was already acknowledged in the 1538 Burgos *Ordonnance*, and subsequently in the 1556 Seville and 1560 Bilbao *Ordonnances*.[178] The Burgos *Ordonnance*, for example, stated that insurers were liable to pay for GA as long as the declaration was made by 'good men'.[179] Insurers also had to pay immediately after GA was awarded, but insurers had the right to challenge the GA calculations and potentially recover the money in a separate procedure.[180] The Seville *Ordonnance* stated that everyone had to contribute to GA, unless there was *force majeure* or the master had made a mistake.[181] That also meant that merchants could pass on their contribution to insurers, but only for GA and not for SA.[182] The Bilbao *Ordonnance* was similar to the two Castilian *Ordonnances*, but more importantly foreshadowed many of the rules that can be found in the Bruges *Hordenanzas*.[183] Unsurprisingly, the Bilbao *Ordonnance* included statements on the valuation of cargo and the contribution of the shipmaster.[184] Most importantly the *Ordonnance* acknowledged the insurability of GA, even if limits were imposed. Artillery, for example, could not be insured, meaning underwriters would not have to pay for the damage even when the ship was insured. Broken cables or masts' costs were reimbursed only if the ship was insured.[185] Consuls were tasked with drawing up the GA calculus, even if insurers had the right to challenge it before those same consuls. Yet, they had to pay their contribution immediately (similar to the 1538 Burgos *Ordonnance*), and before litigating, similar to the *namptissement* procedure in Antwerp and other parts of Europe.[186] Insurers were not allowed to insure both the ship and the cargo at the same time to prevent moral hazard.[187] The Bilbao *Ordonnance* included some protections for insurers. Reclaiming GA from insurers was only allowed for damage incurred during the voyage and for the duration of the insurance policy. Moreover, testimonies had to be recorded by a notary so as

177 Van Niekerk, *The Development*, 76–80.
178 Rossi, *Insurance in Elizabethan England*, 20–21 & 151–153.
179 The 1538 Burgos *Ordonnance* is found in: Pardessus, *Collection* (Vol. 6), 135–194, Article 19.
180 Ibidem.
181 The 1556 Seville *Ordonnance* is found in: Ibidem, 76–103, Art. 36.
182 Ibidem, Art. 46.
183 The 1560 Bilbao *Ordonnance* can be found in: Pardessus, *Collection* (Vol. 6), 195–252.
184 Ibidem, Art. 47.
185 Ibidem, Art. 64.
186 Ibidem, Art. 67.
187 Ibidem, Art. 68.

to provide solid evidence in litigation.[188] An appeal was possible at the Bilbao *Consulado*.[189]

The principle that insurers had to pay for GA claims was highly influential in the Southern Low Countries (as shown in the 1608 *Compilatae*, see below), although we cannot say with certainty that Castilian merchants introduced this principle in the Low Countries. In various Italian cities, the principle was already known, for example as early as the 1380s in Florence.[190] In 1524, the Florentine *Statuti di Sicurtà* explicitly included the liability of the insurer to pay for GA claims, and it was allowed in Tuscany and Genoa as well.[191] Yet there is no extant evidence that any of the Italian *nationes* introduced this principle in the Low Countries or referred to it in GA cases, making the question of the origin of the rule in Antwerp legal practice near-impossible to solve for a lack of conclusive evidence.

As Guido Rossi has shown, the *Hordenanzas* was strongly influenced by the Castilian *Ordonnances* and subsequently made an impact on legislation in Northern Europe, especially in the London insurance market.[192] In the Low Countries, the liability of the insurer for GA payments was only officially acknowledged in the 1608 *Compilatae* of Antwerp municipal law, for which the *Hordenanzas* provided an important influence.[193] Title X, article 6 explicitly mentioned that GA had to be paid by the insurer, whereas Title XIII, article 1 dealt with this subject in more detail.[194] The issue of privateering and piracy was, following the threats by the French and Scottish in the 1540s and 1550s,

188 Notaries played an important role in GA procedure as well in the sixteenth-century Low Countries, for example recording freight contracts and providing legal security by recording testimonies from shipmasters or crew members. See Chapter 4 and: De Groote, *De zeeassurantie*, 143.

189 1560 Bilbao *Ordonnance*, Art. 69.

190 See E. Bensa, *Il Contratto di assicurazione nel medio evo: studi e richerche* (Genoa 1884), 75–76. This was not a direct clause, but simply included all sorts of damage under the insurance protection. In Tuscany, it appears that this was allowed as early as the late fourteenth century. Venice was the exception, as Venetian insurance contracts often included so-called 'free of Average' clauses. See: Nehlsen-Van Stryk, *Die venezianische Seeversicherung*, 165–180. I thank Andra Addobbati for sending me the Bensa reference.

191 See: A. Iodice & Piccinno, 'Managing Shipping Risk: General Average and Marine Insurance in Early Modern Genoa', in: Hellwege & Rossi (eds.), *Maritime Risk Management*, 83–110, there 89–91. I thank both authors, as well as Jake Dyble, Maria Fusaro, Andrea Addobbati and Giovanni Cecarelli for answering my questions on the history of Italian insurance legislation.

192 Rossi, *Insurance in Elizabethan England*, 20–21 & 151–153.

193 The 1608 *Compilatae* were in this respect strongly influenced by the *Hordenanzas*. See: Van Hofstraeten, *Juridisch humanisme*, 111–117.

194 *Hordenanzas* 1569, Title X, Art. 6 & Ibidem, Title XIII, Art. 1.

particularly important. The *Hordenanzas* for example stipulated that the insurer was liable to reimburse GA when cargo was bought back from pirates, following the purchasing price paid to the pirates.[195] Cargo voluntarily given up to pirates (i.e. without putting up a fight) could not be brought into GA, unless a shipmaster could make it clear that this deliberate action had prevented the pirates from doing even more damage to the ship and cargo, echoing Roman law.[196]

The *Hordenanzas* was quite strict when it came to the liability of the insurer. It stated for example that the insurer was liable for cargo 'of all qualities', even if lost in an imperfect state.[197] Only some foodstuffs were exempted, as common GA procedure did not include those either.[198] Another issue arose when a shipmaster abandoned the ship or the cargo. In such a case, it was up to insurers to recover the cargo, whist they had to pay out the insured sum.[199] The *Hordenanzas* stated that the insurers could be held liable for damage incurred upon abandonment as long as GA procedure was followed.[200] Insured cargo could be partly abandoned, for example when only half of the cargo was damaged. Ships could, logically, only be abandoned in full. In cases of partial abandonment, the *Hordenanzas* stipulated that GA could be declared for the non-abandoned cargo if deliberate damage had taken place to save the venture.[201] Insurers could be expected to pay for both abandoned cargo and GA.[202] When a ship changed course out of necessity, for example to escape pirates, the insurer was held to pay potential damages as in a case of GA.[203]

To what extent the *Hordenanzas* was in force outside the Spanish *natio* is still unclear. Philip II promulgated the *Hordenanzas* as princely legislation in 1570, making the compilation applicable law in the Low Countries, yet there is no evidence of the actual application of the *Hordenanzas* in the Antwerp municipal court.[204] The timing of Philip's codification was strange, given the fact that the Duke of Alva had only just allowed the use of insurance again.[205] The influence of the *Hordenanzas* was durable, however, because of its

195 Ibidem, Title XIII, Art. 9.

196 Ibidem, Art. 14.

197 Ibidem, Title XIII, Art. 3.

198 Ibidem, Art. 10.

199 Ibidem.

200 Ibidem, Arts. 12 & 13.

201 Ibidem, Title XIV, Art. 8.

202 Ibidem, Art. 9.

203 Ibidem, Title VII, Art. 2.

204 See: Gilliodts-Van Severen, *Espagne*, 431–434.

205 The text is printed in Reatz, as are the *Ordonnances* on insurance from 1570 and 1571: Reatz, 'Ordonnances'.

dissemination in Antwerp municipal law. We will now turn our focus onto that subject.

3.2.5 *The Antwerp* Costuymen, *Specifically the 1608* Compilatae

Maritime issues were already regulated in Antwerp municipal laws as early as 1419, when the aldermen published the so-called *Keurboeck* setting rules on, among other issues, maritime labour law.[206] Neither the *Gulden Boeck* (1510–*c.*1537) nor the 1548 *Antiquissimae*, however, mentioned maritime issues.[207] The 1570 *In Antiquis* contained the first reference to private maritime law, unsurprisingly on insurance,[208] specifically mentioning the abandonment to the insurer when cargo was damaged.[209] The 1582 *Impressae* contained clauses on insurance as well.[210] The 1608 *Compilatae* did therefore also contain a lot of insurance legislation, but in addition, paid extensive attention to other issues of maritime law. Bram van Hofstraeten, based on contemporary notes (the so-called *Memoriën op de Costuymen*), quantified how many of the rules were based on *usus* (custom).[211] Compared to the other versions of the *Costuymen*, the *Compilatae* contained many new rules (according to Van Hofstraeten, 97.6% of the rules were new for Title VIII, which *inter alia* concerned GA).[212] On maritime laws, some 25% of these were drawn from local customs, but many more were drawn from sources such as the *Hordenanzas* and the royal *Ordonnances* of 1550, 1551 and 1563.[213] For GA, a minority of rules were based on the 1563 *Ordonnance*, with those dealing with the insurability of GA primarily taken instead from the *Hordenanzas*.[214] The GA clauses were, for the remainder, largely based on *usus* (custom).[215] Although no explicit mentions were made of the *Vonnisse van Damme* or the Amsterdam *Ordonnantie*, these

---

206 Text printed in: G. De Longé (ed.), *Coutumes du Pays et Duché de Brabant, Quartier d'Anvers. Coutumes de la ville d'Anvers* (Vol. 1) (hereafter: De Longé, *Coutumes*), 1–90, there 50–51.

207 Text of the *Gulden Boeck* printed in: Ibidem, 379–428; The *Antiquissimae* in: Ibidem, 91–377, there 194–231.

208 Text printed in: Ibidem, 428–705, there 598–604. For the legal framework on insurance during the sixteenth century, see: De ruysscher, 'Antwerp 1490–1590', 89–95.

209 1570 *In Antiquis*, p. 602.

210 The text of the *Impressae* can found in: De Longé, *Coutumes* (Vol. 2), there 400–407 for insurance.

211 See: Van Hofstraeten, *Juridisch humanisme*, 111–117. See for *usus* also: De ruysscher, 'Customs and Municipal Law'.

212 Ibidem, 111.

213 Idem, 'Recording Customs', 292–293.

214 Idem, *Juridisch humanisme*, 113–114.

215 Ibidem, 114.

collections were of course influential in princely legislation and thus indirectly in the *Compilatae*.[216] The Wisby Laws and even the *Guidon de la Mer*, in contrast, were directly referred to.[217] Both Hanseatic maritime law and the *Consolat del Mar* were absent, hinting that those compilations had either only limited impact or were subsumed by other influences.[218] Learned maritime law, such as the treatises of Weytsen and Pieter Peckius,[219] was also completely absent, at least on GA.[220] Finally, there were only five references to the Digest on maritime law, although none of those concerned GA.[221]

Part IV, Title VIII of the *Compilatae* was dedicated to the various tools of risk and cost management, including GA, SA, PA and bottomry. This part ran to some 200 articles, while Title XI on insurance ran over 300 articles.[222] Most articles followed precedent (for example from the 1563 *Ordonnance*), with rules such as the masters' negligence could not be reason for contribution.[223] Moreover, dead seamen and the cost of their funeral could be brought into GA when pirate or privateer attacks were successfully fought off;[224] *lotegelt* still existed;[225] the costs for treating seamen after fighting pirates or privateers could also be brought into GA;[226] lighter ships could be used when a ship had run aground in a storm (even if the cargo were spoilt as a result);[227] salvaged cargo had to be given back to the rightful owner and could not be brought into GA;[228] the heaviest and cheapest cargo had to be jettisoned first;[229] cargo was

216 Ibidem, 114–115. For a similar view: Goudsmit, *Geschiedenis*, 231.

217 Ibidem, 115.

218 Ibidem, 116–117. On the other hand, the Wisby Laws were of course strongly influenced by Hanseatic maritime law, whereas royal legislation and the *Hordenanzas* were of course examples *par excellence* of Castilian influence.

219 See for Peckius: De ruysscher, 'Pieter Peck, Ad rem nauticam', in: Dauchy., Marty., Musson, Pihlajamäki & Wijffels, (eds.), *The Formation and Transmission of Western Legal Culture. 150 Books that made the Law in the Age of Printing* (Heidelberg 2016), 110–113. For the original: V.C.P. Peckius, *Ad Rem Nauticam Pertinentes, commentarii quibus nunc accedunt notae cum ampla dote variorum circa rem Navalem Observationum* (Leuven 1556).

220 Van Hofstraeten, *Juridisch humanisme*, 116–117. On insurance, this was different, as was for example Stracca's treatise.

221 Ibidem, 112.

222 The text of the *Compilatae* can be found in: De Longé, *Coutumes* (Vols. 3/4). Part 4 of the *Compilatae* deals with maritime law. See Vol. 4, Part 4, Title VIII (pp. 86–171) for the chapters on GA and bottomry & Vol. 4, Part 4, Title XI (pp. 198–333) for the titles on insurance.

223 *Compilatae*, Part 4, Title VIII, Art. 28.

224 Ibidem, Art. 77.

225 Ibidem, Art. 78.

226 Ibidem, Arts. 92 & 93. See Art. 77 for a similar clause.

227 Ibidem, Arts. 126 & 127.

228 Ibidem, Art. 74.

229 Ibidem, Art. 82.

calculated according to the market value at the place of destination;[230] merchants were allowed to choose how the shipmaster contributed (via freight or value of the ship);[231] and the standard procedure from the *Rôles* was incorporated in case of jettison.[232] On the issue of pilotage, precedent was also followed as a GA declaration could only be requested when the master could prove the extraordinary pilotage was necessary, with the difference that the six pounds *Grooten Vlaams* limit for SA was scrapped.[233]

Piracy was, of course, also discussed. The rules were stretched to the limit compared to those in the princely *Ordonnances*, as even costs associated with delays resulting from attacks at sea were accepted into GA.[234] GA costs incurred by attacks had to be paid by insurers, at least when the policy included piracy.[235] When negotiations with pirates led to a partial damage to cargo this could also be brought into GA.[236] Damage following pirate attacks were shared by GA first before a potential profit could be shared among the crew, for example when something was taken from the pirate.[237] If they took cargo from a pirate in a counterattack (i.e. they engaged in taking a Prize), they could share the profits after cost compensation among them, barring any specific rules from the relevant competent Admiralty.[238] The master would receive 1/3 of the Prize, the crew 2/3.[239] When pirates hijacked a ship but paid the master to steer the ship safely into port, the income of the master also had to be shared among the interest community, as GA normally would.[240]

In short, the majority of rules in the *Compilatae* were very similar to the older medieval compilations and princely legislation, sometimes even expanding on them.[241] The major contribution of the 1608 *Compilatae* to the Laws of General Average instead lay primarily in two areas: the description of Particular Average (PA) as a third category next to GA and SA, and the interaction between

230 Ibidem, Art. 143.
231 Ibidem.
232 Ibidem, Arts. 79 & 81.
233 Ibidem, Arts. 122–125, 144 & 148. A similar clause to the latter can be found in: H. De Groot, *Inleidinge tot de Hollandsche rechts-geleerdheid* (The Hague 1631) (Part 3) Art. 29.
234 Ibidem, Title XI, Art. 94.
235 Ibidem, Art. 192.
236 Ibidem, Art. 99.
237 Ibidem, Art. 117.
238 Ibidem, Art. 118.
239 Ibidem.
240 Ibidem, Art. 101.
241 This was not to everyone's liking, for there was contemporary debate over whether the *Compilatae* reflected Antwerp customs. See: De ruysscher, *"Naer het Romeinsch recht"*, 66–67; Van Hofstraeten, *Juridisch humanisme*, 57–60.

various instruments of risk management. The latter did not solely concern the insurability of GA, but also the interaction between emergency bottomry and GA. The 1608 *Costuymen* formally acknowledged, for the first time, three different forms of Averages: *averij-grosse* (GA), *averij-commune* (SA) and *simpele averij* (PA).[242] No mention however was made of Contractual Average (CA).[243] Similar to princely legislation, Antwerp municipal law was also making an effort to define general principles rather than rules of thumb as in the past.[244] In the *Compilatae*, GA was defined as deliberate damage or an act to limit further damage, listing jettison, mast cutting, voluntarily running aground and piracy as causes.[245] When a ship voluntarily ran aground, the master had to contribute via his freight, so as not to discourage him from saving the venture.[246] The *Compilatae* defined SA (*averij-commune*) as foreseeable costs, such as port duties and ordinary pilotage,[247] whereas PA (*averij-simpel*) was damage caused by accidents, for example damage to the mast after a thunderstorm.[248] SA was shared among the shipmaster and the cargo owners (e.g. in a freight contract), whereas PA was damage borne by the interested party.[249] The standard rules on the liability of the shipmaster applied, drawn from princely legislation.[250] Barratry (fraud) was strictly prohibited, although it was allowed to be incorporated in insurance policies (in contrast to the 1563 *Ordonnance*).[251]

On the subject of insurance and GA, the *Compilatae* followed the *Hordenanzas* as insurers could be held liable for GA payments (but not for SA).[252] Some protection for insurers was added, compared to the *Hordenanzas*. The insurer could for example be held liable only for claims made within half a year of arriving at the destination, otherwise the liability of the insurer was dropped.[253] Other protections concerned abandonment. For example, if a ship could be repaired within a month, it was prohibited to abandon the ship to the insurer. In that case, the costs for these reparations, as well as the extra wages for the crew, were shared through GA.[254] Masters were not allowed to leave

242 1608 *Compilatae*, Part 4, Title VIII, Art. 66.
243 Van Niekerk, *The Development*, 65–66.
244 De ruysscher, 'Maxims, Principles and Legal Change'.
245 1608 *Compilatae*, Part 4, Title VIII, Arts. 67 & 79.
246 Ibidem, Art. 75.
247 Ibidem, Arts. 156 & 157.
248 Ibidem, Arts. 153–155.
249 Van Niekerk, *The Development*, 63–64.
250 1608 *Compilatae*, Part 4, Title VIII, Art. 85–86, 155 & 178.
251 Ibidem, Art. 109.
252 Ibidem, Title XI, Arts. 177–178 & 180.
253 Ibidem, Art. 283.
254 Ibidem, Art. 225.

their ships when in port, even if the crew arrested by a sovereign, or brought into a port of privateers (i.e. under a Letter of Marque).[255] All the costs that resulted from 'privateering' could also be brought into GA because insurers could not be held liable for arrests by a foreign 'prince', although in principle this deviated from the rule of deliberate damage for the common benefit.[256]

The *Compilatae* moreover noted (and this was really 'new') that insurers could contract themselves 'free of Average', one of the few examples found in Low Countries sources from the sixteenth and early seventeenth centuries.[257] An exception occurred when pirates robbed the cargo or when the cargo was fully lost.[258] These clauses were most likely very rare, contradicting the earlier notion that the interest community had to be preserved even when individuals took out insurance.[259] More common were so-called 'franchise' clauses, whereby the liability of the insurer was dropped when the GA claim did not pass a certain percentual threshold.[260] Given the fact that Antwerp legal practice had already accepted the liability of the insurer to pay for GA in the 1540s, such clauses were probably included for two reasons: first, to protect insurers from numerous small claims which would unduly raise transaction costs; second, they can be seen as a sort of pushback by insurers against their liability. In the 1571 *Ordonnance* and the 1608 *Compilatae* the franchise was 1%, meaning there was already precedent in princely legislation as well.[261] No solid evidence can be found for the application of this rule in Antwerp legal practice during the sixteenth century, although such rules were common in seventeenth-century Amsterdam.[262] Other tools of risk management and the combination of those tools were also discussed. When a GA act led to the loss of bottomry money, the bottomry money and interest payment could be shared via GA.[263] This was probably a rare coincidence (but see section 4.5.2).

The 1608 *Compilatae* was the only collection of Antwerp municipal law that included rules on GA. Despite the initial unwillingness of Antwerp to collect

255 Ibidem, Art 229.
256 Ibidem, Art. 141.
257 Ibidem, Art. 210. In contrast, this was common in Venetian insurance contracts.
258 Ibidem.
259 Van Niekerk, *The Development*, 1037.
260 Ibidem, 1040–1043.
261 See for the 1571 *Ordonnance*: Ibidem, 1042–1043; L. Couvreur, 'Recht en zeeverzekeringspraktijk in de 17e en 18e eeuwen', *Tijdschrift voor Rechtsgeschiedenis*, 16, 2 (1939), 184–214, there 198. See for the *Compilatae*: 1608 *Compilatae*, Part 4, Title XI, Arts. 203 & 204. In the eighteenth-century Dutch Republic the franchise was raised to 3%. See: Van Niekerk, *The Development*, 1043–1044.
262 Van Niekerk, *The Development*, 1043–1044.
263 1608 *Compilatae*, Part 4, Title VIII, Art. 65.

its customs, the city set up multiple projects in the second half of the sixteenth century, culminating in the *Compilatae*. It did include new rules, for example defining PA and the 'free of Average' clauses, but otherwise showed continuity in most aspects of GA (e.g. with princely legislation and the *Hordenanzas*).The *Compilatae* offered the most wide-ranging rules on GA, but also on other tools of risk management such as insurance and bottomry. It clarified the exact applicability of all these instruments, and combinations thereof. As a result, the *Compilatae* show evidence of the thesis that an operationally efficient combination of risk management institutions for maritime trade developed in the sixteenth-century Low Countries.

3.3 GA, Salvage, Shipwreck, and Ship Collisions: Shifting Legal Boundaries

3.3.1 *GA, Salvage and Shipwreck*

When an act of GA was unsuccessful, the ship could of course be lost. From a legal perspective this meant that the boundaries between GA and shipwreck needed clarification.[264] Still, the distinction was not always clear. In medieval times, the European laws of wreck were still strongly based on concepts from Roman law.[265] In English, accidentally lost cargo was (and is) called *flotsam*, as opposed to *jetsam* which described deliberately jettisoned cargo.[266] This also had implications for salvage rights. The laws of wreck were considered as so-called *Strandrecht* (law of the beach) in Hanseatic law, rather than maritime law.[267] The 1550 and 1551 *Ordonnances* stipulated that merchants had to be able to visit the ship in advance of departure, and that a master could not leave without having taken advice from the merchants involved as to whether the ship was seaworthy.[268] Visits by officials of the central government to

264 The two issues are often taken together. See for example: Frankot, "*Of Laws of Ships*", 28–46.

265 R. Melikan, 'Shippers, Salvors, and Sovereigns: Competing Interests in the Medieval Law of Shipwreck', *Journal of Legal History*, 11, 2 (1990), 163–182.

266 Flotsam may always be claimed by the owner of the cargo, whereas jetsam in present-day maritime law may be claimed by whoever finds it. See the *Oxford English Dictionary* for both words: https://www.oed.com/view/Entry/71946?redirectedFrom=flotsam#eid & https://www.oed.com/view/Entry/101177#eid40368110 {Retrieved 25/06/2020}. See also: Melikan, 'Shippers, Salvors, and Sovereigns', especially 177–178; Frankot, "*Of Laws of Ships*", 28–31.

267 Cordes, 'Lex Maritima?', 78–79.

268 Sicking, *Neptune and the Netherlands*, 252: Craeybeckx, 'De organisatie en konvooiering', 190–191.

inspect the ships before sailing out were later made compulsory.[269] Yet the *Ordonnances* offered no description of shipwreck or the circumstances in which it could be declared.

The 1563 *Ordonnance* was the first legislative effort which paid attention to shipwreck, but primarily stipulated measures to prevent it. It started by stating that seamen had to do their best to save the venture, and when damage occurred due to their negligence or incompetence, the master was responsible.[270] Moreover, seamen and other personnel on board lost their wages when a ship was lost.[271] Rules were also instituted for cases where the GA declaration was already drawn up, but cargo was still salvaged after the GA payment had been made. In those cases, the GA already paid had to be paid back by the master. If a seaman salvaged cargo after jettison he could require a payment for this effort (so-called *bergeloon*). Under this form of *negotiorium gestio*, the rights of the owner of the cargo whose cargo was salvaged were well-protected.[272] Articles 66 to 78 in Title VIII in the 1608 *Compilatae* dealt with shipwreck, even if there was no clear definition of what the legal boundaries of shipwreck constituted. It contained similar measures to those in the 1563 *Ordonnance*.[273] GA, shipwreck and salvage were thus connected, though their legal boundaries were blurred.[274] The existing, expansive rules on GA hint to the fact that the use of GA was (unsurprisingly) strongly preferred to shipwreck: leaving the legal rules on shipwreck unclear may well have incentivised masters and seamen to prevent shipwrecks, as liability could fall on them, whereas the proper use of GA would absolve them of liability. Moreover, this solution was more equitable and minimised damage or losses, broadly lowering transaction costs.

3.3.2 *Ship Collisions, Contributory Negligence and GA*

Ship collisions were another contentious issue. In most medieval compilations the issue was often mentioned briefly. The *Vonnisse van Damme* for example included a clause on it, stating that accidental collisions would require a contribution by both parties, as did the *Ordonnantie* and the *Gulden Boeck*.[275] In late

269 Ibidem.

270 1563 *Ordonnance*, Title IV, Art. 1.

271 Wisby Laws, Art. 15.

272 Ashburner, *The Rhodian Sea-Law*, cclxxxviii.

273 1563 *Ordonnance*, Title IV, Art. 2. Interestingly, no reference was made to bottomry loans.

274 The issue was only properly addressed in seventeenth-century French royal legislation. See: Trivellato, '"Amphibious Power": The Law of Wreck, Maritime Customs, and Sovereignty in Richelieu's France', *Law and History Review*, 33, 4 (2015), 915–944.

275 *Vonnisse van Damme*, Art. 15. See also: Frankot, "*Of Laws of Ships*", 47–50; Goudsmit, *Geschiedenis*, 309.

medieval Europe, ship collisions were often solved by a legal principle called 'contributory negligence' (*adiuvantia negligentia provenit*), which nowadays still exists in some Common Law jurisdictions.[276] This describes the principle whereby an injured party is also held (partly) at fault for the accident itself. The classic example from Roman law is the case of an injured man who was held partly at fault for running over an athletics field when a javelin, thrown by someone practising, hit him.[277] This was a much-discussed topic for jurists in both classical Roman law and *Ius Commune*, but for our purposes the contribution of Roman-Dutch jurists in particular is of specific interest.[278] They applied the concept of contributory negligence to ship collisions, seeing it as a useful concept to determine liability.[279] They dealt at length with accidental collisions of ships, cases where one master and/or ship was at fault, and cases where both sides were at fault.

Both the 1551 and 1563 *Ordonnances* and the 1608 *Compilatae* also paid attention to the problem. The 1551 *Ordonnance* contained four articles on the subject,[280] whilst the 1563 *Ordonnance* contained a full chapter on it. Neither of them allowed for GA on such occasions, following the *Vonnisse*.[281] The 1551 and 1563 *Ordonnances* largely followed the same order, with the first articles of both *Ordonnances* being phrased similarly.[282] The first article of the 1551 and 1563 *Ordonnance* stipulated that damages had to be equally shared when no party was at fault, and stated that weather conditions did not play a role in deciding fault.[283] The 1551 *Ordonnance* also contained the rule that when anchors or ropes accidentally slipped and the ship hit another ship in the port, the former ship would have to contribute half of the damages, also found in the 1563 *Ordonnance*.[284] The 1551 *Ordonnance* stated that the damage had to be

276 An excellent work on the history of contributory negligence is: E.H.D. Van Dongen, *Contributory Negligence: A Historical and Comparative Study* (Leiden/Boston 2014). Especially pages 241–255, on the contribution of Roman-Dutch jurists in case of ship collisions, are extremely interesting and useful for studying this subject.

277 Ibidem, 54–78.

278 Ibidem, 241–255.

279 Ibidem, 245–254. Yet not everyone agreed to this solution. The exact objections are not of particular interest for this book, but (for example) the jurist Cornelis van Bijnkershoek stated that the 50–50% divisions of the damages were not useful in ship collisions, since the interested parties often had not incurred exactly similar costs following damage to the ship.

280 The *Ordonnance* can be found in: Pardessus, *Collection* (Vol. 4), 44–63.

281 *Vonnisse van Damme*, Art. 15.

282 1551 Art. 46 matched 1563 Title V, Art. 1.

283 1551 *Ordonnance*, Art. 46 & 1563 *Ordonnance*, Title V, Art. 1.

284 1551 *Ordonnance*, Art. 47 & 1563 *Ordonnance*, Title V, Art. 2.

fully reimbursed unless there was *force majeure*;[285] the 1563 *Ordonnance* distinguished between accidents (50% contribution) and intentional collisions (100%).[286] Both 1551 and 1563 *Ordonnances* therefore largely followed established practice from medieval compilations.

The 1608 *Compilatae*, in contrast, allowed for accidental ship collisions to be shared by means of GA, although crucially it had to be declared by mutual agreement among the parties involved.[287] The phrasing of the applicable article was almost word-for-word that of the first article of the 1563 *Ordonnance*, barring the fact that it added GA, sharing the costs over the two involved ships and their cargo. When it was the shipmaster's fault, the compensation would be shared and calculated based on the value of the ship which had hit the other. When a ship had to cut mast or ropes to avoid collision, or when ships hit each other and wine or oil was leaked, the costs could be brought into GA as well (i.e. over the two ships and their cargo).[288] When sailing into port and accidentally hitting a ship, GA could also be declared, as long as the master and crew swore an oath stating it was not their fault.[289] If he declined to swear an oath or when the damaged ship's master could prove that damage to his ship resulted from negligent behaviour by the other master, a full contribution was due anyway.[290] When a ship was firmly anchored but still hit another ship by accident, GA was the preferred solution, but always by mutual agreement.[291] A final rule stated that abandonment always was dependent on the damage, although the perpetrator was advised to help the master of the damaged ship.[292] While seventeenth-century Roman-Dutch Law treated accidental ship collisions within the framework of contributory negligence, Antwerp 1608 *Compilatae* allowed for GA to be shared after accidental collisions, with both ships and cargo contributing. In legal practice (section 4.5.3), this was also common. Why this was the case remains unclear, although we could speculate this solution was more equitable than 'contributory negligence', which necessitated the admittance of guilt on both sides.

285 1551 *Ordonnance*, Arts. 48 & 49.
286 1563 *Ordonnance*, Title V, Arts. 3–5.
287 1608 *Costuymen*, Part 4, Title VIII, Art. 133.
288 Ibidem, Art. 134.
289 Ibidem, Art. 135.
290 Ibidem, Art. 136.
291 Ibidem, Arts. 137 & 138.
292 Ibidem, Art. 141.

3.4 Weytsen's *Tractaet van Avarien*

One of the most important sources on the Laws of General Average in the sixteenth-century Low Countries is the treatise by Quintin Weytsen, born in Vlissingen in the province of Zeeland and active as a lawyer in the Court of Holland. Even if the first-known printed edition of the treatise dates from 1619, the treatise was probably written in 1564 or 1565 as Weytsen died in 1565.[293] This section analyses Weytsen's short treatise in detail. As this close reading will show, this text was influenced by princely legislation and the Digest, although references to both local and foreign customs and the Wisby Laws were also included. The text most likely aimed to legitimise and act as an intellectual companion to the 1563 *Ordonnance*, offering legal support to the *Ordonnance*.[294] Given the enormous authority that medieval jurists attributed to Roman law (*auctoritas*), no legal treatise was complete without plentiful references to the Digest and how any legal norm fitted into its framework. Weytsen, inspired by the legal-humanist method, hence made multiple linguistic and historical references to the *lex rhodia* and the Digest to bolster his credentials.[295] The text was the first doctrinal work in the Low Countries to distinguish systematically between GA and SA (*averij-grosse* and *averij-commune*) and provide clear examples of the two.[296] Following 1551 princely legislation, Weytsen thus offered a definition of GA and SA, trying to clarify the issue within the Low Countries' legal framework.[297] Weytsen's explanations also shed light on why SA was often called Common Average in the sixteenth-century Low Countries (*averij-commune*).[298] Moreover, it explains the intimate connection between tolls, duties and Averages, a subject to which we will return in Chapter 5.[299]

As per the distinction between GA and SA,[300] he mentioned pilotage as the prime example of SA.[301] Pilotage costs to take a ship out of a port should also

293 Both Otto Vervaart and Dave De ruysscher have made valuable suggestions regarding the origin of the text, for which I am grateful. See also: Dreijer & O. Vervaart, 'Een Tractaet van Avarien – 1617', *Pro Memorie*, 21, 2 (2019), 38–41. The edition most commonly used is the 1631 stand-alone edition, which will also function as the source used here.

294 See again: Dreijer & Vervaart, 'Een Tractaet van Avarien', 38–39.

295 De ruysscher, 'Maxims, Principles and Legal Change'.

296 Weytsen, *Een Tractaet van Avarien* (Haarlem 1631), 1.

297 De ruysscher, 'Maxims, Principles and Legal Change'.

298 Ibidem.

299 Ibidem. See also section 5.3.1 for a more detailed analysis.

300 Weytsen, *Een Tractaet van Avarien*, 1.

301 Ibidem.

be shared as SA by the cargo, not the ship.[302] Pilotage was generally regarded as SA, unless the sum exceeded six pounds *Grooten Vlaams*, similar to the clause in the 1563 *Ordonnance*.[303] Principal acts of GA were confirmed to be either jettison or mast and/or rope cutting as deliberate acts.[304] Negligence was no reason to declare GA, for example if this meant that cargo was spoilt or too wet to sell.[305] However, Weytsen noted that it was customary to include spoilt cargo, resulting from pumping away water on the deck.[306] In most medieval compilations, perishable cargo was not admissible in GA, but Weytsen argued that, in some instances, this was admissible. As De ruysscher has pointed out, this was probably the consequence of the large grain cargo transports in Holland, which only contained perishable cargo and hence needed solutions to carry damage.[307]

Referring to Roman law, the treatise went on to argue that an early jettison was always preferred to minimise overall costs, especially if all on board agreed that this was necessary.[308] Weytsen then alluded to the Digest (without a specific reference) to argue that merchants could not be expected to contribute more than the value they had put into the ship, similar to the arguments made later by Van Glins (see section 2.3).[309] Insurers could thus not be expected to pay more than the value they had insured by means of GA either, an indirect recognition of the liability of the insurer to pay for GA.[310] Corresponding to Antwerp customs, the valuation of jettisoned cargo was different according to the place where the act of jettison occurred.[311]

An important question was what should contribute to the GA claim, especially when it came to money and precious gems as part of the cargo. According to Weytsen, *turben* in Antwerp gave different answers to this question.[312] Some merchants argued that money, jewels, and other valuable items should be

302 Ibidem, 2.
303 Ibidem. See also 1563 *Ordonnance*, Title IV, Art. 9.
304 Ibidem.
305 Ibidem, 3.
306 Ibidem.
307 De ruysscher, 'Maxims, Principles and Legal Change', 267. Before the sixteenth century, 'perishables' were primarily foodstuffs for crew members, meaning they did not count in the freightage and therefore could not be included in GA.
308 Weytsen, *Een Tractaet van Avarien*, 3.
309 Ibidem, 3. See also: Van Glins, *Aenmerckingen*, 62–65.
310 Ibidem, 4.
311 During the first half of the voyage, the price at the place of loading should be counted, whereas cargo jettison in the second half of the voyage should be calculated according to the selling price in the port of destination. Ibidem.
312 Ibidem, 4–5.

counted in GA as long as this saved the voyage as a whole, in line with the 1550 *Ordonnance* of Charles V.[313] If money was incorporated in the bill of lading (*cognossement* in Dutch), then merchants were liable to contribute into GA if the money was jettisoned. Other merchants had, in contrast, argued in these *turben* that it was a long-followed custom that jettisoned money did not contribute to GA, citing the example of Charles V jettisoning money in a storm on his way to the Low Countries in 1549.[314] While the Antwerp municipal court argued for the inclusion, the Council of Brabant had reached the opposite conclusion in a 1548 case, just before Charles' jettison.[315] Weytsen appeared to argue for the inclusion of money in GA claims (consistent with the 1563 *Ordonnance*), even if no clear solution is advocated in the text.[316]

Another major question, unsurprisingly, was that of piracy. If pirates only stole cargo, there would be no GA, consistent with the *lex rhodia de iactu* and subsequent glosses, because the damage had not been deliberate.[317] If a master was, however, able to negotiate with pirates to take part of the cargo, the compensation could be incorporated in a GA claim because this action had prevented greater damage or outright losses.[318] Ransom money could be counted in GA, but voluntarily giving up money could not.[319] In short, there would have to be a certain act of resistance before expenses could be brought into GA. If a shipmaster was held by pirates, merchants were liable to pay for his freedom, but not via GA.[320] Consistent with the princely *Ordonnances*, expenses related to dead seamen, their burials and the remainder of their wages to the widows were to be paid by means of GA.[321] Weytsen thus clearly acknowledged that besides jettison and mast cutting, other actions could also be a reason for contribution.

Weytsen then moved on to treat some very specific, yet more tricky cases. If large ships sailed into a port and the cargo was divided over several smaller ships, these costs were generally incorporated into SA as pilotage costs. However, when a large ship and cargo was saved in this operation, these costs could be brought into GA.[322] Similarly, everyone who had cargo on the larger ship

313 Ibidem, 5.
314 Ibidem.
315 Ibidem. See also: De ruysscher, 'Maxims, Principles and Legal Change', 267.
316 Ibidem, 5–6.
317 Ibidem, 6.
318 Ibidem.
319 Ibidem.
320 Ibidem.
321 Ibidem, 6–7. See also 1551 *Ordonnance*, Art. 28.
322 Ibidem.

was meant to contribute to GA when the cargo on smaller lighter ships was jettisoned.[323] Only when damage ensued by accident during unloading, the costs would be borne by the owners of the cargo.[324] The thorny question of salvage was also treated by Weytsen. He described an example whereby a ship had incurred damage that would lead to GA but was wrecked before it could reach the port safely. The owners of cargo indeed had to pay for GA, but the salvage costs were not shared by means of GA, as it had not contributed to the saving of the venture.[325] Weytsen argued that this was the wrong solution, referring to the Digest.[326] He wrote that the value of salvaged cargo had to be incorporated into the GA declaration, so that owners of jettisoned cargo would also contribute to this act for the common benefit. It would be unfair, Weytsen argued, if someone whose cargo was not lost had to pay more into the GA contribution than those whose cargo was lost and then salvaged.[327] On the valuation of the cargo, Weytsen advocated a similar line to the rules in Antwerp insurance law.[328] Weytsen added that impartial arbitrators had to determine its selling price.[329] Merchants furthermore had the right, within six hours after the arrival of the ship, to come and inspect the cargo. They then had the option to buy the damaged cargo and try to sell it, or otherwise accept the contributions made in GA.[330] Since shipmasters' fraud was considered to be a major problem, Weytsen also remarked that it was, at the time of writing, customary for French and Biscayer masters to contribute to GA claims for 1/3 after damages to cargo, with the merchants taking on the other 2/3.[331] Weytsen therefore clearly noted different customs from formal sources of law, accepting this when there was a clear rationale.[332] This was also an acknowledgement of the fact that the rules on GA could be different across Europe, as local solutions took precedence in specified cases.[333]

Subsequently, Weytsen paid attention to some procedural aspects. Because not all merchants travelled with their cargo, Weytsen allowed for a majority of

---

323 Ibidem.
324 Ibidem, 7–8.
325 Ibidem, 8.
326 Ibidem, 9.
327 Ibidem.
328 Ibidem.
329 Ibidem.
330 Ibidem, 9–10.
331 Ibidem, 10.
332 As *Ius Commune* accepted general customs as overriding other sources of law, this was not unprecedented.
333 In line with; Frankot, "*Of Laws of Ships*".

the crew to agree to a jettison.[334] This was of course common. Crew members moreover had to contribute in GA if they had more than one chest on board, although Weytsen also remarked that this was often deliberately overlooked by merchants since they did not mind for the crew to have some more personal cargo on board.[335] When the cargo of merchants was saved, the strict legal rules (*ex stricto jure*) were put aside for the moment. Only if they had clearly prioritised saving their own cargo over the merchants' cargo, crew members were expected to contribute. This was an odd rule, for merchants tended to be against more space for seamen for multiple reasons, including smuggling opportunities. Again, Weytsen however appeared to accept general customs as overruling formal law.

Weytsen then moved on to answer some final questions. He described a special case when accidental damage had occurred, and the ship was in danger of being wrecked. When additional actions were taken to prevent further damage or to save the venture, those latter costs were a cause for GA (but not the costs arising from the accident in the first place).[336] Another issue was the consequences of an additional stop. If a ship sailing from Spain to Arnemuiden (Zeeland) made a necessary stop in Dover after encountering a storm, took on additional wool as cargo there and subsequently jettisoned this newly-bought wool, did the Spanish merchants also have to contribute?[337] Weytsen answered affirmatively, but only under the condition that the largest part of the crew members on board agreed, and the diversion to Dover had been strictly necessary.[338] When a master took another route to search for cargo for his own profit, merchants did no longer had to pay the freight. This was obviously a point of contention, because in case of need a shipmaster was often allowed to diverge, leading to a grey area regarding which place was *en route* and which was not. Of course, different routes were possible (and Dover, for example, could reasonably be defined as being on the Spain-Low Countries route). Whether there was a clause prohibiting diverting from the route depended on the policy.[339] When only one merchant freighted the ship, compensation was shared via the 1/3–2/3 principle, the master paying the 2/3 share.[340]

Weytsen's work sheds light on the legal development of GA in the Low Countries during the sixteenth century, and in many respects was aligned with

334 Weytsen, *Een Tractaet van Avarien*, 10.
335 Ibidem.
336 Ibidem, 10–11.
337 Ibidem, 11.
338 Ibidem.
339 Ibidem, 11–12.
340 Ibidem, 12.

the 1563 *Ordonnance*.[341] The frequent references to the Digest and legal scholarship on the Digest (for example referring to a gloss on the *lex rhodia*) were aimed at providing an intellectual foundation for the 1563 *Ordonnance*, but Weytsen also described various developments from legal practice, providing practical information on GA procedure. Moreover, he allowed for some exceptions, noting long-held general customs as valid and allowing it to override formal sources of law, such as the *Ordonnance*. Weytsen's work shows the multiple and complex influences of maritime law in the sixteenth-century Low Countries. His work established the principles of GA and SA and acted as a manual on how to apportion GA claims and how to deal with certain tricky issues, such as extra stops and piracy and privateering. Weytsen's work thus acted both as a learned legal treatise and as a manual for merchants and Average adjusters.[342] It aimed to legitimise the decisions made in the 1551 and 1563 *Ordonnances* on GA by giving it a proper learned legal background. Given its durable influence on discussions over GA in the early modern period, Weytsen was largely successful in doing so.[343]

3.5 Conclusion

Whilst rules stipulating a contribution after jettison or mast cutting were commonly known throughout Europe and even beyond, the development of GA in the Southern Low Countries only accelerated after 1550. Four important trends have been traced in this chapter: first, the shipmaster's position was increasingly circumscribed, but he was also given greater freedom of action; second, new causes for GA emerged, such as uninsurable costs and costs to prevent (greater) damage; third, new varieties of Averages, such as SA and PA, were defined in princely legislation and Antwerp municipal law; fourth, the insurability of GA developed. As there were some important differences between the various sources (e.g. on ordinary pilotage or the insurability of GA), the existence of a *lex maritima* can be disproven by the study of formal sources of law only. Yet workable norms were established, for which princely legislation was particularly important as it moved from rules of thumb (e.g. 'jettison means

341 Dreijer & Vervaart, 'Een Tractaet van Avarien', 38–39.

342 A similar argument is made in: Ibidem. It was for example also incorporated in: S.A., *'t Boeck der Zee-Rechten, Inhoudende Dat hoogste ende oudste Godtlantsche Water-recht / dat de gemeene kooplieden ende Schippers geordineert ende gemaeckt hebben tot Wisbuy* (Amsterdam 1678).

343 Dreijer & Vervaart, 'Een Tractaet van Avarien', 38–40.

Average') to general principles, offering greater legal security.[344] Viewed as a whole, there was largely continuity in the application of rules on GA, a many new rules simply expanded on older rules or even incorporated the older rules into the *iura mercatorum*, the layered set of legal sources which governed late medieval and early modern trade.

Whilst there were disagreements over the application of GA and, especially, insurance, particularly between the merchant communities and the central government, the parties engaged in the maritime sector were nevertheless able to find new solutions given the constraints. A major example was the folding of uninsurable costs following a privateer or pirate attack under GA, where both the Castilians and the central government had to compromise. GA's application was therefore widened, but only as part of a package on maritime laws, also including insurance and bottomry.[345] Yet Antwerp, generally willing to allow wide-ranging insurance legislation, kept this clause in the *Compilatae*, cementing this operationally efficient solution. This was the result of the lengthy negotiations where multiple parties used their bargaining power to seek the preferred outcome. Power struggles trumped economic concerns in this matter, clearly showing that GA influenced both the 'size of the pie' and the 'slices of the pie'.[346] In the end, this arrangement appeared to satisfy most parties in the maritime sector.

---

344 De ruysscher, 'Maxims, Principles and Legal Change'.

345 As also emphasised by: Ogilvie, '"Whatever is, is Right?"', 681.

346 Ibidem, 662.

CHAPTER 4

GA in Legal Practice

4.1 Introduction

Formal developments in the Laws of General Average were important to facilitate commercial development and enable risk management. But as legal historians often focus on doctrine, *Ius Commune* and formal legislative sources, the study of legal practice is sometimes underappreciated.[1] How did legal practice and formal law interact? This chapter investigates this question by studying evidence from legal practice on GA in the Southern Low Countries. Next to court cases from Antwerp, Bruges and the Great Council, this chapter will also include a small batch of court cases from Zeeland for comparison.[2] Moreover, the chapter draws on notarial records, insurance ledgers and Antwerp aldermen records such as certifications and Average adjustments.[3] The chapter will show that legal practice in many respects preceded formal law on GA: merchants welcomed the legal security as jurists incorporated these mercantile customs into formal sources of law. The chapter thus supports Dave De

1 In the history of commercial law, combining 'formal sources' of law and legal practice is more common. See for an example on Antwerp: De ruysscher, "*Naer het Romeinsch recht*".

2 Zeeland was allowed to tax the trans-shipment of wine from 1524 onwards. This privilege was called *verbodeming*, a term which is rather hard to translate. A literal translation would be 'rebottoming' or, potentially, 'bottom privilege'. A Dutch definition states that it simply concerns bringing cargo from one ship to another, a term originating in medieval staple rights law. See: https://www.debinnenvaart.nl/binnenvaarttaal/index.php?woord=ver#verbodemen {Retrieved 27/04/2020}. See also: Wijffels, 'Ius Commune and International Wine Trade – a Revision', *Tijdschrift voor Rechtsgeschiedenis*, 71, 3 (2003), 289–317, there 289–290; Zijlmans, *Troebele betrekkingen*, 270–276; Scheltjens, *Dutch Deltas*, 31–33, 46 & 54.

3 In legal history, notarial archives are rarely used to examine legal-practical questions. Most works concern procedural aspects, even if the notarial records offer great potential for the history of commercial law, among other subjects. Most research into the notarial records has hence been the terrain of economic historians. See for legal-historical approaches: H. Callewier, 'Brugge, vijftiende-eeuws centrum van het notariaat in de Nederlanden', *Tijdschrift voor Rechtgeschiedenis*, 77 (2009), 73–102; M. Oosterbosch, '"Van groote abuysen ende ongeregelheden": overheidsbemoeiingen met het Antwerpse notariaat tijdens de XVIde eeuw', *Tijdschrift voor Rechtsgeschiedenis*, 63, 1–2 (1995), 83–101; Murray, 'Failure of Corporation: Notaries Public in Medieval Bruges', *Journal of Medieval History*, 12, 2 (1986), 155–166; Idem, 'The Profession of Notary Public in Medieval Flanders', *Tijdschrift voor Rechtsgeschiedenis*, 61 (1993), 3–31.

 | DOI:10.1163/9789004540354_005

ruysscher's claim that Antwerp incorporated innovations from commercial practice into the existing legal framework, enhancing legal security for merchants.[4]

The chapter is structured in four parts. First, the introductory section 4.2 analyses GA procedure in Bruges and Antwerp, focusing on the complex relationship between the various governmental layers (e.g. the *nationes*, municipality and central government) and private actors (notaries, insurers, average adjusters and arbitrators). It argues that GA moved towards becoming an open-access institution in Antwerp, as GA claims were enforceable before the municipal court, whereas before numerous particularised institutions were involved. This followed a more general trend in Antwerp, as the aldermen claimed back jurisdiction over mercantile cases from the *nationes*, lowering enforcement costs.[5] Although the municipal court was indeed important for enforcement, many private actors were involved in the nominally public-order institutions created by Antwerp.

Second, the chapter examines legal strategies by examining the various steps in GA procedures, first focusing on the role of the shipmaster in section 4.3. His role was crucial in GA procedures: whilst merchants often tried to pin liability on him, the shipmaster, in contrast, aimed to evade liability via PA, of whom the very few legal practice records are also studied in section 4.3.5. Section 4.4 discusses litigation in the next phase of dispute resolution, highlighting the interaction between legal practice and formal law on the insurability of GA which Antwerp already allowed in the late 1540s, showing new dynamics in the interest community as the result of the liability of the insurer to cover GA claims. Section 4.5 studies 'atypical' GA cases. These cases could not easily be solved by applying precedent, formal law or contract law, primarily in cases of ship collisions, the combination of emergency bottomry loans and GA and jurisdictional disputes. Here, research into legal practice has its clearest added value, as it shows how courts dealt with new issues arising from GA claims. It argues that courts were on the whole conservative in applying new norms without explicit rules or general principles in place to draw on, although for ship collisions the Antwerp municipal court and Great Council were relatively willing to apply GA to solve disputes.

The chapter draws heavily on primary source material, primarily on legal practice from Antwerp, as the significant majority of GA cases were litigated before its municipal court. For the period between 1545 and 1582, forty cases

4 De ruysscher, "*Naer het Romeinsch recht*", 381; Idem, 'Maxims, Principles and Legal Change'. A similar but more general argument is made in: Friedman, *The Legal System*.

5 Puttevils, *Merchants and Trading*, 143–145; De ruysscher, "*Naer het Romeinsch recht*", 117–121.

involving GA are preserved in the Antwerp *Vonnisboeken* (Judgement Books).[6] Before 1545, only one case was heard before the Antwerp municipal court, suggesting that the issue of GA either only became a legal problem during the mid-sixteenth century, or that GA cases were mostly handled by private actors before the 1540s. An increasing caseload is a well-observed phenomenon in the literature on sixteenth-century Europe, although we do not have hard numbers for a rising caseload in the sixteenth-century Low Countries.[7] The increase in maritime litigation can probably be explained by two additional reasons: first, this period was an especially violent time on Europe's waters, even as the Antwerp trade was at peak in terms of volume;[8] second, the Antwerp municipal court made an active effort to control jurisdiction over cases of commercial and maritime law after 1550.[9] All this coincided with more sophisticated legal strategies of both plaintiffs and defendants and a complex jurisdictional situation.[10] Therefore the temporal focus of the chapter is primarily on the post-1540 period.

4.2 The Governance of GA Procedure in Bruges and Antwerp

This section analyses the development of the governance system of GA procedure during the fifteenth and sixteenth centuries in the Southern Low Countries. In principle, GA procedure in early modern Europe was straightforward. When a venture suffered a deliberate damage for the common benefit, the shipmaster had to sail to the first port and file for GA. However, procedures differed across Europe. In the Italian Peninsula, most city-states required the shipmaster to apply for GA at designated courts, such as the *Consoli di Mare*

6 Cases on GA can be found in: BE-SAA, Stadsbestuur, Rechtspraak, Raadkamer, Vonnisboeken, inv. V#1235, fol. 26v; V#1241, fol. 130v–131r, 283r–v; V1242, fol. 127r; V#1244, fol. 60v–61r, 126v–127v, 128r–130r, 130r–v; V#1245, fol. 1r, 56r–v, 60r, 104r, 120r–121r, 174r–v, 186v–187r, 187r; V#1246, fol. 60v–61r; V#1247, fol. 269r–v; V#1249, fol. 4v, 204r–205r, 237v–238r, 265r–v; V#1250, fol. 11v–12v, 126v–127r, 139r, 186v–187v, 236r; V#1251, fol. 45v–46v, 104r–v; V#1252, fol. 53r–v, 125v, 130v–131r, 168r–v; V#1253, fol. 4v–5v, 101v–102r; V#1254, 107r–v, 147v–148v, unknown folio; V#1255, fol. 221v–225r; V#1256, fol. 58v–59v, 78v–79v. V#1248 is unfortunately missing from the archives, V#1257 did not contain GA cases. Part of the cases were already noted by De ruysscher & Puttevils. See: De ruysscher & Puttevils, 'The Art of Compromise', 34, there note 28.

7 Richard Kagan termed this period as one of the 'legal revolution'. See: R. Kagan, *Lawsuits and Litigants in Castile, 1500–1700* (Chapel Hill, NC 1981).

8 Van der Wee, *The Growth* (Vol. 2), 209–244.

9 De ruysscher, "*Naer het Romeinsch recht*", 125–136.

10 See again: Donlan & Heirbaut, "'A Patchwork of Accommodations'".

in Pisa or the *Conservatori del Mare* in Genoa.[11] Judges at these courts nominated experts as Average adjusters, acting under the supervision of the local authorities. In the Low Countries, no courts specialising in maritime matters existed in the sixteenth century, meaning jurisdiction on maritime matters in Bruges and Antwerp formally fell under the respective municipal courts. Sections 4.2.1 to 4.2.3 analyse chronologically the regulation of GA procedure, whereas sections 4.2.4 to 4.2.6 analyse specific aspects of it: the role of insurers, consular courts and appeals against private arbitration panels. Although both local and foreign merchants were consulted on many procedural changes, merchants rarely entered into the Bruges or Antwerp governmental circles, as opposed to 'merchant republics' like Amsterdam and Hamburg.[12]

As jurisdiction over internal maritime affairs was a major competence for the consuls of the foreign *nationes*, in the Low Countries, a shipmaster had two basic options to apply for GA; the first option was to apply to the consuls, but this was only allowed when both shipmaster and merchants investing in the venture belonged to the same *natio*. The Portuguese and Castilian consuls for example both possessed this privilege.[13] They sometimes acted as Average adjusters themselves, but more often outsourced the calculation process to trusted experts. The consular option is introduced in greater detail in section 4.2.5, focusing on the Castilian consular court.[14] The other option, more commonly used as many sixteenth-century ventures included investors from various regions, was for the shipmaster to apply for GA by appointing a panel of arbitrators, specialised Average adjusters or notaries in agreement with representatives from the merchants and other parties in the interest community, such as the ship-owner(s).[15] Yet over time GA procedure changed, mostly influenced by the changes to marine insurance legislation and governance, with which the development of GA procedure and regulation became

---

11 The subject of the PhD dissertations of Jake Dyble and Antonio Iodice. See: https://humanities.exeter.ac.uk/history/research/centres/maritime/research/avetransrisk/team/ {Retrieved 14/04/2020}.

12 M. Lindemann, *The Merchant Republics: Amsterdam, Antwerp, and Hamburg, 1648–1790* (Cambridge 2017). This is also confirmed by the recent work of Janna Everaert: Everaert, *Macht in de metropool: politieke elitevorming tijdens de demografische en economische bloeifase van Antwerpen (ca. 1400–1550)* (Unpublished PhD thesis, Vrije Universiteit Brussel & University of Antwerp 2020). See also: K. Wouters, 'Een open oligarchie? De machtstructuur in de Antwerpse magistraat tijdens de periode 1520–1555', *Revue belge de philologie et d'histoire*, 82, 4 (2004), 905–934.

13 De Groote, *De zeeassurantie*, 22–23; Goris, *Étude*, 44–45.

14 The records of the Castilian consular court are the only extant archival records in the Low Countries of the consular court: for the other *nationes*, solely the privileges have survived.

15 See for the definition: Van Niekerk, *The Development*, 61–62.

intertwined.[16] As such, the first three sections also pay attention to the development of insurance as this is necessary to understand the background to the various regulations. This also emphasises the importance of the interplay between different institutions.[17]

4.2.1 GA *Procedure in Bruges (1400s–1490s)*

In contrast to GA, the literature on marine insurance in the Low Countries is well-developed.[18] Yet for Bruges information is relatively scarce on insurance as well. Insurance arrived in the city with Italian merchants during the fourteenth century, although both Carl Reatz and Jan-Albert Goris offered the now-refuted theory that the technique was introduced in the Low Countries by the Portuguese.[19] We are largely left in the dark about its development until the early sixteenth century, as sources are scarce.[20] Most likely, insurance was primarily used by merchants from Southern Europe, who congregated on the local stock exchange to find underwriters for insurance policies, and to trade signed policies to third parties, for risk management and speculation

16 As marine insurance was, until the seventeenth century, the only form of insurance, the term 'insurance' in this paragraph refers throughout to marine insurance. See: Van Niekerk, *The Development*, 271–418.

17 Ogilvie, '"Whatever is, is Right?"', 681.

18 The most important publications are: Goris, *Étude*, 180–193; Van Niekerk, *The Development*; Brulez, *De firma Della Faille*, 156–157 & 528–529; De ruysscher, 'Antwerp 1490–1590'; Idem, 'Van kade naar stadhuis: informatieuitwisseling, fraudebestrijding en gereglementeerde innovatie in Antwerpse zeeverzekeringen (ca. 1550–ca. 1700)', *Tijdschrift voor Geschiedenis*, 125, 3 (2012), 366–383; Wijffels, 'Een Antwerpse zeeverzekeringspolis uit het jaar 1557', *Handelingen van de Koninklijke Commissie voor Geschiedenis*, 63, 1–2 (1948), 95–103; Reatz, 'Ordonnances'; Couvreur, 'Recht en zeeverzekeringspraktijk'; De Groote, *De zeeassurantie*; Idem, 'Onuitgegeven zestiende-eeuwse Antwerpse polissen', *Bijdragen tot de Geschiedenis*, 57, 3–4 (1974), 153–170; Idem, 'Zeeverzekering', in: Asaert *et al* (eds.), *Maritieme Geschiedenis der Nederlanden* (Vol. 1), 206–219; Puttevils & Deloof, 'Marketing and Pricing Risk'; Verlinden, 'De zeeverzekeringen der Spaanse kooplui in de Nederlanden gedurende de XVIe eeuw', *Bijdragen voor de Geschiedenis der Nederlanden*, 2 (1946), 191–216; Van der Wee, *The Growth* (Vol. 2), 327–328. A peculiar article by Ebert argues that Atlantic trade led to the rise of marine insurance in Antwerp, but this is unlikely given that it was already commonly practiced by Castilian merchants before this time in Antwerp: C. Ebert, 'Early Modern Atlantic Trade and the Development of Maritime Insurance to 1630', *Past and Present*, 213 (2011), 87–114.

19 Edler-De Roover, 'Early Examples', 191–194 & 198–199; Reatz, *Geschichte*, 42–55; Goris, *Étude*, 178–179. See for the refutation: Verlinden, 'De zeeverzekeringen', 191–193. Verlinden rightly pointed out that this was a sort of mutual insurance rather than premium-based insurance.

20 De ruysscher, 'Belgium', 114–115.

purposes.[21] Although the Bruges municipal court had formal jurisdiction over insurance cases, it only heard a handful of cases during this period. Regulation of insurance was non-existent, barring a 1458 *Ordonnance* by Philip the Good on procedural rules, whereas for GA customary compilations such as the *Vonnisse* could be used.

Although it is therefore likely that GA was used in most cases where maritime damage occurred, information on GA procedure is scant as well.[22] From the few GA disputes that reached the court, it appears that private arbitrators handled most of the GA applications that could not be handled by consuls. In fifteenth-century Bruges, arbitrators were often trusted merchants, sometimes even appointed by the municipal court when a complex GA case reached the aldermen.[23] The arbitrators would hear testimonies, calculate the damages and issue a judgement. Appeals were only possible at the municipal court but were extremely rare.[24] Although the governance system appears rather 'private-order', on closer inspection this is not the case, as the Bruges municipal court kept a close eye on the GA proceedings and had final jurisdiction when disputes would arise from the GA calculations. Moreover, it had final oversight over the decisions of the consular courts, making appeals in principle possible.

4.2.2 *GA Procedure in Antwerp (1500s–1540s)*

The development of marine insurance in Antwerp is, in contrast to Bruges, well-documented.[25] Besides Italian merchants, Castilian merchants were particularly enthusiastic users of insurance in the city.[26] During the first half of the sixteenth century, Antwerp insurance existed in a relatively thin legal framework, as the city willingly accommodated customary insurance practice.[27] The 1537 *Ordonnance* of Charles V established procedural rules such as the *namptissement* procedure,[28] but was one of the few legislative efforts to reg-

21 Idem, 'Antwerp 1490–1590', 94–95; Van der Wee, *The Growth* (Vol. 2), 328–329.

22 Idem, 'Belgium', 114–115.

23 See for example: Gilliodts-Van Severen, *Espagne*, 137–139 & 214. The first case was an *avería de nación* case, the second case a GA case.

24 De ruysscher, 'Belgium', 113–115; De Groote, *De zeeassurantie*, 13–18.

25 See footnote 18 of this chapter.

26 Verlinden, 'De zeeverzekeringen'; Casado Alonso, 'Juan Henriquez, un corredor de seguros de Amberes a mediados del Siglo XVI', in: J.C. Pérez Manrique (ed.), *Palabras de archivo: homenaje a Milagros Moratinos Palomero* (Burgos 2018), 49–68.

27 De ruysscher, 'Antwerp 1490–1590', 85–87.

28 The *namptissement* procedure required insurers to conditionally pay the insurance indemnity before litigating, whilst the insured party had to pay a deposit with the court. See for the procedure in Antwerp: De ruysscher, "*Naer het Romeinsch recht*", 46 & 285. The *namptissement* procedure existed in many European commercial cities and states. Both

ulate insurance as most trade happened in overland or riverine settings in the 1520s and 1530s.[29] Up to the 1560s, only a handful of policies remain, the earliest one coming from 1531 when a Hanseatic merchant signed an insurance policy.[30] Several other policies have survived in the ledgers of Willem Streyt and other notaries (see below), dating from the 1530s and 1540s.[31] Carlos Wyffels and Rudolf Häpke have also published about Antwerp policies from 1557 and 1566.[32] It appears that in the absence of an extensive legal framework on insurance (as opposed to other major insurance centres such as Burgos and Florence[33]), insurance was primarily a speculative opportunity rather than a technique of risk management until the 1550s.[34] This was particularly the case for the supply side of the market, as the Southern European merchants moved into financial services.[35]

GA was not as regulated as insurance, as we have seen in the previous chapter. Moreover, until the liability of insurers to pay for GA claims became a norm in Antwerp legal practice in the late 1540s, there was in principle no direct connection between GA and insurance, except that they were both instruments of risk management that complemented each other. Yet in practice, the governance systems of insurance and GA were quite similar. As the municipal court Antwerp pursued a policy of self-regulation among merchants on these subjects, cases on either GA or insurance rarely reached the (Antwerp) municipal court until the late 1540s. Consuls and notaries were the primary beneficiaries of this system, as the aldermen largely delegated the work of conflict resolution to them. Many *nationes* possessed the privilege of jurisdiction over maritime affairs, for example the Portuguese in Antwerp.[36] Similar to the situation in Bruges, arbitrators under the formal supervision of the Antwerp municipal court may have solved most cases until the 1520s.[37]

---

sixteenth-century Tuscany and seventeenth-century France for example had similar procedures. See for example: Addobbati, 'Italy 1500–1800', 52–53.

29 Van der Wee, *The Growth* (Vol. 2), 326–328.

30 A. Hofmeister, 'Eine hansische Seeversicherung aus dem Jahre 1531', *Hansische Geschichtsblätter*, 5 (1886), 169–177. See also: De Groote, *De zeeassurantie*, 96.

31 De Groote, *De zeeassurantie*, 96.

32 Wijffels, 'Een Antwerpse zeeverzekeringspolis'; E.L.G. Den Dooren de Jong, 'Lombard Street', *Het Verzekerings-archief*, 5 (1924–5), 11–21. The latter contains a reprint of Häpke's insurance policy.

33 De ruysscher, 'Antwerp 1490–1590', 98.

34 Ibidem, 96; Van der Wee, *The Growth* (Vol. 2), 327–328.

35 Puttevils, *Merchants and Trading*, 19–48.

36 De ruysscher, "*Naer het Romeinsch recht*", 120–121.

37 As a sole case from 1517 indicates: BE-SAA, Vonnisboeken, V#1235, fol. 26v.

Private arbitrators' documentation is non-existent for Antwerp. More material has been left by the Antwerp notaries, whose services were frequently used by foreign merchants and who from the 1520s onwards started to play an important role in Antwerp GA procedure next to the arbitrators.[38] Four notaries were prominent in the maritime sector: Jacob De Platea, Willem Streyt and both father and son Zeeger 'S-Hertoghen. The papers of De Platea are kept in Antwerp's state archives, and those of the other three can be found in Antwerp's municipal archives.[39] These notarial archives have already been studied in detail, and as such useful source editions exist.[40] Notaries had multiple tasks to guarantee a smooth legal process in maritime ventures following their important role in *Ius Commune* legal theory. As written evidence contained dates and witnesses, this trumped all claims on contrary oral agreements. To strengthen legal security, many merchants therefore recorded freight contracts and testimonies with a notary.[41] Local authorities moreover strengthened this system by placing both notaries and brokers under oath, trying to secure the honesty of those middlemen in recording economic transactions.

Most notaries appeared to serve relatively small circles of clients, specialising for example in Iberian or Southern German merchants.[42] The notaries knew each other and formed a circle of trust, acting as witnesses when other notaries concluded freight contracts. One 1535 freight contract concluded by Streyt for example recorded 's-Hertoghen sr. as a witness.[43] Streyt's ledgers for the years of 1535 and 1540 (the only years to have survived), contain the most significant information on GA procedure, as well as information on Averages in freight contracts and insurance.[44] Streyt primarily served Iberian merchants.[45]

38 De Groote, *De zeeassurantie*, 143–144.

39 BE-SAA, Private Archieven, Notariaat, Antwerpen 1480–1810, Notariaat Streyt, inv. N#3132–#3133 & Notariaat 'S-Hertoghen, inv. N#2070–#2078; Rijksarchief Antwerpen (hereafter BE-RAA), Notariaat, inv. R02, Notariaat De Platea, nr. 1, fol. 63r–64r.

40 Primarily so in: J. Strieder, *Aus Antwerpener Notariatsarchiven: Quellen zur deutschen Wirtschaftgeschichte des 16. Jahrhunderts* (Berlin 1930) (hereafter: Strieder, *Notariatsarchiven*). Other useful descriptive works include: Fagel, *De Hispano-Vlaamse wereld*, 72–73; De Groote, *De zeeassurantie*, 143; Goris, *Étude*, 161–171.

41 Under the *Ius Commune*, the sign of a notary was an important prerequisite for proof. See: T. Rüfner, 'Substance of medieval Roman law: The Development of Private Law', in: Pihlajamäki, Dubber & Godfrey (eds.), *The Oxford Handbook of European Legal History*, 309–333, there 323–325.

42 Ibidem, 100–106.

43 BE-SAA, Notariaat Streyt, N#3132, fol. 70r. Also in: Strieder, *Notariatsarchiven*, 343–346 (nr. 667).

44 Goris, *Étude*, 161–167: BE-SAA, Notariaat Streyt, N#3132 & N#3133. For insurance: De Groote, *De zeeassurantie*, 96.

45 Fagel, *De Hispano-Vlaamse wereld*, 70–73 & 100–106.

In the absence of a Consulate where they could bring (GA) disputes, Castilian merchants in the city opted for this option to solve internal disputes.[46] Catalan-Aragonese merchants also regularly used Streyt's services.[47]

Early in 1535, Streyt drew up a GA calculus for the ship *Santa Maria de Consolaçion*.[48] This is the oldest known GA calculation in the Southern Low Countries, and one of the few that is left for the sixteenth century.[49] Streyt divided the costs into GA and SA and assigned contributions to the participants of the interest community. The calculus was rather straightforward as only two merchants and the master were involved, and there was not much damage. Under GA, Streyt included cable and anchor cutting before the coast of Dunkirk to salvage the vessel (i.e. the active mass).[50] Under SA, Streyt categorised common pilotage costs and the wage for the unloaders of the cargo (*descargadores*).[51] Moreover, Streyt calculated the so-called active mass, the contributory value of the cargo, as described in section 2.3.[52] Streyt used the freight that was to be received by the shipmaster to calculate his contribution, which appears to have been common in the 1530s in Antwerp.[53] In this case, Streyt used 6.25% of the freight as the contributory value to GA, after deducting the crew's allowances from the total value of the cargo.[54] The fact that only a part of the freight was taken into account can be explained by the fact that in Antwerp freight was always calculated as a fixed fee per unit, taking the freight

46 Goris, *Étude*, 58–66.

47 See for example: Goris, *Étude*, 610–611. This is a transcription of: BE-SAA, Notariaat Streyt, inv. N#3132, fol. 96r–v. Fagel has however doubted that Streyt held a monopoly position, pointing to the fact that they used many other notaries, although these records are mostly lost. See: Fagel, *De Hispano-Vlaamse wereld*, 100–106.

48 BE-SAA, Notariaat Streyt, inv. N#3132, fol. 8v–9v. It is printed with some deficiencies in Goris, *Étude*, 173–174. See also: De Groote, *De zeeassurantie*, 144. From here on, Castilian GA calculus shall be named as *Rotulo de averías*, as this appears to be the common term for Castilian Average adjustments, primarily in the ledgers of Streyt. In the Castilian consular court, both *carta de averías* and *rotulo de averías* are used (apparently interchangeably), but for clarity we shall stick to *rotulo de averías*. See also: Van Niekerk, *The Development*, 694, footnote 245. Thanks to Marta García Garralón for checking the transcription in Goris and pointing out the deficiencies.

49 De Groote, *De zeeassurantie*, 144.

50 BE-SAA, Notariaat Streyt, inv. N#3132, fol. 9r.

51 Ibidem.

52 This can be found as "*carga de la nao*" in the calculus on folio 8v. Both Antonio Ruyz and Diego Pardo calculated by their cargo, a total of 866 livres.

53 De ruysscher, 'Maxims, Principles and Legal Change', 263. According to Weytsen, it subsequently became common to take half the value of the ship and half the value of the freight for the contribution, but Antwerp appears to have stuck to the freightage.

54 The so-called *penning zestien* (6.25%). See: Ibidem, *n23*.

for the lost cargo as the basis for the contribution by the master.[55] Streyt also provided a rationale for his calculations, stating that he had made the calculus on the basis of oaths by the Castilian merchants and shipmaster, which had been recorded by the notary Antoon van Male in Middelburg (Zeeland).[56] Such a declaration was added to vouch for the reliability of the calculus. This may have been useful when the Castilian master would take the calculus to other merchants to demand their contribution.

Besides drawing up a GA calculus, Streyt also vouched for the reliability of *calculi* made by other notaries. He provided a declaration in 1535 that a calculus made in Middelburg was of sufficient quality and drawn up by trustworthy men.[57] Streyt also recorded notices of ship-owners declaring shipwreck.[58] Sometimes, GA was declared even when a shipwreck followed the act of GA. In 1535, for example, Streyt declared GA despite the occurrence of a shipwreck before the coast of the Scilly Isles, since various parts of the cargo were saved by transferring them to smaller lighter ships before the ship was wrecked, which benefited everyone involved in the venture.[59] Both the master and some crew members testified that this was indeed the case, with merchants involved in the venture recording an oath agreeing to this solution. This solution did not comply with formal law, but Streyt's solution in this case was accepted by all those in the interest community: the custom was agreed upon by all.

4.2.3 *Power Struggles and Reform of Antwerp GA Procedure (1550s–1590s)*

Governance of insurance and GA changed from the 1550s onwards, for three interconnected reasons. One reason was the increasing specialisation in the maritime sector, leading to greater specialisation in both the insurance and GA 'market'. Jeroen Puttevils and Marc Deloof have argued, based on the ledgers of Juan Henriquez, that the Antwerp insurance market during this period was highly individualistic, meaning individuals rather than companies were the major players on the market.[60] Moreover, governance structures of the insurance market were largely based on a thin legal framework and self-regulation until the 1560s.[61] A second reason was the fact that the Antwerp aldermen asserted control over mercantile and maritime jurisdiction after 1550, clawing back on the particularised jurisdictions of the *nationes* and perhaps the private

55 Ibidem, 4: Brulez, *De firma Della Faille*, 161–164.
56 BE-SAA, Notariaat Streyt, N#3132, fol. 9v.
57 Ibidem, fol. 6r–7r. Transcription in: Goris, *Étude*, 635–637.
58 See for an overview: Goris, *Étude*, 162–167.
59 BE-SAA, Notariaat Streyt, N#3132, fol. 95r–v.
60 Puttevils & Deloof, 'Marketing and Pricing Risk'.
61 De ruysscher, 'Antwerp 1490–1590', 95–96.

arbiters.[62] Moreover, the aldermen established a licence system for Average adjusters, meaning that both notaries and Average adjusters were placed under the control of the aldermen.[63] It was no coincidence that some forty GA cases were heard by the Antwerp municipal court between 1545 and 1582, whereas it heard the grand total of one case during the first half of the century.

A third, related reason was the fact that from 1550 onwards, tensions between the central government and the Antwerp municipal government with many of the merchants residing in the city increased markedly, especially on the use of insurance.[64] Both Charles and Philip on the one hand and Antwerp on the other forcefully tried to assert jurisdictional control over insurance procedure and wanted to be the authority to set the rules on insurance, which in practice led to lengthy negotiations.[65] In the 1563 *Ordonnance*, Philip II proposed a standard insurance policy and limits on the value of goods that could be insured up to 90%.[66] The standard insurance policy was strongly opposed by most merchants, both foreign and local, for being too restrictive. In its wake, GA governance was also significantly reformed, although this has been largely neglected in the literature.[67]

Private actors outside of the Antwerp aldermen and the central government also played a major role in attempting to reform the system. In 1555 and 1557, the Piedmontese merchant Jean-Baptiste Ferrufini proposed a central insurance brokers office, setting off a long trail of complex negotiations until the 1570s.[68] The repercussions for the insurance market have been studied by others at length, so we will focus only on its relevance for GA development.[69] Ferrufini proposed both the compulsory registration of insurance policies signed in Antwerp with the office, and a standard insurance policy, leading to significant protests among the various foreign merchant communities in

62 Idem, "*Naer het Romeinsch recht*", 117–120.

63 De Groote, *De zeeassurantie*, 143–148.

64 De ruysscher & Puttevils, 'The Art of Compromise'.

65 Ibidem.

66 De Groote, *De zeeassurantie*, 34–37.

67 De Groote grapples briefly with the consequences for the governance on GA. De Groote, *De zeeassurantie*, 89 & 143–148. See also: Couvreur, 'Recht en zeeverzekeringspraktijk', 201–202.

68 See for example: Couvreur, 'Recht en zeeverzekeringspraktijk', 186; De ruysscher, 'Antwerp 1490–1590', 93–95; De Groote, *De zeeassurantie*, 66–91. The transcribed documents can be found in: P. Génard, *Jean-Baptiste Ferrufini et les assurances maritimes à Anvers au XVIe siècle* (Antwerp 1882).

69 See for an overview: De ruysscher & Puttevils, 'The Art of Compromise', 37–40.

the city.[70] A watered-down version of the office was established after lengthy negotiations. Yet merchants appear to have largely ignored the office and defied the compulsory registration. The Antwerp municipal court did not even stop hearing insurance cases on policies which did not comply with the new rules.[71]

The controversial Ferrufini proposal also led to a discussion on the role of Average adjusters, in Dutch called *dispacheurs*.[72] As the insurability of GA was common practice in Antwerp by this point (late 1550s–early 1560s), specialised Average adjusters had appeared in Antwerp, even if notaries also still regularly played this role, whereas private arbitrators appear to have diminished in number.[73] Specialised Average adjusters were responsible for GA adjustments, requiring a fee for their service from the interest community. During the 1560s, following tensions over the insurance business, the Antwerp municipal government intervened in the sector, regulating Average adjusters. Aldermen received several complaints about the trustworthiness of some of the Average adjusters, as their fee being based on a percentage of the total of the calculus had apparently led to questionable assessments (e.g. the calculation of cargo) to increase the fee.[74] Sometime during the late 1550s or early 1560s, the Antwerp government decided to instate an official license system for Average adjusters. Private Average adjusters thus played an important role in Antwerp from around this period onwards, reinforcing the dispersed and individualistic nature of the GA governance system,[75] echoing the local insurance market.[76] Yet the private Average adjusters firmly remained under the public-order oversight of the Antwerp aldermen.

The licence system for Average adjusters must have been established before 1564, although a *terminus ad quo* is impossible to give. That year, the aldermen heard a complaint against three Average adjusters (Guillaume Rubyn, Philippe Dauxy, and Juan de Castro) acting without a licence.[77] A group of more than 600 insurance underwriters argued that they were disadvantaged because the Average adjusters often possessed more information about losses than the

70 Ibidem.

71 De ruysscher, 'Antwerp 1490–1590', 95–96.

72 De Groote, *De zeeassurantie*, 143–148.

73 Ibidem, 144. In 1560, for example, the notary Antoon van Male drew up two Average adjustments in Castilian (May 30 & June 25). See: BE-SAA, *Verzameling 'Raeckt den handel'*, 1559–1561 N. de Negro en J.B. Spinola, inv. PK#1020.

74 Ibidem, 144–146.

75 Ibidem, 145.

76 Puttevils & Deloof, 'Marketing and Pricing Risk'.

77 BE-SAA, Privilegiekamer, *Rekwestboeken 1564–1565 deel 2*, inv. PK#636, fol. 28r–29r. Case described in: De Groote, *De zeeassurantie*, 144–145.

insurers did. They complained about unfair practices by the three Average adjusters, such as using relatively high valuations for lost cargo. In contrast, a declaration signed by some fifty merchants vouched for the good reputation of the three. Following this complaint, the aldermen (re-)certified the first two Average adjusters, but not De Castro, for unknown reasons.[78] Records of the notary Peter van Ghele show that, two years later, Rubyn and Dauxy indeed acted as licensed Average adjusters in Antwerp.[79] Only in 1571 was De Castro finally granted a licence.[80] This, perhaps surprisingly, only happened after he was charged again with illegally writing up a GA claim, as a group of shipmasters and merchants filed an anonymous appeal arguing that he had written up several GA calculations. As De Castro was a trusted Average adjuster of the Castilian community in Antwerp, the Bruges-based Castilian consuls vouched for his reliability. The Antwerp aldermen subsequently certified him to become an official average adjuster.[81]

Although the Antwerp aldermen claimed back jurisdictional powers from the *nationes* from the 1540s onwards, they were still wary of adjusting Average claims themselves. For some complex international matters, the aldermen nevertheless did issue certificates to proceed with GA claims. In 1564, Juan Curiel applied for GA after his ship had incurred damage before the coast of Barbary (North Africa).[82] Curiel had then sailed to the Canary Islands, where the GA declaration was drawn up. Merchants involved in the venture, however, resisted the GA payment, claiming it was too dangerous to sail there and the insurance policy prohibited this. The aldermen however decided that this would be allowed since the declaration had been made by trusted arbitrators in the Canary Islands and the master and seamen had sworn an oath before a notary.[83] In 1592, another request forced the aldermen to intervene in a complex dispute, as Hamburg-based insurers complained about an Average adjustment drawn up in Livorno, after the masters of the (Antwerp-loaded) ships *Abraham* and *Jonas* had jettisoned grain.[84] The insurers filed a request with the

78 Ibidem, fol. 29r. See also: De Groote, *De zeeassurantie*, 144–145. It is unclear whether this Juan de Castro was related to the De Castro family studied by Raymond Fagel for the 1530s and 1540s. See: Fagel, *De Hispano-Vlaamse wereld*, 56–60.

79 See also: De Groote, *De zeeassurantie*, 145.

80 BE-SAA, Stadsbestuur, Vrijwillige Rechtspraak, Certificatieboeken, 1572, inv. CERT#32, fol. 121r–v. See also: De Groote, *De zeeassurantie*, 145.

81 Ibidem.

82 Idem, *Rekwestboeken 1559–1560*, inv. PK#633, fol. 88v. Case described in; Goris, *Étude*, 176. It was allowed to sail to Africa, and some insurance policies are known from this period, even if they were rare. See: De Groote, *De zeeassurantie*, 159.

83 Ibidem.

84 Idem, Stadsbestuur, Vrijwillige Rechtspraak, Schepenregisters 1550–1599, 1592 Register MN I, inv. SR#404. See also De Groote, *De Zeeassurantie*, 24–25. Since the Hamburg and

aldermen to de-certify the calculus, claiming that the negligence of the master had caused the losses.[85] The aldermen did not accede to this request.

The licence system was Antwerp's answer to the growing pressure to regulate Average adjusters. The central government of Philip II instead focused on insurance and pushed hard for the creation of the Antwerp-based central insurance office.[86] Following the protracted negotiations after Ferrufini's proposal, as a compromise solution the brokers' function was scrapped, but the compulsory registration remained. Despite the persistence of the central government, merchants generally ignored it and concluded insurance policies before notaries or among themselves. In an effort to legitimise the office and attract more business, the lead commissioner and registrar Diego Gonzalez Gante in 1565 decided that office employees also would act as Average adjusters in Antwerp, bypassing municipal control over the licences.[87] The Duke of Alva subsequently acknowledged this function of the office.[88] Gante's successor, Diego de Peralta, was indeed recorded in 1585 as the 'commissioner for insurance and policies and Average adjustment'.[89] According to Roy Couvreur, the office must have handled numerous Average claims between 1565 and 1585, but there is no extant documentary evidence that confirms this.[90]

Following the failed attempt to curb insurance by either princely legislation or by supporting the Ferrufini proposal, Philip II moved decisively to do so after lengthy negotiations on the 1563 *Ordonnance* had failed to provide progress. The Duke of Alva published an *Ordonnance* in 1569 prohibiting all insurance policies after negotiations had broken down.[91] Alva had been a driving force behind the establishment of the central office and was strongly opposed to the speculative aspects of insurance. Nearly all merchants and the city of Antwerp revolted against this decision, forcing him to come back to the negotiation table. In 1570, Philip II and Alva published another *Ordonnance* resulting from negotiations, including a compromise on a standard insurance policy. In 1571, another *Ordonnance* followed with additional measures.[92] The Antwerp

Antwerp insurance markets were closely related, this is not necessarily surprising. See: De Groote, *De zeeassurantie*, 124.

85 Ibidem.

86 De ruysscher, 'Antwerp 1490–1590', 93–95; Idem & Puttevils, 'The Art of Compromise', 40–46.

87 Goris, *Étude*, 46, 140 & 189.

88 Couvreur, 'Recht en zeeverzekeringspraktijk', 202.

89 Ibidem.

90 Ibidem.

91 De ruysscher, 'Antwerp 1490–1590', 95–97. See for the various *Ordonnances*: Reatz, 'Ordonnances'.

92 Ibidem.

aldermen agreed to these measures, but alongside its merchant community largely neglected the contents. The municipal court for example heard cases on policies which did not conform to the rules of the 1570 and 1571 *Ordonnances*.[93] Neither did the 1570 *In Antiquis* correspond to the rules set by the central government. The 1582 *Impressae* and 1608 *Compilatae* included clauses taken from the Habsburg *Ordonnances*, but also many other sources, including the *Hordenanzas*.[94] Although its governance structures were based on compromise and lengthy negotiations, Antwerp was still largely able to set the rules on both insurance and GA, offering a fairly generalised and open-access legal system that left room for the input of private actors.[95]

After the proclamation of the 1571 *Ordonnance*, the central government mostly neglected the governance of GA, as it had to focus on the Dutch Revolt. Antwerp's licence system persisted and appears to have held more legitimacy under the merchant community at large. From 1578 onwards, an arbitration panel of trusted merchants based at the Antwerp stock exchange acted as the primary Average adjusters in the city.[96] Antwerp thereby resorted to its pre-1550 style of minimal oversight and self-regulation, although it did probably licence the members of the arbitration panel. In a sign that the Brussels-based central government accepted defeat in the matter, the duke of Alva also certified the arbitration panel.[97] Evidence is scarce, however. The example of two merchants, Maximiliaan Lanckhals and Anthonie Vranckx, referring to themselves as 'merchants of the bourse of Antwerp', is the sole evidence that this system existed. On 14 October 1592, they were appointed by a number of insurers and merchants to arbitrate a dispute, after receiving a licence from the aldermen.[98] Subsequently, they also acted as Average adjusters on 12 July and 28 October 1593 in different cases.[99] One 1593 judgement of the 'Commission on Averages and Insurances' has also survived.[100] This was most likely Peralta's

93 Ibidem, 96.

94 Van Hofstraeten, *Juridisch humanisme*, 113–117. The text is published both in French and Castilian. Transcription in: Verlinden, 'Código de seguros'; Idem, 'Code d'assurances'. See for more recent, correct interpretations: Coronas González, 'La Ordenenza'; Rossi, *Insurance in Elizabethan England*, 148–157; De Groote, *De zeeassurantie*, 52–58.

95 As also argued by Van Niekerk: Van Niekerk, *The Development*, 60–80.

96 De Groote, *De zeeassurantie*, 146–147.

97 Ibidem.

98 Ibidem, 145–146.

99 Ibidem.

100 See: Nederlands Economisch-Historisch Archief (hereafter NL-NEHA), Collectie Velle, nr. 2.4.15, piece nr. 7. Velle, a former Antwerp archivist, stole the document(s) from the Antwerp municipal archives. Upon his death, the records were sold to the NEHA which explains why the documents are found in Amsterdam rather than Antwerp.

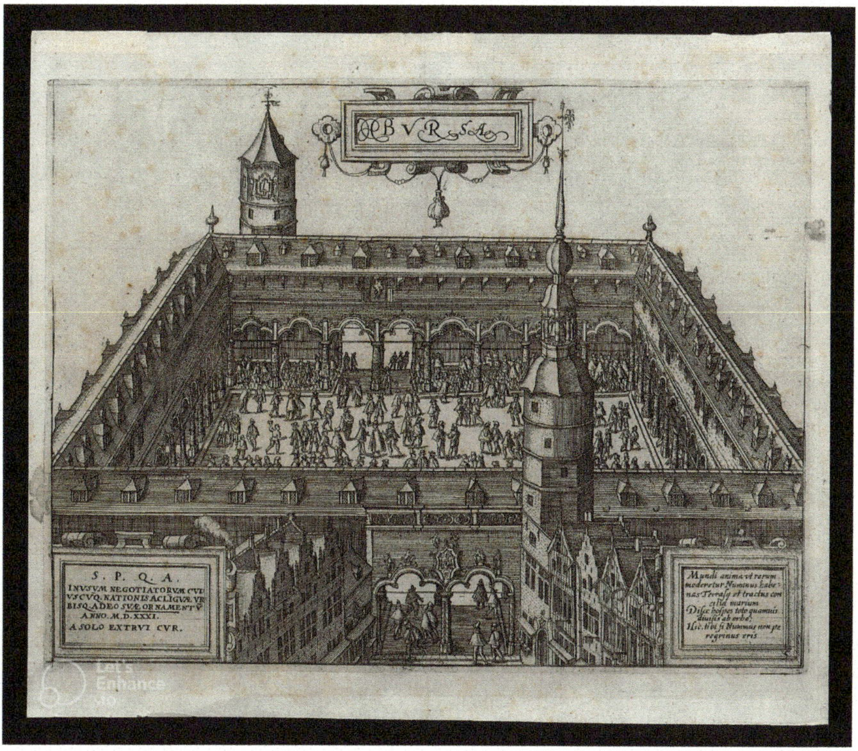

IMAGE 8 Anonymous, Antwerp's bourse (1612–1648)

office. The Commission decided that 34 insurers had to pay for GA losses, after a ship sailing from Lübeck to Genoa had jettisoned grain in a storm before the coast of Portugal and filed for GA in La Coruña.[101] Even if this was the central-government certified office, it does not appear to have gained much traction with the Antwerp merchant community.[102]

In the end, Antwerp's aldermen were able to assert control over GA procedure, even if the central government aimed to control GA procedure in the wake of its crusade against insurance and its manifold regulations. In practice, private actors largely neglected the central government's regulations with Antwerp's municipal authorities quiet backing. The aldermen moved from a practice of self-regulation, probably based on Bruges' example, to a more forceful assertion of jurisdiction and public-order backing of GA procedure, placing the notaries under oath, establishing a licence system for specialised

101 Ibidem. Besides the jettisoned grain, the master had abandoned the ship and the remainder of the spoilt grain, which was also part of the verdict but did not concern GA.

102 Couvreur, 'Recht en zeeverzekeringspraktijk', 202.

Average adjusters and hearing a substantial number of GA cases after 1545. We can draw four conclusions from this: first, public-order backing was crucial for the system to operate, and, in this case, particularly Antwerp's backing; second, private actors played a major role in the system, also acting themselves at times to push and advocate for reform; third, GA governance moved towards a generalised, open-access institution, although Antwerp was unable to recoup the jurisdiction over maritime affairs of the Portuguese *natio*;[103] and fourth, that the interplay between GA and insurance was key to understanding the development of GA's governance.[104]

4.2.4 *Insurance and GA: The Example of Juan Henriquez*

At least from the 1540s onwards, the widespread use of insurance in Antwerp meant that participants in the interest community could also turn to insurers to take over the payment of their GA contribution.[105] Similar to notaries, insurers often served a small circle of customers.[106] Despite limited available evidence of actual insurance policies for the sixteenth century, we can see that insurance played a major role after 1550 thanks to two surviving ledgers of the Antwerp-based Castilian insurer Juan Henriquez for the years 1562–1563.[107] His policies mostly covered ventures between the Low Countries and France and the Iberian Peninsula, as only two policies covered the Baltic area (Danzig and Stockholm, see Table 8 and Maps 1 & 2). Since Henriquez also noted other underwriters in his ledgers, as well as all payments, damage, shipwrecks and other events, this source gives us precious and unique insights into the insurability of GA and the role of insurers.[108]

Insurers were liable both for the payment of the remaining loss after a GA contribution by others in the interest community, and when insured cargo was used to determine the GA contribution to someone else.[109] This was no different for the Iberian insurers in the city, who had more or less monopolised the local market, as Italians largely moved into banking.[110] Besides policies for voyages

103 De ruysscher, "*Naer het Romeinsch recht*", 120–121.
104 Following Ogilvie, '"Whatever is, is Right?"', 681.
105 See section 4.4.2 for additional evidence on this matter.
106 Fagel, *De Hispano-Vlaamse wereld*, 60–64.
107 The work by Alain Wastiels remains the best place to start research of the ledgers. See: A. Wastiels, *Juan Henriquez, makelaar in zeeverzekeringen*. Other work is: Puttevils & Deloof, 'Marketing and Pricing Risk', especially 824–825. A small amount of policies also concerned life insurance: Casado Alonso, 'Insuring Life', 81–82.
108 Full data can be found in the appendix.
109 Van Niekerk, *The Development*, 76–80.
110 Puttevils & Deloof, 'Marketing and Pricing Risk', 796–800; Goris, *Étude*, 178–190; Verlinden, 'De zeeverzekeringen', 191–197; De ruysscher, 'Antwerp 1490–1590', 87–92.

starting or ending in Antwerp, Henriquez also offered policies for voyages starting in other ports, for example in Zeeland (Middelburg or Arnemuiden), Hamburg, France, or even Italy and Lisbon.[111] Given the Europe-wide reach of the Antwerp insurance market, this should be no surprise. In this section, we will limit ourselves to what is of interest to GA procedure. Based on research by Jeroen Puttevils and Marc Deloof, Table 5 shows that underwriters like Henriquez paid out some 14.6% of the premiums they received to cover GA claims. This stands in sharp contrast to the analysis of Henry de Groote on the same ledgers (Table 6), who argued that some 58.05% of insurance premiums was used to hedge against GA claims.[112]

TABLE 5 GA contributions and losses paid by Juan Henriquez (1562–1563)

Henriquez as underwriter of marine insurance	£ Fl. gr.
Marine insurance premiums	763
Payment of average	−112
Payment of total losses	−302
Total profit	349

SOURCE: PUTTEVILS & DELOOF, 'MARKETING AND PRICE RISK', 824.

TABLE 6 GA contributions paid by Juan Henriquez (1562–1563)

Destination	Amount in guilders
Britain	1.203.3.6
France	5.371.0.9
Iberian peninsula	11.369.2.5
Mediterranean sea	373.11.4
Africa	4.649.14.3
Total	22.966.12.3

SOURCE: DE GROOTE, *DE ZEEASSURANTIE*, 150.

111 De ruysscher, 'Antwerp 1490–1590', 88–89.

112 De Groote, *De zeeassurantie*, 150.

Puttevils and Deloof's numbers are based on the actual archival documents and a sophisticated statistical analysis, and their work is therefore preferable to De Groote's, who does not specify the routes. Based on Wastiels' detailed analysis of Henriquez ledgers, it is possible to investigate the exact routes and payments by underwriters for GA losses. In total, the ledgers offer 165 observations of GA payments by the underwriters. Table 7 shows the number of observations in the ledgers. Table 8 shows the routes on which GA occurred.[113]

TABLE 7 Number of GA payments by insurers in the ledgers of Juan Henriquez, by the percentage of the insured sum (1562–1563)

Percentage of GA of insurance indemnity (%)	Number of observations
0–0.99%	45
1–4.99%	79
5–24.99%	28
>25%	13
Total	165

SOURCE: DATABASE AUTHOR BASED ON WASTIELS, *JUAN HENRIQUEZ* (PARTS 2–4). SEE APPENDIX FOR FULL DATA.

TABLE 8 Routes on which GA occurred, based on the ledgers of Juan Henriquez (1562–1563) (n = 165)

Route	Number of observations
Amsterdam-Bordeaux	4
Amsterdam-Lisbon	4
Antwerp-Saint Valeri	8
Antwerp-Villa Nova	4
Antwerp-Seville	4
Antwerp-Rouen	1
Antwerp-Saint Malo	1
Antwerp-Lisbon	8
Antwerp-Tavira	1

113 For those interested in the full data, I refer to the appendix.

TABLE 8 Routes on which GA occurred, based on the ledgers of Juan Henriquez (*cont.*)

Route	Number of observations
Antwerp-Mazaron	1
Antwerp-Nantes	1
Ayamonte-Antwerp	1
Antwerp-Bordeaux	2
Bordeaux-Antwerp	35
Bordeaux-Zeeland	1
Bordeaux-London	1
Bristol-Antwerp	1
Cádiz-Livorno	1
Cádiz-Antwerp	1
Cognac-Antwerp	1
Danzigv -Lisbon	1
Dartmouth-Antwerp	1
Lisbon-Antwerp	41
Malaga-Antwerp	12
Marseille-Antwerp	3
Nantes-Antwerp	2
Rouen-Sevilla	1
Rouen-Antwerp	1
Saint Malo-Antwerp	2
Saint Malo-Faro	1
Stockholm-Antwerp	3
Tavira-Antwerp	1
Flushing-Nantes	1
Zeeland-La Rochelle	1
Zeeland-Bordeaux	8

SOURCE: SEE TABLE 4.3. SEE APPENDIX FOR FULL DATA.

Most GA payments were relatively small compared to the sum insured. Around 27% of the GA claims amounted to less than 1% of the insurance indemnity.[114] As a result, insurers mostly had to pay a small sum which could

114 Which may explain why franchise clauses became more common in late sixteenth-century Antwerp, see section 3.2.5.

MAP 1 Spatial distribution of the insured routes of Juan Henriquez (1562–1563)
SOURCE: MADE WITH GOOGLE MAPS, SEE HTTPS://WWW.GOOGLE.COM/MAPS/D/U/0/EDIT?MID=1Y0L3ZAV_4UDYRONOV27AGROSQKAIJVIE&USP=SHARING FOR THE MAP. ANTWERP IS IN GREEN

be covered by the premium (since they were mostly 5–10% for the routes to the Iberian Peninsula at this time).[115] This confirms the implicit argument of Puttevils and Deloof that insurers could absorb costs for GA damages rather easily. Moreover, premiums were often paid only after a voyage was safely completed: if the amount of damage was roughly similar to the premium, it is likely that the contract would be declared void by mutual approval and no pay-out was made. This may also explain why litigation was rare. Insurers of course primarily paid common losses, but even when some cargo was salvaged the costs could be high. When a near-shipwreck occurred, GA payments could quickly skyrocket, although this was uncommon. On one 1563 voyage from Bordeaux to Antwerp, for example, a ship suffered such severe damage that insurers were held liable for around 90% of the damage by means of GA.[116]

115 See De Groote, *De zeeassurantie*, 135–138.
116 Wastiels, *Juan Henriquez* (Vol. II), 345.

MAP 2 Spatial distribution of the insured routes of Juan Henriquez (1562–1563), Western Europe only
SOURCE: MADE WITH GOOGLE MAPS, SEE HTTPS://WWW.GOOGLE.COM/MAPS/D/U/0/EDIT?MID=1Y0L3ZAV_4UDYRONOV27AGROSQKAIJVIE&USP=SHARING FOR THE MAP. ANTWERP IS IN GREEN

4.2.5 GA *Procedure in the Castilian Consular Court*

Now that we have established one part of the common GA procedure, this section sheds light on GA procedure in the Castilian consular court in Bruges. The consular court was the place where most, if not all, intra-*natio* GA procedures took place. For shipmasters, the consular option was the standard option when only compatriots were involved in the venture. In many cases, this also meant it was the more straightforward option. The records of the court (recorded in the so-called *libro de pleitos ordinarios*) are preserved for the period between 1545 and 1561, allowing for an in-depth analysis of GA procedure within the *natio* as a significant number of cases about GA and other Averages (see next chapter) are included.[117] These are the only consular court records extant in

117 The so-called *Ayuntamientos* registers are also available for the seventeenth century, containing a handful of documents dealing with GA. Two GA cases from 1664 and 1665, for example, are still preserved in these records, which was the general meeting of the

the Low Countries.[118] The large majority of cases heard by the consuls concerned issues of what we would define today as commercial law. A significant number of them dealt with maritime issues, disputes about freight, insurance, GA or other varieties of Averages.[119] Although the consular option was in principle limited to members of the *natio*, Portuguese shipmasters and merchants also appeared twice before the consuls to enforce a GA-related claim in 1546 and 1548.[120] This shows that it was possible to appeal to a consular court whilst not being a member, although this was probably rare and formally an option: it does however show that the dichotomy between particularised and generalised institutions was not always clear. Moreover, the peculiar structure of the Castilian and Biscayer trade meant that the 'Flanders fleet' was often combined between the two *nationes* (via the so-called *rotulo* system[121]): as a result, Biscayer merchants could also apply to the Castilian consular court for disputes arising from joint ventures.[122]

According to Louis Gilliodts-Van Severen, 75% of suits arising in Bruges during the fifteenth century involving Castilian merchants were arbitrated.[123] He does not, however, contextualise this number or provide hard evidence for this claim. For the sixteenth century no reliable numbers exist either on the percentage of arbitration cases compared to those which were addressed at the consular court. Between 1545 and 1561, the consuls on average heard

natio. Since they fall outside of the temporal scope of this book, I will not discuss these cases. See: BE-SAB, Oud Archief, Spaans Consulaat, inv. 304, nr. II.A.1, *Ayuntamientos*, fol. 162v–165v & 177r–179r.

118 As noted in the introduction, there may be records of the Portuguese consular court in the Low Countries in Lisbon.

119 The first article dealing specifically with the insurance activities of the 'Spanish' merchants in Bruges and Antwerp was: Verlinden, 'De zeeverzekeringen'. Recently, much more has been written on their activities as insurers. See: Puttevils & Deloof, 'Marketing and Pricing Risk'; Casado Alonso, 'Juan Henriquez'.

120 BE-SAB, *Libro de pleytos ordinarios*, fol. 11r–v & 46v. This was not wholly uncommon: Miranda has already pointed out that Flemish merchants sometimes sought recourse to the Portuguese consular court in Bruges as well. See: Miranda, 'Commerce, conflits et justice', 8–9.

121 The *rotulo de averías* or *privilegio de rotulación* system concerned the joint allocation of ships by the Burgos and Bilbao *Consulados* for the transport of wool to Flanders. When there were not enough ships available, private ships could be hired, whereby merchants were given the right to load at least half of the ship's bottom by signing a sort of freight contract. See: Guiard y Laurrauri, *Historia*, 64–65. I thank Marta García Garralón for explaining this detail.

122 And this may well have been the case the other way around.

123 Gilliodts-Van Severen, *Espagne*, 35. See also: Ogilvie, *Institutions and European trade*, 298.

twenty-five cases a year,[124] which is a relatively high number given the fact that the Castilian community in Bruges was rather small (between forty and sixty merchants were present in Bruges at any time during the sixteenth century).[125] Procedure was rather straightforward: the consuls heard arguments from both sides and issued a judgment (although they could request additional evidence). Most aspects of the more sophisticated Romano-canonical procedure, such as written evidence, the possibility of delay, or the intervention of trained lawyers, were largely absent.[126] One aspect of the Romano-canonical procedure, the possibility to appeal, was present, as members could appeal to the Bruges municipal court, although this seems to have been a rarity.[127] The judgements primarily rested on Castilian customs and laws of the *Consulado*, and various references to the 1538 *Ordonnance* for the Burgos *Consulado* can for example be traced in the archives. Although the consular court had an official status, the procedure largely mimicked arbitration.

Only a handful of GA cases or related issues remain in the archival records of the consular court. The consuls often decided whether the declaration of GA was allowed but subsequently outsourced the work of actual calculations to trusted members of the Castilian community.[128] Sometimes, a master could also bring his own calculations following the declaration of GA with private average adjusters and request a certification from the consuls, as a 1554 case shows.[129] Often the consuls declared damage incurred to be a *caso fortuito* (an uncontrollable event leading to damage[130]) and from there decided whether GA was justifiable based on the testimonies of the master and other crew members.[131] In many ways, Castilian consuls thus followed the Bruges and Antwerp

124 Although this varied widely per year. For example, in 1555 three cases were heard, whereas, in 1548, 62 cases were heard. Dave De ruysscher has counted the cases per year. These notes were sent to the author by personal communication: 1546: 20; 1547: 44; 1548: 62; 1549: 45; 1550: 36; 1551: 24; 1552: 24; 1553: 51; 1554: 8'1555: 3; 1556: 4; 1557: 17; 1558: 15; 1559: 28; 1560: 32; 1561: 6.

125 Fagel, *De Hispano-Vlaamse wereld*, 17–19.

126 The Great Council and other courts, in contrast, by and large used this procedure to hear their cases. See: Van Rhee, *Litigation and legislation*, 15–25.

127 See for an example: Gilliodts-Van Severen, *Espagne*, 34.

128 See for example: BE-SAB, *Libro de pleytos ordinarios*, fol. 75v–76r & 108r–v.

129 Ibidem, fol. 145r.

130 The meaning of the *caso fortuito*, or *casus fortuitus* in Latin, is a rather polysemic term which does not figure often in sources in the Low Countries. Yet other project members of the *AveTransRisk* team have discussed this at length. I refer here to the project Glossary which will be available in 2022 or 2023: https://humanities.exeter.ac.uk/history/research/centres/maritime/research/avetransrisk/glossary/ {Retrieved 30/06/2020}.

131 See e.g. BE-SAB, *Libro de pleytos ordinarios*, 115r–v, where GA was not allowed after a *caso fortuito* where cables and artillery were damaged.

municipal courts in exercising final oversight over GA procedure by deciding on these matters, while outsourcing much of the actual work to trusted private average adjusters. Frequently, the consuls referred to the 'customs' or *custombre* of the *natio* to justify a judgement. In 1552, for example, the consuls decided that salvaged cargo after a shipwreck could be included as GA.[132] This was largely congruent with Castilian customs from the New World trade, where even shipwrecks could be included in GA claims.[133] In the Low Countries, this could not be the case, in principle, although the courts did not always follow the letter of the law strictly in GA cases (see section 4.5). The Castilian consuls therefore relied on Castilian customs rather than local ones in deciding internal GA disputes.

4.2.6 *Arbitration and Appeals*

Arbitration was probably a common way to solve GA disputes, although archival evidence is again scarce. Clauses in (freight) contracts could prohibit merchants to seek an appeal at a court. Yet in practice, those dissatisfied with the outcome of arbitration could always seek an appeal at various courts. Often, arbitration agreements included clauses that did not allow for an appeal, but in practice merchants or shipmasters did violate these clauses.[134] Both the Antwerp municipal court and the Great Council heard GA cases that had supposedly been solved by arbitration, seeking to keep formal supervision over GA disputes. Arbitration, as per Douglass North and others, has often been presented as an efficient way to solve disputes through speedy resolution as opposed to the slow official courts.[135] Albrecht Cordes and Philip Höhn have questioned this view and pointed out that arbitration was often costlier, as the participants in the process were disappointed with the outcome and started litigation anyway.[136] Court records from Antwerp and the Great Council appear

132 Ibidem, 108r–v.

133 García Garralón, 'The Nautical Republic', 31.

134 Even today, the connection between arbitration and 'formal' appeals are a matter of debate, as 'Alternative Dispute Resolution' (ADR) is still a common way to solve disputes. See for historical informed work: Wubs-Mrozewicz, 'Conflict Management', especially 93–96. An impossibility of appeal was often part of the clauses of arbitration panels, although in practice this was difficult to enforce. Both parties would appoint one arbitrator. The two arbitrators then jointly decided on the third arbitrators. See for its historical origins: F. Marrella & A. Mozzato (eds.), *Alle origini dell'arbitrato commerciale internazionale: l'arbitrato a Venezia tra medioevo ed età moderna* (Padova 2001).

135 See for example: Milgrom, North & Weingast, 'The Role of Institutions'; Gelderblom, *Cities of commerce*, 106–108. Gelderblom does not advocate for the existence of a *lex mercatoria*, but does argue that arbitration was an efficient way to solve disputes. See: Gelderblom: *Cities of Commerce*, 106–108 & 133–136.

136 Cordes & Höhn, 'Extra-Legal and Legal Conflict Management'.

to confirm Cordes and Höhn's thesis, as some GA disputes indeed went anyway to a court to overturn a judgement. Moreover, these cases support Justyna Wubs-Mrozewicz's idea that merchants always used multiple strategies to manage disputes and could, depending on the circumstances, escalate or de-escalate disputes.[137] Paradoxically, in most cases the decision of the arbitration panel was upheld by the courts on procedural grounds.[138]

One 1567 case from the Antwerp municipal court offers an excellent example of competing demands. A Castilian shipmaster for example filed a case in Antwerp, supported by several Castilian insurers and merchants, against local merchants participating in the short venture from Dieppe (France) to Zeeland.[139] The ship incurred damage just before arriving in Middelburg, making it impossible to reach port without jettisoning cargo. The master decided not to jettison the merchants' cargo, but rather the remaining food for the crew. The local merchants, however, declined to pay for GA, which was not unreasonable given the fact that perishable cargo was generally not brought into GA, but was rather incorporated as SA as standard operational costs paid via the freight.[140] The local merchants argued that the master could have easily escaped the storm or could have sailed to Arnemuiden, another port in Zeeland. The parties had sought to solve the issue by arbitration, but the local merchants were disappointed with the outcome as they were held to contribute to GA. The arbitrators argued that this was deliberate damage to save the venture, which was the case, strictly speaking. On the other hand, common knowledge would state that food was perishable and hence not subject to a GA contribution. Both outcomes were, in short, tenable. Based on the freight contract, the court decided that the arbitration was binding as the arbitration clause was clear. The procedural arguments thus overrode the formal rules of GA, as the rationale was clear, and the arbitration agreement was considered binding.

The Great Council also heard appeals against arbitrations. Both in 1553, 1554 and 1564, the court decided to hear first instance cases filed as appeals against arbitration agreements.[141] In one of the cases, three Zeeland merchants successfully argued for an SA contribution rather than a GA contribution after

137 Wubs-Mrozewicz, 'Conflict Management', 102–107.

138 Appeals against arbitration outcomes were formally possible when there were strong procedural grounds to question the actual outcome, but as the cases studied here show, courts were unlikely to alter the judgement of the arbitrators.

139 BE-SAA, *Vonnisboeken*, V#1249, fol. 204r–205r.

140 De ruysscher, 'Maxims, Principles and Legal Change'.

141 BE-ARB, Grote Raad, *Processen*, nr. 595 (*sine folio*) & nr. 608 (*sine folio*); Idem, *Beroepen uit Holland*, inv. A106, nr. 581. The latter case is transcribed in: Van Answaarden, *Les Portugais*, nr. 55 (pp. 319–320).

the shipmaster had taken out pilotage, pointing to the newly promulgated 1551 *Ordonnance*,[142] but in the two other cases this strategy was unsuccessful, once as the Great Council simply confirmed the arbitrational sentence albeit acknowledging flaws in its judgements,[143] and in a second case as the defendant, the Genoese Gregorio Nigrone, declined to appear before the Great Council after an arbitration panel had allowed the shipmaster Ghysbrecht Pieterszoon to levy a GA contribution from him.[144] In the latter case, the appeal may have been a way to force Nigrone to the negotiating table.[145]

This small sample relative to GA cases confirms the view that arbitration was not a panacea for efficient mercantile dispute resolution.[146] Only in the 1553 case did the application of the 1551 *Ordonnance* override procedural rules, implying that only when weighty considerations were in play was the Great Council willing to do so. In trying to avoid GA payments, challenging arbitral agreements was clearly a disadvantageous strategy for merchants, simply raising enforcement costs without clear benefits. It did however show that both courts were willing to hear these cases, offering another forum for those dissatisfied with arbitration outcomes.[147] As the previous sections on Average adjustment in Antwerp also showed, arbitration could work when regulation by the aldermen was in place, but a private-order solution did not always work well to adjudicate GA disputes.

4.3 The Position of the Shipmaster and Legal Strategies

Much like present-day GA procedure largely taking place outside of the public view, shipmasters in the Low Countries in the first instance turned to their consuls or to private average adjusters to adjudicate damages and compensation following an act of GA. Formal litigation before a municipal court was hence rare until the late 1540s, when the city of Antwerp asserted greater jurisdictional control over GA procedure (see above). For fifteenth-century Bruges,

142 Ibidem, nr. 595 (*sine folio*).

143 Idem, nr. 608 (*sine folio*).

144 Idem, *Beroepen uit Holland*, nr. 581. The case is transcribed in: Van Answaarden, *Les Portugais*, nr. 55 (pp. 319–320).

145 In line with: Wubs-Mrozewicz, 'Conflict Management', 102–107.

146 Milgrom, North & Weingast, 'The Role of Institutions'; Gelderblom, *Cities of Commerce*, 106–108. Lewis Wade's PhD dissertation makes similar arguments for seventeenth-century France, questioning the effectiveness of arbitration. See: L. Wade, *Privilege at a Premium: Insurance, Maritime Law and Political Economy in Early Modern France, 1664–c. 1710* (Unpublished PhD thesis, University of Exeter 2021).

147 Following Cordes & Höhn, 'Extra-Legal and Legal Conflict Management'.

only a handful of cases survive as a result. In sixteenth-century Antwerp, evidence for some forty GA cases survived for the period 1545–1582; but for the first half of the century, there is evidence for only one case.[148] Even rarer were cases at central courts, probably because the sum involved did not justify the high fees that central courts charged.[149]

This section focuses on the pivotal role of the shipmaster. Note that we have concluded in Chapter 3 that there was a double-edged development in his position: on the one hand, his liability was tightened, but on the other hand he was given greater leeway to act.[150] Merchants whose cargo was not lost obviously wished to shift payment onto other parties inside or outside the interest community. Commonly the first step for merchants was to try to pin the responsibility on the shipmaster. For merchants, trying to shoot a hole in the testimony of the shipmaster was the preferred legal strategy. When liability could be pinned on him, all the costs and reimbursements were carried by the shipmaster and his crew.[151] According to Guido Rossi, civil law courts were not as strict as common law courts in pinning liability on the shipmaster, relying instead on a series of presumptions and causations to establish fault or negligence.[152] As the cases studied here show, the courts in the Southern Low Countries indeed approached this issue in GA cases in a nuanced way, as (a lack of) proof often made straightforward judgements impossible. The Antwerp municipal court distinguished between negligence (negligent but not criminal behaviour) and barratry (criminal behaviour), a common distinction in continental Europe which relied on a causality of events and a complex degree system of fault.[153] The latter was explicit fraud (for example selling cargo whilst saying that a jettison was necessary), whilst the former was not (for example not taking the necessary measures to prevent damage). Although the development of the doctrine of barratry became a more pressing issue in sixteenth-century Europe, it appears that in the Low Countries the bar to prove barratry was rather high.[154]

Shipmasters were of course not passive actors in this process. As a counterstrategy, masters could for example pre-emptively record testimony with a

148 See footnote 6 of this chapter for the applicable references.
149 In line with: Gelderblom, *Cities of Commerce*, 127–128.
150 Rossi, 'The Liability of the Shipmaster'.
151 Ibidem.
152 Ibidem.
153 Idem, 'The Barratry of the Shipmaster (I)' and Idem, 'The Barratry of the Shipmaster (II)'. See also: 1608 *Compilatae*, Part IV, Title XI, Art. 210.
154 Ibidem.

notary, along with crew members to protect themselves.[155] For masters, a declaration of PA was often the best way, for the damage then fell to the merchant(s) owning the cargo. Although PA did not yet formally exist, there were a small number of cases where shipmasters clearly tried this tactic (section 4.3.4). If this was impossible, GA was probably the next-preferred option, since it required only a partial contribution by the shipmaster via the value of his ship or via the value of the freight. Moreover, the ship-owner could also be expected to share the damage which befell the ship. In the former case, the master could try to persuade the average adjuster to value the ship at a lower price. In formal law, the choice was still commonly between the value of the ship and that of freight: in Antwerp legal practice, the value of the freight was commonly used, implying that masters were agents most of the time.[156] In the Low Countries, the choice of contribution of the shipmaster was the merchants', to limit moral hazard on behalf of the shipmaster, even if he was simply an agent of the venture. Assuming liability for the damage to cargo or the ship was of course detrimental to the shipmasters' interest and hence was always the least-preferred option. In many cases, this would mean severe damage or outright insolvency for shipmasters. In short, the interests of merchants and those of the shipmaster were diametrically opposed in cases of damage.

Two cases, one from Middelburg and one from Antwerp, might be taken as exemplary cases of standard GA in which the role of the shipmaster was disputed. The Middelburg case, dating from 2 May 1517, concerned a dispute on GA between a Biscayer merchant and a Biscayer skipper.[157] Although they generally tried to keep their intra-*natio* disputes within the small circle of the *natio*, this case apparently left the Biscayer merchant with no option other than to seek redress at the Middelburg municipal court. The merchant, Pedro Caveliero, filed a complaint against Pedro de Arrenes, a Bilbao-born master, whose ship (the *Andries*) was still in the port of Arnemuiden. A quantity of figs, which were destined to be sold to Caveliero, were lost because they had been stored on the deck of the ship, rather than in the dedicated storage areas at the back of the ship.[158] Although masters in the Low Countries did generally not store cargo themselves, they were formally in charge of the

155 Streyt recorded some of those testimonies, see for example: BE-SAA, Notariaat Streyt, N#3133, fol. 77. See also: Strieder, *Notariatsarchiven*, 355–356 (nr. 683).

156 De ruysscher, 'Maxims, Principles and Legal Change', 263.

157 Unger, *Bronnen tot de geschiedenis van Middelburg in den landsheerlijken* (Vol. 3) (hereafter Unger, *Bronnen Middelburg*) (The Hague 1931), 264 (nr. 363). Based on: NL-RA, Groote register civijl, fol. 193. This archive is now lost, making historians dependent on these source editions.

158 Ibidem.

process.[159] Caveliero demanded compensation, but De Arrenes argued that his ship had encountered a storm which had forced him to cut the mast and jettison some of the cargo, including the figs.[160] He expected that the cargo could later be salvaged, but this had not happened.[161] De Arrenes moreover argued that the Biscayer *natio* did not contribute to protection costs such as artillery, increasing the risk of damage. The municipal court asked various merchants for advice and decided that the master had to reimburse Caveliero, as it was common knowledge in Spain that figs had to be stored in the back. However, it also decided that the jettison was done in accordance with proper GA procedure and that Caveliero subsequently had to pay for the GA declaration of the remainder of the cargo: as such, it partly accepted Spanish customs but also applied common GA rules, deciding the shipmaster had acted appropriately.

In a case from 1555, the question was how damage incurred by crew members should be dealt with.[162] A number of ships sailing from Antwerp had been damaged soon after they had left the Scheldt under the convoy leadership of the shipmaster Silvester Ratingij. Ratingij subsequently filed a GA declaration as his ship was attacked by privateers near Bordeaux (no mention was made of the other ships). The crew was able to fend off the attack, but the ship was severely damaged: mast and cables were cut as a result. Moreover, most of the crew members' provisions (mainly malt) were jettisoned. Ratingij thus had to buy (expensive) new food in Bordeaux. On its way back, the ship did not take the shortest route, but rather took a long passage via the English coast. According to Ratingij, he had decided to use this route to minimise the chances of encountering privateers or pirates again. All these costs (mast cutting, food jettison, extra cargo and longer travel time) were included in the subsequent GA declaration. Some of the merchants who had loaded cargo onto Ratingij's ship protested this GA declaration at the municipal court, claiming that their contributions would simply enrich the master and the crew.[163] They questioned whether the mast cutting was strictly necessary, and argued that the detour via England had been unnecessary. The aldermen requested advice from a panel

159 In the Low Countries, there was sometimes a dedicated employee for loading and unloading, the *kommis*. Yet in many cases this was simply fixed in the freight contract. See: http://humanities.exeter.ac.uk/history/research/centres/maritime/research/modernity/roles/ {Retrieved 21/01/2021}. In Castile, the *contramaestre* for example was responsible for loading under supervision of the *maestre*. See: http://humanities.exeter.ac.uk/media/level1/academicserviceswebsite/it/documents/avetransrisk/RolesOnBoardSpanishShips.pdf {Retrieved 21/01/2021}.

160 Unger, *Bronnen Middelburg*, 264 (nr. 363).

161 See for this principle: Férrandiz, 'Will the Circle be Unbroken?', 50–52.

162 BE-SAA, *Vonnisboeken*, V#1244, fol. 60v–61r.

163 Ibidem, fol. 61r: the claim would be "*tot sijne eigene profyt*" ('to his own profit').

of trusted merchants, deciding that the GA costs were exorbitantly high.[164] The arbitration panel was subsequently asked to draw up a new GA declaration for a smaller sum according to the customary norms of the 'Bourse of Antwerp' and the 'customs of the sea' (*costuymen vander zee*), the standard yet vague phrase which was often invoked in such disputes.[165] The aldermen would then sign off the GA declaration after the panel of experts reported back to them.

4.3.1 *The Position of the Shipmaster in the Bruges Municipal Court*

Two cases from the Bruges municipal court concerned the position of the shipmaster, showing that this was already an issue in the fourteenth and fifteenth century. One dating from 1377 was incorporated in the so-called *Wittenboeck*, a compilation of municipal privileges, probably as an exemplary case for future reference. It concerned a Genoese merchant, Morael de Mari, who requested reclaiming for damage to his cargo from the Spanish shipmaster Gautier Ludovici, who had jettisoned almonds and sugar during a storm on his way to Bruges, but later salvaged much of the cargo.[166] The municipal court stated that Ludovici was to deliver the salvaged cargo to De Mari, but otherwise ruled that the master had stuck to the commonly applied rules of jettison in a storm. This, indeed, followed standard rules on GA and salvage.

In 1467 the Florentine merchant Anthoine de Medicis requested a reimbursement from the shipmaster after his cargo was lost in a storm, accusing him of not taking the necessary precautions to prevent damage.[167] The Bruges municipal court appointed an arbitration panel to deal with the dispute, which decided that the damage was partly the result of the master's negligence and lack of preparations.[168] They however also pointed out that the bad weather had certainly played a part. As a result, the arbitration panel awarded De Medicis compensation for negligent behaviour by the master, in the form of a reduction of freight money, although they also sentenced De Medicis to contribute for GA for part of the lost cargo. The sum however was not mentioned, potentially cancelling out the contributions to each other. In this case, the Bruges municipal court apparently sought to placate both parties.

---

164 Ibidem: the aldermen decided that "*groote moderaties*" ('great moderations') were necessary.

165 This was regularly used in verdicts by the Antwerp aldermen. This might indicate that the aldermen largely followed the Wisby Laws, although there is only circumstantial evidence for this.

166 Gilliodts-Van Severen, *Cartulaire* (Vol. 1), nr. 361 (pp. 280–181).

167 Ibidem (Vol. 2), nr. 1091.

168 As was common in Bruges. See for example: Idem, *Espagne*, 73–75 & 95–97.

4.3.2 *The Position of the Shipmaster in the Antwerp Municipal Court*

The position of the shipmaster was no less important in the Antwerp municipal court. In fact, the only GA case before 1548 centred on the issue. It originated in 1517 when the Castilian master Francisco de Mosira started proceedings against local and Castilian merchants, who had concluded a freight contract with him to transport cargo from the Iberian Peninsula to Antwerp.[169] Just before arriving in Antwerp, the ship had encountered a storm and jettisoned cargo. This forced De Mosira to stop in a Zeeland port and repair the ship, a common requirement.[170] De Mosira required a contribution from the merchants for both the jettisoned cargo and other costs (e.g. the costs for the delay as well as the actual repairs), which the Average adjusters confirmed. Since payment was not forthcoming, De Mosira filed a case at the municipal court. The merchants countered that some of the jettisoned cargo had been salvaged but was still incorporated in the GA calculus. Salvaged cargo could not be included in GA declarations, but the Average adjusters had nevertheless allowed this. The merchants requested a court-appointed arbitration panel rather than the arbitration panel which had, in their opinion, been biased towards De Mosira. The court however gave De Mosira the right to demand payment from the merchants, because the arbitration panel's decision was considered binding.[171] In a similar case from 1547, the municipal court even allowed the master Bastiaan vanden Velde to take the merchant in question, Jacob Bangie, hostage and seize his belongings because Bangie declined to pay for GA.[172] A court-appointed *procureur* would assist Vanden Velde.

A December 1575 case provides a clear illustration of the legal problems the courts faced when potential fraudulent behaviour by a master came to light.[173] An Antwerp merchant complained that the master had voluntarily jettisoned cargo without consulting his crew. According to his testimony recorded before a notary, he encountered a storm soon after leaving Antwerp on his way to Genoa and thereafter (via land) Lombardy. He decided voluntarily to jettison some cargo as a precautionary measure, jettisoning the heaviest and cheapest

169 BE-SAA, *Vonnisboeken*, V#1235, fol. 26v.

170 For example in the 1563 *Ordonnance*, Title IV, Art. 3.

171 This case also supports Cordes and Höhn's claims that arbitration was not necessarily faster or more efficient than litigation, as enforcement could only be effectively ordered by the Antwerp aldermen. See: Cordes & Höhn, 'Extra-Legal and Legal Conflict Management', 520–521. See also section 4.2.6 for similar arguments.

172 BE-SAA, *Vonnisboeken*, V#1241, fol. 130v–131r.

173 Idem, V#1254, Unknown folio. The folio is unknown because the archival file is damaged and the last folios of this specific Judgement Book are partly illegible.

cargo according to the applicable rules in the 1563 *Ordonnance*.[174] The master argued that the freight contract gave him the freedom to do so. In contrast, the unnamed merchant argued that the master wished to apply for GA to share the costs and to receive payment for the GA claim on top of his freight money. Only when the merchant filed a case at the municipal court accusing the master of barratrous behaviour did the master change his narrative. Unable to find any back-up for his story from his crew members, he offered a voluntary compensation for the lost cargo to the merchants.[175] The master argued that he had acted in good faith, but because no one was willing to support him, the judges sentenced him to reimburse the merchant for the lost cargo. It did not, however, convict the master for criminal behaviour, confirming Rossi's argument that civil law courts did make a difference between fault and negligence.[176] As it was rather hard to find proof for explicit barratrous behaviour (as opposed to (contributory) negligence), the Antwerp municipal court did not criminally convict the master.

4.3.3 *The Position of the Shipmaster before the Great Council*

Whilst Habsburg legislation paid attention to the position of the shipmaster and GA, cases on the issue only rarely reached central courts. Two cases survive in the archives, and it is no coincidence that both were filed by widows of deceased shipmasters, as widows were privileged litigants at the Great Council (as so-called *personae miserabiles*).[177] The first case (dated 24 September 1552) was an appeal by (the widow of) Jean Peres d'Arresti (also Juan Pérez de Arístregui), a Castilian shipmaster based in Arnemuiden.[178] The Great Council however decided to hear the case in the first instance, arguing that the initial judgement from the Middelburg aldermen was based on flawed legal reasoning, against the wishes of the Portuguese defendants in the case.[179] When the suit started in 1549, Arresti was still alive, but by the time of the

174 1563 *Ordonnance*, Title IV, Art. 5.

175 A so-called *vrijwillige indemnatie*.

176 Rossi, 'The Liability of the Shipmaster'.

177 Van Rhee, *Litigation and Legislation*, 41 *n*65. According to the jurist Filips van Wielant, both widows and orphans were *personae miserabiles*, probably as they needed greater protection. Other privileged litigants were commonly high-status members (e.g. nobility or high administrative personnel), making *personae miserabiles* a slightly odd inclusion, but perhaps they needed protection for the exact opposite reason of the other included categories.

178 BE-ARB, Grote Raad, *Registers, geëxentendeerde sententiën*, inv. T107, nr. 853.65 (pp. 817–825). Case also in: Van Answaarden, *Les Portugais*, nr. 49 (pp. 310–312).

179 Ibidem, p. 817. The Great Council did indeed have the right to do so. See for another example Chapter 5.

final judgement he had died.[180] On his behalf, the widow claimed compensation from the Portuguese merchants, who were represented by the Portuguese factor João Rebello.[181] In his initial defence of 1549, Arresti claimed that the Portuguese merchants had incurred damage to the front of the ship to save their cargo, although this had not been necessary. Yet, he claimed that the damage was the result of 'fortunes of the sea'.[182] He agreed to contribute to GA for both the damage to the ship and salvage costs, at the same rate as that of the merchants.[183] Because Arresti owned his ship, he proposed to use the value of the ship to determine the contribution. Rebello, in contrast, argued that Arresti's negligence was the reason the damage to the ship were necessary in the first place.[184] Moreover, Rebello argued that Arresti had not acted when the venture was clearly in danger. He thus requested compensation from Arresti both for the lost cargo, and for all the costs made to salvage the cargo.[185] The Great Council was unable to reach a decision in 1549 citing a lack of evidence, but in 1552 the court did issue a decision after the Portuguese offered additional testimonies. The Great Council agreed with the Portuguese defendants, judging that the widow had to bear all the costs they requested.[186] No mention was made about Arresti's death or how this impacted the judgement in the case.

Katheline vanden Driessche, the Ghent-born widow of the shipmaster Jan van Leancourt Arentszoon, filed an appeal in October 1565.[187] She had won the case before the aldermen of Ghent but had lost the appeal at the Council of Flanders.[188] The defendant, Pieter Romboult, had been sentenced by the aldermen of Ghent to pay a GA contribution after the death of Arentszoon, following the rules from the 1551 and 1563 *Ordonnance*.[189] Vanden Driessche alleged that Romboult had put an extra hundred sacks of grain on the ship without the

180 This suggests that the case may not have been filed under the guise of *personae miserabiles*, but under the competence of the Great Council as the superior court in matters of maritime transport (*ratione materiae*). Yet the case may well have been filed before the Great Council only when Arresti had passed away. See: Van Rhee, *Litigation and Legislation*, 42–43.

181 Van Answaarden, *Les Portugais*, 310.

182 Ibidem, 311. See also BE-ARB, Grote Raad, *Registers*, nr. 853.65, p. 823.

183 BE-ARB, Grote Raad, *Registers*, nr. 853.65, pp. 817–818.

184 Ibidem, pp. 819–820.

185 Ibidem, pp. 821–823.

186 Ibidem, pp. 824–825. Transcription also in: Van Answaarden, *Les Portugais*, 312.

187 Idem, nr. 866.44 (pp. 639–652).

188 Ibidem, pp. 639–640.

189 Ibidem. This was, of course, primarily, the case in pirate attacks, but the Ghent aldermen apparently interpreted this clause broadly.

consent of the shipmaster Arentszoon, alleging that this had led to the sinking of the ship.[190] The Gent aldermen imprisoned Romboult by the Ghent aldermen for not paying, also allowing Vanden Driessche to lay claim to Romboult's possessions as compensation.[191] Both the Council of Flanders and the Great Council, however, heard new evidence that Arentszoon had himself allowed the hundred sacks to be on board. Moreover, Romboult alleged, there was written proof that all merchants involved had consented to this, as was proven by the hundred pounds *Grooten Vlaams* that he had paid as a deposit to the merchants.[192] Romboult furthermore alleged that Arentszoon had been drunk while supervising the loading of the ship. This claim was, crucially, backed up by the testimonies of various seamen.[193] As a result, Romboult was acquitted of all charges.[194] Again, the question of proof was essential: in both cases, the Great Council acquitted the shipmaster of wrongdoing as it was impossible to prove barratrous behaviour.

4.3.4 *The Liability of the Shipmaster and the Development of Particular Average (PA)*

Particular Average was first defined in the 1608 *Compilatae*.[195] Its legal definition was important primarily as the use of insurance became more widespread, because the distinction between GA and PA clarified the exact liability of the insurer: when PA was declared, the insurer had to reimburse the full damage.[196] But as PA was not yet formally defined, there are only a small number of PA cases from the sixteenth century, as 'common' damage (i.e. attributable to 'Acts of God') were covered by insurance. Yet, a few examples of PA have survived without being named as such, mostly dealing with conflicting stories about 'common' damage. In these cases, the liability of the shipmaster was also often the major question, as merchants tried to hold shipmasters liable for negligence whereas their countertactic was to pin the loss on the merchant. The cases were therefore closely related to those studied in the previous sections.

In 1540, the Antwerp shipmaster Jacob Simonszoon recorded a testimony with Streyt that his ship had suffered damage near the coast of Portugal in

190 Ibidem, pp. 642–645: according to Vanden Driessche, the merchant did not 'carry the consent' ("*consent gedragen*") of Arentszoon.

191 Ibidem, pp. 641–644.

192 Ibidem, pp. 642 & 648.

193 Ibidem, pp. 645–646 & 649–650.

194 Ibidem, pp. 645–646 & 648–652.

195 1608 *Compilatae*, Part 4, Title VIII, Art. 66.

196 Van Niekerk, *The Development*, 64–65.

a storm.[197] The silver the ship transported, owned by the famous Augsburg Fugger family, was thereby lost.[198] By recording this testimony, Simonszoon probably aimed to reduce the chances of him being held liable for negligence or GA costs. Indeed, two of his crew members also backed him up by providing testimony. No dispute between Simonszoon and the Fuggers was subsequently recorded. The few remaining PA cases primarily revolve around responsibility and shipmaster liability. Two cases in the Antwerp municipal court, from 1568 and 1571, for example, concerned the responsibility of the master after damage was incurred during loading or unloading.[199] To have PA declared was after all a convenient way for the shipmaster to escape liability, although the tactic was unsuccessful, as in both cases the masters lost the case.

One PA case heard before the Council of Flanders of 8 October 1569 is worth examining in greater detail, as it provides a clear view of the issues at hand in PA cases. The case also concerned the responsibility for the loading of cargo.[200] The Castilian shipmaster Pedro de Bassano had agreed to transport bales of wool from St. André to Sluis. According to the charter party De Bassano would only be paid when he loaded the cargo in a proper condition. If a damaged sack of wool was found in Bruges after unloading, the contract allowed the Castilian consuls to appoint experts to judge the case, without the possibility of an appeal. Upon arrival, many of the bales of wool were indeed found to be damaged or spoilt. The merchants nevertheless offered to pay freight money but asked the consuls to decrease the amount relative to the damage incurred to the cargo. The consuls agreed to this and decided that the merchants only had to pay half of the freight money. Despite the impossibility of the appeal stated in the charter party, De Bassano appealed to the Bruges municipal court, which agreed to hear the case.[201] De Bassano argued that the damage had occurred in a storm and that he could not be held responsible for the damage resulting from this accident. The court ruled that the merchants had to pay De Bassano the full freight money and bear the damage, judging

197 BE-SAA, Notariaat Streyt, N#3133, fol. 77r–v. Also in: Strieder, *Notariatsarchiven*, 355–356 (nr. 683).

198 See for the Fuggers: Eherenberg, *Das Zeitalter der Fugger*.

199 BE-SAA, *Vonnisboeken*, V#1250, fol. 126v–127r; Idem, V#1252, fol. 53r–v. In the second case, a shipmaster tried to have PA declared after a supposed accident of unloading, but testimonies of crew members unveiled that the ship was attacked by Barbary corsairs. As a result, the shipmaster was held liable to reimburse the merchants for the damage as a result of negligence.

200 Gilliodts-Van Severen, *Espagne*, 436–437.

201 Similar to cases in section 4.4.4, where we saw a number of cases litigated despite the arbitration clause.

his case to be a 'good cause' (*bonne cause*).[202] The court also issued an order of payment (*procuratie*), leading the merchants to immediately file an appeal with the Council of Flanders. The judges, somewhat paradoxically, cited the charter party which stated that the decision of the consuls was binding and that no appeal was possible, cancelling the sentence of the municipal court.[203] De Bassano was moreover sentenced to pay for the trial costs.

In short, the small number of PA cases studied here primarily concern the liability for damage following perceived negligence, rather common questions when GA or PA damage arose. PA cases were rare, as the importance of defining PA only became necessary at the end of the sixteenth century as insurance became more widely used. Before this time, PA cases primarily revolved around the liability of the shipmaster, similar to the many GA cases dealing with this issue.

4.4 The Insurability of GA, Moral Hazard and Changes in Risk Distribution

This section studies the link between insurance and GA in legal practice, following our observation that the institutions should be studied in interaction with other institutions.[204] The liability of insurers to pay for GA was a significant cause of disputes arising before the Antwerp municipal court. Although we have seen that Juan Henriquez accepted this liability in the 1560s, other underwriters still regularly sought to avoid paying their contribution. As GA damage could be defrayed to a third party, this shifted incentives for both shipmaster and merchants and increased moral hazard in the interest community to take out insurance and defray both PA and GA damage to the insurer. Indeed, twenty-five out of forty GA cases (i.e. 62.5%) heard in sixteenth-century Antwerp were either concerned with insurers complaining about GA payments, or with merchants trying to enforce payment from the insurer. On the other hand, the strategy to defray the costs to the insurer may well have raised transaction costs, as enforcement costs rose as well (at least temporarily).

In the Low Countries, Antwerp was probably the first to allow for the insurability of GA, as Bruges for example did not yet allow for this, despite some scholarly assertions to the contrary.[205] According to Henry de Groote, the liability of

202 Ibidem, 437.
203 See also section 4.2.5.
204 Ogilvie, '"Whatever is, is Right?"', 681.
205 De Groote, *De zeeassurantie*, 15.

insurers for GA was the topic of a dispute in the Bruges municipal court in 1441, but a close reading of the actual archival file reveals it does not say anything about insurance.[206] Although most Italian city-states (with the notable exception of Venice) already allowed for the insurability in the fourteenth or fifteenth century, it appears that the introduction of the principle in the Low Countries should be dated to the mid-sixteenth century.[207] Coupled with the evidence from the Juan Henriquez ledgers, it appears safe to assume that the insurability of GA in the Low Countries was a development that should be dated to the 1540s, although an exact date is hard to pinpoint. This development may have been inspired by Castilian normative practice, although the records of the Castilian consular court do not provide conclusive evidence either: and nor can we take into account the influence of Italian normative practice for lack of sources.[208]

4.4.1 *Insurance and GA before the Antwerp Municipal Court*

All cases heard between 1545 and 1582 in the Antwerp municipal court on the insurability of GA damage were either merchants requesting their insurers to pay for a GA claim, or insurers filing a claim against the shipmaster for perceived negligent behaviour.[209] Insurers rarely won those cases. As merchants often did not file a case against the shipmaster when cargo was insured, these cases offer an early example of moral hazard as the incentive shifted as losses could be defrayed to the insurer without significant cost to merchant and shipmaster in the interest community.[210] Moreover, this may have contributed to diminishing the speculative aspect of insurance, as the liability of insurers to pay for GA left them with less options not to pay out claims.[211] If the municipal

206 See: Gilliodts-Van Severen, *Espagne*, 83; see for the actual file BE-SAB, Spaans Consulaat, nr. VII, Charters, nr. 22. The case revolves around the payment of Averages and will be treated in further detail in Chapter 6.

207 See footnotes 190–191 of Chapter 3.

208 I analyse the Castilian contribution to GA legislation in the Low Countries in greater detail in: Dreijer, 'Castilian Normative Practice and the Development of General Average in the Southern Low Countries (sixteenth century)', in: Fusaro, Addobbati & Piccinno (eds.), *General Average*, forthcoming. See also for Italian practice: Iodice & Piccino, 'Managing Shipping Risk', 85–90.

209 BE-SAA, *Vonnisboeken*, V#1241, fol. 283r–v; V#1242, fol. 127r; V#1244, fol. 128r–130r; V#1245, fol. 120r–121r & 174r–v; V#1246, fol. 62r–v; V#1247, fol. 82v–84v, 148r–151r & 269r–v; V#1249, fol. 1r–v, 6v–7v, 130r, 204r–205r; V#1250, fol. 139r, 150v–151r & 241r–v; V#1251, fol. 45v–46v, 71v–72r & 104r–v; V#1252, fol. 78r–v & 168r–v; V#1254, fol. 107r–v & 147v–148v; V#1255, fol. 221v–225r; V#1256, fol. 58v–59v.

210 See also: Heimer, *Reactive Risk and Rational Action*, 123–125.

211 For the speculative aspect: De ruysscher, '1490–1590', 95–96; Van der Wee, *The Growth* (Vol. 2), 327–328.

court allowed for further hearings, it often expected the insurer to pay the *namptissement* (the conditional pay-out) first, before litigating further. This procedure was established to discourage insurers from taking legal action, especially for small sums. Yet some insurers tried their luck. Since there were many similar cases, we will only treat a few typical cases here.

The first insurance-and-GA case dates from 1548.[212] On 8 March, the insurer Cornelis de Jonge filed a case at the municipal court against Joost de Mellar, whose cargo was jettisoned after a ship coming from Dover encountered a storm before the coast of Zeeland. De Mellar claimed the money for GA costs for the remainder of the damage back from De Jonge, who declined to pay and filed a case to avoid liability. De Jonge filed a case at the Antwerp municipal court, hoping that the court would allow him to avoid paying for the GA claim based on exceptions in the insurance policy. De Mellar, in contrast, claimed that the 'customs of the sea' (*costuymen vander zee*) allowed him to levy the costs for GA from his insurer.[213] De Jonge claimed protection against payment on two grounds. First, that the master had brought additional cargo on board for his own profit; and second, that the storm was not heavy enough to justify jettisoning the cargo. This would mean that the conditions of the insurance policy were violated because the necessary measures to protect cargo were not taken. The court however concurred with De Mellar and forced De Jonge to pay. The reference to the 'customs of the sea' is most intriguing here, as these sometimes referred to the Wisby Laws. Yet as the Wisby Laws did not state anything on insurance or the insurability of GA, a different explanation must be sought. As we have noted before, the 'customs of the sea' were primarily a rhetorical tool, reinforcing legal pluralism and allowing merchants or masters to apply their own customs.

Two further cases, one from 1567 and one from 1575, offer a clear look on the legal problems following from the application of the principle of the insurability of GA. The 1567 case dealt with a pirate attack and its fall-out.[214] A Portuguese ship sailing from Antwerp to Lisbon was heavily damaged in a pirate attack before the coast of France, losing all cargo. The pirates also forced the master to set sail to an unnamed French port, where they released master and crew. The master immediately abandoned the ship to the insurer, meaning the ship was now the insurer's property (although still in the hands of the

212 BE-SAA, *Vonnisboeken*, V#1241, fol. 283r–v.

213 By this, he may have meant the Wisby Laws. This however did not note anything on the insurability of GA, even if it was 'customary' in the Low Countries at this point.

214 BE-SAA, *Vonnisboeken*, V#1249, fol. 6v–7v.

pirates).[215] Some of the cargo had been lost due to a jettison, which according to him had been an attempt to sail faster and escape the pirates. Hence, he filed for GA for that portion of cargo. Although the insurers agreed with the act of abandonment, they were unwilling to pay for the GA claim as well, citing the failure of the attempt: and strictly speaking, they were right. The court however judged that the insurers had to pay the *namptissement* notwithstanding this failure, leaving them with an abandoned ship in the hands of pirates and payment for a GA claim for jettisoned cargo.

Insurers having to pay the *namptissement* in cases where they were also liable for GA was common.[216] The 1575 case speaks volumes about the relationship between insurers and GA. A Castilian ship jettisoned wool near Dover after encountering a storm.[217] A repair was necessary, but on its way to the Normandy port of Dieppe, incompetent pilots incurred additional damage to the ship. As a result, more wool was jettisoned. All this wool was insured by Lombard insurers based in Antwerp, who agreed to pay for the first but not for the second jettison. They filed a case at the municipal court, arguing that hiring incompetent pilots was not their responsibility, but rather the masters'. The court largely agreed with the insurers, decreeing that the costs for the repair of the ship and the pilotage costs had to be paid by the master. Nevertheless, the jettisoned wool had to be paid for, the first jettison by means of GA and the second by 'normal' insurance. Although insurers tried to avoid payment, they were either unsuccessful or only partly successful as shipmasters and merchants allied to win the cases.

Antwerp legal practice included the liability of insurers to pay for GA before the *Hordenanzas* and the *Compilatae* incorporated the principle into formal law. It appears that the fine-meshed distinction from Roman-Dutch law about the various liabilities of insurers were not yet developed, as only the direct reimbursement for GA damage was the object of litigation.[218] The Antwerp aldermen were innovative in allowing for this (at least in north-western Europe), protecting the interest community but thereby creating incentives to defray damage to insurers.

---

215 See for the rules regarding abandonment: Rossi, 'The Abandonment to the Insurers in Sixteenth Century Insurance Practice: Comparative Remarks and (a Few) Methodological Notes', in: Pihlajamäki, Cordes, Dauchy & De ruysscher (eds.), *Understanding the Sources*, 87–118, there 91–95.

216 See for example the following cases: BE-SAA, *Vonnisboeken*, V#1245, fol. 1r, 60r, 174r–v; V#1247, fol. 269r–v; V#1250, fol. 139r; V#1251, fol. 140r–v; V#1252, fol. 125v, 130v–131r; V#1256, fol. 78v–79v.

217 Idem, V#1255, fol. 221v–225r.

218 Van Niekerk, *The Development*, 76–80.

4.4.2 *Insurance and* GA *before the Castilian Consular Court*

Although a number of insurance cases were heard in the Castilian consular court, these cases rarely concerned complaints about the GA payment (as was the case in Antwerp around the same time). As Chapter 3 already analysed, both the 1538 Burgos and 1556 Seville *Ordonnance* already allowed for the insurability of GA, making it likely that Castilian merchants in the Low Countries applied similar rules, as were of course later also incorporated into the *Hordenanzas*.[219] Yet only one case has survived in the archives of the Castilian consular court, dating from 1560.[220] Eight insurers at that time applied to the consuls to declare void an insurance policy after a ship incurred damage to the wool on its way from Portugalete to Bruges, complaining that the shipmaster had not taken the necessary precautions to prevent the damage.[221] Besides the fact that they were held to reimburse the merchants whose cargo was lost, the insurers were subsequently also held liable to contribute to the GA damage of the merchants who had not insured their cargo, as the insured cargo was used to estimate the contribution to the uninsured cargo.[222] As a result, the insurers complained that they had to contribute twice for the same cargo. The consuls did not scrap this obligation, but ordered the Average adjusters to lower the valuation of the cargo used for the contribution, thereby lowering the sum of the GA contribution.[223]

The interaction between Castilian legislation and normative practice and Antwerp normative legal practice is not fully clear. Although from this case we may infer that the Castilians in Bruges also held insurers liable for GA claims, the Antwerp archival evidence provides clearer, repeated evidence for this fact that was standing practice from the 1540s onwards. Yet for reasons sketched in Chapter 3, the available material does not enable us to solve the issue of the introduction of the principle with certainty.

4.5 'Atypical' GA Cases

In the cases studied in the previous sections, precedent or procedural rules could be applied with relative ease. Even on the insurability of GA, precedence could be found in Castilian and Italian normative practice. Some cases were

219 Rossi, *Insurance in Elizabethan England*, 148–157.

220 BE-SAB, *Libro de pleytos ordinarios*, fol. 205v–208r.

221 Ibidem, fol. 205v–206v.

222 Ibidem, fol. 207r–207v. See also: Van Niekerk, *The Development*, 76–80.

223 Ibidem, fol. 208r.

however so complex that courts had to be more creative to solve the issue. These cases form the heart of research into legal practice, because they provide new insights into how legal actors perceived the legal system at large. Moreover, it sheds light on its flexibility. This section aims to study some of these atypical cases, showing that (in particular) the Great Council displayed remarkable flexibility in applying new concepts. Given its historiographical reputation for slow proceedings,[224] this may come as a surprise, especially as the Antwerp municipal court stuck to precedent more faithfully. Cases studied below were more eclectic or especially complex in their nature. A first group of cases concerns two examples where both emergency bottomry and GA was involved, a less common combination in the Low Countries' evidence in contrast to insurance and GA.[225] A second group consisted of ship collisions, already discussed in Chapter 2 on a doctrinal level. A third category concerned complex jurisdictional arrangements, where different privileges of the *nationes* overlapped and conflicted with each other, making it difficult to simply uphold privileges. The first two categories of cases clearly show that legal practice preceded eventual codification in formal law, particularly Antwerp municipal law.[226]

4.5.1 *Bottomry and GA*

We have seen how the relationship between insurance and GA was clarified in legal practice and formal law during the sixteenth century. Less clear was the relationship between other instruments of risk management. In the 1608 Antwerp *Compilatae*, only a few clauses on the combination between bottomry loans and GA were included, stating that the combination was not allowed unless the bottomry loan was jettisoned in extraordinary circumstances.[227] In practice, this meant that incidents involving both instruments had to be solved by a court that could not rely on explicit precedent or formal law. Nor was the topic of great importance in legal practice, meaning courts had to solve these rare disputes without recourse to formal law.

One case from 7 January 1534 heard before the Bruges municipal court shows how such a case was solved in practice.[228] Jehan de Martinen de Luggera, the

---

224 Van Rhee, *Litigation and Legislation*, 313–342.

225 Whilst in Italy for example this was relatively common, even in the eighteenth century. See: Addobbati, 'Italy 1500–1800', 69.

226 Following Friedman, *The Legal System*.

227 See chapter 3: 1608 *Compilatae*, Part 4, Title VIII, Art. 65. In the reference to the bottomry loan, the actual cash money was meant.

228 Gilliodts-Van Severen, *Espagne*, 299–302. See for the sequence of cases in Bruges: BE-SAB, Oud Archief, Civiele Sententiën Vierschaar 1533–34, inv. 157, fol. 65, n. 1, fol. 77v, n. 1, fol. 84v, n. 2, fol. 126v, n. 1, fol. 154v, n. 2, fol. 162v, n. 2, fol. 221v, n. 1.

Biscayer shipmaster of the *Sainct Pierre*, was called to appear before the municipal court, after the Castilian consuls, representing a number of Castilian merchants who had freighted the ship, had filed a case.[229] Despite the wishes of the merchants and majority of the crew members, De Luggera had declined to hire a pilot to transport the cargo into the port of Flushing (Zeeland) when the ship encountered a heavy storm. Subsequently, the ship ran on the rocks and was shipwrecked just before the coast of Westcappelle and Zoutelande (also Zeeland).[230] Most of the cargo was saved, but the ship had incurred heavy damage and had to be repaired in Zeeland. The Biscayer consuls, administering the procedure, decided that these costs could be claimed back from the merchants through the risk-sharing of an emergency bottomry loan, but the Castilian consuls (of whom two were also freighters) complained. They filed a lawsuit at the Bruges municipal court, where they accused the shipmaster of acting in bad faith.[231] Moreover, they alleged that there were discrepancies in the testimonies of shipmaster and crew, while they were also not allowed on the ship to survey the damage.

The shipmaster and some of his crew members argued that they had, in fact, acted in good faith, making sure that most of the cargo would end up safely onshore rather than in the sea. This was however not a deliberate act to save the ship, and hence the *lex rhodia de iactu* could not be used in this case, according to De Luggera, explicitly referring to Roman law.[232] He proposed that damage had to be borne by the owners of the cargo, next to the merchants' bottomry loan to repair the damage to the ship. The court however decided that he and his crew members had to pay the large sum of 2,200 ducats for the damage.[233] De Luggera then tried to sell some of the ship equipment to lower the costs for himself, but subsequent appeals by the Castilians made sure that this would not be allowed. In the end, two aldermen were appointed to make sure that nothing from the ship could be sold without explicit consent of the Castilians.[234] Although the court declined to approve of the emergency bottomry loan, it did not declare GA either, returning a potential decision to declare GA to the Biscayer consuls.

A similarly complex case can be found in a 1550 Great Council appeal case filed by Lievin van Weylant against Pieter de Posa, a Castilian residing

229 Ibidem, 299.
230 Ibidem, 300.
231 Ibidem, 300–301.
232 Ibidem.
233 Ibidem, 302. The text does not specify which ducats were used, but given the timing these were probably Venetian ducats, the preferred currency of merchants at the time.
234 Ibidem.

in Middelburg.[235] Van Weylant had participated in a venture organised by De Posa that went to Cadiz from Middelburg. The venture, led by master Steven Stevenszoon, had however incurred damage to the ship on the way back. In Cádiz, Stevenszoon had received money from the Flemish merchant Lievin de la Haye, who resided there. The money was meant to be paid to Van Weylant to buy cargo in Flanders. However, because of the damage, Stevenszoon had used the sum of 180 *escuderos* to pay for an emergency repair in Bristol.[236] Stevenszoon filed an appeal against De Posa because he was responsible for the venture. Because the money was, however, used for the common safety of the ship, the judge in Middelburg had decided that Stevenszoon had been justified in using the money to repair the ship in Bristol.[237] The Great Council confirmed this judgement, by pointing to the damage incurred by the ship, and ruled that Stevenszoon had been right to use the money for the repair, rather than to borrow extra money through a bottomry loan (*notbodmerei*).[238] Moreover, the master had followed the advice of his crew and sailed to Bristol.[239]

However, not all of the money was spent on the repair. Some of the money was also given to De Posa, despite the fact that it was meant to be paid to Van Weylant.[240] The Great Council therefore ruled that Stevenszoon had broken with the 'customs of the sea'.[241] Stevenszoon also testified, arguing that his actions had saved most of the cargo. The Great Council acknowledged this, pointing out that Stevenszoons' actions had prevented further damage.[242] Van Weylant tried another line of attack focusing on the extra loan supposedly made by Stevenszoon, for which the judges could not find evidence.[243] According to Van Weylant, Stevenszoon had used that money and some of the profits on the cargo sold (from which the money came from in Cádiz) to enrich himself.[244] The judges ruled that De Posa was not at fault and that the costs for the delay were to be shared by all merchants involved in the venture.[245] Nonetheless, Stevenszoon still had to pay back the profits from the cargo sold: after all, De Posa should have collected the money. As such, Stevenszoon had to

235 BE-ARB, Grote Raad, *Registers*, nr. 851.9 (pp. 93–100).
236 Ibidem, pp. 93–95.
237 Ibidem, pp. 93–94.
238 Ibidem, p. 98.
239 Ibidem, pp. 96–97.
240 Ibidem, p. 97.
241 Ibidem, pp. 99–100. No specific references were made to what these 'customs of the sea' should mean.
242 Ibidem, pp. 97–98.
243 Ibidem, p. 97.
244 Ibidem.
245 Ibidem, pp. 99–100.

pay back the profits to Van Weylant, notwithstanding the fact that his actions had saved the ship.[246] The interest community carried the costs for the repair by means of GA.

As the 1608 *Compilatae* attested, combining (emergency) bottomry with GA was uncommon and even discouraged by Antwerp municipal law, which was normally quite accommodating to new risk management techniques or a combination of those techniques (e.g. insurance and GA).[247] Only in unique situations could the two instruments interact, as in the two cases described above. No useful precedent or legislation existed to decide in these two cases. The court therefore looked at the rules on the liability of the shipmaster, deciding that Stevenszoon had largely acted appropriately. By repairing the ship in Bristol to everyone's benefit, Stevenszoon incurred limited GA costs but managed to avoid taking out an expensive bottomry loan (notwithstanding his later efforts to make a profit out of the situation). Article 2 of the 1563 *Ordonnance*, which stipulated that a ship would have to be repaired in a month, and only afterwards could GA be declared, had a similar rationale to avoid taking out emergency bottomry loans.[248] But even without this written rule, both the Bruges court and the Great Council decided that taking out emergency bottomry loans was not acceptable even in a crisis. In both cases, the courts focused strongly on the actions of the shipmaster as the key to judging the dispute, which made sense given the applicable norms on the role of the shipmaster. Both courts therefore fell back on commonly applied rules to judge the dispute.

4.5.2 *Ship Collisions*

Ship collision cases were rarely heard by courts in the Low Countries, but some evidence has survived in the Great Council archives. This issue was treated in the 1563 *Ordonnance* of Philip II, but by means of contributory negligence and not as GA. The 1608 *Compilatae* in contrast did allow for GA when two ships accidentally collided, even if shipmasters of course were expected to prevent the collision of ships.[249] Similar to the insurability of GA, legal practice preceded this rule. A 1556 case from the Antwerp municipal court for example concerned a ship collision before the coast of Sardinia.[250] One of the

246 Ibidem.

247 1608 *Compilatae*, Title VIII, Art. 65.

248 1563 *Ordonnance*, Chapter IV, Art. 2.

249 In the 1563 *Ordonnance*, this was still treated from the viewpoint of *dolus* and *culpa*, going back to Roman law. In the 1608 *Costuymen*, an accidental collision could be treated as GA. See: Van Dongen, *Contributory negligence*, 245–254.

250 BE-SAA, Vonnisboeken, V#1244, fol. 126v–127v.

merchants involved in the venture, Albert Peeters, complained about the GA calculus. Following the collision, the master Sarganus Lazzano kept the ship in the port for a couple of days to make necessary reparations and load new alum, because part of the alum was spoilt during the collision. The costs for this delay were incorporated into the GA declaration, which was quickly drawn up when the ship arrived in Bruges, based on testimonies Lazzano had registered with a notary in Sardinia. The Average adjusters, notably, solved the issue of the ship collision by GA, indicating this was common mercantile practice.[251] Peeters, supported by other merchants involved in the venture, claimed that the collision was the result of mistakes by Lazzano and his crew when they moored the ship. Hence, Peeters proposed that the costs incurred by the collision had to be borne by Lazzano. Lazzano, in contrast, maintained that the collision was an accident and no one's fault. Lazzano also pointed out that the alum was insured and proposed that much of the damage could be covered by the insurers.[252] The aldermen consulted a merchant panel and decided that Peeters and the other merchants had to contribute for both the spoilt cargo and the delay to the voyage, in line with what Weytsen claimed. In case they were able to offer new evidence, they were nevertheless allowed to litigate their case again. The question of proof was essential. Since Peeters could not provide evidence that Lazzano or his crew had acted in bad faith, he lost the case. Yet Peeters appeared not to contest the principle that ship collisions could be solved by GA. Whilst written legal sources commonly described the liability and responsibility of the shipmaster in detail, legal practice did not always provide clear-cut cases where legislation could easily apply.[253]

Two Great Council appeals (from Holland) were concerned with ship collisions and surprisingly, the Great Council also applied the 'Antwerp rules' solving ship collisions by means of GA.[254] The first from 1569 was an *incidenteel beroep* (an appeal by both sides[255]) in a case that had originally been litigated at the Admiralty in Veere and subsequently the Court of Holland.[256] Shipowners Vesterman, Willemszoon, and Corneliszoon *cum suis* from Enkhuizen (Holland), sued Groot, a shipmaster from the same town. The ship of the three

251 See also section 4.5.3.

252 This was an interesting point, which may also explain the litigation of insurers about GA payments (see section 4.4.2): because insurance was more widely used, this may theoretically have led to a less strict application of what could count as GA, since most of the damages could be pinned on insurers anyway.

253 Compare: Rossi, 'The Liability of the Shipmaster'.

254 BE-ARB, Grote Raad, *Registers*, nrs. 870.68 (pp. 1019–1038) & 872.42 (pp. 667–691).

255 See Van Rhee, *Litigation and Legislation*, 81–82.

256 BE-ARB, Grote Raad, *Registers*, nr. 870.68 (pp. 1019–1038), pp. 1019–1020 & 1025.

ship-owners, sailing from Portugal to the Low Countries with salt, had collided with the ship of Groot, with both ships incurring damage.[257] Both lower courts judged that both parties were at fault, solving the issue by contributory negligence (rather than GA).[258] The Court of Holland also held Corneliszoon, the master on his part-owned ship, liable for the fact that Groot's ship had sunk as a result of the collision, sentencing him to pay 50% of the total damages to Groot's sunk ship.[259] Moreover, the Court of Holland ruled that Corneliszoon and his crew did not help Groot and his crew to assemble some of the lost cargo, nor did they attempt to save his crew.[260] Both the Court of Holland and the Admiralty also noted that Groot had made mistakes, besides the bad weather conditions: for these two reasons, Corneliszoon would have to assume liability as well.[261] Groot accepted his liability and testified that both ships could have avoided the collision.[262] Because of the collision, his mast had broken down and subsequently the ship had sunk.[263] Attempts to salvage the ship were in vain.[264] Referring to the maritime laws of Westcappelle, the Great Council ruled that both parties had behaved negligently, and compensation for the sunken ship had to be shared by all. It hence largely followed the rulings of the lower courts but came to a different solution, as it used GA rather than contributory negligence to solve the case. Both parties had to contribute 50% of the damages of the other ship on the basis of GA rather than contributory negligence, meaning the Great Council had already applied a solution which was not commonly found in formal law at the time.[265]

Another 1571 appeal from Holland concerned the case between Aert Joncker and Willem Steenbicker.[266] The latter was sailing from Hamburg to Amsterdam with alum on board, when his boat was hit by Joncker's fishing boat near Harderwijk (Guelders) in the Zuiderzee.[267] Both ships were damaged, and Joncker had incurred damage so heavy that he jettisoned all equipment onboard and abandoned ship.[268] By abandoning the ship, he hoped not to be held liable for a potential GA claim, on the basis of 'eternal traditions'.[269]

257 Ibidem, p. 1019.
258 Ibidem, p. 1025.
259 Ibidem, pp. 1022–1024 & 1029.
260 Ibidem.
261 Ibidem, p. 1026.
262 Ibidem: they could have stayed "*costeloos ende sgadeloos*".
263 Ibidem, p. 1031.
264 Ibidem, p. 1022.
265 See: Van Dongen, *Contributory Negligence*, 241–255.
266 BE-ARB, Grote Raad, *Registers*, nr. 872.42 (pp. 667–691).
267 Ibidem, pp. 668–670.
268 Ibidem, pp. 674–675.
269 Ibidem, p. 674: "*eeuwige tradities conform de costuymme*".

However Steenbicker, on the basis of the Amsterdam *Ordonnantie* and the 1551 *Ordonnance*, claimed that Joncker should be held liable for at least half of the damage, besides paying Steenbicker a contribution for spoilt and lost cargo, which he had to jettison to save the venture.[270] Moreover, he claimed that Joncker could have contributed voluntarily to the damage within eight days of the incident (apparently a local custom), which Joncker had neglected to do.[271] As a result, both the municipal court of Muiden (in Holland) and the Court of Holland had ruled in favour of Steenbicker, stating that negligent behaviour by Joncker indeed was a reason for compensation by means of GA.[272] The Great Council agreed with the other two courts, arguing that Joncker's recklessness had caused the collision and the subsequent damage.[273] There was, as such, not a problem of contributory negligence, since Steenbicker was not accused of negligent behaviour himself. The court declared Joncker's voluntary abandonment to be void and judged that he should pay for the damage suffered by Steenbicker to ship and cargo by means of GA, as well as to contribute to the lost profits.[274] Not only the Great Council, but the lower courts also acknowledged the rationale for GA in this case. References to well-known legal norms helped Steenbicker to win the case, although no explanations to the exact norms were named.[275]

Both the Antwerp municipal court and the Great Council solved disputes by applying GA where formal law did not require or stipulate this. Legal practice deviated clearly from formal law here. Most surprisingly, it was the Great Council that applied GA to solve disputes, rather than use contributory negligence. We are left to speculate why this was the case.[276] It may well have been the most equitable way to solve the dispute, offering more ways to value the damage than contributory negligence. Clearly, merchants appearing before the Great Council often referred to the relevant laws to further their cause, although the references to 'customs of the sea' or the 1551 *Ordonnance* were fairly generic. Concepts from Roman law rarely figured in the judgements of the Great Council on maritime law: only De Luggera mentioned the *lex rhodia* before the Bruges municipal court but to no avail.[277] The opposition between

270 Ibidem, pp. 674–676.

271 Ibidem, p. 684.

272 Ibidem, pp. 686–687.

273 Ibidem, p. 685.

274 Ibidem, pp. 688–691.

275 Indicating that this was more a form of *captatio benevolentiae* than 'legal literacy', as claimed in: Lambert, 'A Legal World Market?', 173–175.

276 It should be borne in mind that the Great Council never explained its reasoning in the extended sentences.

277 Gelderblom, *Cities of Commerce*, 133–139, states that the municipal courts actively incorporated legal sources into their legal practice, including Roman law.

the use of Roman law in municipal and central courts should thus not be overstated. It furthermore underlines the opportunistic nature of merchants in appealing to legal norms.[278] Notably, however, the courts applied new rules long before the *Compilatae* included this. In Antwerp, this may not be particularly surprising as the city also allowed for the insurability of GA long before it incorporated the rule into municipal legislation. But for the Great Council, this *was* surprising as it contradicted official Habsburg legislation. Both courts and merchants nevertheless sought practical solutions by combining existing rules, for example on the liability of the shipmaster and GA.

4.5.3 *Jurisdictional Disputes*

Jurisdictional disputes over GA were relatively common, but finding a solution was not necessarily easy. For the parties, often the consuls of the *nationes*, jurisdiction over GA cases was a major privilege. Deciding these cases were tricky because a court had to deal with long-held privileges and political sensitivities. More than in other cases, both parties could be right to a certain extent, but a decision still had to be made. Two types of privileges were vigorously defended before the various courts in the Low Countries: until the 1540s, the *avería de nación* privilege was the most important subject, often litigated before the Great Council (see Chapter 6). As Antwerp consolidated jurisdiction from the 1540s onwards, jurisdictional disputes dating from the second half of the sixteenth century (primarily dealing with jurisdiction for *nationes* over GA 'proper') were all heard in the Antwerp municipal court. The jurisdictional problems were especially pronounced after roughly 1560, when the Antwerp-based Castilian community (without a *natio*) and Portuguese *natio* in the city clashed several times. This coincided with Antwerp's consolidation of jurisdiction, as the merchant communities sought conflict resolution at the Antwerp municipal court rather than at the Great Council.[279]

4.5.3.1 Jurisdictional Disputes in the Bruges Municipal Court

The first extant jurisdictional dispute dates from 15 July 1441.[280] A Castilian commercial fleet sailed from Burgos to Bruges with a cargo of iron and wool. They encountered a storm and one of the ships jettisoned cargo. Both Biscayer

278 Lambert, 'A Legal World Market?', 173–175.

279 Gelderbom, *Cities of Commerce*, 127–133.

280 De Groote, *De zeeassurantie*, 13; Gilliodts-Van Severen, *Coutumes des Pays en Comté de Flandre. Quartier de Bruges, Coutume de la Ville de Bruges* (2. Vols.) (Brussels 1874) (hereafter: Gilliodts-Van Severen, *Coutumes*) (Vol. 2), 109.

and Castilian merchants participated in the venture, but neither agreed to contribute to GA since both parties argued that the ship was too heavily loaded because of the other party's cargo. The ship arrived in Sluis, an ante-port of Bruges.[281] Even if the parties could have brought their case before the Sluis municipal court, they decided to litigate in Bruges.[282] The Castilian consuls referred to their privilege to judge GA cases in the consular court given their civil jurisdiction over members of the *natio*.[283] The municipal court did not agree with this argument since both parties had invested to a similar extent in the venture. This meant it could not be considered the privilege of the Castilian consuls to draw up the calculations. As a result, both parties were summoned to contribute to GA for exactly half of the damage, echoing the solutions courts chose in cases that had to be solved formally by contributory negligence.[284]

Although consuls had jurisdiction in charge of GA proceedings, their verdicts could be challenged in municipal courts. This rarely happened, as there appears to be only one 1488 GA case concerning a group of ten Portuguese merchants filing an appeal against a decision by their consuls.[285] The consuls had appointed the Portuguese merchant Stevin Yanes and the Florentine merchant Renault de Ricassoly (Ricasoli) to survey the damage and draw up the calculus, but the group of Portuguese merchants (for unknown reasons) did not agree with their appointment. Their cargo on two ships, the *La Olivero* and the *La Pigarre*, was damaged, but they were not allowed to reclaim the cargo or survey the damage themselves. The municipal court's decision is unfortunately not known, but the fact that Portuguese merchants were willing to challenge the authority of their consuls on matters of GA is noteworthy.

It was not just individual merchants who appealed in the municipal court. In 1521, the consuls of the Catalan-Aragonese *natio*, who had already *de facto* moved their Consulate to Antwerp before the *de jure* move in 1527, filed a lawsuit at the Bruges municipal court to obtain GA payments from several Spanish merchants (whose membership of a *natio* is not noted in the source).[286] The

281 See for the role of Sluis in the Zwin Estuary system: Leloup & Dumolyn, 'The Zwin Estuary', 206–208.

282 Bruges' control over the towns in the Zwin Estuary was well-established during the fifteenth century, and this was hence a logical decision. See: Ibidem, 209–210.

283 Gilliodts-Van Severen, *Coutumes* (Vol. 2), 109. The Castilians had civil jurisdiction over its merchants since 1343. See: Gilliodts-Van Severen, *Espagne*, 8–12.

284 In that sense, the judgement mimicked 'contributory negligence'. See: Van Dongen, *Contributory negligence*, 241–255.

285 Gilliodts-Van Severen, *Cartulaire* (Vol. 2), nr. 1245.

286 Ibidem, nr. 1496.

consuls sent a document to the municipal court explaining that a GA calculus had been drawn up by them, which required a contribution by various merchants residing in Bruges. Since they had no jurisdictional power to force them to pay, they requested an order of payment (*procuratie*) from the Bruges municipal court. The Catalan-Aragonese consuls, present at the court proceedings, explained that they drew up the calculus in good faith and brought with them written oaths from crew and the master of the ship, recorded by an unnamed Antwerp notary. After seeing this evidence, the court acceded to their demands and issued the order. Since the Catalan-Aragonese were still formally based in Bruges, this would *de jure* have meant they did not need a sign from a notary to have the order issued in the municipal court. Their *de facto* move to Antwerp however made the consuls take additional measures to guarantee a favourable outcome, bringing the sign of a trusted Antwerp notary with them for additional legal security.[287]

4.5.3.2 Jurisdictional Disputes in Zeeland

Given the presence of foreign merchants in Zeeland, the municipal courts in Veere, Middelburg, and Arnemuiden also dealt with complex cases. There was a strong rivalry between the various cities and towns in Zeeland, each of them offering extensive privileges to lure foreign merchants.[288] Besides the presence of the Andalusians from 1505 onwards in Middelburg,[289] from the mid-fifteenth century onwards most Iberian ships sailed to the large natural ports of Zeeland (e.g. Arnemuiden and Middelburg).[290] The Castilian *natio* even appointed several officials in Middelburg, the comptroller-general (*controlador*) and some men to load and unload ships (*discargadores*) to make sure all Castilian ships paid their duties and contributions.[291] The Scottish *natio* settled in Veere during the fifteenth century, after they were ejected from both Bruges and Antwerp by the more powerful Hanseatic merchants and the

287 Ibidem.

288 Gelderblom's thesis on municipal competition seems well-suited to towns and cities in Zeeland. Middelburg, Arnemuiden and Veere competed with each other to attract foreign merchants and provided multiple privileges to those foreign merchants, as well as a wide range of maritime services. They were nevertheless second-tier cities in the economic ecosystem in which Bruges and Antwerp, and potentially Rotterdam and Dordrecht to the north, dominated, which may well have influenced the Zeeland's towns strategies. They were moreover negatively affecting each other, for example by blocking jurisdiction and litigating extensively over tolls and custom duties.

289 Fagel, 'Spaanse kooplieden', 22–25.

290 Degryse, 'Brugge en de pilotage'.

291 Gilliodts-Van Severen, *Espagne*, 412–415. For the various functions of the Consulate: Maréchal, 'La colonie espagnole', 22–28.

English Merchant Adventurers. This small Scottish community remained there until the late seventeenth century.[292]

Members of the Scottish *natio* twice appeared before Veere's municipal court in GA related matters. On 11 July 1516, Cornelis de Heerder appeared before the municipal court, as his ship had been attacked by an English 'man of war' (*man van oirlooge*) taking four pieces of cloth in the attack.[293] The Scottish merchant Andries Oodtwaert, who participated in the venture, argued that this was a case of privateering and that he did not have to contribute in GA as there had been no deliberate damage for the common benefit. He was supported by the Scottish consuls, who claimed jurisdiction over the case as one of their members was involved. The court nevertheless decided that Oodtwaert had to contribute to GA, on the grounds that De Heerder had taken all the necessary measures to protect the ship and cargo against attacks from war ships. Moreover, De Heerder and his crew had tried to fight off the attack, successfully defending the ship but not all of the cargo, making the damage to an extent 'deliberate'. The court thus decided that the act was sufficiently successful to justify a GA contribution. Moreover, Veere's aldermen denied the jurisdiction of the Scottish consuls over the case, as the aldermen pointed out that the shipmasters' origin was decisive in allocating jurisdiction over the case. As De Heerder was a local shipmaster, this meant the Veere municipal court claimed jurisdiction.

Another case dating from 6 November 1534 shows further evidence of the jurisdictional problems over GA claims of the Scottish *natio*.[294] Similar to the arguments of many Antwerp-based *nationes*, the Scottish *natio* claimed a right to decide GA cases within the consular court when the venture concerned solely Scottish cargo. In this case, the non-Scottish shipmaster Amant Adriaenssoon of Veere, claimed a GA contribution from a couple of Scottish merchants named Robert Black and Andro Mor, represented in court by their consul Symon Patricxzoon. Adriaenssoon had recently sailed from Scotland to Veere, jettisoning a large pack of wool because of a storm. He demanded

---

292 The two major works on the Scottish *natio* in Veere date from the early twentieth century: M.P. Rooseboom, *The Scottish Staple in the Netherlands: An Account of the Trade Relations between Scotland and the Low Countries from 1292 till 1676, with a Calendar of Illustrative Documents* (The Hague 1910); J. Davidson & A. Gray, *The Scottish Staple at Veere: A Study in the Economic History of Scotland* (London/New York/Bombay/Calcutta 1909).

293 Smit, *Bronnen Engeland*, nr. 304. The case was transcribed from Rijksarchief Middelburg (hereafter NL-RA), Archief van de Vierschaar 1456–1811, Rol 1514–1517, fol. 253v. The archive was incorporated into NL-ZA, RAZE, inv. 2.1.1.1, until it was lost in 1940 due to German bombardments.

294 Smit, *Bronnen Engeland*, (nr. 563). The case is based on: NL-RA, Archief van de Vierschaar 1456–1811, Rol 1534–1537, fol. 47r. The original is, again, lost.

that the Scottish merchants contributed to GA, but the Scottish consul sent a statement that this case should be decided by the Scottish consular court rather than the municipal court of Veere, for the ship genuinely only contained Scottish cargo.[295] The court did not agree with this and obliged the consul to reply in person at the court, even though the court did not issue a decision on the case itself. There is a coda to the story. In 1537, Adriaenssoon dispatched another skipper, Sander Kyen, to Scotland to force the merchants involved in the venture to pay for the GA contribution, which apparently had not yet happened.[296] The diplomatic offensive had no effect since there was contribution noted, but neither was the case heard again before the municipal court. No decision was recorded, although it was again clear that the origin of the shipmaster decided jurisdiction, even if the Scottish consuls had tried to claim jurisdiction.

4.5.3.3 Jurisdictional Disputes in the Antwerp Municipal Court

The presence of foreign merchants in Antwerp often led to jurisdictional problems on GA claims, especially between the Portuguese *natio* and the Castilian colony in the city. The two groups often participated in joint ventures and this could lead to jurisdictional problems.[297] The Portuguese were largely able to keep their jurisdictional privileges in maritime affairs, whilst the Castilians failed to establish a Consulate in the city despite repeated efforts.[298] In one 1557 case, the Portuguese consuls in Antwerp drew up a GA claim for damage that a ship incurred on its way from Lisbon to Antwerp.[299] The Portuguese merchants whose cargo was jettisoned filed a case against the (Castilian) insurers of the cargo, having insured it in Antwerp. The Castilian insurers were unwilling to pay, arguing that they could not be forced to pay for GA claims they had not been able to help draw up. Moreover, they claimed that they would only accept GA claims made under the auspices of the Castilian *natio* in Bruges, their *forum domicilii*. As many Castilian insurers may well have argued for a separate Antwerp-based Castilian *natio* around 1550, this was not a particularly strong argument. The municipal court, in its decision, pointed to the privileges of the Portuguese *natio* to draw up the calculus, even if it also cautioned that a GA calculus was generally drawn up with the input of everyone involved, including the insurers. The court ruled that the calculus was to be followed, but also

295 Ibidem. See for the consular jurisdiction: Davidson & Gray, *The Scottish Staple*, 361–404.
296 Ibidem, note 3.
297 De ruysscher, "*Naer het Romeinsch recht*", 117–120.
298 Goris, *Étude*, 46 & 66–68.
299 BE-SAA, *Vonnisboeken*, V#1245, fol. 120r–121r.

offered that the aldermen could act as brokers between the Castilian insurers and the Portuguese consuls to solve the dispute when trouble persisted.

A similar case was presented to the Antwerp aldermen in 1568. Two Castilian merchants, the brothers Alonso and Juan De Palma, requested the Antwerp aldermen to appoint a city official to aid the notary Jan de Berlaymont in adjusting a GA claim resulting from damage to a combined Castilian-Portuguese ship coming from São Tomé.[300] Initially, the aldermen granted this request, so that the calculus could be sent to the Iberian Peninsula for insurance purposes. The Portuguese secretary of the *natio*, Jehan Fernandes, filed a complaint claiming jurisdiction over the case. The Antwerp aldermen subsequently decided that the Portuguese consuls indeed had the inalienable right to draw up the calculus based on their privilege, as all ships coming from Portugal fell under the Portuguese *natio*. The Castilian merchants thus failed in their effort to justify their solution by seeking the blessing of the aldermen to draw up the calculus by their favoured average adjuster. This also confirms the importance of public backing for enforcement in Antwerp, notwithstanding that most actors in the GA and insurance business were private actors.

In 1579, the Castilians were finally able to win a GA case against the Portuguese. A Castilian ship was meant to sail from Portugal to Antwerp, but after a planned stop in the Bay of Biscay to load more cargo, the ship ended up in a French port as it was arrested by pirates. The cargo was unloaded there, meaning that the master did not stick to what had been agreed upon in the bill of lading and freight contract. The average adjusters appointed by the Castilian master had agreed to include the costs of the delay and the arrests into the GA calculus, meaning the Portuguese merchants had to contribute as well. The Portuguese, represented by their consuls, defended themselves with two arguments: first, the Portuguese consuls should have had the right to administer the case, because the ship came from Portugal; and second, the deviation of the route was unexplained, which cast doubt on the reason for the increased costs. The Portuguese therefore declined to pay both the freight money for the cargo and the GA claim, claiming jurisdiction over the case as well as accusing the shipmaster of negligence. The aldermen, however, decided that the arbitration clause included in the freight contract was binding and forced the Portuguese to pay. Moreover, the ship was considered Castilian as the shipmaster was Castilian, and so a common criterium applied. This shows that the

---

300 Idem, *Rekwestboeken 1566–1567*, inv. PK#640, fol. 148v–149v. The case is also described in: De Groote, *De zeeassurantie*, 22–23 & 144.

privileges were not considered to be binding, as the arbitration clause took precedence here.[301]

Courts had to deal with the long-held privileges of the *nationes*, which the latter of course vigorously defended in the power struggle over jurisdictional competence. Antwerp for example was unable to claw back jurisdiction from the Portuguese *natio* in the 1570s (as opposed to many other *nationes*), meaning the municipal court also had to comply with these agreements which were for example cemented in the 1582 *Impressae*.[302] Courts were generally rather reluctant to break with established practice anyway: both in Antwerp and Veere the origin of the shipmaster simply decided who had jurisdiction over GA cases, even if the *nationes* applied pressure in legal cases to claim jurisdiction. Despite the many private actors in the process, public-order backing was eventually crucial for GA procedure. This ensured predictability, and on jurisdiction the municipal courts were not willing to be innovative or apply new norms, wary of offending long-held privileges or meddling in sensitive controversies.

4.6 Conclusion

When a shipmaster incurred damage to cargo or ship, he had two basic options. The consular option was probably the most common one, but it had limited jurisdictional reach when inter-*natio* ventures became more common over the course of the sixteenth century. GA procedure for those ventures was, at first sight, largely a private-order solution, for notaries and private arbitrators solved almost all cases. However, this governance structure was clearly backed by the aldermen in Bruges and Antwerp, indicating the importance of the public-order backing.[303] From the late 1540s onwards, Antwerp asserted control over GA procedure in three ways, slowly freeing itself from the constraints set by Philip II and the Duke of Alva in the negotiations over the insurance framework: first, the court started hearing more GA cases itself; second, it clawed back on the jurisdiction of the *nationes*; and third, it established a licence system for Average adjusters.[304] Thereby it was able to largely offer

301 Idem, *Vonnisboeken*, V#1256, fol. 58v–59v.

302 Martyn, 'De Portugese natie', 83–84.

303 See Edwards & Ogilvie, 'What Lessons?'. See also section 4.4.4 for a rebuke of North's arguments about the perceived efficiency of arbitration.

304 De ruysscher, "*Naer het Romeinsch recht*", 118–121; De Groote, *De zeeassurantie*, 143–144.

open-access proceedings for GA disputes, in contrast to Bruges' governance system which was public-order but also relied heavily on the *nationes* for enforcement. Only a few *nationes* escaped Antwerp's assertive jurisdictional reach, the Portuguese among them: as the latter still had a wide jurisdiction over maritime affairs, enforcement remained particularised to a limited extent.[305] When the battle over control over GA procedure against the central government was won around 1578, Antwerp appeared to reverse to its former position of self-regulation by merchants and minimal oversight, although there is very little archival material for this period. As the Castilians remained in Bruges, intra-*natio* cases were still commonly heard by the Castilian consuls, although they were flexible in allowing various procedures when damage occurred.

The position of the shipmaster significantly changed during the sixteenth century, as he increasingly became an employee and agent of the venture. As a result, formal legislation had to set new rules for his position, responsibilities, and liability. A consequence was that increasingly merchants and masters had diametrically opposed interests when damage occurred. Pinning liability on the shipmaster was a common strategy for merchants to avoid payment of GA, which explains the increasing focus of formal legislation on what constituted negligence or barratrous behaviour by the master. In practice, however, providing proof was rather hard. Masters had, to a certain extent, an information advantage, as they filed GA claims and thus could control the start of the procedure, often trying to have PA declared to evade liability for any contribution. When no crew members turned on the shipmaster, merchants had a hard time proving fraudulent or negligent behaviour. Only in glaring cases of fraudulent behaviour were shipmasters unmasked, and this explains why GA or PA cases were rarely litigated.

When liability could not be put explicitly on shipmasters' negligence, merchants sought other strategies to evade payment of GA. Starting in the late 1540s, a new strategy was to shift payment to the insurer. Although hard to prove, this tactic may have contributed to the rise in GA cases, as merchants and shipmasters could collude to force an insurer to cover the damage. A certain degree of moral hazard was clear: rather than opposing the shipmaster, an alliance with the master against the insurer was more advantageous for merchants to pass on their GA contribution to a third party (i.e. the underwriter). This was made easier by precedents set by the municipal court of Antwerp, which from at least 1548 onwards accepted the liability of the insurer to pay for GA contributions. The assertion that Bruges also allowed for this principle cannot be sustained

305 Ibidem.

by the available evidence, making it a distinct sixteenth-century development in the Low Countries.[306]

Although most GA cases could be solved in a straightforward manner, in some cases courts had to find solutions outside of established norms. The chapter considered three such legal practice questions: bottomry and GA, ship collisions, and jurisdictional disputes. Regarding bottomry, courts generally tended to tread carefully, whereas on ship collisions courts opted for solutions that did not (yet) exist in formal law. Foreshadowing the 1608 *Compilatae*, both the Antwerp municipal court and the Great Council allowed cases to be solved by GA rather than contributory negligence. This was particularly surprising for the Great Council, as the solution formally contradicted the Habsburg *Ordonnances*. In Antwerp, most solutions preceded formal law. In contrast, most courts took a conservative line in jurisdictional disputes, taking the origin of the shipmaster as the deciding factor in allocating jurisdiction. In the case of the Portuguese, the Antwerp municipal court for example held up their privileges as Antwerp was unable to claw down on the jurisdiction of that *natio*. Both the Antwerp municipal court and Great Council were however willing to provide legal security to merchants by following precedence and equity as much as possible, as De ruysscher has already pointed out for Antwerp.[307]

Developments in mercantile and legal practice were crucial to clarify the role of the various risk management tools available to merchants, particularly as merchants increasingly used a number of tools at the same time. At various points in time, different interests decided what strategy parties in the interest community followed, necessarily leading to disputes over the exact application of GA. As merchants were confronted with new risks, applying GA to a new situation could be useful, even if formal law did not yet accept this solution.[308] Faced with the increased use of insurance, Antwerp legal practice allowed for the liability of insurers to pay for GA claims in the 1540s, potentially diminishing the speculative use of insurance as insurers were now also liable for GA claims. The aldermen offered legal security by consistently ruling on cases arising and eventually incorporating the principle into the 1608 *Compilatae*.[309] It thus provided an unofficial legal rule of thumb ('insurers should pay for GA damage') before it finally incorporated this legal principle into municipal law. This contributed to the operationally efficient combination of risk management institutions even before formal law had accepted this. Yet this was the result of the

306 De Groote, *De zeeassurantie*, 23.

307 De ruysscher, "*Naer het Romeinsch recht*", 381.

308 Following Friedman, *The Legal System*.

309 In line with: Ibidem; Idem, 'Maxims, Principles and Legal Change'.

long negotiations between interested stakeholders, both over governance and content aspects of both GA and insurance. Therefore, we can again observe that the interplay *between* institutions was key, as the development of GA was part of a larger package of institutional development.[310] GA subsequently contributed to the transfer from 'uncertainty' to 'risk' as it covered anticipatable hazards *ex post* next to the *ex ante* transfer of risk under insurance.[311]

---

310 Ogilvie, '"Whatever is, is Right?"', 681.

311 Knight, *Risk, Uncertainty, and Profit*, 247–253; North, *Institutions*, 126; Dreijer, 'Maritime Averages'.

PART 2

Varieties of Averages and Cost Management

CHAPTER 5

Contractual Varieties of Averages and Cost Management

5.1 Introduction

This chapter studies the development of varieties of Averages and how this established a system of *cost* management next to a system of *risk* management. It focuses both on the cost management varieties developed in the Low Countries itself and the Castilian *flete y averías*. As Chapter 3 showed, Small or Common Average (SA) was defined in formal law in the 1551 *Ordonnance*. However, in legal practice SA was already commonly used. Merchants in Antwerp, for example, already used SA in the 1520s under that very name, *averij-commune*.[1] Varieties of Averages allowed merchants to manage costs that could not be covered by tools of risk management, as these costs were both predictable and foreseeable and therefore would always be incurred. Ongoing developments in cost management made it clear who in the interest community should be held liable for certain costs, offering legal security to all involved. Proper cost management lowered transaction costs, particularly enforcement costs. Secondly, it also limited risk, for example as ordinary pilotage was covered in a freight contract, diminishing the risk of damage when sailing into port. Yet the development of varieties of Averages, and more specifically Contractual Average (CA), requires further analysis, as Averages were deliberately 'contractualised' (i.e. put into a freight contract).[2] Although there is no evidence that merchants were unhappy with the existence of GA, they were searching for greater legal security even when this meant covering the operational or protection costs of a venture. It appears that from the mid-fifteenth century onwards, merchants used similar instruments to manage costs as precisely as possible. Merchants, notaries and lawyers reoriented freight contracts to cover the common operational costs of the venture.

This chapter also returns to the debate on the *lex maritima*. As sections 5.3.1 and 5.3.2 show, freight contracts partitioning Averages often contained phrases like the 'customs of the sea' (*costuymen vander zee*). For 'mercatorists', this may

1 De ruysscher, 'Maxims, Principles and Legal Change'.

2 See Van Niekerk, *The Development*, 64–65.

 DOI:10.1163/9789004540354_006

well sound like evidence which proves their theory that merchants developed a customary mercantile law to which they could appeal.[3] However, as Chapter 3 also showed, the existence of the *lex maritima* is based on a misguided view of the medieval and early modern world. In the Antwerp freight contracts, the term 'customs of the sea' were common as references. For merchants from various regions across Europe, such a reference could establish a base line in freight contracts, but it could by no means stop them from applying their own norms and customs when applying to courts. The chapter therefore argues that explanations other than a *lex maritima* should be sought. Instead, as freight was a fixed sum and the 'Averages' (i.e. the operational costs of the venture) could vary, the phrase rather gave the shipmaster the necessary flexibility to incur costs such as pilotage, without an exact monetary contribution that was already defined before the venture. Phrases such as 'customs of the sea' thus implied this flexibility rather than autonomous rules on GA.

This chapter relies on similar notarial records and court cases as studied in the last chapter, with a particular focus on the France-Low Countries trade and records from Zeeland, as most ventures ended or started there.[4] In a prelude (section 5.2.1), the section first explores the link between freight, Averages and the operational costs of a maritime venture. Sections 5.2.2 and 5.2.3 analyse the inclusion of operational costs in freight contracts and its legal development, showing the development from early Averages used for common operational costs up to the more sophisticated use of Contractual Average which also included protection costs or even PA losses. Section 5.2.4 studies the (limited number of) disputes on the cost management varieties that were heard by the various courts. Section 5.3.1 analyses the *flete y averías*, pointing out both the similarities and the differences to the local cost management varieties, whilst section 5.3.2 offers an in-depth look at the negotiations over pilotage costs by the Castilians included in the *flete y averías*. The chapter then concludes (section 5.4), returning to the issues of risk versus cost management and the *lex maritima*.

---

3 See for example: Tetley, 'The General Maritime Law'.

4 There are two reasons for this. First, most sixteenth-century voyages started or ended in Zeeland, turning the coastal towns into hubs of maritime transport; second, source editions are very easily accessible and complete, even if the actual archival files were destroyed by German bombardments in World War II. See for example: Z.W. Sneller & Unger (eds.), *Bronnen tot de geschiedenis van de handel met Frankrijk* (2 Vols.) (The Hague 1930–1942) (hereafter: Sneller & Unger, *Bronnen Frankrijk*); Unger, *Bronnen Middelburg*.

5.2 Contractual Varieties of Averages

5.2.1 *Prelude: Freight, Averages and Cost Management*

Quintin Weytsen's statement that tolls, duties and Averages were closely related may seem somewhat bewildering at first sight.[5] On closer inspection, however, such a statement makes sense considering the structure of the maritime economy and the operational role of the shipmaster. As the following sections show, freight contracts often included promises to pay 'freight and Average' to the shipmaster after the venture. In the Low Countries, freight (i.e. the wage of the shipmaster) and all other operational costs were strictly separated in the freight contracts, although they had to be paid at the same time, namely upon safe arrival. The operational costs included pilotage, tolls and custom duties; in short, every expense that ensured the safe arrival of the voyage.[6] During the sixteenth century these operational costs were called Common or Small Average (SA), but were also simply named 'Average' before that time, signifying a contribution made by merchants towards the common operational costs of the interest community.[7] Among other costs such as pilotage, this included tolls and custom duties.

Tolls were common as feudal rights were still exercised during the late medieval period.[8] Bruges consolidated jurisdictional control over most ante-ports (such as Damme) in the mid-fourteenth century, with the notable exception of Sluis.[9] Sluis constantly infringed on the staple rights of Bruges.[10] Under the staple rights, merchants simply paid once and were henceforward excepted from additional duties. Foreign merchants were generally exempt from most tolls and duties, except for the ones levied by the *natio* itself.[11] Yet in the Zwin area, both Sluis and Bruges acted as staples and levied tolls, duties and taxes, with Sluis even constructing a comital castle in 1385 to control access to the Zwin militarily.[12] The silting of the Zwin led many foreign merchants to sail

---

5 See for an in-depth analysis of Weytsen's work and its connection to SA: De ruysscher, 'Maxims, Principles and Legal Change'.

6 These were the most common costs noted in the freight contracts, but many other costs were included, such as food for the crew members, ropes, and the anchor.

7 Addobbati, 'Principles and Inferences'.

8 Goris, *Étude*, 176–177; Degryse, 'Brugge en de pilotage', 267; De Smedt, *De Engelse natie* (Vol. 2), 208–240; Maes, 'Twee arresten', 167–188; Zijlmans, *Troebele betrekkingen*, 267–277; Doeleman, 'Zeggenschap op de Honte'; Idem, 'Le tonlieu Zélandaise'.

9 Dumolyn & Leloup, 'The Zwin Estuary', 208–209.

10 Ibidem. See also section 1.5.

11 Goris, *Étude*, 175–178.

12 Dumolyn & Leloup, 'The Zwin Estuary', 208–209.

to Zeeland and load the cargo onto smaller ships for pilotage to Bruges.[13] In 1486–1487, Maximilian of Austria reorganised the toll regime in Sluis, giving the local skippers' guild the opportunity to levy a duty on all incoming ships, including Iberian ones, further undermining Bruges' control over the Zwin following her support for the Flemish Revolt (whereas Sluis was allied with Maximilian).[14] This proxy dispute between Bruges and Sluis therefore severely impacted foreign merchants' transaction costs, as tolls were levied both by Sluis and Bruges.

In the Scheldt area, tolls on the Honte (today called the Western Scheldt) were also the subject of battles over political and economic control.[15] Antwerp, Bergen-op-Zoom and several towns in Zeeland for example tried to control the Honte. Long before access to the Honte became a political problem between the Dutch Republic and the Southern Netherlands, the question of who was allowed to extract tolls there was already a major political and legal question, leading to repeated litigation at the Great Council.[16] Jurisdiction over the levying of tolls on the river was not properly fixed as multiple towns and cities claimed jurisdiction (all levying their own tolls), also raising transaction costs for merchants.[17] This was the case until in 1531, Antwerp outbid the other towns for control over the toll by paying the central government for this privilege, consolidating control over the Honte.[18] Yet this was not the only toll that had to be paid before entering Antwerp. There was also the so-called *Riddertol* and some lesser ones, although foreign *nationes* were mostly exempted.[19] The way the tolls were levied changed: until the late fifteenth century, these were mainly levied on ships rather than cargo (hence the connection to the operational costs of the ship), whilst those levied on cargo became more common during the sixteenth century.[20] This shifted the costs largely to merchants, although the 1563 *Ordonnance* still stipulated a contribution by the shipmaster as well.[21] Weytsen also appeared unsure as to how the costs for tolls should

---

13 Degryse, 'Brugge en de pilotage', 108–109.

14 Gilliodts-Van Severen & Gaillard, *Inventaire* (Vol. 6), 274–277, specifically 275–276; Dumolyn & Leloup, 'The Zwin Estuary', 208–209.

15 Maes, 'Twee arresten', 172–183; Wijffels, 'Ius Commune and International Wine Trade', 289–292; Idem, 'Flanders and the Scheldt Question: A Mirror of the Law of International Relations and its Actors', *Sartoniana*, 15 (2002), 213–280, there 214–232; Zijlmans, *Troebele betrekkingen*, 267–277.

16 Maes, 'Twee arresten'; Wijffels, 'Ius Commune'; Doeleman, 'Zeggenschap op de Honte'.

17 Zijlman, *Troebele betrekkingen*, 267–274.

18 Ibidem, 274–275.

19 Goris, *Étude*, 176–177.

20 De ruysscher, 'Maxims, Principles and Legal Change', 269–270.

21 Ibidem.

be redistributed among the interest community, for he acknowledged that the master was often simply an agent for the venture rather than a stakeholder, but did still stick to a contribution to the operational costs by the master.[22]

Besides tolls, shipmasters also had to pay several port duties on behalf of the interest community. These payments also had to be paid to the shipmaster together with the freight, although again these costs fell under the 'Average' category specified in freight contracts. Port duties included so-called *lichgelt*, a duty paid to keep a ship in port;[23] *cranegelt*, a duty to use the crane in a port to unload cargo;[24] and so-called *ankeragegeld* (anchor money), a duty paid when a ship docked in Zeeland.[25] Sometimes temporary tolls were levied on foreign merchants as well, as we have also seen above in the case of Sluis and the Castilian merchants.[26] This raised costs for merchants, although in times of peace this did probably not impede too much on merchants' ability to trade.

5.2.2 *'Freight and Average' in the France-Low Countries Wine and Woad Trade*

In fifteenth-century and early sixteenth-century notarial archives, the term 'freight and Average' can often be found in the context of the France-Low Countries trade, more specifically wine and woad from Bordeaux and La Rochelle to Zeeland.[27] Freight contracts often stated that merchants promised to pay 'freight and Average' to the shipmaster when he delivered cargo in a proper state (i.e. upon safe arrival).[28] 'Freight and Average' did not denote a specific variety of Average, but the Average specified in those contracts would later be named SA. Freight contracts were primarily used to regulate the pooling and sharing of common costs.[29] In short, freight contracts are an excellent

22 Ibidem.

23 See below for the 1557 settlement for *lichgelt*.

24 Goris, *Étude*, 170–171.

25 De Smedt, *De Engelse natie* (Vol. 2), 236–237.

26 Ibidem, 237–240.

27 Woad was a plant necessary for the dyeing industry and was commonly grown in France. See for an overview of the France-Low Countries trade and the role of woad: Coornaert, *Les Francais* (Vol. 2), 98–121. Yet 'freight and Average' was not a specifically north-western European phenomenon. Evidence for similar structures can be found in Portugal, for example. In 1460, 'freight and Average' was paid by the shipmaster of the *Lodrea* on the Lisbon-Porto Pisano route, specified by cargo. See: *Fondazione Istituto Internazionale di Storia Economica "F. Datini"* (hereafter IT-DAT), Fondo Archivio Federigo Melis, inv. III.IV.7/9, nr. 248, cc. 97s/d. I thank Maria Fusaro for help and Francesco Ammannati and Federica Nigro for sending scans of the documents.

28 See for safe arrival and Averages: De ruysscher, 'Maxims, Principles and Legal Change', 270–271.

29 Ibidem.

source to study the use of Averages for cost management purposes before such varieties were acknowledged in formal sources of law. Conflicts about these Averages were rare, as the point of these freight contracts was precisely to provide legal security and prevent conflict.[30] This, in turn, lowered transaction costs for all parties in the venture, as enforcement costs were lowered. Disputes were primarily handled by notaries. Despite the relative vagueness of the 'freight and Average' clause, it was commonly included in fifteenth- and sixteenth-century freight contracts. The subsequent development of 'proper' Contractual Average often specified in greater detail the liability of all the parties, aiming to further minimise conflict about cost management.

The freight contracts studied here were primarily recorded by French notaries, yet shipmasters and merchants from the Low Countries figure prominently. These freight contracts also show that 'Averages' often included tolls and port duties.[31] In these fifteenth-century contracts, the clause of safe arrival was the singular prerequisite for the payment of 'freight and Average' by merchants. Safe arrival, more specifically, meant the safe unloading and delivery of cargo in the port of arrival: the *crane* usually formed the marker as the end-point of the shipping voyage.[32] This was important as it demarcated clearly to what extent and up to what point merchants and masters had to contribute to the cost management exercise. One notarial deed, dating from 8 February 1460, recorded a promise by three Zeeland innkeepers, on behalf of their foreign guests, that 'freight and Average' would be paid when the shipmaster delivered wine at the *crane* in Middelburg, Zeeland.[33] If any additional Averages or damage occurred after this point, hostellers and merchants had to pay these

30 For this research, two source collections have been primarily used: Sneller & Unger, *Bronnen Frankrijk*; Unger, *Bronnen Middelburg*. I have also taken samples as a check from source editions of French notarial archives, which in some cases overlap with the two source editions named above. Volume 1 covers the notarial records of La Rochelle, Volume 2 covers Bordeaux. See: M.A. Drost (ed.), *Documents pour server à l'histoire du commerce des Pays-Bas avec la France jusqu'à 1585* (Vol. 1) (The Hague 1983) (hereafter: Drost, *Documents*), nrs. 467 & 468; Idem (Vol. 2) (The Hague 1989), nrs. 74, 93, 126, 137, 138, 190, 239, 273. This latter source edition contains over 50 references to Averages, including pilotage and 'freight and Average'. I refer to the number of the document in the source edition rather than the pages, since the index also refers to these numbers.

31 Weytsen, *Een Tractaet van Avarien*, 10; De ruysscher, 'Maxims, Principles and Legal Change'. Indeed, pilotage costs between Flushing and Antwerp were considered 'common': Coornaert, *Les Français* (Vol. 2), 218.

32 The *crane* was a convenient landmark signalling the formal end of the shipping passage, but the instrument was used to lift heavy cargo from a ship, for which a contribution was paid by those in the interest community. To be clear, the duty to use the *crane* and unload the cargo was often still included in the Averages.

33 Sneller & Unger, *Bronnen Frankrijk* (Vol. 1), nr. 206.

costs.[34] In a Bruges municipal court judgement dating from 2 March 1469, two Castilian merchants were summoned to pay for 'freight and Average' after wine in a ship leaked after a collision in the port of Sluis.[35] The municipal court referred to Article 15 of the *Vonnisse*, stating that both parties had to contribute half of the compensation by means of contributory negligence.[36] Since the shipmaster had fulfilled his contractual duties (i.e. safe arrival), the merchants were forced to pay for freight and additional costs (i.e. Averages).

A significant number of freight contracts stated that merchants were liable for 'all Averages' (*de toutes avaries*).[37] As merchants were of course also liable for potential GA, this was true in theory.[38] However, in most cases this would have meant the operational costs, as most freight contracts stipulated that this meant tolls, duties and other costs associated with the operational aspect of the venture. This also explains why these costs were legally distinct from the freight, as the latter was a fixed sum, while Averages, in contrast, could vary. In the sixteenth century, a number of freight contracts stated that 'freight and Average' would be paid after the 'customs of the sea' or similar wordings.[39] As has already been argued, this gave parties leeway to interpret the rules according to local customs (hence stimulating legal pluralism), for example when a dispute came before a French court rather than in the Low Countries, or vice-versa. Rather than being symbolic of a *lex maritima*, it probably had the opposite effect. This may also explain why defined monetary contributions were rare: occurring in only one contract from 1531, when the merchant Pierre de Sabaros promised to pay a contribution of four pounds *Grooten Vlaams* for Averages.[40] Otherwise, the exact liability was left in the void so as to give flexibility to the shipmaster to incur costs for the voyage within certain limits.

---

34 Ibidem.

35 Gilliodts-Van Severen, *Coutumes* (Vol. 2), 109. See also: BE-SAB, Civiele Sententiën Vierschaar, 1469–70, inv. 157, fol. 42v, nr. 1. They were summoned to pay 21 lb. Great Flemish pounds.

36 Ibidem. *Vonnisse van Damme*, Art. 15. See also section 3.3.2. This is one of the few remaining references to the *Vonnisse* in judgements from the Bruges' municipal court, at least to my knowledge.

37 Sneller & Unger, *Bronnen Frankrijk* (Vol. 1), nrs. 406, 407, 431, 447, 457, 461, 467, 593, 637, 682 & 720.

38 As for example Ibidem, nr. 431 shows. See also nr. 447.

39 See for example Sneller & Unger, *Bronnen Frankrijk* (Vol. 1), nrs. 580, 637, 682, 715, 718 & 720; Ibidem, *Bronnen Frankrijk* (Vol. 2), nr. 827; Coornaert, *Les Français* (Vol. 2), 225, footnote 5 & 232 for some other examples of similar clauses. Other documents confirm this. See for example: Drost, *Documents* (Vol. 1), nrs. 467 & 468; Idem (Vol. 2), nrs, 74, 93, 126, 137, 138, 190, 239, 273.

40 Ibidem, nr. 593.

Besides the French notarial archives, one can find indications for the common use of 'freight and Average' in the France-Low Countries trade in archives across Zeeland and Holland.[41] Already in 1460, three Middelburg merchants promised in an oath before the city's aldermen to pay the La Rochelle shipmaster Jan Dolo 'freight and Average' when the wine would be delivered.[42] Other freight contracts and court cases from the sixteenth century contain similar clauses.[43] Again, 'customs of the sea' and similar phrases appeared frequently.[44]

In short, all sorts of operational costs were covered by Averages, including tolls, custom and port duties. All these costs would later be termed Small or Common Average (SA, *averij-commune* in Dutch), a clear nod to the operational 'common' costs it was supposed to cover, which did not significantly differ from 'freight and Average' except that it was more frequently included in freight contracts via Contractual Average (CA).[45] These clauses support the hypothesis that parties in maritime ventures preferred stable and foreseeable costs, and hence established these techniques of cost management. Although the costs for Average could vary according to the circumstances, the inclusion of such clauses offered clarity about liability for all parties in the interest community.

5.2.3 *The Development of Contractual Average*

Following the widespread use of 'freight and Average' clauses, Contractual Average (CA) developed during the sixteenth century in Antwerp. Van Niekerk has been the sole author pointing to the existence of Contractual Average in the early modern Low Countries.[46] Van Niekerk however interpreted the instrument as one for contractualising GA, something that is not supported by the available sources for Antwerp. Contractual Average was primarily used to record liability for both foreseeable costs and small damage between participants in the venture, combining costs of Small Average and (more rarely) protection costs and Particular Average.[47] The inclusion of small damage (i.e. PA) and explicit protection costs such as artillery was the major difference between 'freight and Average' and SA on the hand and CA on the other. CA aimed to minimise conflict after the voyage, and provided merchants with predictable foreseeable costs and hence lower transaction costs. Even if CA simply

41 For the remainder of this section, I refer primarily to: Unger, *Bronnen Middelburg*.
42 Unger, *Bronnen Middelburg* (Vol. 3), nr. 237.
43 Smit, *Bronnen Engeland*, nrs. 236 & 280.
44 Sneller & Unger, *Bronnen Frankrijk* (Vol. 2), nrs. 19, 58, 69, 88, 126 & 130.
45 Van Niekerk, *The Development*, 64.
46 Ibidem, 65–66.
47 Ibidem; Goris, *Étude*, 71.

recorded liability for SA and (potential) PA costs, it was a popular instrument among Antwerp merchants.[48]

The development of CA coincided with a more widespread use of contributions for SA.[49] Freight contracts of CA could also contain clauses to divide potential damage, in effect mutualising PA among the interest community. Moreover, as artillery was uninsurable, new ways had to be found to cover damage to artillery when GA did not apply. This may have been inspired by the Spanish varieties, although we should note the important difference that under CA the obligation was contractual and paid after the voyage.[50] Merchants and shipmaster could for example share damages to the ship, something which should normally only be borne by the ship-owners. This technique was especially common when the use of shipping insurance was not yet widespread in Antwerp during the 1520s and 1530s.[51] CA was always recorded in the freight contract by notaries, similar to 'freight and Average': moreover, they largely handled potential conflicts afterwards.[52] Freight contracts could, in principle, also be registered with the Antwerp aldermen.[53] CA was also used by English and German merchants, who were generally more reluctant than Iberian merchants to adopt new techniques for managing maritime risk, as they preferred more conservative techniques such as cargo spreading.[54] For example, in 1564 the English merchant Thomas Heyden promised to pay SA costs to the shipmaster Anthonis Nobel for a journey to Topsham and Bordeaux.[55] Because the English Merchant Adventurers strictly enforced their monopoly on the cloth

48 Dreijer, 'Maritime Averages', 46–49.

49 De ruysscher, 'Belgium', 113 & 116; Idem, 'Maxims, Principles and Legal Change'. This development was of course already also observable in the fifteenth century.

50 Fagel, *De Hispano-Vlaamse wereld*, 484.

51 Idem, 'Antwerp 1490–1590', 96; Van der Wee, *The Growth* (Vol. 2), 327–328.

52 BE- SAA, Notariaat Streyt, inv. N#3132 & N#3133; Notariaat 's-Hertoghen, inv. N#2070–N#2078; BE-RAA, Notariaat De Platae, nr. 1, fol. 63r–64r.

53 Two 1557 freight contracts were for example registered with the Antwerp aldermen, both containing clauses on Averages. See: BE-SAA, Schepenregisters 1550–1599, 1557 Register GA I, inv. SR#265, fol. 168v–169v & 290r. See also: Cassiers, *Bijdrage*, 77–78. Due to time limitations, I have decided to focus on the notarial archives, given that most freight contracts were probably registered with notaries and most are both in form and content rather similar to each other. See for the notaries: BE-SAA, Notariaat Streyt, inv. N#3132 & N#3133; Idem, Notariaat 's-Hertoghen, inv. N#2070–N#2078; BE-RAA, Notariaat De Platea, nr. 1, fol. 63r–64r.

54 De Smedt, *De Engelse natie* (Vol. 2), 259–261 & 297–303; Harreld, *High Germans*, 174. 'S-Hertoghen appears to have functioned as a 'trusted notary' for Southern German and Hanseatic merchants.

55 BE-SAA, Vonnisboeken, V1246, fol. 197v: "*gemeyne avarye naer usantie van der zee*".

trade, merchants often loaded onto ships owned by the Merchant Adventurers, decreasing the necessity for individual freight contracts in many cases.[56]

Jan-Albert Goris already noted that Iberian merchants regularly included SA in freight contracts, as the compulsory contributions could not be used for every venture but mutual protection costs had to be covered.[57] Indeed, as sixteenth-century freight contracts often included multiple merchants, the division of liability between the merchants should also be made clear. Since pilotage costs could be steep, it was often decided that these costs would be split among the partners in the venture, enabling merchants to assess the costs upfront. Indeed, a freight contract recorded by Willem Streyt on 14 June 1535 shows that SA was divided among various Spanish merchants before a voyage.[58] This did not only enable cost management, but also helped in the transfer from uncertainty to risk.[59] In a GA calculation of 1535, Streyt also included SA costs (*avería comun*), primarily for pilotage on the river and to avoid running aground on a shoal.[60] The ship had also incurred additional damage, which was brought into GA, including costs for the notary in Seville who had registered testimonies there.[61] Examples of CA abound in the Antwerp notarial archives.[62] Almost all clauses referred to the 'customs and usages of the sea' or a very similar phrase, similar to 'freight and Average'.[63] In many freight contracts, operational costs such as tolls and duties were included in the Averages. Streyt however also included uninsurable costs such as artillery in a freight contract by CA.[64] In such cases, both the upfront costs for artillery and potential damage to the artillery were borne by the participants in the venture.

56 De Smedt, *De Engelse natie* (Vol. 2), 240–248.

57 Goris, *Étude*, 173.

58 BE-SAA, Notariaat Streyt, N#3132 (1535), fol. 57v–58r.

59 Following Knight, *Risk, Uncertainty, and Profit*, 247–253.

60 BE-SAA, Notariaat Streyt, N#3132 (1535), fol. 9r–v. See also Chapter 4 for the tables and the role of notaries in GA calculations.

61 Ibidem.

62 See for a more expansive analysis of CA: Dreijer, 'Maritime Averages', 46–49. As the contracts are very repetitive, I have chosen to simply refer to them in the footnotes.

63 For example: BE-RAA, Notariaat De Platea, nr. 1, fol. 63r–64r; BE-SAA, Notariaat 's-Hertoghen, N#2072 (1545), fol. 70r–73r; Idem, N#2073 (1547), fol. 13r–14r; Idem, Notariaat Streyt, N#3132, fols. 56r–57v, 57v–58r, 70r, 71r–72r, 95r–v; N#3133, fol. 165r–166r. Transcription of the latter also in: Goris, *Étude*, 630–632; Idem, Notariaat Streyt, N#3132, fol. 52v–53r, for example states: "*avecques toutes les avaries communes, tant dela que decha – sans toutesfois l'ancoirage – en telle sorte et maniere*". See also : Sneller & Unger, *Bronnen Frankrijk* (Vol. 2), nr. 23; Goris, *Étude*, 639. Based on: Archives of the Museum Plantin-Moretus (hereafter BE-MPM), *Handel en Scheepvaart Varia*, nr. 1074–1; Van Answaarden, *Les Portugais*, nr. 42 (p. 295). Based on: BE-ARB, Grote Raad, *Beroepen uit Holland*, inv. A110, nr. 904. For tolls: BE-SAA, Notariaat Streyt, N#1232, fol. 58v–59r & fol. 71v–72r.

64 BE-SAA, Notariaat Streyt, N#1232, fol. 56r–57v & 71v–72r; N#3133 (1540), fol. 96v–97v.

Why did merchants use CA? Since only Johan van Niekerk has identified the phenomenon, we are largely left in the dark about this subject.[65] CA was not only common practice in the Southern Low Countries, but also in late sixteenth- and early seventeenth-century Amsterdam.[66] Amsterdam's international market made contractual and legal security important, but that was the case for Antwerp as well. In sixteenth-century Antwerp, CA was commonly used by merchants, pointing to a need for the greater legal security which cost management in a freight contract could offer. The increasing 'juridification' of mercantile practice and the need for greater legal security benefited notaries, as their signature improved power in court under the *Ius Commune*.[67] Clearly, Contractual Average was not a technique set in stone, and could be used by parties in the interest community as they wished. Because it was unregulated it could contain both PA and SA.[68] There were no strict rules about the partition of costs in the interest community, although it appears that there were some customary rules.

Take the example of ordinary pilotage, where a shipmaster customarily paid 2/3 of the costs, while the merchants involved covered the remaining 1/3.[69] One the one hand, the master had to be knowledgeable about the route, but in some ports compulsory pilotage was required, or a master decided that it was better to take out pilots to diminish the chance of damage to the ship or cargo.[70] This was thus a pragmatic solution, for it made sure the shipmaster was given the freedom to act to arrive safely, but also limited costs. In Antwerp, the safe arrival clause so commonly found in the fifteenth-century contracts was quietly replaced, as this made shipmasters hesitant to jettison cargo or make other necessary decisions to save the venture.[71] Safe arrival was of course still the goal, but in the Antwerp freight contracts there was a double-edged development towards increasing masters' liability and a greater freedom of action for the master, allowing the master and crew to take necessary decisions and minimise damage. Although no calculation was made beforehand, freight contracts show that merchants actively worked to manage foreseeable costs upfront.

---

65 Van Niekerk, *The Development*, 65–66.

66 I wish to thank Cátia Antunes (Leiden University) for providing access to a database of Amsterdam notarial archives, with the following numbers: 1/615v; 68/59; 32/11/76; 50/39v; 81/108; 82/170. All these documents include references to CA.

67 De ruysscher, "*Naer het Romeinsch recht*", 17–18.

68 Van Niekerk, *The Development*, 65–66.

69 Weytsen, *Een Tractaet van Avarien*, 10; De ruysscher, 'Maxims, Principles and Legal Change'.

70 Ibidem. See also: Rossi, 'The Liability of the Shipmaster', 29–33.

71 De ruysscher, 'Maxims, Principles and Legal Change', 270.

5.2.4 *Disputes at the Municipal Courts*

Even if contractual forms of Averages were meant to prevent conflicts, disputes could still arise, yet they appear to have been extremely rare. Most were solved by the same notary who had drafted the contract to minimise costs. However, some disputes on the operational costs of the venture reached the Antwerp municipal court and those offer some (limited) insights on the structures of cost management. The issue of pilotage was one of the few contentious topics.

Both in Bruges and Antwerp, one can find a few disputes on operational costs. In Bruges, one case concerned the payment of 'freight and Average', when the Genoese merchant Andulo Lommelin (Lomellini) in 1452 claimed small damage to a ship from Berdard Salat, who represented the Catalan merchant Saldon Ferrier in Bruges.[72] By mutual agreement, the court appointed an arbitration panel of three Florentine merchants to assess the damage, which they estimated at sixteen pounds *Grooten Vlaams*.[73] These costs were to be paid independently of the freight and other Averages (i.e. the operational costs) and shared between the two parties, with Andulo promising to bring the assessment to the municipal court for homologation (i.e. approval). This shows that 'freight and Average' indeed did not concern damage, which had to be divided outside of the freight contract. On 30 April 1532, a shipmaster only named as Machuyt filed a complaint at the Veere municipal court against the son of Lieven Stevens, who acted as the representative for the German merchant Jacob Welser.[74] During a heavy storm, Machuyt had jettisoned Welser's cargo.[75] Stevens claimed that he and Welser did not have to pay for the GA claim since the freight contract excluded payments of Averages to the shipmaster.[76] The Veere aldermen however sentenced Stevens to pay the damages *pro rata*, as it was likely impossible to contractualise oneself out of GA at this point in time.[77] Similar cases are found in the Antwerp archives from 1567 and 1570, in both cases following complaints by merchants unwilling to pay for (additional) SA costs, having already agreed on a range of contributions before the voyage.[78]

72 Gilliodts-Van Severen, *Espagne*, 52; Idem, *Cartulaire* (Vol. 2), nr. 915.

73 Ibidem.

74 Sneller & Unger, *Bronnen Frankrijk* (Vol. 2), nr. 18.

75 Ibidem.

76 Ibidem. These contracts, so-called *vrij van avarij* ('free of Average') did exist in the Dutch Republic but were very uncommon before the seventeenth century. See: Van Niekerk, *The Development*, 1035–1052.

77 See section 3.2.5 for 'free of Average' clauses in Antwerp municipal law.

78 BE-SAA, V#1250, fol. 236r; Idem, V#1253, fol. 4v–5v.

Pilotage was an especially contentious topic and was discussed at length in the 1608 *Compilatae* and in Weytsen's work, for example.[79] In one 1566 case heard in Antwerp, the shipmaster was allowed to levy additional SA costs on merchants after testifying that he had done everything in his power to minimise those costs.[80] Although he had incurred additional, unforeseen, pilotage costs, the master also left crew members onshore in both Bordeaux and an unnamed English port to minimise crew wages and food costs. Only after crew members testified to this end, both a notary and the Antwerp municipal court ordered merchants to pay additional Averages to the master. A 1570 Antwerp municipal court case concerned a complaint that the costs for ordinary pilotage were too high.[81] The plaintiff claimed that he had already contributed to Averages for these purposes, although the shipmaster had requested another contribution for common pilotage. According to the merchant, the master himself should also have contributed. In the end, the court allowed the merchant file a case at the municipal court, but only under the condition that he conditionally paid a *namptissement*. The conclusion of this case is not recorded.

Merchants started litigation on the operational costs in only a very limited number of cases, for example when costs skyrocketed. As freight contracts often clearly demarcated the liabilities of everyone involved in the venture, disputes were rare. We could therefore say that the tools for cost management were relatively successful, as the freight contracts both minimised disputes and managed costs effectively.

5.3 The *flete y averías* as a Cost Management Structure

5.3.1 *The* flete y averías

The *flete y averías* was a cost management structure for the operational costs of the venture, administered by the respective *Consulados* and *nationes* of Burgos and Bilbao. It thus differed from the local cost management structures such as SA in that the obligation did not (solely) lie in the underlying interest community of the venture, but also in the obligation to pay the respective *Consulado* or *natio* administering the payment and setting the rules. Yet in most other respects, the instrument was very similar: for merchants, the advantage must have been in the fact that the *natio* bargained for collective lower costs which

79 1608 *Costuymen*, Part 4, Title VIII, Arts. 120–132; Weytsen, *Een tractaet van avarien*, 1–2.

80 BE-SAA, *Vonnisboeken*, V#1249, fol. 4v.

81 Idem, V#1252, fol. 125v.

were paid by the *flete y averías*, most importantly on pilotage (see next section). It is not mentioned in any of the privileges for the Iberian *nationes*, but as both the Burgos and Bilbao *Consulado* had the privilege to levy and administer the *flete y averías* (sometimes also called *flete mas averías*), the *nationes* may by extension have had the same privilege, or were forced to participate by their mother-organisation.[82] This also makes it likely that control over the instrument was granted to the merchant organisations at the end of the fifteenth or early sixteenth century: the first recorded evidence of payment by a Castilian merchant in the Low Countries comes from 1511.[83] As the archival records of the Biscayers have not survived, the already limited information on the instrument besides the mention in the privileges of the *Consulados* is restricted to the Castilian case. The Castilian consuls strictly enforced payment, punished those who tried to evade payment, and therefore appointed a comptroller-general (the *controlador*) in Zeeland.[84]

Most likely, merchants and the shipmaster paid the *flete y averías* both when arriving in Bruges after having sold their wool, and upon returning to Burgos. The system thus existed specifically for the monopolistic routes the *Consulados* controlled for its wool exports, for example the routes to Bruges and Nantes.[85] Due to the limited availability of material, it is not exactly known what was covered by the *flete y averías*, although pilotage costs were definitely part of it, as there is abundant proof that the Castilians bargained with local skippers' guilds for low, fixed costs. Raymond Fagel has been able to calculate the *flete y averías* for the years 1511–1514 (Table 9), based on the ledgers of the Bruges-based merchant Juan de Estella.[86] Even if this only concerns four years, it sheds some light on the matter. The *flete y averías* hovered between 4.6–5.3% of the profits of De Estella on the sale of wool.[87] This means that whilst the costs fluctuated somewhat (for example as freight or pilotage costs rose or fell), the costs were probably relatively predictable for merchants to deal with in this period, similar to the goals of the cost management varieties studied in section 5.2.

82 See for the Burgos *Consulado*: Basas Fernández, 'Priores y Cónsules de la Universidad de Mercaderes y Consulado de Burgos en el siglo XVI', *Boletón de la Institución Fernán González*, 42, 161 (1963), 679–691, there 684. For the Bilbao *Consulado*: Guiard y Larrauri, *Historia*, 68–84. For the situation in Bruges under the Castilian *natio*: Fagel, *De Hispano-Vlaamse wereld*, 484.

83 Fagel, *De Hispano-Vlaamse wereld*, 484.

84 See for the structure of the Consulate: Maréchal, 'La colonie espagnole', 28–29.

85 Basas Fernández, 'Priores y Cónsules', 684.

86 Fagel, *De Hispano-Vlaamse wereld*, 41–55 & 484. For the *controlador*: Gilliodts-Van Severen, *Espagne*, 243–245.

87 Ibidem, 484.

TABLE 9 Payments of the *flete y avérias* as a percentage of profits, based on the ledgers of the merchant Juan de Estella (1511–1514)

Year	Percentage *flete y averías* of total profit (dineros)
1511	4,79%
1512	5,2%
1513	5,31%
1514	4,59%

SOURCE: FAGEL, *DE HISPANO-VLAAMSE WERELD*, 484.

Whilst complaints were rare at the start of the sixteenth century, this changed in the 1550s. The *natio* obliged everyone to pay the *flete y averías* for the incurred costs even if damage occurred. That meant merchants were liable for both the costs of a maritime venture (e.g. pilotage) and for potential damage, such as lost cargo. As costs of the *flete y averías* appears to have risen around the 1550s as a result of the new measures taken to combat privateering, complaints by members of the *natio* about the high costs increased, particularly as the risk of paying damages also increased.[88] In most cases, merchants were obliged to pay despite their protests. In 1553, for example, eight Castilian shipmasters requested the consuls to establish clear rules on the subject.[89] The shipmasters were awaiting payment for the freight, but up to this point had not received any money from the consuls. The merchants, appearing before the consuls, complained that they also had to pay the *flete y averías* in Burgos, leading to an unfair rise in costs, particularly when they had to use the compulsory *rotulo* system, which allowed the *Consulados* to use available ships for transport to the Low Countries (see section 4.2.5).[90] The shipmasters subsequently proposed that the costs be included in the *carta de averías*, the document where all the costs for a venture were written down.[91] Both the Burgos *Consulado*[92] and the Castilian consuls in Bruges[93] subsequently confirmed the right of the

88 See for example: BE-SAB, *Libro de pleytos ordinarios*, fol. 6v, 82r, 82v, 129r–130r, 130v, 131v–132r, 132v, 133r, 133v, 134r, 134v, 135r, 135v, 136r, 150v–151r, 151v–152r, 160v–161v, 183v, 188v–190v, 211r–v, 212r–v, 213r–v, 214r & 214v–215r.

89 Ibidem, fol. 129r–130r, 130v, 131v–132r, 132v, 133r, 133v, 134r, 134v, 135r, 135v, 136r.

90 Ibidem, fol. 130v.

91 Ibidem, fol. 129r.

92 Ibidem, fol. 130v & 131v.

93 Ibidem, fol. 132v.

shipmasters to request the freight, also sentencing the merchants to pay for the other operational costs to the *natio*.

In the wake of these decisions, the merchant Juan de la Peña however also registered a testimony before the consular court noting that master Pedro de Ribas had incurred much additional damage to his sacks of wool, and wanted to claim back costs associated with the damage, such as having to rent a warehouse for the sacks of wool and the cost of litigation.[94] The consul Diego de Lerma decided that if it was proven true, he would have the right to reclaim this money on De Ribas, but stated nothing about the *flete y averías* which would remain the prerequisite of the *natio*.[95] The case hence led to multiple costs which De la Peña had to cover, both before the voyage and after the voyage, as damage had occurred. In 1560, the consuls re-affirmed their right to levy the *flete y averías* after numerous merchants complained about the high costs.[96] A group of Castilian merchants claimed they had already paid the shipmaster for freight and operational costs, whilst the shipmaster tried to reclaim the *flete y averías* from the merchants. In the end, the consuls allowed the shipmaster to reclaim the costs, as arbitration had failed. Whereas the goal of the *flete y averías* was to offer predictable costs to merchants, the cases show that this goal was not necessarily reached.

5.3.2 *The Castilian natio and Pilotage between Zeeland and Bruges*

Pilotage was an important element of the *flete y averías* for two related reasons: first, both Burgos and Bruges lay inland, necessitating riverine pilotage; second, pilotage was compulsory both in Zeeland (where most Spanish ships docked) and in Sluis. This was also the case in Portugalete, where most ships under Castilian or Biscayer control (i.e. with Castilian or Biscayer shipmasters) left or returned.[97] As such, it made sense for the *Consulado* and *natio* to bargain with the relevant skippers' guild for low and predictable prices, especially as the Flanders fleet was an important customer for the skippers' guilds in Portugalete, Zeeland and Sluis.[98] The Castilians used their market power to bargain for low and predictable prices: from the 1560s onwards, the Castilians often negotiated alongside the Biscayers and Navarrese to strengthen their negotiating power. As Roger Degryse has shown, the privilege to pilot Iberian cargo to Bruges and Antwerp was important given the quantities of wool and

94 Ibidem, fol. 136r–v.
95 Ibidem, fol. 136v.
96 Ibidem, fol. 211r–v, 212r–v, 213r–v, 214r & 214v–215r.
97 Fagel, *De Hispano-Vlaamse wereld*, 145. Fagel notes that most ships left from Bilbao, but Portugalete was Bilbao's port.
98 Degryse, 'Brugge en de pilotage'.

other cargo imported.[99] In lengthy negotiations with the skippers' guilds of Middelburg, Arnemuiden and Bruges, the Castilian *controlador* tried to provide predictable costs for its members and pin down the liability for damage on the pilots. As the skippers' guilds also competed amongst each other, the Castilians could bargain for low prices and shift risks to the pilots.[100]

Source material permits us to study the problem in remarkable detail and tease out the connections to *flete y averías*. For transport and pilotage from Zeeland to Bruges, Castilian merchants were dependent on the Middelburg and Arnemuiden skippers' guild after at least 1525. The skippers' guild in that year obtained the privilege to transport cargo to Brabant or Flanders if a ship arriving in a Zeeland port had wine as cargo.[101] In practice, pilotage from Zeeland to Bruges and/or Antwerp was common from the late fifteenth century onwards, when most Iberian ships docked at ports in Zeeland anyway for more practical reasons as the Zwin river silted up and both Sluis and Bruges claimed staple rights on the Zwin.[102] Wine was not a common Iberian import product, the wool trade of course being of overarching importance.[103] The docking at Zeeland however presented its own jurisdictional problems, as the cargo piloted from Zeeland to the Zwin had to be trans-shipped to other pilot ships in Sluis, from where the Bruges skippers' guild held the monopoly for the final transport to Bruges.[104]

The Castilians generally agreed to cover part of the SA costs for the pilots' voyages but pinned actual damage on the pilots, absolving the shipmaster of the responsibility for liability.[105] The Castilians thus agreed to pay a fixed part of the operational costs. Both the Castilians and the Portuguese received such a right as part of their 1367 and 1438 privileges.[106] In 1531, the first agreement with the Middelburg and Arnemuiden skippers' guild was agreed upon, stating that

99 Ibidem.

100 In 1470, the Bruges' skippers' guild for example complained about the low prices the Middelburg guild charged. See: Gilliodts-Van Severen, *Espagne*, 243–245. A decision was reached, which was again confirmed in 1517 after additional disputes arose.

101 Zijlmans, *Troebele betrekkingen*, 274–275. This was called the right of *voorlading* (literally 'pre-loading').

102 Degryse, 'Brugge en de pilotage', 108–109; Dumolyn & Leloup, 'The Zwin Estuary', 208–209.

103 Philips, 'Spanish Merchants and the Wool Trade'; Philips jr. 'Merchants of the Fleece'.

104 See: Degryse, 'Brugge en de pilotage', 105–120. The distance between Sluis and Bruges by the canal is only fifteen kilometres (some nine miles).

105 Gilliodts-Van Severen, *Espagne*, 244, 287, 289–291, 311, 332, 364–365, 375, 412–415, 419–420, 426–428.

106 Finot, *Étude de Espagne*, 100. Art 26 states. Moreover, the Castilians could request to use other pilots when they were unhappy with the services. See: Gilliodts-Van Severen, *Espagne*, 307–311. For the Portuguese: Braamcamp Freire, *Noticias*, 52.

pilots jettisoning cargo had to pay twelve pounds *Grooten Vlaams* to the *natio* as a compensation, without regard to the reason of the action.[107] In 1539, a dispute between the two parties heard by the Middelburg Magistrate changed this agreement.[108] The Castilians agreed to scrap the compensation, although damage could still be deducted from the freight.[109] Moreover, they agreed to cover a greater share of the SA costs, primarily port duties, which even the skippers' guilds themselves had to pay.[110] In 1549, a pilot was even summoned to appear before the Castilian consuls after having incurred damage between Zeeland and Bruges, but as the pilot declined to appear, negotiations were the only option left for the Castilians, having no formal jurisdictional means to force the pilot to contribute.[111] In 1539, as well as in 1552 and 1557, disputes between the *natio* and the skippers' guild followed, until a new agreement was concluded in 1568 between the Castilian, Biscayer and Navarrese *nationes* and the Zeeland skippers' guild.[112] It only complemented the 1531 agreement, but pinned an even stricter liability on pilots to prevent damage.[113] No GA could be declared, and neither could a Castilian merchant be held liable for any kind of damage resulting from jettison. The compensation was deducted from the freight.[114] The costs for *lichghelt*, the duty to remain in port for a ship, were borne by the *natio* by paying a contribution to the pilots.[115] A similar agreement was concluded in November 1568 with the Bruges' skippers guild (also by the three *nationes* together).[116] According to this agreement, damage had to be paid for by the *natio*, although they were given significant jurisdictional and procedural powers to determine the costs.[117] In short, the Castilians were able to shift the liability for damage during the pilots' voyage to the skippers'

107 Gilliodts-Van Severen, *Espagne*, 287–291. See also: Wijffels, 'Ius Commune and International Wine Trade'. A similar agreement was concluded with the Bruges skippers' guild in 1545. See: Gilliodts-Van Severen, *Espagne*, 332–335.

108 Ibidem, 311–313. Other points of dispute included the payment of freight until the port of Sluis and the trans-shipment in port.

109 Ibidem, 312.

110 Ibidem.

111 BE-SAB, *Libro de pleytos ordinarios*, fol. 60v–61r.

112 Gilliodts-Van Severen, *Espagne*, 364–365, 365–366, 371 & 412–415. The 1539 disputes concerned the payment of *lichgeld* (port duties); the other disputes were concerned with payment enforcement. The Navarese *natio* had become a *natio* in 1530, with new privileges granted in 1556. See: Ibidem, 242–245 & 370–371.

113 Ibidem, 413, Article 8.

114 Ibidem, 414, Article 10.

115 Ibidem, 414–415, Article 17.

116 Ibidem, 426–428.

117 Ibidem, 428.

guild, whilst often only paying freight and a part of the SA costs (primarily port duties).

The Castilians, represented by the *controlador*, were able to negotiate stable pilotage costs with the local skippers' guilds. The Burgos *Consulado* concluded a similar agreement with the skippers' guild in Portugalete in 1547, securing low costs and proper service for the compulsory pilotage.[118] Both the *Consulado* and *natio* hence made efforts to keep the costs for the compulsory pilotage low. These negotiations make clear that the Castilians actively tried to manage the costs of pilotage and acted to keep the *flete y averías* low for its members, using its market power to bargain for low costs. These negotiations may thus also explain why the *flete y averías* was administered by the *controlador*, as only the *natio* as an organisation could bargain for low costs for the compulsory service, and hence lower bargaining costs for its members. In that way, they were able to use their market power to navigate the complex jurisdictional and political reality as control over tolls and pilotage was one part of the power struggles between the central government and the Flemish cities in the wake of the Flemish Revolt, with Sluis acting as a proxy for the central government.

5.4 Conclusion: Averages and Cost Management

This chapter has studied the development of cost management varieties of Averages. Denoting the common operational costs of a venture as 'Average' was important for merchants and shipmasters as it enabled those in the interest community to incorporate foreseeable costs in business dealings. Although cost management was the goal, it subsequently also lowered risk, for example as pilotage would limit the risk of damage upon entering port. Varieties of Averages thus function as an excellent illustration of the multiple functions of institutions.[119] Moreover, it supports Edwin Hunt's and James Murray's arguments that innovations in mercantile techniques were often built on older techniques, rather than being the result of radical innovation.[120] Most innovations studied here originated in mercantile practice and were only included in formal law much later (e.g. the 1551 *Ordonnance* or the 1608 *Compilatae*), which did offer legal security by incorporating the definition into the broader legal framework.[121] In contrast, Contractual Average was left unregulated, making it

118 Basas Fernández, *El Consulado*, 42–43.
119 Ogilvie, '"Whatever is, is Right?"', 681.
120 Hunt & Murray, *A History of Business*, 178–179 & 249.
121 De ruysscher, 'Maxims, Principles and Legal Change'.

was a very flexible instrument to cover whatever costs the parties in the interest community found necessary to cover, including protection costs and even common PA damage.

The operational costs for the voyage were separated from the freight during the fifteenth century and thence included in the freight contracts *ex ante*. This was the logic behind Contractual Average, offering predictable cost management to the interest community. Both pilotage and artillery were frequently incorporated. To minimise conflict after a voyage and offer predictable transaction costs to all parties, the increasing use of freight contracts was an important way to guarantee legal security. For operational costs or uninsurable costs such as artillery, insurance was largely unavailable, making the development of varieties of Averages a necessity. The additional advantage was that transaction costs were lower, as enforcement costs remained low. Indeed, disputes were very rare: neither the notaries nor the municipal courts of Bruges and Antwerp appeared to hear disputes on cost management varieties of Averages very often, indicating that the instruments were to a large extent a success in evading elaborate disputes about costs afterwards, and thereby lowering enforcement costs. In the Castilian case, the *natio* decided to take control over payment to negotiate lower prices for pilotage in (politically) unstable times through the *flete y averías*.[122] In this the *natio* was successful, although complaints were common in the 1550s as costs rose.

Most contractual clauses did not explicitly state monetary contributions but rather clauses like 'customs of the sea', which gave masters the freedom to incur common costs for the venture as was necessary. Rather than evidence of a *lex maritima*, this was rather a reflection of this system whereby 'freight' was a defined sum and 'Average' were the common operational costs which could vary according to local customs, giving the interest community, notaries and courts the necessary flexibility to keep the system flowing. Next to a system of risk management, a system of cost management was therefore established which reflected the common interests of all involved in a venture, contributing to an operationally efficient system of institutions for maritime trade.

122 Fagel, *De Hispano-Vlaamse wereld*, 139–148 & 484.

CHAPTER 6

Consular Averages, Compulsory Contributions and Protection Costs

6.1 Introduction

The extant evidence in the Southern Low Countries offers a wealth of information on the innovative ways in which Iberian merchants developed instruments to manage (protection) costs in their monopolistic wool trade.[1] Notwithstanding their fondness for insurance and their lobbying for a more expansive definition of GA,[2] one of their most important contributions to the development of Averages in the Low Countries was to develop their so-called 'consular Averages' to cover protection costs, such as artillery and convoy ships. Crucially, these costs were paid in advance of the venture rather than upon arrival, setting it apart from the cost management varieties studied in Chapter 5. Moreover, they were non-contractual, as the obligation for payment lay in the ability of the *natio* to levy a 'consular Average'. Averages were therefore intimately connected to the issue of protection costs, as the aptly named *avería de nación* and the *avería(s)* studied in this chapter show. This chapter analyses this complex interplay through the prism of Frederic Lane's theory of protection costs, as this theorem fits the historical reality of Castilian sixteenth-century trade better than the transaction costs theorem, for which this solution had ambivalent effects.[3] The compulsory contributions[4] based on the privilege to levy the 'consular Averages' of the Castilian and Biscayer *nationes* were an effort to create protection rents for the members of the *natio*, with ambivalent effects on transaction costs.[5] There is still substantial linguistic and conceptual confusion over the compulsory contributions of the Iberian merchants in the Low Countries, as Spanish 'Averages' are a complex tale of power, money and polysemy.[6] This confusion was to a large extent also present

1 See for an overview of the Spanish-Low Countries trade: Fagel, *De Hispano-Vlaamse wereld*, 135–162.

2 Verlinden, 'De zeeverzekeringen'; Sicking, 'Los grupos de intereses'.

3 Lane, *Profits from Power.*

4 For the Low Countries, I prefer the term 'compulsory contribution' rather than tax, as the *nationes* were not state-like entities.

5 Lane, *Profits from Power*, 12–21.

6 Gilliodts-Van Severen, *Espagne*, 595–596; De Smidt *et al*, *Chronologische lijsten van de geëxtendeerde sententiën en procesbundels (dossiers) berustende in het archief van de Grote Raad*

 | DOI:10.1163/9789004540354_007

during the sixteenth century, as the polysemic aspects of the consular Averages became part of numerous legal arguments between 1460 and 1550.[7]

The largest part of the chapter looks at the *avería de nación*, the 'original' form of the consular Average allowed in the privileges of the Castilian and Biscayer *nationes*. The (limited) literature on the *avería de nación*, following Louis Gilliodts-Van Severen, has categorised all the similar (compulsory) contributions to the Southern European *nationes* under the name *droit d'avarie* ('right of Average').[8] This chapter, through a close reading of the privileges and court records, will however show that the privileges of the *nationes* differed, as the Portuguese *direito da nação* and Genoese *massaria* were solely used for the 'ordinary' costs of the *natio* (such as political representational costs and devotional costs), whereas the Spanish *avería de nación* explicitly covered maritime protection costs next to similar ordinary costs. This had major implications for cost management and explains the connection to Averages. Moreover, when inter-*natio* ventures, primarily those on Biscayer and Castilian ships, became more common during the sixteenth century, the question arose of whether foreign merchants could be obliged to contribute to the protection costs of the venture, paid for by the *avería de nación*. This was a battle that could only be decided in legal practice, which was eventually solved to the advantage of the Castilian and Biscayer *nationes* (section 6.4): the origin of the shipmaster proved key here, and hence when we speak about a 'Biscayer ship' in this chapter this means that the shipmaster was Biscayan.

For sections 6.2 and 6.3 this chapter relies primarily on three excellent source editions detailing the privileges of the various Southern European merchant communities, as well as secondary literature on the *Consulados* and their compulsory contributions.[9] The chapter focuses primarily on the Castilians,

---

van Mechelen (6 vols.) (Brussels 1988) (hereafter: De Smidt, *Sententiën*), also lumps together the *droit d'avarie* of the various Southern European *nationes*.

7 See particularly section 6.4 for the disputes before the various courts.

8 Gilliodts-Van Severen, *Espagne*, 595–596.

9 For the Castilians and other 'Spanish' *nationes*: Gilliodts-Van Severen, *Espagne*; Fagel, *De Hispano-Vlaamse wereld*; González Arce, 'La Universidad'; Vandewalle, 'El Consulado'; Finot, *Étude de Espagne*; Goris, *Étude*, 55–70. For the Genoese: C. Desimoni & L.T. Belgrano (eds.), *Documenti riguardanti le relazione di Genova col Brabante, La Fiandra e la Borgogna: raccolti ed ordinati* (Genoa 1871) (hereafter: Desimoni & Belgrano, *Documenti*); Braekevelt, 'Entre profit et dommage'; Finot, *Étude de Gênes*; Goris, *Étude*, 75–78. For the Portuguese: A. Braamcamp Freire, *Noticias da feitoria de Flandres precedidas dos brandies poetas do cancioneiro* (Lisbon 1920) (hereafter: Braamcamp Freire, *Noticias*); Pohl, *Die Portugiesen*; Martyn, 'De Portugese natie'; Miranda, 'Conflict Management in Western Europe: The Case of Portuguese Merchants in England, Flanders and Normandy, 1250–1500', *Continuity and Change*, 31, 1 (2017), 11–36; Idem, 'Commerce, conflits et justice: les marchands portugais en Flandre à la fin du Moyen Âge', *Annales de Bretagne et des Pays de l'Ouest*, 117, 1 (2010), 1–16. Paviot, 'Les Portugais à Bruges'; Goris, *Étude*, 37–55; Van Answaarden, *Les Portugais*.

Biscayers, Portuguese and Genoese, as these *nationes* were among the most important, also leaving extensive paper trails behind. Moreover, the chapter presents litigation from the Castilian consular court, Antwerp and Bruges municipal courts and Great Council to analyse how the tension between transaction and protection costs played out on the ground, chiefly so in section 6.4. Section 6.2 first examines the *avería*, a well-studied compulsory contribution to cover protection costs for the New World Trade to set the stage and offer a clearer view of how compulsory contributions were used by Castilian merchants.[10] Section 6.3 compares the privileges of the Southern European *nationes* and explains the crucial differences between the Spanish case on the one hand and the Portuguese and Italian cases on the other, distinguishing the protection costs and average element as the key difference. Section 6.4 studies litigation on the *avería de nación*, as only legal practice could clarify whether the *avería de nación* could also be levied on foreign merchants (more specifically Italians) using Castilian or Biscayer ships for transport. Most material comes from the Bruges municipal court and records of the Great Council. Section 6.5 shortly discusses the *avería(s)*, the second compulsory contribution developed by the Castilians to cover protection costs following the 1551 *Ordonnance*, on which extant material is very scarce.[11] Note that when we speak of the *avería*, it means the Seville compulsory contribution for protection costs in the New World trade, but when we speak of the *avería(s)*, it means a similar compulsory contribution particularly for protection costs in the Low Countries.[12] Section 6.6 concludes and fleshes out the connection between the political organisation of the two Spanish *nationes* and the use of consular Averages for protection costs in the Castilian and Biscayer case.

6.2 The Seville *avería* as an Example of Protection Costs

The consular Averages, as introduced in Chapter 2, were a key privilege for the *Consulados* and *nationes*. Whilst they started as compulsory contributions for

---

10 This particular type of *avería* has attracted much attention from historians and thus serves as an excellent case study for the compulsory contributions levied in the Spanish case. See for example: Céspedes del Castillo, 'La Avería'; Talavan, 'La Avería'. Of course, insurance in this respect has also been covered. See: Céspedes del Castillo, 'El seguro marítimo en la Carrera de Indias', *Anuario de Historia del derecho Espanol*, 19 (1948–1949), 57–103; Casado Alonso, 'El seguro marítimo en la Carrera de Indias en la época de Felipe II', in: J.J. Iglesias Ródriguez *et al* (eds.), *Comercio y cultura en la Edad Moderna* (Seville 2015), 1253–1270.

11 Fagel, *De Hispano-Vlaamse wereld*, 484.

12 Ibidem, 419–422.

the ordinary costs of the merchant organisations, separate compulsory contributions were also established to cover specific expenses, often for protection costs.[13] One example on which the Spanish historiography has focused in detail is the peculiar case of the *avería*, offering a useful framework to study the compulsory contributions used in the Low Countries. The *avería* has rarely been studied explicitly in the framework of protection cost and rents, although it functions as an excellent case study of the issues in play.[14] The *avería*, an *ex ante*, non-contractual compulsory contribution, was established in 1521 by the *Casa de Contratación* and levied on imports and exports.[15] In 1543, the Seville *Consulado* acquired control over the instrument, an important privilege for the *Consulado* as it was allowed to levy money from its members.[16] The *avería* was levied to cover the protection costs for the voyage to and from the New World, for example convoy ships and artillery on the value of cargo in a ship as a percentage of the imports and exports.[17] At first, it was relatively low (around 1%), but during the sixteenth century it rose to around 5%, before falling again at the end of the century (see Graph 1).[18] According to Robert Smith, it varied widely during the sixteenth century, but took on a fixed amount at the end of that century, namely one *maravedí* on each ducat, which was itself worth 375 *maravedí*.[19] Guillermo Céspedes del Castillo has provided more detailed numbers (Graph 1), which indicate that the tax indeed varied over the years.[20] All the available evidence confirms that the *avería* fluctuated across the century, although it in the long run it rose.

Over time, the bureaucracy tasked with levying the *avería* grew. The *Consulado* of Seville for example appointed a receiver-general to account for

13 Smith, *The Spanish Guild Merchant*, 87–91.

14 Lane, *Profits from Power*, 12–22, 37 & 44.

15 The *Casa de Contratación* (established 1503) was the organisation in charge of organising the New World trade, at least until the establishment of the Council of the Indies in 1524 which from then on held final power. From 1524 onwards, the *Casa* was primarily in charge of the daily administrative matters, although it kept significant jurisdictional powers as well, for example over GA. See: García Garralón, 'The nautical republic' and bibliography therein quoted.

16 Vila Villar, 'Algunas consideraciones', 55–56.

17 Céspedes del Castillo, 'La Avería', 524–532 & 549–552.

18 C.H. Haring, *Trade and Navigation between Spain and the Indies in the Time of the Hapsburgs* (Cambridge, MA 1918), 76; Céspedes del Castillo, 'La Avería', 671–672.

19 Smith, *The Spanish Guild Merchant*, 88.

20 Céspedes del Castillo, 'La Avería', 671–672. According to Haring, the *avería* hovered around 5% around 1550, which appears justified only for the latter part of the decade. See: Haring, *Trade and Navigation*, 76.

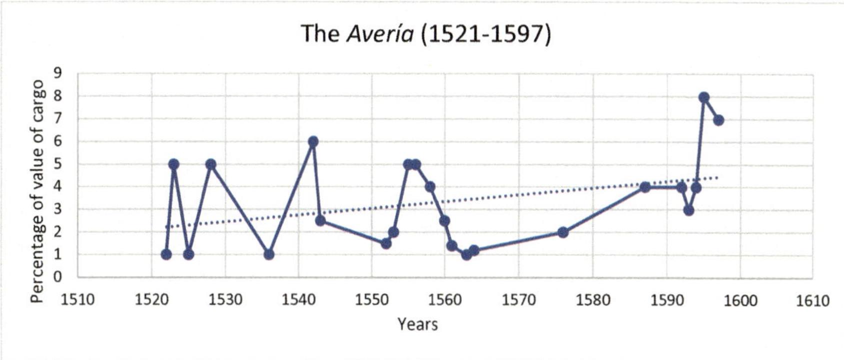

GRAPH 1 The avería (1521–1597, selected years)
SOURCE: CÉSPEDES DEL CASTILLO, 'LA AVERÍA', 671–672

all the import and export taxes, similar to the position of the *controlador* in the Castilian *natio*.[21] As Céspedes del Castillo has argued, the *avería* was the first clear (Castilian) attempt to distinguish between costs on the one hand, and damage on the other (*averías-gastos* – costs, and *averías-daños* – damage), a distinction that is consistent with the polysemic nature of Averages we have already observed in Chapter 2.[22] Compensation was shared by means of GA under the tacit agreement that underpinned GA, whilst protection costs were levied by the *Consulado* to provide protection as a club good and manage the associated costs.[23] Although the *avería* was meant to cover protection costs for the New World trade, the *avería* soon included other costs such as a payment for the consuls of the *Consulado*.[24] Contributions to the poor were often also included.[25] A secondary effect of the *avería* was risk-related, as the protection measures in turn also lowered risk for the participants. Moreover, the protection costs to an extent lowered the moral hazard resulting from insurance, as the protection costs were obligatorily shared by everyone in the interest community, whereas under insurance an in individual merchant shifted the measures and associated costs to the ship-owner and/or shipmaster.[26]

21 Haring, *Trade and Navigation*, 72–73. This was similar to the bureaucratic structure of the *flete y averías*.
22 Céspedes del Castillo, 'La Avería', 518.
23 Ibidem.
24 Smith, *The Spanish Guild Merchant*, 87.
25 Ibidem.
26 See: Heimer, *Reactive Risk and Rational Action*, 123–125.

6.3 Privileges and the *droit d'avarie*: False Friends?

In the Low Countries, the compulsory contributions to the Southern European *nationes* were generally called the *droit d'avarie* ('right of Average'), drawn from the privileges that were the result of negotiations between the home sovereign and the host government, be it central state, municipality, or both.[27] According to Gilliodts-Van Severen, they were similar for the Iberian and Italian *nationes*, but a close reading reveals there were important differences in the application of the contributions to the *natio*. In short, the Spanish *nationes* used the so-called *avería de nación* (following from the privilege to levy the consular Averages, the *echar las averías*) both for ordinary costs (e.g. legal fees, political representation and devotional costs) and for maritime protection costs, whilst the Portuguese (*direito da nação*) and Genoese, Florentines and Lucchese (*massaria*) used the contribution solely for ordinary costs of the *natio*. The only maritime expenses both the Portuguese and Genoese made from the contributions was to salvage ships and cargo in case of shipwreck, but no mention of 'Average' or protection costs were made in the privileges.[28] In the Castilian and Biscayer cases, the monopolistic wool trade necessitated additional protection measures for the ships, which explains the inclusion of protection costs.[29] Whilst the 'deeper' goals of the compulsory contributions were similar, the Spanish consular Averages had broader applications (e.g. maritime protection costs).

6.3.1 *Consulados and* nationes

Both the Iberian *Consulados* and the Spanish *nationes* were instrumental in developing the compulsory contributions, besides their important role in developing other tools of risk management.[30] Before we can study the compulsory contributions of the various Southern European *nationes*, a closer look at both the *Consulados*, the *nationes* and the maritime organisation of the Iberian-Low Countries wool trade is in order. Merchant guilds commonly existed in the Iberian Peninsula.[31] During the fifteenth and sixteenth

27 Gilliodts-Van Severen, *Espagne*, 595–596.

28 Although the Portuguese registered the *direito da nação* in the so-called *rol das averías*, there is no evidence that they used this for maritime protection costs. See: Pohl, *Die Portugiesen*, 54.

29 Lane, *Profits from Power*.

30 For insurance: Verlinden, 'De zeeverzekeringen'; Casado Alonso, 'Juan Henriquez'; Puttevils & Deloof, 'Marketing and Pricing Risk'. For Averages: Fagel, *De Hispano-Vlaamse wereld*, 129–138 & 484.

31 Smith, *The Spanish Guild Merchant*, 67–70.

century, some merchant organisations received royal protection and became a *Consulado*, with a significant mercantile jurisdiction.[32] In Burgos, the *Consulado* received royal privileges in 1494; Bilbao followed in 1512, whilst the Seville *Consulado* followed in 1543.[33] Both the *Consulados* of Burgos and Bilbao primarily focused on trade to 'the North' (e.g. Flanders, France and England), while Seville's *Consulado* was focused on the Atlantic trade.

The development of uses of the consular Averages for protection costs was the consequence of both the way the Iberian-Low Countries trade was organised and of exogenous factors, such as the increase in privateering before the coast of France.[34] Most of the information known to historians comes from the Castilians, which therefore also informs the discussion here. Their wool exports fluctuated throughout the sixteenth century, but generally the exports rose until they reached a peak in 1548–1549.[35] Thereafter the wool export steadily declined, largely as the numerous Habsburg wars and the increase in privateering attacks during the 1550s severely impacted the ability to make a profit, despite the best efforts of the merchant guilds to incorporate protection costs.[36] The organisation of the 'Flanders fleet' fell under the responsibility of the *Consulados*. Although the Burgos one was formally in charge of the chartering of ships, most were chartered by individual merchants and ship-owners with the blessing of the *Consulado*.[37] Most ship-owners owned only one or two ships, hiring shipmasters for the venture.[38] The *Consulado*, dependent on the wool exports of their members for income, provided protection by chartering convoy ships and artillery for the fleet. In economic terms, the *Consulado* thus provided 'club goods', protection for ships chartered by its members which was

32 A general introduction to the *Consulado* structure can be found in: Smith, *The Spanish Guild Merchant*, especially 67–111; M. Milagres del Vas Mingo, *Los consulados en el tráfico indiano* (Madrid 2000), especially 36–63 for the three *Consulados* studied here. See also: De ruysscher, *Gedisciplineerde vrijheid: een geschiedenis van het handels- en economisch recht* (Antwerp/Apeldoorn 2013), 31–36, for a wider European perspective on the *Consulados*. For their place in Castilian politics: Yun-Casalilla, *Iberian World Empires*, 84–86 & 215–225.

33 See for the Seville *Consulado* the footnote below. See for the Burgos *Consulado*: Basas Fernández, *El Consulado*; Idem, 'Priores y Cónsules'. See for the Bilbao *Consulado*: Guiard y Laurrauri, *Historia*.

34 The promulgation of the 1550 and 1551 *Ordonnances* was also connected to the protection of the 'Spanish' wool fleets. See: Sicking, 'Les marchands espagnols et portugais'; Idem, 'Stratégies de réduction de risque'.

35 Fagel, *De Hispano-Vlaamse wereld*, 144–147.

36 Ibidem, 147–149.

37 Ibidem, 153–155.

38 Ibidem, 155. See also: Philips jr., 'Spain's Northern Shipping Industry'.

not accessible to others.[39] This task explains the use of the consular average for the matter, as this allowed the *Consulado* to defray to costs to its members. Members were dependent on the *Consulado* for the supply of wool, as the *Consulado* did most of the bargaining on behalf of the merchants.[40] On the other hand, they were relatively free to charter ships as they wished.[41] The Bruges-based *natio* was in charge of the protection of the return fleet, which primarily included fabrics.[42] For the return fleet, local ships were regularly chartered, emphasising the distinctly private-public nature of the Iberian-Low Countries trade under the flag of the *Consulado* and *natio*.[43]

The relationship between the Burgos *Consulado* and the Castilian *natio* was (in theory) close, as the *Consulado* formally had to approve the consuls in Bruges and theoretically had final jurisdiction over internal disputes. In practice, the *natio* possessed significant autonomy in commercial and administrative matters, the only obligation being to send a report on income and costs every year to Burgos.[44] The Bilbao *Consulado* and the Biscayer *natio* functioned along similar lines.[45] Both in Castile and the Low Countries, relationships between the two groups (Castilians and Biscayers) were often tense. As a result of the 1494 agreement, the Biscayers also established their own *natio* in Bruges (see next section). As the Burgos *Consulado* received the monopoly to transport goods northwards that year, this meant that the Bilbao-based merchant guild lost its overseas business.[46] On the other hand, Burgos lay inland and had to use the ports of Bilbao or Santander to transport goods overseas.[47] As a result, the Burgos *Consulado* and the Bilbao merchant guild agreed on sharing the monopoly in 1496, a solution blessed by King Ferdinand of Castile in his *Pragmática*, before the Bilbao merchant guild became a *Consulado* as well in 1512.[48] Rivalry however always existed between the Burgos and Bilbao *Consulados* throughout the sixteenth century: in 1547, the Burgos *Consulado* for example concluded an agreement with the port town of Portugalete (near

39 See for protection costs: Lane, *Profits from power*. For club goods in the Hanseatic context: E. Lindberg, 'Club Goods and Inefficient Institutions: Why Danzig and Lübeck Failed in the Early Modern Period', *The Economic History Review*, 62, 3 (2009), 604–628.

40 Basas Fernández, *El Consulado*, 231–245; Guiard y Laurrauri, *Historia*, 35–53.

41 Fagel, *De Hispano-Vlaamse wereld*, 148–150.

42 Ibidem, 151. The 'fabrics' are not specified but were most likely finished cloth and similar commodities. See: Ibidem, 152.

43 Ibidem, 152.

44 Basas Fernández, *El Consulado*, 81. See also: González Arce, 'La Universidad'.

45 Guiard y Laurrauri, *Historia*, 20–21 & 68–84.

46 Vas Mingo, *Los Consulados*, 38–39 & 43–44.

47 Ibidem, 38–39.

48 Basas Fernández, *El Consulado*, 37–39.

Bilbao), ensuring all custom rights to charter its fleet from there, despite repeated protests from Bilbao's *Consulado*.[49] In the Low Countries, the rivalry was less pronounced as the *nationes* often worked together out of necessity or opportunism.[50]

6.3.2 *The 'Spanish'* nationes *in the Low Countries*

Following the demise of the Champagne Fairs, Iberian merchants, alongside the Italians, were quick to arrive in the Low Countries. The first record of privileges for Castilian merchants in Bruges dates from 1343.[51] Both Bruges, as a member of the *Drie Leden* (Three Members), a collective of the cities of Bruges, Ghent, and Ypres, and the Count of Flanders, acknowledged these privileges, which mainly concerned protection against arbitrary imprisonment. Further privileges (1348, 1421 and 1428) both confirmed and elaborated on the previous ones. The 1348 ones, for example, expanded the legal protection for Castilian merchants and gave them staple rights.[52] By 1389, Aragonese merchants had also received their own privileges to trade to and from the Low Countries.[53] In 1447, merchants from Biscay negotiated their own privileges in Bruges, following the legal battles in Castile between the Burgos and Bilbao merchant guilds over the privileges back home.[54] Following developments in Castile, from 1494 onwards 'Spanish' merchants in the Low Countries were divided into three *nationes*: the Castilian, Biscayer, and Catalan-Aragonese.[55] In 1500, the Andalusians also received privileges in Antwerp, before moving to Middelburg (Zeeland) in 1505.[56] The Navarrese received privileges in Bruges in 1530, which were renewed in 1556.[57] The privileges however differed per *natio*. The Castilians received the most extensive ones, including wide jurisdiction in civil matters.[58] Crucially, only the Castilians and Biscayers possessed the privilege to levy the *avería de nación* for protection costs, whilst the Catalan-Aragonese only received the privilege to levy a compulsory contribution for ordinary costs.[59]

---

49 Ibidem, 42–43. It also concluded an agreement about pilotage: see section 6.5.3.

50 See also: Dreijer, 'Identity'.

51 Gilliodts-Van Severen, *Cartulaire* (Vol. 1), 8–12.

52 Ibidem, 13.

53 Ibidem, 19–21.

54 Ibidem, 31.

55 The standard text on the Spanish *nationes* is still: Maréchal, 'La colonie espagnole', particularly 7–10. See also: Idem, 'Le depart'; Casado Alonso, 'La colonie', 233–251; Idem, 'La nation', 61–77.

56 Fagel, 'Spaanse kooplieden', 22–23.

57 Gilliodts-Van Severen, *Espagne*, 242–245 & 370–371.

58 De ruysscher, *Gedisciplineerde vrijheid*, 33.

59 Gilliodts-Van Severen, *Espagne*, 163–167 & 594–596. See also section 6.3.5.

As a result of the disputes between the Castilian and Biscayer merchants, the emancipation of the Biscayer merchants from the Castilians proceeded slowly.[60] Both in 1447 and 1455, the Biscayers already received limited privileges to form their own so-called *universitas*, which was explicitly not a fully-fledged *natio*. This changed in 1465, when the Castilian *natio* and the Biscayer *universitas* came to an agreement about the rights and duties of the two merchant communities.[61] On the *avería de nación*, the agreement stated that both communities had the right to levy the compulsory contribution on their own members or ships. The Castilians also retained the right to levy the *avería de nación* on Andalusian merchants.[62] Portuguese merchants had to pay a compulsory contribution to their own *Consulado*, unless they made a stop on the Biscayer or Guipuzcoan coast.[63] This agreement apparently did not solve all problems, since the Castilian King Ferdinand ordered an inquiry into the jurisdictional competence of the two merchant communities in the 1480s. In 1485, he published his decision, with further revisions made as part of the 1494 reforms.[64] The Burgos *Consulado* requested greater control over the Castilian *natio* in Bruges to combat fraud, including an annual report of Averages levied by the consuls of the Spanish *nationes* (i.e. not solely the Castilians, but also the Biscayers and the Aragonese).[65] Although the report stated that the *Consulado* kept ultimate jurisdiction over the foreign branches, it did not touch upon the *avería de nación*.[66] In 1496 Ferdinand's *Pragmática* stated that merchants from Castile and Biscay could load cargo anywhere in his kingdom without having to pay additional taxes and contributions, although merchants still had to pay common SA costs.[67] The Biscayers and Castilians would have a 2.5% exemption from paying the *avería de nación* to the other *natio*.[68] After a request from the Biscayer consuls in Bruges, a second revision was published in 1501.[69] The Biscayer consuls complained that the Castilians often kept their own revenues from the *avería de nación*, even if there were joint ventures or when ships came from the Biscayer region.[70] They referred to the municipal law of Bruges to justify their position, a clear nod to the fact that foreign merchants appealed to

60 Maréchal, 'La colonie espagnole', 7–10.
61 Gilliodts-Van Severen, *Espagne*, 84–86.
62 Ibidem, 85.
63 Ibidem.
64 Ibidem, 124–130.
65 Ibidem, 125.
66 Ibidem, 127–128.
67 Ibidem, 128.
68 Ibidem, 298.
69 Ibidem, 129–130.
70 Ibidem, 129.

local municipal laws.[71] The Castilian consuls in Bruges retorted that they were allowed to levy the *avería de nación* partly for SA costs, potentially pilotage.[72] Although Ferdinand agreed to this point in principle, he urged moderation in collecting the compulsory contribution so that it was fair for both parties.[73]

In 1493, the Bruges Magistrate confirmed new privileges for the Biscayer *natio*.[74] The Biscayer consuls could henceforward levy the *avería de nación* when Biscayer ships arrived in Flanders, also on all foreign merchants using Biscayer ships for transport.[75] The (port of) origin of the shipmaster was the leading factor in this matter (see below). Soon afterwards the Castilians also received privileges from the city of Bruges in September 1494, which confirmed their right to levy the *avería de nación*.[76] In 1569, the *Hordenanzas* also included a similar clause.[77]

Yet, the partitioning of the Spanish *nationes* did not mean that conflicts vanished. In 1503, a dispute between the Castilians and the Biscayers for example reached the Great Council, as Bruges' Magistrate requested an opinion from the Great Council on the subject of the *avería de nación*.[78] Both parties argued that due to the various Italian Wars, protection costs had shot up.[79] Hence they were unwilling to pay the *avería de nación* to the other *natio*, but the Great Council decided that both parties had to pay the compulsory contributions 'without delay'.[80] In 1504, the Castilian consuls also tried to recover jurisdictional privileges over the Andalusian merchants, primarily to levy the *avería de nación* on them.[81] The Andalusians were granted privileges in Antwerp in 1500, although they soon moved on to Middelburg in 1505.[82] The case at hand concerned the lawfulness of these privileges, since Philip the Fair had not ratified the privileges given by Antwerp to the Andalusians, which was part of the

71 Lambert, 'A Legal World Market?', 170–173.

72 Gilliodts-Van Severen, *Espagne*, 129.

73 Ibidem, 130.

74 Ibidem, 151–162.

75 Ibidem, 155. The *avería de nación* had to be paid as soon as possible upon arriving and when foreign merchants used Biscayer ships, the Biscayer consuls had to liaise with the consuls of the *natio* of the merchant to make sure the *avería de nación* was not paid twice. See: Ibidem, Art. 17. See also Art. 42.

76 Ibidem, 170–183, there 173, Art. 6. These privileges were also confirmed by both Maximilian of Austria (in 1494) and Philip the Fair (in 1499). See: Ibidem, 183 & 194.

77 1569 *Hordenanzas*, Title XII, Art. 4.

78 Gilliodts-Van Severen, *Espagne*, 206.

79 Ibidem.

80 Ibidem.

81 Which was still allowed in 1465, when the agreement between the Biscayers and Castilians stipulated this.

82 Fagel, 'Spaanse kooplieden', 22–23.

Kingdom of Castile since 1492.[83] The Castilian consuls, for this reason, argued that they still retained the privilege to levy the *avería de nación* on Andalusian merchants in the Low Countries. They requested the notary Leonard Hughe to pass a public pronouncement stating that the Andalusians did not have such a right, although it remains unclear what this aimed to achieve, besides putting pressure on the Andalusians.[84] Unsurprisingly, the Andalusians simply rejected the allegations on 2 May 1504 in a letter to Hughe, after which no further actions can be found.[85]

Although the two Spanish *nationes* clearly had the right to levy the *avería de nación* on its members, sometimes even its own members protested. Both in 1439 and 1464 merchants complained that they had to pay for GA after a venture had suffered damage, despite the fact that they had already paid for the *avería de nación* before the voyage to cover protection costs.[86] In 1504, the Biscayer consuls had to seek enforcement of a decision at the Bruges municipal court, after they had forcefully claimed the *avería de nación* payment from three Bilbao shipmasters arriving in Sluis, who were using Castilian ships rather than Biscayer ones.[87] This may have been a con to avoid paying for the compulsory contribution, although the various privileges clearly stated that the port of origin of the shipmaster decided to which *natio* the *avería de nación* had to be paid. In 1550, the Castilian merchant Fernando Orosco filed a case at the Bruges municipal court after the Castilian consuls had confiscated Orosco's and others' wool bales, as Orosco *cum suis* had not paid for the *avería de nación*.[88] Again, the Bruges municipal court upheld the right of the consuls to claim the compulsory contribution. In 1551, the *tesorero* (treasurer) of the *natio* requested an enforcement order against Jéronimo Pardo Lerma who had repeatedly declined to pay the *avería de nación*, indicating that problems remained as merchants resisted the payment.[89] In 1559, another claim in the

83 Yun-Casalilla, *Iberian World Empires*, 13–14.

84 Gilliodts-Van Severen, *Espagne*, 208–209.

85 Ibidem, 209.

86 Idem, *Cartulaire* (Vol. 1), nr. 756 (p. 618–619); Idem, *Espagne*, 83; De Groote, *De zeeassurantie*, 15. De Groote, wrongly notes that the case was about insurers, but nowhere this is actually mentioned in the source edition of Gilliodts-Van Severen. The actual archival file (BE-SAB, Spaans Consulaat, inv. 304, *Collectie Charters*, nr. 22) does not mention anything about insurers either. This case probably set a precedent, which might explain why it was included in the charters of the Castilian *natio*.

87 Idem, *Espagne*, 214.

88 Ibidem, 354.

89 BE-SAB, *Libro de pleytos ordinarios*, fol. 97r–98v. A similar case can be found on fol. 104v–105r.

consular court, for a merchant's request to be absolved from paying the compulsory contribution, was also declined.[90]

Around 1550, the large Castilian colony in Antwerp tried to set up its own *natio* in the city.[91] Although Castilian subjects in Antwerp often acted as though they were a *natio*, they had not received the extensive privileges that their countrymen cherished so much in Bruges. Although the Bruges-based consuls had appointed a representative for legal matters in Antwerp, for first instance cases Antwerp-based merchants formally had to travel to Bruges. As we have seen in Chapter 3, the Castilians in Antwerp subsequently devised their own system to resolve conflicts by appointing trusted notaries.[92] In 1551, the Antwerp-based Castilian colony established a consular court with the support of the Antwerp aldermen.[93] Of course, the consuls in Bruges did not agree with this unilateral move: both the Great Council and Charles V himself had thwarted earlier efforts to establish a separate Consulate in Antwerp.[94] After negotiations between the two Consulates failed, the Bruges Consulate staged a blockade for Castilian ships sailing to Antwerp.[95] Both Charles V and Philip II subsequently confirmed that the Bruges Consulate was the only lawful Castilian *natio* in the Low Countries.[96] The Antwerp-based Castilians were never able to establish a proper *natio* during the sixteenth century.[97] As a result, they still had to contribute to the *avería de nación* of the Castilian *natio* in Bruges.

6.3.3 *The Portuguese*

The Portuguese received privileges in Flanders early in the fourteenth century. The Portuguese community there was a strange construct, because it consisted of three interlinked organisations: the *bolsa*, the *feitoria* (factory) and the actual *natio*.[98] The *bolsa* was the voluntary association of Portuguese merchants

90 Ibidem, fol. 173r.

91 This episode is recounted in: Goris, *Étude*, 55–66. See also: Fagel, *De Hispano-Vlaamse wereld*, 78–82.

92 Fagel, *De Hispano-Vlaamse wereld*, 52–54 & 100–104.

93 Goris, *Étude*, 62–63.

94 Ibidem, 59.

95 Ibidem, 64–65.

96 Ibidem, 65–66.

97 The archives of the Castilians in Antwerp contain material on the request for privileges, whilst arbitrated cases only come from the mid-seventeenth century. See: BE-SAA, Natie van Spanje, inv. PK#1079.

98 I. Elbl, 'Nation, Bolsa, and Factory: Three Institutions of Late-Medieval Portuguese Trade with Flanders', *International History Review*, 14, 1 (1992), 1–22. See also: Sicking, 'The Medieval Origin of the Factory or the Institutional Foundations of Overseas Trade: Toward

trading with Flanders (a sort of proto-merchant guild) under royal patronage, which later morphed into the *natio*.[99] The leader of the *feitoria*, the *feitor*, was appointed by the Portuguese king to make sure that the monopolistic trade to and from Portugal was done according to the rules, for example in sugar, ivory and African gold.[100] Both the *feitoria* and *natio* had to negotiate privileges with the Flemish Counts, although the *feitoria* as an expression of royal monopoly could more easily negotiate privileges via diplomatic means. Although merchants working under the *feitoria* could be members of the Portuguese *natio* in Bruges, this was not a prerequisite. In 1470, however, one of the four Portuguese consuls also acted as the royal *feitor*, suggesting that the two organisations were at least close.[101] As Portugal expanded its African trade, the King also tightened his grip on the trade with Flanders during the late fifteenth century, moving the *feitoria* to Antwerp in 1499.[102]

The *natio* functioned like most other foreign merchant communities, negotiating privileges for merchants to act on the market. Yet as the Portuguese King also controlled part of the trade, the trade under the *natio* was more limited compared to the Spanish or Italian *nationes*. Some cargo, such as sugar, was under the King's royal monopoly and could not be freely traded on the Antwerp market without explicit consent from the *feitor*.[103] Moreover, the *feitor* taxed some of the imports and exports on the king's behalf. The king also intervened in disputes in the Low Countries by conducting extensive diplomacy, probably to protect his monopoly on the trade.[104] Privileges for the Portuguese *natio* were given and (re)confirmed in 1386, 1411, 1421, 1438, 1442 and 1469 by the Flemish Counts.[105] After the *natio* moved to Antwerp, the city also granted extensive privileges in 1511, 1539, 1542, 1545 and 1554.[106] The actual *natio* functioned like the other Southern European *nationes*, with the members electing consuls, although these were subject to the King's approval. In the 1582 *Costuymen* of Antwerp, the extensive privileges were again confirmed, safeguarding the first instance jurisdiction of the Portuguese.[107] Even

---

a Model for Global Comparison', *Journal of World History*, 31, 2 (2020), 295–326, there 302–304.

99 Ibidem, 1–2.

100 Sicking, 'The Medieval Origin', 303.

101 Ibidem.

102 Ibidem, 302–304.

103 Ibidem, 303.

104 Miranda, 'Commerce, conflits et justice', 8–9; Idem, 'Conflict Management in Western Europe', 25–27.

105 Martyn, 'De Portugese natie', 81.

106 Ibidem, 83.

107 1582 *Impressae*, Title XI. Printed in: De Longé, *Coutumes* (Vol. 2), 36.

their jurisdiction over maritime affairs largely remained intact,[108] whilst other *nationes* were faced with a gradual encroachment over their jurisdiction from the late 1540s onwards.[109]

According to Hans Pohl, the Portuguese *natio* could already levy the so-called *direito da nação* in the mid-fifteenth century, as their version of the compulsory contribution was known.[110] In 1459 the King proclaimed that Portuguese merchants henceforth had to use Portuguese ships for transport, whilst foreign merchants using Portuguese ships had to pay for the *direito da nação* as well.[111] He referred to a 1458 case before the Bruges municipal court, which allowed the Biscayer *natio* to levy the *avería de naçion* on foreign merchants when the latter used foreign ships (see below), taking this as precedent.[112] The 1459 *Ordonnance* also urged Portuguese merchants to record their freight contracts at a notary so that the consuls could levy the compulsory contribution.[113] In 1512, the king decreed that Portuguese notaries could not record freight contracts when the compulsory contribution was not paid first, and also that every Portuguese merchant in the Low Countries had to pay for the contribution even if they did not live in Antwerp.[114] The estates of both Flanders and Brabant later recognised this document in response to two litigated cases on the subject from 1512 and 1516.[115] In 1518, the Portuguese king again reprimanded merchants for not paying the *direito da nação*.[116]

The specific privilege of the *direito da nação* was subsequently (re)confirmed by Margareta of Austria in 1512, by king Manuel in 1518 and in 1527 by Charles V.[117] In the Portuguese case the *direito da nação* corresponded to 1/240 levied on the imports and exports of cargo, amounting to a 0.41% contribution.[118] In 1513, the consuls were allowed to appoint a superintendent to collect it, similar to the position of *controlador* in the Castilian case.[119] As the *direito da nação* was levied on the imports and exports via maritime transport, this might indicate that it was connected to Averages, but on closer

108 Goris, *Étude*, 46–47.

109 De ruysscher, *"Naer het Romeinsch recht"*, 117–120.

110 Pohl, *Die Portugiesen*, 53–54.

111 Braamcamp Freire, *Noticias*, 69–70.

112 Ibidem. This may have referred to the 1458 case between Castilian consuls and a Pisan merchant, although this remains unclear.

113 Ibidem.

114 Ibidem, 99–100.

115 Ibidem, 176–177.

116 Ibidem, 183–184.

117 Ibidem, 100.

118 Ibidem; Goris, *Étude*, 52; Van Answaarden, *Les Portugais*, 208.

119 Braamcamp Freire, *Noticias*, 100.

inspection this is not the case. It was primarily used to cover the maintenance of the chapel and legal fees, although it could also be used to salvage cargo from wrecked ships.[120] The *direito da nação* was thus not a contribution for maritime protection costs.

Disputes within the *natio* about the *direito da nação* were not uncommon, especially following the Flemish Revolt as the Portuguese *natio* moved back and forth from Bruges to Antwerp. The Portuguese twice encountered problems with merchants unwilling to pay, leading to the 1512 *Ordonnance* of the Portuguese king. The first case in 1512 concerned Thomé Lopez, who declined to pay for the *direito da naçao* since he lived in Flanders and could not profit from the chapel of the *natio* in Antwerp.[121] The Portuguese King intervened personally and ordered that the compulsory contribution was also used for legal fees and representational costs, from which he profited, even if he did not live in Brabant.[122] Another merchant, named Loupes de Calvos, proved more stubborn. De Calvos had already returned to Bruges in 1496, apparently blessed by the (at that point) Antwerp-based consuls. The decision was also recorded by the Antwerp aldermen.[123] Yet, the Portuguese consuls filed a case in the Antwerp municipal court the same year against De Calvos to force him to pay the *direito da nação*.[124] The Antwerp aldermen lacked jurisdiction and sent the case to the Council of Brabant, which decided on 23 December 1497 that the Portuguese could not have jurisdiction over all merchants in the Low Countries, thus absolving De Calvos.[125] Subsequently, the records are silent until 1516, when the Portuguese consuls filed a case at the Great Council against De Calvos.[126] The consuls wanted to confirm their right to levy the *direito da nação* on De Calvos again after formally moving to Antwerp in 1511, but De Calvos successfully argued that since he was based in Flanders, he could not benefit from the assistance of the Portuguese consuls, pointing to an example when a ship of his was recently shipwrecked and the consuls had declined to help him.[127] The Portuguese consuls made one final effort to prove that the legal reasoning of the Council of Brabant had been wrong by pointing to their

120 Martyn, 'De Portugese natie', 80; Pohl, *Die Portugiesen*, 54; Van Answaarden, *Les Portugais*, 208–209.

121 Braamcamp Freire, *Noticias*, 99–100.

122 Ibidem.

123 Ibidem, fol. 235v.

124 Van Answaarden, *Les Portugais*, 209.

125 Ibidem. The registers of the Council of Brabant for civil law cases unfortunately only start in 1510, meaning this case has not survived in the archives.

126 BE-ARB, Grote Raad, *Registers*, nr. 816.33 (fol. 232–242). This case is also described in: Van Answaarden, *Les Portugais*, 208–220 & 221–222.

127 Ibidem, fol. 232r.

renewed privileges in Antwerp which were also acknowledged by Margareta of Austria.[128] Notwithstanding these new privileges the Great Council decided that the *direito da nação* could not be levied by the Portuguese consuls on a merchant in Bruges, in line with the sentence of the Council of Brabant.[129]

This judgement did not stop the Portuguese consuls from litigating again against De Calvos three years later.[130] De Calvos declined to appear, citing the Bruges municipal court as his *forum domicilii*. On 2 April 1519, the Great Council denied him the opportunity to lay claim to what was effectively the *Ius de non evocando* for himself, and ordered him to appear in May. However, no more cases were found by Rudy Van Answaarden.[131] Both cases clearly show the nature of the *direito da nação*. Although the contribution was levied on the transport of Portuguese ships, the costs were clearly 'common' costs, such as the maintenance of a chapel (in Lopez' case), legal fees and general costs. Salvage costs in case of shipwrecks were included and mentioned by De Calvos, but these were the only reference to maritime costs. No allusion was made to maritime protection costs.

6.3.4 *The Genoese*

The first known privileges the received by the Genoese in the Low Countries date from 1395, as the Burgundians and Genoese concluded a friendship treaty.[132] This included privileges for Genoese merchants in the Low Countries, allowing them to form a *natio*. Relations between Genoa and the Low Countries were shaky throughout the centuries. Troubles for the Genoese community thus persisted throughout the fifteenth century, depending on the wider European political situation.[133] In 1414, the Genoese in Bruges were granted further privileges in the form of tax exemptions, but in 1476 they were temporarily banned from the city, suspected of supporting France, with whom the Burgundians were at war.[134] The Consulate *de facto* moved to Antwerp in 1509, but *de jure* remained in Bruges until 1522 when Antwerp confirmed their privileges.[135] The Antwerp privileges were subsequently confirmed by Charles V and Philip II in 1532 and

128 Ibidem, fol. 236r–237r.

129 Ibidem, fol. 238r–239r.

130 Van Answaarden, *Les Portugais*, 221–222; BE-ARB, Grote Raad, *Registers*, nr. 983.509, fol. 100r. As De Calvos was not a *poorter* (citizen of Bruges), this was not necessarily a convincing argument.

131 Ibidem.

132 Braekevelt, 'Entre profit et dommage', 119. See also: Petti Balbi, *Mercanti e* nationes *nelle Fiandre: I genovesi in èta bassomedievale* (Pisa 1996), 19–45.

133 Ibidem, 121–129; Petti Balbi, *Mercanti*, 19–36.

134 Ibidem, 121–123; Goris, *Étude*, 75.

135 Goris, *Étude*, 75.

1556.[136] Despite the political troubles between Genoa and the Habsburgs at the end of the fifteenth and early sixteenth centuries, Genoese merchants could often trade in relative freedom.[137] After 1529, when their hostilities ended with the Peace of Cambrai, the importance of the Genoese within the Habsburg Empire, and hence in the Low Countries, quickly rose. They became major financiers for Charles V and Philip II, providing ample credit on the Antwerp market to the Habsburg sovereigns, playing a major role in credit relations alongside the large Southern German family firms.[138]

The Genoese had already received the right to levy the so-called *massaria* in 1395.[139] The *massaria* was sometimes also used to denote the financial administration of the *natio*, but in the context of this chapter it will mean the compulsory contribution.[140] The *massaria* already existed as a term denoting both the financial administration of Genoese merchant colonies and a contribution for their ordinary costs, for example in Cairo or the Ottoman Empire.[141] The sum the Genoese could levy was lower than the *avería de nación* of the Castilians (0.5% versus 1%) and was administered by the *Senato* back in Genoa until 1496, rather than by the consuls in the Low Countries.[142] According to the privilege, this was primarily meant to pay for the construction and the maintenance of the house of the *natio*.[143] This also explains the absence of a mention of 'Average' in the name of the *massaria*, since it was not used to cover maritime protection costs.[144] In 1496 the *Senato* agreed to a request by the Genoese consuls to give them control over the costs made by the yield of the compulsory contribution.[145] The consuls were also allowed by the *Senato* to judge disputes between their members, although this was not a formal jurisdiction.[146] In 1501, when a large number of Genoese merchants had already

136 Ibidem, 76.

137 See for an overview of their activities in Antwerp: C. Beck, 'Éléments sociaux et économiques de la vie des marchands génois a Anvers entre 1528 et 1555', *Revue du Nord*, 64, 254–255 (1982), 759–784.

138 Haemers & Stabel, 'From Bruges to Antwerp', 31–36.

139 Gilliodts-Van Severen, *Cartulaire* (Vol. 1), nr. 469 (p. 391–396).

140 Idem, *Espagne*, 595–596.

141 See footnote 110 of Chapter 2 for the relevant literature.

142 Gilliodts-Van Severen, *Cartulaire* (Vol. 1), nr. 469 (pp. 394–396); Goris, *Étude*, 77; Finot, *Étude de Gênes*, 202.

143 Finot, *Étude de Gênes*, 202.

144 Ibidem, 205.

145 Ibidem, 202–204.

146 Desimoni & Belgrano, *Documenti*, 455–457. Interestingly, this document was recorded and signed by 's-Hertoghen, one of the notaries from the family playing a major role in sixteenth-century Antwerp.

moved to Antwerp but the Consulate was still in Bruges, the consuls received permission from Philip the Fair to levy the *massaria* from the Genoese merchants in Antwerp.[147] According to Philip, some merchants had refused to pay for the compulsory contribution, arguing that they no longer used the chapel (see below).[148] In this privilege the Genoese were also allowed to use the *massaria* to cover the costs incurred by shipwreck, among other costs including bursaries for Genoese students studying abroad.[149] In contrast to the Iberian *nationes*, it could not cover the legal fees of members of the *natio*. Similar to the *direito de nação*, salvage costs were thus included, but mutual protection costs were not, as was the case with the *avería de nación*.

In 1522, the Genoese requested to have all their privileges moved from Bruges to Antwerp, which was allowed by Antwerp.[150] This privilege also allowed them to levy the *massaria* on all Genoese merchants in the Low Countries.[151] Further instructions in 1536 and 1564 were primarily concerned with combatting fraud.[152] Nevertheless the consuls were granted consular jurisdiction in 1564 by the Antwerp aldermen, which was acknowledged by Philip II in 1571.[153] According to De ruysscher, it is likely that the Genoese only used this jurisdiction sparingly, given the fact that no judgements were signed off by the Antwerp municipal court.[154] In the later sixteenth and early seventeenth century, the privileges of the Genoese *natio* were broadened to also include Genoese merchants in Cologne (1583) and all provinces of the Low Countries (1612).[155]

Similar to the Portuguese case, internal disputes came out into the open during the late fifteenth and early sixteenth century as merchants and *nationes* transferred back and forth from Bruges to Antwerp. An important and exemplary case revolved around Leonard Gentil, a Genoese merchant who lived in Antwerp and declined to pay for the *massaria* to the (at that point) Bruges-based *natio*.[156] In 1502, the Genoese consuls appeared before the Great

147 Gilliodts-Van Severen, *Cartulaire* (Vol.2), nr. 1331 (pp. 342–344).

148 Ibidem, 343–344.

149 Finot, *Étude de Gênes*, 206–207.

150 Gilliodts-Van Severen, *Cartulaire* (Vol. 2), 344; Ibidem, nr. 1524 (pp. 558–561); Finot, *Étude de Gênes*, 211–216 & 218–219; Desimoni & Belgrano, *Documenti*, 479–483. This document was also signed by Zeeger 's-Hertoghen, see Desimoni & Belgrano, *Documenti*, 483.

151 Finot, *Étude de Gênes*, 213–214; Desimoni & Belgrano, *Documenti*, 471–473. It was also confirmed by the Genoese *Doge*. See: Finot, *Étude de Gênes*, 222–226.

152 Desimoni & Belgrano, *Documenti*, 484–490; Finot, *Étude de Gênes*, 225–227; Goris, *Étude*, 76.

153 Goris, *Étude*, 76; Finot, *Étude de Gênes*, 227–228; De ruyscher, "*Naer het Romeinsch recht*", 120.

154 De ruysscher, "*Naer het Romeinsch recht*", 120.

155 Finot, *Étude de Gênes*, 229–230.

156 Goris, *Étude*, 76.

Council, bringing a notarial deed of the Bruges notary Leonard Hughe with them to certify the privileges.[157] Hughe had already passed a condemnation in 1501, demanding that Gentil should pay, apparently to no effect.[158] The Genoese *Senato* issued a statement supporting the consuls, stating that the privileges (and thus the *massaria*) were also valid outside of Flanders. In 1502, another notary, Jehan Bertin, signed and recorded the consuls' order obliging Gentil to pay.[159] Hughe also issued another order (*procuratie*) in 1503 to no avail.[160] Gentil still declined to pay, and he did not wish to appear before the Great Council in 1502 when the Genoese started legal proceedings.[161] The Great Council heard the case only in 1504, deciding that Gentil should be arrested and imprisoned until he paid for the *massaria*.[162] The court argued that the Genoese Statute and their privileges overrode all other concerns, extending the Flemish privileges to Brabant as well. Both Philip the Fair and the Council of Brabant ratified this judgement, the former also providing an implementation order for the agreement.[163] This case notably contrasts with the Portuguese case of De Calvos, where in very similar circumstances the Great Council decided otherwise, as the Portuguese privileges could only be applied in Flanders. Again, the files on Gentil make no mention of maritime protection costs or issues about Averages, but rather about the ordinary costs of the *natio*.

6.3.5 *Other* nationes *in Bruges & Antwerp*

Three other Italian merchant communities established Consulates in the Low Countries: Venetians, Florentines and Lucchese. The Venetians were important traders in fifteenth-century Bruges, but quickly faded into obscurity and (most likely) did not form a formal *natio* in Antwerp.[164] In contrast, Florentines and Lucchese were major players in the Antwerp credit market.[165] The Lucchese formed a *natio* in Bruges and received privileges in Antwerp in

157 Ibidem, 76–77; Gilliodts-Van Severen, *Cartulaire* (Vol. 2), nr. 1333 (p. 345).

158 Desimoni & Belgrano, *Documenti*, 457. See for the *condempnation*: https://www.oed.com/view/Entry/38477?redirectedFrom=condemnation#eid {Retrieved 19/01/2021}.

159 Ibidem, 462 & 463.

160 Ibidem, 463.

161 Ibidem, 463–464.

162 Ibidem, 464. Long delays were not uncommon at the Great Council: Van Rhee, *Litigation and Legislation*, 319–342.

163 Goris, *Étude*, 77; Desimoni & Belgrano, *Documenti*, 464–465.

164 Stabel, 'Italian Merchants', 140–148; Idem, 'De gewenste vreemdeling', 200–205.

165 Haemers & Stabel, 'From Bruges to Antwerp', 26–31; Lambert, *The City, the Duke and their Banker*; De Roover, *Money, Banking and Credit*. As the Genoese and Southern Germans rose in Antwerp, the Florentines became less important. See: Haemers & Stabel, 'From Bruges to Antwerp', 35; Goris, *Étude*, 78–80 & 347–350.

1501, including the right to levy the *massaria*.[166] Their *massaria* however had rather limited uses: it could only be used to salvage cargo and ships in cases of shipwreck, and for chapel maintenance.[167] In 1556, these privileges were reconfirmed by Antwerp.[168] The Florentines *de jure* moved their Consulate to Antwerp in 1510, although they received formal privileges, including the right to levy the *massaria*, only in 1546.[169] In 1564, the Florentines were granted civil jurisdiction.[170] For both the Lucchese and the Florentines, the *massaria* had limited applications.

The Catalan-Aragonese *natio*, formally based in Bruges until 1527, also levied a compulsory contribution on its members, but solely for ordinary costs, as a 1455 case proves. The Catalan merchant and *natio* representative Saldone Ferrier confiscated the contribution to protection costs made by three Aragonese merchants before a venture left, arguing that they had not paid for the maintenance of the chapel (the *Notre Dame des Carmes*) as stipulated by the privileges.[171] The merchants, meanwhile, argued that the contribution they had paid could only be used for protection costs of the venture. The Bruges municipal court ruled in the merchants' favour, arguing that the payment was unlawful and that it should be returned to the shipmaster Adrien Screvel. Yet they were also held to pay their annual compulsory contribution for the maintenance of the chapel separately, suggesting the Catalan-Aragonese did not use their compulsory contribution for maritime protection costs but solely for ordinary costs, similar to the Genoese and Portuguese.[172] This shows that the Castilians and Biscayers were unique in their uses of their compulsory contribution to cover maritime protection costs, as even other 'Spanish' *nationes* did not do so.

The Antwerp municipal archives also preserve the privileges of multiple other *nationes*, including various smaller and less-studied merchant communities such as the Scottish and 'Greek' *natio* of Constantinople.[173] These do not include privileges to levy a compulsory contribution, but mostly basic

166 Goris, *Étude*, 79–80; BE-SAA, Vreemde natieën, Natie van Lucca, inv. PK#1076 (1501). See for the Lucchese in Bruges: De Roover, 'La communauté'.

167 BE-SAA, Natie van Lucca, inv. PK#1076.

168 Goris, *Étude*, 80.

169 Ibidem, 79.

170 Finot, *Étude de Gênes*, 228.

171 Gilliodts-Van Severen, *Espagne*, 65–66.

172 Ibidem, 66.

173 See for example: BE-SAA, Vreemde natieën, Griekse natie (Natie van Constantinopel), inv. PK#1080 (1582); Idem, Natie van Schotland, inv. PK#1081 (1540). See for the Greeks of Constantinople: E. Dursteler, *Venetians in Constantinople: Nation, Identity and Coexistence in the Early Modern Mediterranean* (Baltimore, MD 2006).

tax exemptions. It appears that Antwerp was less forthcoming than Bruges in offering extensive privileges, unless these were long held in Bruges. In those cases, Antwerp simply confirmed that the privileges from Bruges were also valid in Antwerp.[174] The Hanseatic merchants were given relatively extensive privileges including civil jurisdiction, exactly as they held in Bruges.[175] The English, alongside the Portuguese, had the most extensive jurisdictional privileges in Antwerp.[176] The English possessed a rather broad civil jurisdiction over its own members, but primarily to make sure that English merchants did not have to go to a local court to litigate.[177] Their ability to levy contributions on their members was rather limited or non-existent. According to Oskar De Smedt, the English levied a small one-off fee when becoming a member, but this was not comparable to the compulsory contribution of the Southern European *nationes*.[178] English merchants paid some common SA costs (e.g. tolls and duties) to the *natio*, but no payments for maritime protection costs.[179]

6.4 Disputes on the *avería de nación*

6.4.1 *Disputes on the* avería de nación *in Bruges and Antwerp*

Now that we have established that the *avería de nación* differed from the compulsory contributions of the other *nationes*, it is time to look at litigation. As we have also seen in some of the above cases, internal questions could often be decided on the basis of the respective privileges. The privileges however did not answer the question of whether the Castilian and Biscayer *nationes* could levy the *avería de nación* on other foreign merchants, as the *avería de nación* was levied on imports and exports. In practice, this primarily concerned Italian merchants, who regularly used Castilian and Biscayer transport services. Legal practice and litigation were the only way to find out. In principle, the answer was affirmative, at least when Italian merchants transported cargo on Spanish ships.[180] The port of origin of the shipmaster was crucial in this respect, for

174 Gelderblom, *Cities of commerce*, 114–116. See for example for the Portuguese: Martyn, 'De Portugese natie', 76–77; Goris, *Étude*, 35–38.

175 Kypta, 'Von Brügge nach Antwerpen', 174–175; De ruysscher, "*Naer het Romeinsch recht*", 120. See also: BE-SAA, Vreemde natieën, Duitse natie (Oosterlingen, Hanzeaten), inv. PK#1061 (1469–1584).

176 De ruysscher, "*Naer het Romeinsch recht*", 117–120.

177 De Smedt, *De Engelse natie* (Vol. 2), 158–175.

178 Ibidem, 30–31.

179 Ibidem, 244–248.

180 The question whether rented ships could count, for example, was never answered.

which signed freight contracts often provided the best proof. However, the jurisdictional complexity of the sixteenth-century Low Countries made enforcement a substantially difficult task, especially as most Italian *nationes* moved to Antwerp during the sixteenth century. In contrast, intra-Spanish disputes presented another answer, as the Bruges municipal court did not allow the Castilians or Biscayers to levy the contribution on Catalan-Aragonese merchants.

6.4.1.1 Disputes with the Genoese

Tensions existed particularly between the Spanish and Genoese *nationes*, as the latter often used the former's ships for cargo transport to the Low Countries. For example, in 1458 a Pisan merchant called Baptiste Aliate refused to pay the *avería de nación* to the Castilian *natio* for a Castilian-led venture transporting his cargo.[181] Aliate preferred to pay the compulsory contribution to the Genoese, claiming membership of the *natio*.[182] The municipal court in Bruges decided that the merchant should pay a contribution specifically for this venture and therefore the *avería de nación* was to be paid to the Castilians. The court however also decided that Aliate should also pay his regular contribution to the Genoese *natio*.[183] In 1472, the Castilian shipmaster Michel de Sancle claimed the right to extract the payment of Averages from the Genoese consuls, whose merchants had used his ship to transport cargo to the Low Countries.[184] The Genoese objected, stating that common costs and protection costs had to be part of the freight agreement, at least according to the Statute of the city of Genoa and their *natio*. According to this Statute, the Genoese were only allowed to pay protection costs and SA to either their own consuls or use ships from Genoa. The Bruges aldermen consulted several foreign merchants and decided that the Genoese nevertheless would have to pay the contribution. This set a precedent for later decisions by the municipal court, a decision also reached by the Great Council in the sixteenth century in the large case between the Biscayers and the Genoese (see below). In January 1482, the municipal court sentenced the Genoese merchant Jean Baptiste Spinulli to pay for protection and common operational costs, although it only required a *namptissement* for now, stating that its judgement would come later.[185] The judgement came two months later, indeed stating that Genoese merchants

---

181 Gilliodts-Van Severen, *Espagne*, 79–80.

182 See for Aliate: Fieremans, "'In the Hope'", 24.

183 Gilliodts-Van Severen, *Espagne*, 80. This may well be the case that the Portuguese King referred to in his privileges, see section 6.3.3.

184 Ibidem, 111.

185 Ibidem, 122.

using Castilian transport facilities had to pay for it.[186] Even if the contribution was not explicitly mentioned in the freight contract, the Bruges municipal court ruled that the freight contract formed the legal basis to extract the compulsory contribution, based on the origin of the shipmaster. In 1505 and 1511 similar cases formed the subject of litigation against Genoese merchants with the same outcome.[187]

6.4.1.2 Intra-Spanish Disputes

Intra-Spanish disputes were also common in the Low Countries, although these cases brought different results. In 1487, the Castilian consuls launched a case at the Bruges municipal court, this time aimed at the consuls of the Catalan-Aragonese *natio* about the *avería de nación*.[188] As Catalonia and Aragon formally remained separate kingdoms from Castile (under the composite monarchy), it is not unthinkable that domestic rivalry played a role here.[189] The Castilians, in this case, wished to reclaim Averages from the Catalan merchant Jan Pasqual.[190] The Castilian consuls claimed their 'ancient right' to levy the contribution on all merchants using Castilian ships.[191] They invoked precedents from similar cases, including cases in favour of the Genoese, Florentine and Lucchese *nationes* in Bruges being allowed to levy the contribution on foreigners.[192] Unfortunately, there are no known records of these specific cases, which is a shame as they could have been interesting to shed light on the 'Italian side' of the story.[193] The Catalan-Aragonese consuls responded that they had held this privilege themselves for 150 years, and that their privileges only allowed them to levy a contribution for the maintenance of their church (see also section 6.3.5).[194] The Castilian consuls retorted that both the Biscayers and the Castilians had the privilege to levy the *avería de nación* for all ventures that made a stop between Gibraltar and Bilbao.[195] The Catalan-Aragonese however argued that their compulsory contribution only included a contribution to the maintenance of the chapel, and that they thus could not be held liable to pay

186 Ibidem, 122–124.
187 Ibidem, 214 & 230–231.
188 Ibidem, 137–139.
189 See: Yun-Casalilla, *Iberian World Empires*, 22–34.
190 He was also named Jehan Pascal, as the 1515 Great Council case shows where this precedent was used in the oral arguments. See section 6.4.4.
191 Gilliodts-Van Severen, *Espagne*, 137.
192 Ibidem.
193 Although some of these cases were referred to in the 1515 Great Council case. See section 6.4.4.
194 Gilliodts-Van Severen, *Espagne*, 138.
195 Ibidem, 138–139.

for the protection costs of another *natio*.[196] They moreover complained that the Castilians did not make a similar claim on members of other *nationes*, such as the Hanseatic, Southern German, Portuguese and Florentine merchants, indicating there was a 'Spanish' political controversy at the root of the dispute.[197] The aldermen bench appointed a panel of a Hanseatic, Portuguese and local merchants, all 'notable men', which decided that the Catalan-Aragonese did not have to pay for the *avería de nación* of the Castilians, referring to their ancient privileges.[198] Notably, this decision differed from those where the Genoese were involved.

The value of the payments became the issue in a case of August 1500.[199] Three Castilian shipmasters filed the case against the Aragonese merchant Baltazar Fave. The masters had delivered wool to Fave, who according to the charter party was supposed to pay Averages per bale of wool.[200] Fave argued that the freight contract stipulating the five pounds *Grooten Vlaams* payment per bale of wool included payments for Averages, although they were not specifically mentioned. Since no damage had occurred, Fave argued that not everything would have to be paid.[201] The court commission decided that in principle the shipmasters had the right to receive the full freight from Fave, but required a *namptissement* by the shipmasters and also ordered them to deliver the bales of wool to Fave.[202] Both parties were given time to develop their arguments further and produce evidence, but no outcome is known since no further developments on this case are recorded. On 20 July 1502, another group of Castilian shipmasters again appeared in court to litigate a case against Biscayer merchants, the latter group having declined to pay for the *avería de nación*.[203] The Biscayer merchants argued that they had also paid Averages in Burgos to the *Consulado* before the venture, and that moreover they customarily only paid part of the Averages to the Castilian *natio*, as would be incorporated in the 1504 *Prágmatica*. The court agreed to this latter point and subsequently decided that the Biscayers only had to pay for a quarter of the requested sum of Averages.

---

196 Ibidem, 139.

197 Ibidem.

198 Ibidem. The decision of the arbitration panel was immediately enforced by the Bruges municipal court.

199 Ibidem, 197–198.

200 Ibidem, 198.

201 Ibidem.

202 Ibidem.

203 Ibidem, 205. The case is only described by Gilliodts, rather than offering a transcription. Part of the information is hence based on the underlying archival file: BE-SAB, Spaans Consulaat, *Collectie Charters*, nr. 73.

Even whilst the Castilians and Biscayers from 1511 onward jointly litigated an important case against the Genoese on the *averia de naçión* (see sections 6.4.2–6.4.5), intra-Spanish disputes on the same subject were still commonplace. Both cases clearly show that the legal strategies of the Castilians were very much based on opportunism, shifting alliances as they saw fit.[204] In April 1517, for example, the Castilian consuls obtained a warrant to enforce payment of the *avería de nación* against both Biscayer and Genoese merchants using their ships.[205] In 1533 another dispute between the Castilians and Biscayers can be traced, as two Castilian shipmasters complained before the Bruges municipal court about the lack of payment by the consuls of the Biscayer *natio* (Pedro de Navarrete, Cristophe de Salines, Fernando Dorosco and Martin de Salines).[206] The Biscayer consuls replied that, according to the agreement between the Castilians and the Biscayers, as well as the 1504 *Pragmática*, they were exempted for 2.5% of Average payments.[207] The shipmasters pointed to the fact that two of the Biscayer consuls and freighters were themselves not actually Biscayers, which meant that the agreement had to be invalid in this case.[208] The court however agreed with the consuls, stating that the exemption was indeed well-known. In 1559, various Biscayer merchants also complained to the Castilian consuls for being forced to pay for the *avería de nación* after using the compulsory *rotulo* system to transport wool to Flanders.[209] They argued that the *avería de nación* they paid also included a contribution for the maintenance of the Castilian chapel in Bruges: for understandable reasons, the Biscayers only wanted to contribute to the maritime protection costs from which they directly profited. Although the consuls did not scrap their contribution fully, they were allowed to pay a lower sum.[210] Even in Antwerp, the two *nationes* fought legal battles over the subject, as a case from 1568 indicates.[211]

In Bruges, the Castilians actively litigated to levy the *avería de nación* on foreign merchants. When it came to Genoese merchants, they were relatively successful. Despite repeated agreements between the Castilians and Biscayers,

204 See: Dreijer, 'Identity'.

205 Gilliodts-Van Severen, *Espagne*, 245.

206 Ibidem, 298–299.

207 Ibidem, 298.

208 This is interesting in itself: Puttevils, focusing primarily on Italian merchants, has already pointed to the fact that the attachment to the various *nationes* was less strict in sixteenth-century Antwerp. See: Puttevils, *Merchants and trading*, 150.

209 BE-SAB, *Libro de pleytos ordinarios*, fol. 187r–v.

210 Ibidem, fol. 187v.

211 BE-SAA, *Vonnisboeken*, V#1251, fol. 193r.

tensions over the *avería de nación* of both *nationes* remained commonplace as well, although they also opportunistically worked together when necessary. Levying the compulsory contribution on other Spanish *nationes* (e.g. the Catalan-Aragonese, or the Andalusians after 1500), however, appeared to be impossible. What accounted for the differences with the Genoese is not fully clear, although political motives may have played a role. The Crown may have been unwilling to disturb the different customs and traditions of the various components of the 'composite monarchy', therefore allowing all the 'Spanish' *nationes* to continue enjoying their long-held privileges even in the Low Countries. Yet this solution inevitably led to an increase in litigation following a different understanding of the reciprocal customs. The Genoese meanwhile did not enjoy this protection within the 'composite monarchy', although there is sparse evidence that some of the Italian *nationes* also tried to levy the compulsory contribution on foreign merchants in response.[212]

6.4.2 *The 1515 Biscayer-Genoese Case: Introduction*

The remainder of this paragraph studies in detail the arguments brought forward in a case filed at the Great Council in July 1515. The case was similar to disputes with Genoese merchants sketched above but turned into a thrilling legal drama with multiple appeals before various courts across the Low Countries. This time, the Biscayer consuls requested this contribution from three Genoese merchants and one Florentine merchant. It is clear that the small yet undefined sum involved was only a proxy for the actual issue at hand. The case set off a chain of legal events, which lasted until the 1540s: although the case is procedurally interesting in itself (see Table 10 for all the extant evidence), we will primarily limit ourselves here to the 1515 case, as the arguments presented shed light on both the legal nature of the *avería de nación* and the role of Averages more broadly in protection costs.[213] The material has also been described in some of the source editions for this period, but the details have been incorrectly interpreted in many places, as the literature followed Gilliodts-Van Severen in lumping together the various compulsory contributions.[214]

212 Gilliodts-Van Severen, *Espagne*, 137.

213 It also sheds light on the legal strategies, but they shall not be discussed in detail here. See: Dreijer, 'Identity, Conflict and Commercial Law'.

214 All the cases are catalogued and described in: De Smidt, *Sententiën*. See table 10 for the references in the various source editions and books. See also: Wijffels, 'Justitia in Commerciis', 48–49. This is a very concise summary of the case, but it does grasp its importance.

TABLE 10 The Biscayer vs. Genoese case (1511–1540s)

Date	Archive / Additional sources	Case	Remarks
1511	BE-ARB, Grote Raad, *Processen*, nr. 294 (*sine folio*)	First instance proceeding before Bruges municipal court	Initiated by Biscayer consuls vs. Genoese and Florentine merchants
1511	–	First instance proceeding before Antwerp municipal court	Initiated by Castilian merchants
1515	BE-ARB, Grote Raad, *Processen*, nr. 294 (*sine folio*)	First instance proceeding before Great Council	Files contain arguments of the parties
1515	Idem, nr. 3519 (*sine folio*)	Idem	Files concern *namptissement* in Bruges
28/07/1515	BE-ARB, Grote Raad, *Registers*, 815.12, fol. 70–88; also in Gilliodts-Van Severen, *Espagne*, 230–240; Desimoni & Belgrano, *Documenti*, 469–470; Finot, *Étude de Gênes*, 160–170	Extended sentence of first instance proceeding	First instance proceeding on *avería de nación* by Biscayers
28/07/1515	Idem, 815.13, fol. 90–106v	Idem	First instance proceeding on *avería de nación* by Castilians
22/05/1518	Idem, 818.28, pp. 283–309	Appeal before Great Council	On *avería de nación*
13/07/1518	Idem, 818.35, pp. 391–405	Idem	On *namptissement*
1518	Idem, *Processen*, nr. 294 (*sine folio*)	Judgement of Secret Council	Archives of Secret Council only start in 1531
28/11/1523	Idem, *Registers*, 823.68, pp. 547–560; also in Desimoni & Belgrano, *Documenti*, 476	Appeal against Secret Council decision (1518)	Appeal by Biscayer consuls on *avería de nación*

TABLE 10 The Biscayer vs. Genoese case (1511–1540s) (*cont.*)

DATE	ARCHIVE / ADDITIONAL SOURCES	CASE	REMARKS
31/03/1524 (1525 n.s.)	Idem, 824.83, pp. 749–755; also in Desimoni & Belgrano, *Documenti*, 476	Idem	Appeal by Biscayer consuls on *avería de nación*
08/07/1524	Desimoni & Belgrano, *Documenti*, 477	Idem	Interlocutory judgement by the Great Council, not found in the archives
06/10/1526	BE-ARB, Grote Raad, *Registers*, 826.68, pp. 567–574.	Request for implementation order (*procuratie*)	Initiated by Biscayer consuls
1526–1549	Idem, *Processen*, nr. 294 (*sine folio*)	Various requests by both parties	

SOURCES: SEE TABLE.

6.4.3 *Prelude: First Instance Proceedings at the Bruges and Antwerp Municipal Courts (1511)*

The case (again) concerned the question of whether the Castilian and Biscayer *nationes* could levy the *avería de nación* contribution on Italian merchants.[215] In 1511, the Biscayer consuls requested a contribution from five Italian merchants for a venture to the Iberian Peninsula: the Genoese merchants Jehan Baptiste Spinelli, Luuc Pinelly, Simon Carga and Nicolas Spingle, and Anthone Rouselin of Florence.[216] All these merchants lived in Antwerp.[217] It followed the arrival of a ship from Bilbao in Zeeland with Genoese and Florentine cargo, for which the Biscayers requested payment of the *avería de nación*.[218] The Biscayer consul started legal proceedings before the Bruges municipal court against the Genoese and Florentine consuls, supported by the Castilian consuls who also sought to have their right to levy the *avería de nación* on foreign merchants

215 Gilliodts-Van Severen, *Espagne*, 230–240.

216 Ibidem, 231.

217 The Genoese *de jure* moved their Consulate to Antwerp in 1522, although *de facto* a large part of the Genoese colony already went in 1509.

218 BE-ARB, Grote Raad, *Processen*, nr. 294 (12/07/1511).

confirmed. At the same time, the two Spanish *nationes* encouraged individual Castilian and Biscayer merchants in Antwerp to start proceedings in Antwerp on the same issue, perhaps foreseeing enforcement problems in Bruges.[219] In Bruges, the Biscayers won the case and the Genoese were forced to pay a *namptissement* to the court's clerk until their merchants paid the contribution or an appeal was made.[220] The Antwerp municipal court, meanwhile, sided with the Italian merchants, citing jurisdictional problems to levy the *avería de nación*.[221]

The Genoese consuls subsequently filed an appeal at the Great Council against the *namptissement* payment they were forced to make in Bruges.[222] They did so supported by the consuls of Venice, Florence and Lucca, also threatened by the precedent of allowing Castilians and Biscayers to levy the *avería de nación* on Italian merchants.[223] Foreseeing trouble on enforcement grounds (the merchants after all lived in Antwerp), the Castilian and Biscayer consuls filed an appeal at the Great Council against the decision of the Antwerp municipal court, representing the individual merchants who had filed the case in Antwerp. Information on the two initial cases before the municipal courts is very sketchy, as references to those cases can only be found in the court briefings in the suit before the Great Council.[224] These cases offer solid evidence of the jurisdictional complexity of the early sixteenth-century Low Countries, something increased by the shift from Bruges to Antwerp.[225] Although an appeal to the Council of Flanders was theoretically a possibility, it appears that both parties agreed that only the Great Council had the proper jurisdiction to judge about the dispute.

6.4.4 *The Arguments before the Great Council (1515)*

The Genoese and Biscayers agreed with the attorney-general (*procureur général*) at the Great Council that the court should hear the first instance proceedings. The Council agreed to hear three separate cases. First, the Biscayers appealed the Bruges verdict against the Genoese;[226] second, the Castilian

219 Idem (28/08/1515).

220 Gilliodts-Van Severen, *Espagne*, 231. See also: BE-ARB, Grote Raad, *Processen*, nr. 294 (12/07/1511).

221 BE-ARB, Grote Raad, *Processen*, nr. 294 (28/08/1515). This was probably an appeal in Antwerp given the date of the case. The *Vonnisboeken* of the Antwerp municipal court have unfortunately not survived for this period.

222 Ibidem.

223 Ibidem.

224 Ibidem.

225 Donlan & Heirbaut, '"A Patchwork of Accommodations"'.

226 BE-ARB, Grote Raad, *Registers*, nr. 815.12, (fol. 70–88); Gilliodts-Van Severen, *Espagne*, 230–240.

consuls appealed against the Antwerp decision;[227] third, the Genoese appealed against the payment of a *namptissement* in Bruges by its town clerk, Johan de Hayon.[228] The first two cases offer specific information on the application of the *avería de nación*, and will therefore be treated in detail here: the third will be referenced only where necessary, as it was primarily a procedural case.

The full record of the first instance case of the Biscayers before the Great Council has been preserved in the archives of the Castilian *natio* and in the Great Council archives themselves, including the arguments of both parties.[229] This offers a unique insight into the perception of the merchants on the compulsory contributions, although the arguments in the court case were sometimes also deliberate misstatements to win the case. In their oral arguments, the Biscayer consuls neatly laid out the differences between three varieties of Averages: GA and SA (*grosse et commune avarie*); PA (*petite*); and the compulsory contribution of the *natio* (*denier de nation*, the French term for the *dinero de nación*, in itself another name for the *avería de nación*).[230] The latter was used for the maintenance of their chapel, but also for protection costs of maritime trade.[231] The Biscayers thence argued that the *avería de nación*, which they claimed to be their form of the *denier de nation*, could also be levied on foreign merchants using their ships.[232] This was a deliberate falsehood, as they equalled the various compulsory contributions to argue for their cause: of course, as the Genoese did not use the *massaria* for protection costs, they could not do the same. The Biscayers therefore deliberately used the polysemic meaning of their 'Consular average' to strengthen the argument. To further support their argument, the Biscayers included precedents and privileges.[233] The Genoese, in response, argued that only members of the *natio* should pay for the compulsory contribution as it covered ordinary costs for the benefit of the members only.[234] Moreover, they stressed that the cited privileges had

227 Idem, nr. 815.13 (fol. 90–106v).

228 Idem, *Processen*, nr. 3519.

229 Printed in: Gilliodts-Van Severen, *Espagne*, 230–240.

230 Ibidem, 231–232.

231 Ibidem, 231.

232 Ibidem.

233 Ibidem, 231–235. They cited for example the 1368 and 1494 privileges, an arbitrational sentence from 1454, court records from 1458, 1471, 1481, 1482 and 1490, an agreement between the Spanish and Italian *nationes* on the subject of the *avería de nación* and 'usages and customs'. See: Ibidem. See for the privileges: BE-ARB, Grote Raad, *Processen*, nr. 294 (15/03/1482), (18/08/1494) & (18/12/1504). See also: BE-SAB, Spaans Consulaat, III.A.1, fol. 18r–23v.

234 Ibidem, 233–234.

been granted to the Castilians and not the Biscayers.[235] Denying that the cases presented by the Biscayers constituted precedent,[236] they also argued that a single payment to the Castilian *natio* (from 1454) could not bind individual merchants for future payments.[237] In addition, they argued that the former judgements were against individual merchants and not against the *natio*.[238] The attorney general offered an interim judgement after these arguments, siding with the Genoese. He argued that levying the *avería de nación* on the Genoese was not an established right of the Biscayers, suggesting they should be fined for bringing this case.[239] After this interim verdict, the parties were allowed to answer and address the points raised.

The Biscayer consuls produced a lengthy answer.[240] They argued that they did not want to claim control over individual Genoese merchants, but that the freight contract signed by a Biscayer shipmaster constituted the legal basis to levy the *avería de nación*, as the shipmaster's port of origin decided where the Averages should be paid.[241] The Genoese had argued that compulsory contributions could only be levied with the blessing of a sovereign, something they implied the Biscayers did not have.[242] Denying that the case of Jan Pasqual (also Jehan Pascal, see above) constituted precedent, the consuls argued that their own privileges took preference as the cited case had only concerned the Catalan and Castilian *natio*.[243] As they had received their own privileges in the meantime, and were also acknowledged by the city of Bruges and the Count of Flanders, these privileges overruled the precedent.[244] Yet both the sovereign and the Bruges aldermen had acknowledged the privilege of the *avería de nación* for the Biscayers.[245] The Biscayers thus held that they had followed the law of Bruges and stuck to every procedural rule to levy the compulsory contribution.[246] Given the fact that individual Genoese merchants had consented to the voyage by means of the freight contract, this was the legal basis for levying the *avería de nación*.[247] According to the Biscayer con-

235 Ibidem, 234.
236 Ibidem. See footnote 233.
237 Ibidem, 234.
238 Ibidem.
239 Ibidem, 235.
240 Ibidem, 235–240.
241 Ibidem, 236.
242 Ibidem.
243 Ibidem.
244 Ibidem, 237.
245 Ibidem, 237–238.
246 Ibidem, 238.
247 Ibidem.

suls, the precedents passed by the municipal court of Bruges showed that this was enough to consider the compulsory contribution binding for the Genoese merchants.[248]

Although the Biscayers may not have known compulsory registration of the freight contracts like the Portuguese, these precedents may well have incentivised the Biscayers to keep the freight contracts meticulously for future purposes. They further claimed that because they had followed the law of Bruges, the *namptissement* needed by them in the first instance case in Bruges was rightfully levied.[249] This followed the precedents set by the Bruges municipal court, for example the 1472 and 1482 cases.[250] The Great Council ruled in favour of the Biscayers, forcing the Genoese to pay for the compulsory contribution on the basis of the cited precedents, and the fact that the freight contract was the legal basis on which compulsory contributions could be levied. This meant the court openly disagreed with the attorney-general.[251] Moreover, they declared that only the Genoese had to pay for the *avería de nación* levied by the Biscayers, but not Rouselin, the Florentine merchant.[252] No reason was given for this by the court, although the document hints at the fact that the Florentine merchant was only a junior partner in the venture.[253]

In the second case, following the Antwerp judgement, the Castilian consuls launched an appeal at the Great Council against the four Italian *nationes*, although the Great Council also decided to hear this case in the first instance.[254] It appears that unnamed Genoese merchants had declined to pay for the *avería de nación*, notwithstanding the fifteenth-century precedents before the Bruges municipal court and the 1492 agreement, although no clear direct reason for the case is given.[255] Most likely, the Castilians also wanted to have their privilege secured by a firm precedent following the Biscayer case. The Castilian consuls explicitly argued that, based on the precedents also cited by the Biscayers, they had the right to levy the *avería de nación* on all Italian merchants using Iberian ships.[256] Only those with substantial interests in the venture had to contribute (meaning a sort of franchise clause was applied), but

248 Ibidem.
249 Ibidem, 239.
250 Ibidem.
251 Ibidem, 240.
252 BE-ARB, Grote Raad, *Registers*, nr. 815.12 (fol. 87v).
253 Ibidem, fol. 88r.
254 Idem, nr. 815.13 (fol. 90r–106v).
255 Ibidem, fol. 90r–v.
256 Ibidem, fol. 91r.

according to the Castilians this was the case for the Genoese.[257] Even if ships arrived in Middelburg instead of the ante-ports of Bruges, the right to levy the *avería de nación* was valid, as the Middelburg aldermen had acknowledged this as well.[258] As a form of *captatio benevolentiae*, the Castilians also referred to the privileges and municipal law of Bruges, without specifying which specific rule would benefit them.[259] The Castilian consuls furthermore argued that the Genoese would at least have to pay a *namptissement* before disputing the fact in court, something the Genoese had failed to do in Antwerp.[260]

The court requested both parties to come up with additional evidence (e.g. freight contracts), especially on the cargo the Genoese had loaded onto Castilian ships.[261] These documents have unfortunately not survived. The Genoese, on behalf of the other Italian *nationes*, defended themselves by arguing that they stuck to the municipal law of Bruges, which allegedly guaranteed their independence by the privileges.[262] They had liaised with the Lucchese, Florentine and Venetian consuls and agreed with them that this case could not be covered by the 1492 agreement on the payment of Averages, since this was only valid for Bruges, but not for Brabant and Antwerp.[263] The Genoese consuls called it 'absurd' that the Castilian consuls had the right to levy the *avería de nación* without consulting the consuls of Italian *nationes*.[264] This infringed on their sovereign rights, because the Genoese consuls at least had to be consulted when levying the *avería de nación* on their members.[265] The Great Council, referring to the 1492 agreement and the precedents from Bruges, decided however that the Genoese indeed had to pay for the *avería de nación* when loading on Castilian ships, deciding this on the same day as the decision in favour of the Biscayers was made (28 July 1515). However, the Florentine, Venetian and Lucchese merchants were absolved from paying it. The court gave no specific reason for this decision.[266]

6.4.5 *Coda: Enforcement Problems (1518–1549)*

Although the Great Council clearly laid out its verdict and also stuck to the precedents from the Bruges municipal court, the case lingered on for decades.

257 Ibidem, fol. 91v.
258 Ibidem, fol. 93r.
259 Ibidem, fol. 94v.
260 Ibidem, fol. 94r & 95v.
261 Ibidem, fol. 96v.
262 Ibidem, fol. 100v.
263 Ibidem, fol. 100r.
264 Ibidem, fol. 101r–v.
265 Ibidem, fol. 105v.
266 Ibidem, fol. 106r–v.

Based on procedural loopholes, the Genoese were able to litigate for years to delay the actual payment (see Table 10). Only in the appeals brought by the Genoese consul Jaspar Sauly in May 1518 were further arguments presented. One concerned the proper *avería de nación* case, the other one the *namptissement* paid in Bruges.[267] For the first case, the sentence has survived, again with the arguments. The Genoese based their appeal for the *avería de nación* case on two grounds: first, the ship transporting the cargo in the 1511 case primarily transported Genoese cargo, meaning the Biscayers had no right to levy a contribution; and second, the Biscayers deliberately inflated the value of the cargo on the ship to receive a higher contribution from the Genoese.[268] Sauly argued that the *avería de nación* could be used to cover SA costs, but not GA costs.[269] According to him, the Biscayers had inflated the value to also hedge against potential GA costs, which was, of course, not the goal of the *avería de nación*. Nor could the contribution be used to hedge against the risk of damage, as the point of the contribution was to manage costs and thence avoid damage.[270] If this was indeed the case, the Biscayers violated the goal of the instrument when levying the contribution on foreign merchants. Rather than allow the Genoese insight into the calculations on the *avería de nación*, the Biscayer consuls had consistently denied the Genoese this.[271] The Biscayers answered by pointing to their 'ancient' privilege to levy the *avería de nación* and the privilege to draw up the necessary calculations.[272] They had calculated the compulsory contribution in a similar manner as they did for their own members, based on the freight contracts underlying the venture.[273] The Great Council agreed with the Biscayers and decided that the ancient privileges of the Biscayers were valid in claiming the compulsory contribution of the Genoese.[274]

This was not the end of the story, however. The Genoese, ever the masters of procedural loopholes, petitioned the supreme court of the Low Countries, the Secret Council, to force the Great Council to revise the verdict.[275] The Secret Council indeed allowed for this on technicalities in 1518, after which the Great Council revised the verdict only in 1524.[276] The Genoese argued there that in a recent case, the Catalan-Aragonese *natio* had been denied the right to levy the

267 Idem, *Registers*, 818.28 (pp. 283–309) & 818.35 (pp. 391–405).

268 Idem 818.28, pp. 285 & 287.

269 Ibidem, p. 289.

270 Ibidem, p. 287.

271 Ibidem, p. 290.

272 Ibidem, p. 288.

273 Ibidem, pp. 303–305.

274 Ibidem, p. 306.

275 Idem, *Processen*, nr. 294 (17/04/1515) & (24/03/1518). See section 1.6.3 for the role of the Secret Council.

276 Ibidem, *Processen*, nr. 294 (24/03/1518).

*avería de nación*on the Genoese. As the Catalan-Aragonese did not use their compulsory contributions for maritime protection costs, this argument could not be put on an equal footing with the arguments on the *avería de nación*, but may have been a useful legal argument for the Genoese.[277] Although the Great Council did not significantly change the verdict, it lowered the amount that the Genoese had to pay: moreover, in another verdict from 1525 it decided that the Biscayers had to share in the litigation costs.[278]

Despite an order of payment from 1526, the case lingered until the late 1540s, as the Genoese invented numerous ways to avoid payment, for example by filing new cases at the Admiralty.[279] Despite the enforcement problems, the case clearly offered a precedent on the *avería de nación* when Italian merchants used Castilian or Biscayer ships to levy the compulsory contribution on them based on the freight contract. Both the Biscayers and Genoese deliberately misrepresented the nature of the *avería de nación* in their legal arguments, for example as the Biscayers falsely equalled their compulsory contributions to the Genoese ones under the name *denier de nation*, whilst the Genoese did not use their compulsory contribution for protection costs; or as the Genoese cited precedents from the Catalan-Aragonese *natio* in 1524. As this thorny issue could only be solved in legal practice, the documents of the Great Council case present a unique insight into the matter. The Great Council largely followed precedent from the Bruges municipal court, although it is not clear why the distinction between Italian and Spanish merchants was made: it may have been the case that the Italian merchant communities were totally dependent on Castilian and Biscayer maritime transport, and that moral hazard was prevented as the Italian merchants profited from the protection arrangements made. What it does show is the specifically Castilian and Biscayer nature of the protection costs issue, as the mercantile and political organisation of the wool trade and its strength in maritime transport led them to go to great lengths to protect the privilege of the *avería de nación*, as this was seen as instrumental to protect the interests of the *natio*, particularly its task to provide protection for the wool trade. Yet insisting on the privilege backfired to a certain extent, as enforcement costs rose, which also significantly impacted the ability of shipmasters and merchants to trade profitably and provide proper protection.

---

277 Idem, *Registers*, 823.68, pp. 551–552.

278 Desimoni & Belgrano, *Documenti*, 477.

279 See for example: BE-ARB, *Processen*, nr. 294 (07/10/1531) & (14/05/1542).

6.5 The *avería(s)*

The developments around the threat of attacks at sea *c.*1550 apparently necessitated the development of a new compulsory contribution levied by the Burgos *Consulado* and Castilian *natio*. Whilst the *avería de nación* of course covered protection costs, this 1% compulsory contribution may well not have been enough to cover the rising protection costs stipulated by the 1550 and 1551 *Ordonnances*. Therefore, a new compulsory contribution was developed, which was (confusingly) called the *avería(s)*.[280] Archival material is scarce and is often rather polysemic, as it as times denoted as *flete y averías gruesas*, *averías gruesas* or *averías gruesas y comunes*.[281] In a previous publication, I have thus confused the *flete y averías* with this 'new' compulsory contribution, reading the available evidence as either *flete y averías* or as GA.[282] While the publication was correct in stating that pilotage costs fell under the *flete y averías*, the article misinterpreted the available evidence on protection costs, as the *flete y averías* did not cover protection costs. In the literature on the Castilians in the Low Countries, only Raymond Fagel has noted that around 1553 a new form of *avería(s)* was established to meet the demands stipulated under the 1551 *Ordonnance*, but did not provide further details.[283] In short, the polysemic meaning of the Spanish Averages is nowhere near as clear (or obscure) as in the case of the *avería(s)* for protection costs.

What is clear is that the demand for protection as a 'club good' rose during the sixteenth century,[284] as privateering was endemic and the endless wars of Charles V and Philip II did not make the seas any safer either. As we have noted in section 6.2, the most famous establishment of a compulsory contribution for protection costs was the *avería* for the New World trade.[285] Yet the issue of protection costs was of course also rather relevant for the Low Countries trade. Whilst we have seen in Chapter 2 that the Castilians and Portuguese opposed the measures of the central government for compulsory protection measures (convoy ships and artillery),[286] internally the Castilians did act to meet the

---

280 Basas Fernández, *El Consulado*, 168–171; Fagel, *De Hispano-Vlaamse wereld*, 419–422; García Garralón, 'The Nautical Republic', 10–11.

281 BE-SAB, *Libro de pleytos ordinarios*, fol. 108r–v, 145r, 151v–152r, 210v & 211r–v, for different notes of these terms.

282 Dreijer, 'Maritime Averages', 49–52.

283 Fagel, *De Hispano-Vlaamse wereld*, 419. See also: Sicking, *Neptune and the Netherlands*, 247–260.

284 See for protection as a 'club good': Lindberg, 'Club Goods and Inefficient Institutions'.

285 García Garralón, 'The Nautical Republic', 10.

286 Sicking, *Neptune and the Netherlands*, 247–260; Idem, 'Les marchands'; Idem, 'Grupos de interesos maritímos'.

new demands by establishing the *avería(s)*, probably around 1553 as Fagel has noted, which might make sense as the first complaint in the Castilian consular court comes from 1552 (see below). Whether the *avería(s)* was established by order of the *Consulado* or by initiative of the *natio* is not fully clear, although Manuel Basas Fernández suggests it was the former.[287]

According to Basas Fernández, the Castilian *natio* registered the payment of the *avería(s)* in Bruges in the so-called *Libros de Rótulos*, but this has not survived in the archives of the Castilian *natio*.[288] This means that except for the circumstantial evidence presented in the secondary literature, there is not much left of the actual proof. Indeed, the records of the Castilian consular court contain a sole case about the issue of protection costs, dating from 1552, just before the *avería(s)* was about to be established as a new duty.[289] An anonymous petition brought to the consuls' attention stated that a ship had incurred damage to the wool near the coast of Flanders, leading to a GA declaration. Yet the merchants also complained that, before the voyage, they had contributed to the artillery and convoy ships, in short, the protection efforts for the venture. As a result, they wished to claim back part of these protection costs, but the consuls did not allow them to do so, pointing out that the Consulate in Burgos had stipulated that these protection costs were compulsory.[290] This shows the danger of 'double contributions', both *ex ante* for protection costs which only diminished the risk of damage, but of course could not eliminate it. In such a case, merchants were liable to pay both for the protection costs and the redistribution of damage, leading to higher transaction costs.

6.6 Conclusion

The compulsory contributions levied by the Castilian and Biscayer *nationes* before a venture were a remarkable adaption of Averages, which had significant repercussions both in the Iberian Peninsula and the Low Countries, following the specific organisational form of the *Consulados* that flowed from the monopolistic wool trade. Neither the Italians nor the Portuguese used the compulsory contribution for protection costs. The protection costs element may have been just one of the many expenses covered by the consular Averages, but

287 Basas Fernández, *El Consulado*, 170.

288 There exists the so-called *Libros de cargaçones*, but this only starts in the 1570s. See: Gilliodts-Van Severen, *Espagne*, 4.

289 BE-SAB, *Libro de pleytos ordinarios*, fol. 107v.

290 Ibidem.

this chapter has argued that given the substantial amount of attention given to this element in legal practice, there was a conceptual difference between the Castilian and Biscayer *avería de nación* and the other compulsory contributions. Levying a non-contractual compulsory contribution based on their privileges of the consular Averages to cover protection costs was thus clearly a Spanish innovation, and the membership fees for the *nationes* have as such been wrongly described as being similar to each other.[291] Although risk was subsequently lowered, the Averages were in the first place a form of cost management, deriving from the specific political organisational form behind the Spanish monopolistic wool trade. From the mid-fifteenth century onwards, the Castilians also levied the *avería de nación* on foreign merchants using their ships for transport, based on the port of origin of the shipmaster.

Following Sheilagh Ogilvie's argument that most institutions fulfilled multiple functions, this can clearly be observed in the case of Spanish Averages: the Spanish *ex ante* compulsory contributions were used to simultaneously manage costs, minimise risks and create protection rents.[292] On all these counts, this solution was only moderately successful: on the one hand the contribution asked of the merchants was not extremely high, but combined with the other duties and contributions merchants had to pay, the compulsory contributions may well have meant significantly higher protection costs for individual merchants. Moreover, enforcement problems also raised transaction costs, as is shown by the 1515 Great Council case. In 1553, when the *avería(s)* was likely established to cover higher protection costs following the 1551 *Ordonnance*, protests against the high contributions rose accordingly, also impacting the ability of the *natio* to provide proper transaction costs. Whilst the examples of the Portuguese, the Dutch East India Company and the Venetian fleet have been invoked to show that the incorporation of protection costs could lead to a profitable monopolistic trade,[293] the evidence for the Castilian and Biscayer cases is more mixed.[294] The instrument did not necessarily create huge protection rents: profits went down significantly during the 1550s, whilst the 'demand' for protection as a 'club good' rose, creating a gap.[295]

The organisational structure of the *Consulados* and the associated *nationes* were key to understand why Averages were connected to protection costs, and why these protection efforts took front and centre place in legal practice. The

291 For example in: Gilliodts-Van Severen, *Espagne*, 595–596.

292 Following Addobbati, 'Principles and Inferences'.

293 Lane, *Profits from Power*, 13, 15–20 & 25–26; Steensgaard, 'The Dutch East India Company'.

294 Sicking, *Neptune and the Netherlands*, 247–253.

295 Fagel, *De Hispano-Vlaamse wereld*, 144–149.

'consular Averages', among the most polysemic terms used to denote a form of Average, were used for the common expenses of the *nationes* but was soon broadened to include protection and other costs. Faced with a rapidly changing business environment and new challenges, both the *Consulados* (e.g. the Seville *Consulado* with the *avería*) and the *nationes* (e.g. the Castilians with the *avería*(*s*)) established new compulsory contributions to cover those costs, based on their privilege to levy consular Averages. This raised protection costs to a significant extent (particularly the *avería*(*s*) for the Low Countries trade): on transaction costs, the effects were likely ambivalent as protection rents did not necessarily occur for the members of the *natio*.

Conclusion

This book has studied the development of GA and other varieties of Averages in the Low Countries in the fifteenth and sixteenth centuries. Part 1 showed that GA was widely used to manage risk in maritime trade in the major commercial cities of Bruges and Antwerp. Part 2 showed that other varieties of averages were also commonly used to manage costs in a maritime venture, either operational or protection costs, in turn also lowering risk. Overall, I have argued that GA and other forms of Averages played an important role in the interplay between institutions in the maritime sector, creating an operationally efficient set of institutions to manage risk and costs, notwithstanding the attempts of multiple governmental (e.g. Antwerp and the central government) and governance (e.g. private actors) layers to control the crucial maritime sector in rapidly changing times of political and social upheaval. Whilst the manifold meanings of Averages are difficult to understand (the 'pains' of polysemy), this analysis has also made the case that the various applications of the instruments were crucial for risk and cost management in the maritime sector (the 'power' of polysemy). This has filled a significant lacuna in the history of the maritime sector and maritime risk management, which is particularly apparent in the case of the Low Countries. Moreover, as the case of the *Ever Given* shows, many of the issues inherent in contemporary maritime trade were also present in sixteenth-century Antwerp, offering a clear-eyed look on the historical roots of maritime risk management and its structure.

Given the unique non-market structure of the instrument, the analytical value of GA is significant for both economic and legal historians.[1] Besides historical insights, it also adds a much-needed nuance to contemporary debate about the 'usefulness' of GA.[2] Assumptions that GA was already obsolete in the medieval or early modern period can easily be challenged: discussions about the instrument were primarily jurisdictional and part of larger negotiations over (control of) the crucial maritime sector, but it was clear that no one doubted (the use of) GA. Rather than question the instrument, GA's application was deliberately broadened during the fifteenth and sixteenth centuries and other varieties were developed to cover different risks and manage costs. GA for example covered uninsurable costs, making new legal arrangements necessary to incorporate both tools into mercantile practice. Whilst the book

1 Fusaro, 'Sharing Risks'.

2 For critical voices on GA see: Selmer, *The Survival*; Mukherjee, 'The Anachronism'. See for another view: Kruit, 'General Average'.

 | DOI:10.1163/9789004540354_008

has argued that this may not have amounted to proper path dependency, it has observed that in the negotiations the constraints for all parties were clear, as no party could push through its will.[3] Although an operationally efficient set of institutions came into existence, the book argued that we cannot explain the development of GA through efficiency alone, but rather through the lens of distributive institutions as the parties in the maritime sector all bargained in a power struggle to get a bigger 'slice of the pie'.[4] Moreover, the development of GA was strongly intertwined with other institutional developments, most notably insurance.[5]

Let us summarise the three main contributions of the book. In the field of legal history, it has contributed to the debate on the existence of the *lex maritima*, for which GA has often served as a *pars pro toto*.[6] The book has made clear that the idea of a *lex maritima* is a myth for the fifteenth- and sixteenth-century Low Countries, as jurisdictional complexity and overlapping sets of rules were omnipresent. This is however does not deny that the various parties in the maritime sector in the Low Countries were able to attain a workable set of norms on GA. Rather than straightforward, applicable rules, an overlapping set of privileges, legislation and customs (the so-called *iura mercatorum*, plural emphasised) existed in the case of GA.[7] Many of these norms developed from political considerations. The book therefore also corroborates Lawrence Friedman's point that socio-political influences on the development of GA were instrumental, rather than purely economic considerations (of 'efficiency') or internal, doctrinal legal change.[8] Of course, seeking legal authority (*auctoritas*) for new rules was common, but this was not what primarily drove legal change. Yet lawyers were instrumental as they transformed the practice-drawn rules of thumb into general legal principles, providing legal security in this way.[9]

The second main contribution of the book concerned maritime risk management. The book argued that it was not solely marine insurance which allowed for the transfer from 'uncertainty' into 'risk', as per Frank Knight's observation.[10] Risks were often covered by a combination of insurance and GA, enabling merchants to transfer the risk *ex ante* and share damages *ex post*.

---

3 North, *Institutions*, 98–99. See also: Bennet & Elman, 'Complex Causal Relationships', 256–259.
4 Ogilvie, '"Whatever is, is Right?"', 649–654, 662–665 & 668–671.
5 Ibidem, 681.
6 For example in: Tetley, 'The General Maritime Law', 110–112. See also: Kruit, 'General Average'.
7 Frankot, "*Of Laws of Ships*"; Cordes, 'Lex Maritima?'; Kadens, 'Order within Law', 42.
8 Friedman, *The Legal System*.
9 De ruysscher, 'Maxims and Cases'.
10 Knight, *Risk, Uncertainty, and Profit*, 247–253. See also: North, *Institutions*, 126.

GA was used to cover uninsurable risks for the interested parties, for example artillery or the costs flowing from fighting off attacks at sea.[11] Moreover, both legal practice and formal law increasingly made clear what kinds of risk could be covered by which instrument. The research supports Edwin Hunt's and James Murray's idea that innovations in business history were often built on older structures and tools, rather than being radical innovations.[12] The development of cost management structures of Averages testifies as much, as they did not radically reinvent risk management but rather developed to manage foreseeable costs such as pilotage and artillery, as merchants preferred legal security over higher profits. In a world where insurance became a more prominent instrument of risk transfer for merchants, averages were a major way to mitigate moral hazard and share protection costs and common operational costs.[13] GA was not, of course, a perfect instrument providing comprehensive coverage against maritime risks (and this is still the case today), but its role in maritime risk management should be properly acknowledged by scholars.[14] Moreover, the diversity of Averages, their polysemic meanings and associated different goals should be included in the study of maritime risk management.

Based on Ogilvie's theory of institutions, the third point made by this book is that GA was a multifaceted institution with strong (re)distributive characteristics.[15] GA is indeed a strange institution that cannot be explained on its own by efficiency, cultural or accidental theories of institutions.[16] The study of GA and other Averages points out the limits of theories of the New Institutional Economics on institutional development, with its focus on lowering transaction costs. GA and other Averages after all present a mixed picture: the contractual cost management varieties for example lowered transaction costs as enforcement costs became somewhat lower, but the jurisdiction of the foreign *nationes* over GA claims may well have raised bargaining and enforcement costs until Antwerp moved towards an (imperfect) system of open-access institutions.[17] Both intrinsically and in terms of its jurisdiction the effect of GA on transaction costs was therefore ambivalent, which necessitates explanations other than solely 'efficiency' for the perseverance and the development of GA in the period and region under study. Whilst an operationally efficient set of institutions emerged, many parties in the lengthy negotiations were

11 1551 *Ordonnance*, Art. 28.
12 Hunt & Murray, *A History of Business*, 178–179 & 249.
13 Heimer, *Reactive Risk and Rational Action*, 123–125.
14 Dreijer, 'Maritime Averages'.
15 Ogilvie, '"Whatever is, is Right?"', 649–654, 662–665 & 668–671.
16 Ibidem.
17 Puttevils, *Merchants and Trading*, 139–150.

constrained in pushing through their wishes, meaning that there were motives of power behind the emergence of this set of institutions as well. The Spanish case of protection costs for example shows clearly that transaction costs could in theory be raised, but could nevertheless have other positive effects (e.g. lowering risk or moral hazard): the frame of protection costs and protection rents therefore fits historical reality better in this case.[18] The study of GA and other Averages shows the importance of studying the interaction with other institutions (e.g. insurance), as the institutions in the maritime sector always interacted with one another.[19]

The study of GA in the Southern Low Countries as a tool for maritime risk management is an interesting start, but much more could (and should) be done. Other studies in the *AveTransRisk* project, for example, look at GA in other European areas, with most case studies often offering quantitative evidence complementing the primarily legal evidence presented in this book.[20] Another potential avenue to study are the effects of new GA rules developed in Antwerp on Amsterdam and London, illuminating cross-influences across early modern north-western Europe (and perhaps beyond the area as well).[21] The relationship with other tools of risk management can also be further explored. The study of bottomry, for example, is another subject in which maritime, legal and economic history should converge to study this. In a broader perspective, the interplay between speculation and risk management would be an excellent topic for study in a historical perspective. As risk management and speculation were two sides of the same coin in sixteenth-century Antwerp,[22] such a starting point may well offer a fitting research agenda for the major commercial cities of the Low Countries, incorporating insurance, GA and bottomry into an integral analysis in a European framework. Bruges and Antwerp, as well as Amsterdam and London, all offer excellent opportunities to do this.[23] Although GA is only a small part of a much-larger puzzle, this book has shown the value of studying GA and other Averages in a broader framework of risk management and institutional development, whilst simultaneously avoiding reductionist narratives on legal change, as exemplified by the *lex maritima*.

18 Lane, *Profits from Power*.

19 Ogilvie, '"Whatever is, is Right?"'.

20 See for a preliminary assessment: https://humanities.exeter.ac.uk/history/research/centres/maritime/research/avetransrisk/datasets/ {Retrieved 06/05/2020}.

21 As has for example been done by Guido Rossi for insurance: Rossi, *Insurance in Elizabethan England*.

22 De ruysscher, 'Antwerp 1490–1590', 96; Van der Wee, *The Growth* (Vol. 2), 365.

23 As has already been shown by Gelderblom: Gelderblom, *Cities of Commerce*.

By way of a coda, I would like to end this book by shortly looking at a counterfactual situation to the situation sketched in the previous pages. Given that GA already existed in Roman law, absence of GA in the sixteenth-century Low Countries is of course an unlikely scenario, but we can run our thoughts over a different, more likely case. What would have happened if GA and other forms of Averages would not have been adapted to the progressive needs of merchants, shipmasters and others in the maritime sector in the sixteenth-century Low Countries? GA would have still been applied in limited cases such as jettison, but it appears highly likely that without the expansion of GA and the legal security that the cost management structures offered, maritime trade in the Low Countries would have been less important than it was now. Rich ship-owners may well have been able to insure their ships against damage, but many shipmasters would have been left with cargo spreading and joint ship ownership to minimise risks, leaving shipmasters to cover for many damages and losses in any case when maritime dangers materialised. Merchants would have had to rely on rather risky techniques such as insurance and bottomry loans.

In such a scenario, insurance may well have developed faster, as it would have been one of the few ways in which many damages to cargo would be covered. Notwithstanding opposition by Church and some governments, it is likely that merchants would have used this for all sorts of cargo, including enslaved people and very risky ventures, leading to a more specialised market that would have progressively distinguished between insurance for common maritime ventures (e.g. Antwerp to London) and very risk endeavours, a development that could to an extent be observed in sixteenth-century Antwerp but which remained at the periphery of the insurance market.[24] Moreover, combinations between insurance and bottomry loans may have become more common, as the risk of bottomry loans was somewhat when the interest could be insured.[25] Yet this would have meant a high-risk, high-profit situation for maritime trade, leaving out those without the means to take these risks. Lobbying for more permissive rules would have in turn led to even more speculative activity. It appears likely that this would have led to a world where only the richest investors could 'financialise' maritime trade, without many of the equitable rules that GA offered and underpinned much of Antwerp's maritime economy.

In sum, the maritime world would have been riskier, leaving particularly those at the lower end of the sector with significant risks to cover, whilst speculation may have taken a larger flight as profit opportunities abounded by

24 De Groote, *De zeeassurantie*, 157.

25 See for cases of this in seventeenth-century France: Wade, 'Privilege at a Premium'.

speculating on risky instruments like insurance.[26] The broader application of GA and the development of other Averages therefore solved very real problems for all those in the interest community, mitigating and complementing the effects of other risk management instruments. Without GA and other Averages, the maritime economy of the Low Countries would have likely suffered the adverse consequences of uncertainty and risk, rather than its profits.

26 See also De ruysscher, 'Antwerp 1490–1590', 96; Van der Wee, *The Growth* (Vol. 2), 365; Knight, *Risk, Uncertainty, and Profit*, 247–253.

Appendix

TABLE 11 GA in Juan Henriquez's Ledgers (1562–1563)

Origin	Destination	Date	GA (%)	Page Wastiels	Part
Amsterdam	Bordeaux	16.4.1563	0.96	445–447	III
Amsterdam	Bordeaux	16.4.1563	1.04	445–447	III
Amsterdam	Lisbon	10.5.1563	2.25	603	III
Amsterdam	Lisbon	27.4.1563	4.55	606	III
Amsterdam	Lisbon	27.4.1563	4.58	606	III
Amsterdam	Lisbon	13.5.1563	32	608	III
Amsterdam	Bordeaux	13.5.1563	34.67	449	III
Amsterdam	Bordeaux	8.2.1563	50	447	III
Antwerp	Saint Valeri	8.8.1563	0.65	192–193	II
Antwerp	Saint Valeri	8.8.1563	0.66	192–193	II
Antwerp	Villa Nova	17.3.1563	0.87	620–622	IV
Antwerp	Villa Nova	17.3.1563	0.88	620–622	IV
Antwerp	Villa Nova	17.3.1563	0.89	620–622	IV
Antwerp	Saint Valeri	8.8.1563	0.9	192–193	II
Antwerp	Villa Nova	17.3.1563	0.93	620–622	IV
Antwerp	Saint Valeri	8.8.1563	1	192–193	II
Antwerp	Seville	6.5.1563	1	661–663	IV
Antwerp	Rouen	18.5.1563	2	215–216	II
Antwerp	Saint Malo	27.8.1563	2.1	232–233	II
Antwerp	Saint Valeri	8.8.1563	2.21	194–195	II
Antwerp	Saint Valeri	8.8.1563	2.25	194–195	II
Antwerp	Saint Valeri	8.8.1563	2.32	194–195	II
Antwerp	Saint Valeri	8.8.1563	2.33	194–195	II
Antwerp	Lisbon	27.8.1562	3.37	543	III
Antwerp	Lisbon	31.12.1562	4	544	III
Antwerp	Lisbon	10.8.1562	4.65	544	III
Antwerp	Lisbon	31.12.1562	5	544	III
Antwerp	Lisbon	26.10.1562	5.08	543	III
Antwerp	Lisbon	19.11.1562	6.75	543	III
Antwerp	Lisbon	7.12.1562	6.75	544	III
Antwerp	Seville	6.9.1563	6.88	661–663	IV
Antwerp	Bordeaux	27.4.1563	9.3	299–300	II
Antwerp	Nantes	15.4.1563	10.9	257–261	II

 | DOI:10.1163/9789004540354_009

TABLE 11 GA in Juan Henriquez's Ledgers (1562–1563) (*cont.*)

Origin	Destination	Date	GA (%)	Page Wastiels	Part
Antwerp	Lisbon	27.8.1562	11	543	III
Antwerp	Seville	24.7.1563	24.5	653	IV
Antwerp	Seville	25.7.1563	24.5	657–659	IV
Antwerp	Bordeaux	8.2.1563	25	299–300	II
Antwerp	Tavira	5.1.1563	33.94	705	IV
Antwerp	Mazaron	26.2.1562	75	735–737	IV
Ayamonte	Antwerp	22.5.1563	2.5	624–626	IV
Bordeaux	Antwerp	13.5.163	0.6	377–380	III
Bordeaux	Antwerp	13.5.163	0.61	377–380	III
Bordeaux	Antwerp	13.5.163	0.62	377–380	III
Bordeaux	Antwerp	13.5.163	0.63	377–380	III
Bordeaux	Antwerp	7.6.1563	1	382–383	III
Bordeaux	Antwerp	20.7.1563	1.01	339	II
Bordeaux	Antwerp	20.7.1563	1.02	339	II
Bordeaux	Antwerp	20.7.1563	1.03	339	II
Bordeaux	Antwerp	20.7.1563	1.05	339	II
Bordeaux	Antwerp	20.7.1563	1.06	339	II
Bordeaux	Antwerp	17.2.1563	1.08	333	II
Bordeaux	Antwerp	22.4.1563	1.16	353–355	II
Bordeaux	Antwerp	13.5.1563	1.25	349	II
Bordeaux	Antwerp	2.3.1563	1.66	349	II
Bordeaux	Antwerp	22.4.1563	1.66	353–355	II
Bordeaux	Antwerp	22.4.1563	1.91	353–355	II
Bordeaux	Antwerp	22.4.1563	1.93	353–355	II
Bordeaux	Antwerp	22.4.1563	1.95	353–355	II
Bordeaux	Antwerp	22.4.1563	1.96	353–355	II
Bordeaux	Antwerp	22.4.1563	1.97	353–355	II
Bordeaux	Antwerp	22.4.1563	1.98	353–355	II
Bordeaux	Antwerp	19.4.1563	2.2	353	II
Bordeaux	Antwerp	19.4.1563	2.25	353	II
Bordeaux	Antwerp	19.4.1563	2.26	353	II
Bordeaux	Antwerp	19.4.1563	2.27	353	II
Bordeaux	Antwerp	19.4.1563	2.28	353	II
Bordeaux	Antwerp	2.3.1563	2.4	347	II
Bordeaux	Antwerp	22.1.1563	2.7	345	II
Bordeaux	Antwerp	20.1.1563	5.72	337	II

TABLE 11 GA in Juan Henriquez's Ledgers (1562–1563) (*cont.*)

Origin	Destination	Date	GA (%)	Page Wastiels	Part
Bordeaux	Antwerp	20.1.1563	5.73	337	II
Bordeaux	Antwerp	20.1.1563	5.77	337	II
Bordeaux	Zeeland	2.3.1563	7.08	441	III
Bordeaux	Antwerp	3.3.1563	7.1	337	II
Bordeaux	London	6.5.1563	24.1	160–161	II
Bordeaux	Antwerp	4.3.1563	68.6	343	II
Bordeaux	Antwerp	29.5.1563	90	345	II
Bordeaux	Antwerp	29.5.1563	90.87	345	II
Bordeaux	Antwerp	29.5.1563	90.91	345	II
Bristol	Antwerp	15.7.1563	1.83	145–146	II
Cádiz	Livorno	18.5.1563	1.62	822–824	IV
Cádiz	Antwerp	21.5.1563	56.65	699	IV
Cognac	Antwerp	7.6.1563	1.05	291–292	II
Cognac	Antwerp	7.6.1563	1.06	291–292	II
Cognac	Antwerp	7.6.1563	1.11	291–292	II
Danzig	Lisbon	28.11.1562	7	128	II
Dartmouth	Antwerp	Na 20.3.1563	2.36	147	II
Dartmouth	Antwerp	Na 20.3.1563	2.41	147	II
Lisbon	Antwerp	19.11.1562	0.21	558	III
Lisbon	Antwerp	9.8.1562	0.22	559	III
Lisbon	Antwerp	9.8.1562	0.23	559	III
Lisbon	Antwerp	9.8.1562	0.24	559	III
Lisbon	Antwerp	9.8.1562	0.25	559	III
Lisbon	Antwerp	9.8.1562	0.26	559	III
Lisbon	Antwerp	19.11.1562	0.29	558	III
Lisbon	Antwerp	6.12.1562	0.3	557	III
Lisbon	Antwerp	31.10.1562	0.3	564	III
Lisbon	Antwerp	31.10.1562	0.3	564–566	III
Lisbon	Antwerp	31.10.1562	0.31	564	III
Lisbon	Antwerp	31.10.1562	0.31	566	III
Lisbon	Antwerp	9.8.1562	0.33	559	III
Lisbon	Antwerp	31.10.1562	0.33	562	III
Lisbon	Antwerp	31.10.1562	0.33	564	III
Lisbon	Antwerp	31.10.1562	0.35	566	III
Lisbon	Antwerp	31.10.1562	0.37	566	III
Lisbon	Antwerp	31.10.1562	0.38	568	III

TABLE 11 GA in Juan Henriquez's Ledgers (1562–1563) (*cont.*)

Origin	Destination	Date	GA (%)	Page Wastiels	Part
Lisbon	Antwerp	31.10.1562	0.4	566	III
Lisbon	Antwerp	31.10.1562	0.4	568	III
Lisbon	Antwerp	31.10.1562	0.41	568	III
Lisbon	Antwerp	31.10.1562	1.2	568	III
Lisbon	Antwerp	16.7.1563	1.73	583	III
Lisbon	Antwerp	24.9.1563	1.73	597	III
Lisbon	Antwerp	19.7.1563	1.75	581–583	III
Lisbon	Antwerp	16.7.1563	1.75	583	III
Lisbon	Antwerp	16.7.1563	1.75	583–585	III
Lisbon	Antwerp	19.8.1563	1.75	587	III
Lisbon	Antwerp	19.8.1563	1.75	587	III
Lisbon	Antwerp	19.8.1563	1.75	587	III
Lisbon	Antwerp	19.8.1563	1.75	589	III
Lisbon	Antwerp	19.8.1563	1.75	589	III
Lisbon	Antwerp	19.7.1563	1.75	591	III
Lisbon	Antwerp	19.7.1563	1.75	593	III
Lisbon	Antwerp	24.7.1563	1.9	579–581	III
Lisbon	Antwerp	31.10.1562	2.1	568	III
Lisbon	Antwerp	19.12.1562	2.1	570	III
Lisbon	Antwerp	6.9.1563	2.5	591	III
Lisbon	Antwerp	20.7.1563	2.6	579	III
Lisbon	Antwerp	31.10.1562	4	566	III
Lisbon	Antwerp	2.3.1563	14.25	557	III
Lisbon	Antwerp	6.8.1562	40	558	III
Malaga	Antwerp	13.5.1563	0.5	718	IV
Malaga	Antwerp	13.5.1563	0.8	718	IV
Malaga	Antwerp	13.5.1563	0.82	718	IV
Malaga	Antwerp	13.5.1563	0.83	718	IV
Malaga	Antwerp	16.4.1563	0.9	720–726	IV
Malaga	Antwerp	30.1.1563	1.16	718	IV
Malaga	Antwerp	7.5.1563	2.2	727–728	IV
Malaga	Antwerp	7.5.1563	2.3	727–728	IV
Malaga	Antwerp	7.5.1563	3.7	727–728	IV
Malaga	Antwerp	7.5.1563	3.8	727–728	IV
Malaga	Antwerp	7.5.1563	7.7	727–728	IV
Malaga	Antwerp	16.4.1563	12.6	720–726	IV

TABLE 11 GA in Juan Henriquez's Ledgers (1562–1563) (*cont.*)

Origin	Destination	Date	GA (%)	Page Wastiels	Part
Marseille	Antwerp	17.5.1563	0.81	787–789	IV
Marseille	Antwerp	17.5.1563	0.83	787–789	IV
Marseille	Antwerp	17.5.1563	0.85	787–789	IV
Nantes	Antwerp	20.7.1563	6.5	267	II
Nantes	Antwerp	20.7.1563	6.58	267	II
Rouen	Seville	31.12.1562	1.2	251	II
Rouen	Antwerp	13.5.1563	2.5	222–223	II
Saint Malo	Antwerp	16.4.1563	1.35	236–237	II
Saint Malo	Antwerp	16.4.1563	1.75	236–237	II
Saint Malo	Faro	16.2.1563	50	248–249	II
Stockholm	Antwerp	31.10.1562	5.5	103–106	II
Stockholm	Antwerp	22.11.1562	5.5	103–106	II
Stockholm	Antwerp	6.12.1562	66.6	103–106	II
Tavira	Antwerp	20.1.1563	11.25	709	IV
Flushing	Nantes	22.1.1563	3.5	273	II
Zeeland	La Rochelle	7.6.1563	1	285–186	II
Zeeland	Bordeaux	7.6.1563	3.4	435	III
Zeeland	Bordeaux	22.1.1563	3.42	432	III
Zeeland	Bordeaux	22.1.1563	3.92	432	III
Zeeland	Bordeaux	20.7.1563	5.1	438	III
Zeeland	Bordeaux	7.6.1563	9.12	435	III
Zeeland	Bordeaux	7.6.1563	9.16	435	III
Zeeland	Bordeaux	4.6.1563	2.08	438	III
Zeeland	Bordeaux	4.6.1563	2.1	438	III

SOURCE: WASTIELS, *JUAN HENRIQUEZ* (PARTS 2–4).

Bibliography

Unpublished Primary Sources

Municipal Archives Bruges (BE-SAB)

Oud Archief, Spaans Consulaat, inv. 304, nr. II.A.1, *Ayuntamientos*.

Oud Archief, Spaans Consulaat, inv. 304, nr. III.A.1, *Libro de las ordenanças*.

Oud Archief, Spaans Consulaat, inv. 304, nr. III.A.2, *Libro de las ordenanças*.

Oud Archief, Spaans Consulaat, inv. 304, nr. V.A., *Libro de pleytos ordinarios*.

Oud Archief, Spaans Consulaat, inv. 304, nr. VII, Charters, nrs. 22 & 73.

Oud Archief, Bijlage 1, nr. 22, Purpurenboek (14e eeuw-1540).

Oud Archief, Civiele sententiën Vierschaar 1469–70 & Civiele sententiën Vierschaar 1533–34, inv. 157.

Felixarchief Antwerp (BE-SAA)

Ancien Régime, Stadsbestuur, Privilegiekamer, Handel en Scheepvaart, Verzameling 'Raeckt den Handel', 1559–1561 N. de Negro en J.B. Spinola, inv. PK#1020 & 1551–1572 Toerusting van Schepen, inv. PK#1021.

Ancien Régime, Stadsbestuur, Privilegiekamer, Rekwestboeken 1559–1600, Rekwestboeken 1564 deel 2, inv. PK#633, Rekwestboeken 1564–1565 deel 2, inv. PK#636, Rekwestboeken 1566–1567, inv. PK#640.

Ancien Régime, Stadsbestuur, Privilegiekamer, Vreemde natiën, Duitse natie (Oosterlingen, Hanzeaten), inv. PK#1061.

Ancien Régime, Stadsbestuur, Privilegiekamer, Vreemde natiën, Natie van Genua, inv. PK#1075.

Ancien Régime, Stadsbestuur, Privilegiekamer, Vreemde natiën, Natie van Lucca, inv. PK#1076.

Ancien Régime, Stadsbestuur, Privilegiekamer, Vreemde natiën, Natie van Spanje, inv. PK#1079.

Ancien Régime, Stadsbestuur, Privilegiekamer, Vreemde natiën, Griekse natie (Natie van Constantinopel), inv. PK#1080.

Ancien Régime, Stadsbestuur, Privilegiekamer, Vreemde natiën, Natie van Schotland, inv. PK#1081.

Ancien Régime, Stadsbestuur, Vrijwillige Rechtspraak, Schepenregisters 1550–1599, 1557 Register GA I, inv. SR#265 & 1592 Register MN I, inv. SR#404.

Ancien Régime, Stadsbestuur, Vrijwillige Rechtspraak, Certificatieboeken, 1572, inv. CERT#32.

Ancien Régime, Stadsbestuur, Rechtspraak, Raadkamer, Vonnisboeken, inv. V#1235, V#1241–V#1242, V#1244–V#1247, V#1249–V#1252, V#1254–V#1256.

Private Archieven, Notariaat, Antwerpen 1480–1810, Notariaat Streyt, inv. N#1232–#1233 & Notariaat 'S-Hertoghen, inv. N#2070–#2078.

Rijksarchief Antwerp (*BE-RAA*)

Notariaat, inv. R02, Notariaat De Platea, nr. 1.

Museum Plantin-Moretus Antwerp (*BE-MPM*)

Handel en Scheepvaart Varia, nr. 1074–1.

Rijksarchief België, Brussels (*BE-ARB*)

Admiraliteitsarchief, inv. T094, nrs. 106, 952–953, 959, 961 & 963–966.

Grote Raad der Nederlanden te Mechelen, *Beroepen uit Holland*, inv. A106, nr. 581 & inv. A110, nr. 904.

Grote Raad der Nederlanden te Mechelen, *Processen in eerste aanleg*, inv. A138, nrs. 294, 595, 608, 3519.

Grote Raad der Nederlanden te Mechelen, *Registers, geëxentendeerde sententiën*, inv. T107, nrs. 815.12 (fol. 70–88), 815.13 (fol. 90–106v), 816.33 (fol. 232–242), 818.28 (pp. 283–309), 818.35 (pp. 391–405), 823.68 (pp. 547–560), 824.83 (pp. 749–755), 826.68 (pp. 567–574), 851.9 (pp. 93–100), 853.65 (pp. 817–825), 866.44 (pp. 639–652), 870.68 (pp. 1019–1038), 872.42 (pp. 667–691), 983.509 (fol. 100r).

Zeeuws Archief Middelburg (*NL-ZA*)

Admiraliteit van Veere, inv. 243, nrs. 1–49.

Rechtszaken Vierschaar, inv. RAZE 341, nrs. 1–33.

Nederlands Economisch-Historisch Archief (*NL-NEHA*), *International Institute for Social History, Amsterdam*

Bijzondere Collecties, Collectie Velle, inv. 471, nr. 2.4.15.7.

Fondazione Istituto Internazionale di Storia Economica "F. Datini" (*IT-DAT*)

Fondo Archivio Federigo Melis, inv. III.IV.7/9, nr. 248, cc. 97s/d.

Published Primary Sources

Braamcamp Freire, A., *Noticias da feitoria de Flandres precedidas dos brandies poetas do cancioneiro* (Lisbon 1920).

Desimoni, C. & Belgrano, L.T. (eds.), *Documenti riguardanti le relazione di Genova col Brabante, La Fiandra e la Borgogna: raccolti ed ordinati* (Genoa 1871).

Drost, M.A. (ed.), *Documents pour server à l'histoire du commerce des Pays-Bas avec la France jusqu'à 1585* (2 vols.) (The Hague 1983–1989).

Gilliodts-Van Severen, L., *Coutumes des Pays en Comté de Flandre. Quartier de Bruges, Coutume de la Ville de Bruges* (2. Vols.) (Brussels 1874).

Gilliodts-Van Severen, L., *Cartulaire de l'ancien consulat d'Espagne à Bruges: recueil de documents concernant le commerce maritime et intérieur, le droit des gens public et privé, et l'histoire économique de la Flandre* (Bruges 1901–1902).

Gilliodts-Van Severen, L., *Cartulaire de l'ancien Estaple de Bruges* (6 vols.) (Bruges 1904–1909).

Gilliodts-Van Severen, L. & Gaillard, E., *Inventaire des Chartes des archives de la ville de Bruges* (9 vols.) (Bruges 1871–1876).

Jahnke, C. (ed.), *Seerecht im Hanseraum des 15. Jahrhunderts. Edition und Kommentar zur Flandrischen Copiar Nr. 9* (Lübeck 2003).

Kiesselbach, T., 'Der Ursprung der rôles d'Oléron und des Seerechts von Damme', *Hansische Geschichtblätter*, 12 (1906), 1–60.

Korthals Altes, A., *Ons oudste zeerecht* (Zwolle 1976).

Lameere, J. (ed.), *Recueil des ordonnances des Pays-Bas. Deuxième série, 1506–1700* (Vol. 6) (Brussels 1922).

De Longé, G. (ed.), *Coutumes du Pays et Duché de Brabant. Quartier d'Anvers, Coutumes de la ville d'Anvers* (4 vols.) (Brussels 1870–1874).

Maes, L.T. & Dogaer, G., 'De oudst bekende tekst van de stichtingsakte van het Parlement van Mechelen (1473)', *Handelingen van de Koninklijke Kring voor Oudheidkunde, Letteren en Kunst van Mechelen*, 71 (1972), 41–60.

Pardessus, J-M., *Collection de lois, maritimes antérieures au XVIIIe siècle* (6 vols., Paris 1828–1845).

De Ruysscher, D., *De ontwikkeling van het Antwerpse privaatrecht in de eerste helft van de zestiende eeuw: uitgave van het Gulden Boeck (ca. 1510–ca. 1537), (ontwerpen van) ordonnanties (1496–ca. 1546), een rechtsboek (ca. 1541–ca. 1545) en proeven van hoofdstukken van de costuymen van 1548* (Brussels 2014).

De Smidt, J.T. *et al* (eds.), *Chronologische lijsten van de geëxtendeerde sententiën en procesbundels (dossiers) berustende in het archief van de Grote Raad van Mechelen* (6 vols.) (Brussels 1988).

Smit, H.J. (ed.), *Bronnen tot de geschiedenis van de handel met Engeland, Schotland en Ierland* (vol. 2, 2 parts) (The Hague 1942–1950).

Sneller, Z.W. & Unger, W.S. (eds.), *Bronnen tot de geschiedenis van de handel met Frankrijk* (2 Vols.) (The Hague 1930–1942).

Spruit, J.E. *et al* (eds.), *Corpus Iuris Civilis: tekst en vertaling* (vol. III, Digesten 11–24) (The Hague 1996).

Strieder, J., *Aus Antwerpener Notariatsarchiven: Quellen zur deutschen Wirtschaftgeschichte des 16. Jahrhunderts* (Berlin 1930).

Telting, A., *Die alt-Niederländischen Seerechte* (The Hague 1907).

Den Tex, C.A., 'Oud-Nederlandsch zeerecht: kritische bewerking van den tekst der Vlaamse Zeeregten', *Bijdragen tot rechtsgeleerdheid en wetgeving*, 5 (1830), 33–62.

Den Tex, C.A., 'Oud-Nederlandsch zeerecht: kritische bewerking van den tekst der Amsterdamse Ordonnantie, *Bijdragen tot rechtsgeleerdheid en wetgeving*, 5 (1830), 170–208.

Twiss, T. (ed.), *The Black Book of Admiralty* (Vol. 3) (Cambridge 2013).

Unger, W.S. (ed.), *Bronnen tot de geschiedenis van Middelburg in den landsheerlijken tijd* (vol. 3) (The Hague 1931).

Verlinden, C., 'Código de seguros marítimos según la costumbre de Amberes: promulgado por le Consulado Español de Brujas en 1569', in: *Sección Española del Instituto de Investigaciones Históricas* (Buenos Aires 1947), 146–193.

Verlinden, C., 'Code d'assurances maritimes selons la coutume d'Anvers, promulgué par le consulat espangol de Bruges en 1569', *Handelingen van de Koninklijke Commissie voor de Uitgave der oude wetten en verordeningen van België*, 16 (1950), 38–142.

Doctrine

Cleirac, E., *Us et coutumes de la mer, divisées en trois parties. I: de la navigation. II: du commerce naval & contracts maritimes. III: de la jurisdiction de la marine. Avec un traicté des termes des marine & reglemens de la nauigation des fleuves & rivieres* (Bordeaux 1647).

Van Glins, T., *Aenmerckingen Ende Bedenckingen over Zee-Rechten, uyt het Placcaet van Konick Philips* (Amsterdam 1665).

De Groot, H., *Inleidinge tot de Hollandsche rechts-geleerdheid* (The Hague 1631).

Malynes, G., *Consuetudo, vel, Lex Mercatoria: or, the Ancient Law-Merchant. In three parts, according to the essentials of Traffick. Necessary for Statesmen, Judges, Magistrates, Temporal and Civil Lawyers, Mint-men, Merchants, Mariners, and all other negotiating in an parts of the world* (London 1629/1686).

Miège, G., *The Ancient Sea-Laws of Oleron, Wisby and the Hanse-Towns still in force* (London 1686).

Peckius, V.C.P., *Ad Rem Nauticam Pertinentes, commentarii quibus nunc accedunt notae cum ampla dote variorum circa rem Navalem Observationum* (Leuven 1556).

S.A., *'t Boeck der Zee-Rechten, Inhoudende Dat hoogste ende oudste Godtlantsche Water-recht / dat de gemeene kooplieden ende Schippers geordineert ende gemaeckt hebben tot Wisbuy* (Amsterdam 1678).

Verwer, A., *Nederlants See-Rechten: Avaryen en Bodemereyen Begrepen in de Gemeene Costuimen vander See; de Placcaten van Keiser Karel den Vijfden 1551 en Knoning*

Filips den II 1563 't Tractaet van Mr Quintyn Weitsen van de Nederlantsche Avaryen (Amsterdam 1711).

Weytsen, Q., *Een Tractaet van Avarien* (Haarlem 1631).

Secondary Literature

Abu-Lughod, J.L., *Before European Hegemony: The World System A.D. 1250–1350* (Oxford 1989).

Acemoglu, D., Johnson, S. & Robinson, J.A., 'Institutions as the Fundamental Cause of Long-Run Growth', in: Aghion, P. & Durlauf, S.N. (eds.), *Handbook of Economic Growth* (Amsterdam/Paris 2005) (Vol. 1A), 385–472.

Acemoglu, D. & Robinson, J.A., *Why Nations Fail: The Origins of Power, Prosperity and Poverty* (London 2013).

Addobbati, A., 'Italy 1500–1800: Cooperation and Competition', in: Leonard, A.P. (ed.), *Marine Insurance: Origins and Institutions* (Basingstoke 2016), 47–78.

Aerts, E., 'Geld en krediet: Brugge als financieel centrum', in: Vermeersch, V. (ed.), *Brugge en Europa* (Antwerp 1992), 56–71.

Aerts, E., 'Wisselruiterij in de Lage Landen. De wisselbrief op de Brugse geldmarkt tijdens de late middeleeuwen', in: Le Clercq, G. (ed.) *Ter Beurze: Geschiedenis van de Aandelenhandel in België, 1300–1900* (Bruges/Antwerp 1992), 32–47.

Aerts, E., 'Italian Presence in the late Medieval Bruges Stock Market', in: Brunori, L., Dauchy, S. Descamps, O. & Prévost, X. (eds.), *Le droit face à l'économie sans travail: l'approche internationale* (Vol. 2), 169–221.

Van Answaarden, R., *Les Portugais devant le Grand Conseil des Pays-Bas (1460–1580)* (Paris 1991).

Antunes, C.A.P. & Pólonia, A., (eds.), *Beyond Empires: Global, Self-Organizing, Cross-Imperial Networks, 1500–1800* (Leiden 2016).

Asaert, G., *De Antwerpse scheepvaart in de XVe eeuw (1394–1480)* (Brussels 1973).

Asaert, G., 'Scheepsbezit en havens', in: Asaert, G., Bosscher, P.M., Bruijn, J.R., Hoboken, W.J., *et al* (eds.), *Maritieme Geschiedenis der Nederlanden, deel 1* (Amsterdam 1976), 180–205.

Asaert, G., 'Hollandse bezoekers in de haven van Antwerpen voor 1585', *Neerlandia*, 89, 3 (1985), 103–114.

Asaert, G., 'Gasten uit Brugge: nieuwe gegevens over Bruggelingen op de Antwerpse markt in de vijftiende eeuw', in: Wijffels, C. (ed.), *Album Carlos Wijffels* (Brussels 1987), 23–41.

Ashburner, W., *The Rhodian Sea-Law* (Oxford 1909).

Astorri, P., *Lutheran Theology and Contract Law in Early Modern Germany (ca. 1520–1720)* (Paderborn 2019).

Aubert, J-J., 'Dealing with the Abyss: The Nature and Purpose of the Rhodian Sea-Law on Jettison (*Lex Rhodia De Iactu*, D 14.2) and the Making of Justinian's Digest', in: Cairns, J.W. & Du Plessis, P.J. (eds.), *Beyond Dogmatics: Law and Society in the Roman World* (Edinburgh 2007), 157–172.

Van den Auweele, D., 'Zeerecht', in: Asaert, G., Bosscher, P.M., Bruijn, J.R., Hoboken, W.J., *et al* (eds.), *Maritieme Geschiedenis der Nederlanden, deel 1* (Amsterdam 1976), 220–226.

Van den Auweele, D., 'Het Brugse zeerecht, schakel in een supranationaal geheel', in: Vermeersch, V. (ed.), *Brugge en de zee: van Bryggia tot Zeebrugge* (Antwerp 1982), 145–155.

Baelde, M., *De collaterale raden onder Karel v en Philips ii (1531–1578): bijdrage tot de geschiedenis van de centrale instellingen in de zestiende eeuw* (Brussels 1965).

Baker, J.H., 'The Law Merchant and the Common Law before 1700', *The Cambridge Law Journal*, 38, 2 (1979), 295–322.

Balard, M., 'The Greeks of Crimea under Genoese Rule in the xivth and xvth Centuries', *Dumbarton Oaks Papers*, 49 (1995), 23–32.

Balard, M., 'La *Massaria* génoise de Famagouste', in: Beihammer, A.D., Parani, M.G. & Schabel, C.D. (eds.), *Diplomatics in the Eastern Mediterranean 1000–1500: Aspects of Cross-Cultural Communication* (Leiden/Boston 2008), 235–250.

Barbour, V., 'Marine Risks and Insurance in the Seventeenth Century', *Journal of Economic and Business History*, 1, 4 (1928–1929), 561–596.

Basas Fernández, M., 'Priores y Cónsules de la Universidad de Mercaderes y Consulado de Burgos en el siglo xvi', *Boletón de la Institución Fernán González*, 42, 161 (1963), 679–691.

Basas Fernández, M., *El Consulado de Burgos en el Siglo xvi* (Madrid 1963).

Basu, K., Jones, E. & Schlicht, E., 'The Growth and Decay of Custom: The Role of the New Institutional Economics in Economic History', *Explorations in Economic History*, 24 (1987), 1–21.

Bateman, V.N., *Markets and Growth in Early Modern Europe* (London 2012).

Baucom, I., *Specters of the Atlantic: Finance, Capital, Slavery and the Philosophy of History* (Durham/London 2005).

Van Bavel, B.J.P., 'History as a Laboratory to Better Understand the Formation of Institutions', *Journal of Institutional Economics*, 11, 1 (2015), 69–91.

Beck, C., 'Éléments sociaux et économiques de la vie des marchands génois a Anvers entre 1528 et 1555', *Revue du Nord*, 64, 254–255 (1982), 759–784.

Bennett, A. & Elman, C., 'Complex Causal Relations and Case Study Methods: The Example of Path Dependence', *Political Analysis*, 14, 3 (2006), 250–267.

Bensa, E., *Il Contratto di assicurazione nel medio evo: studi e richerche* (Genoa 1884).

Benson, B.L., 'The Spontaneous Evolution of Commercial Law', *Southern Economic Journal*, 55, 3 (1989), 644–661.

Berman, H.J., *Law and Revolution: the Formation of the Western Legal Tradition* (Cambridge, MA 1983).

Bielsa, P.D., 'El Consulado Catalán de Brujas (1330–1488)', in: Gros, C.O. (ed.), *Aragón en la Edad Media. XIV–XV. Homenaje a la profesora Carmen Orcástegui Gros* (Zaragoza 1999), 375–390.

Blakemore, R.J., 'Law and the Sea', in: Jowitt, C., Lambert, C. & Mentz, S. (eds.), *The Routledge Companion to Marine and Maritime Worlds, 1400–1800* (London/New York 2020), 388–425.

Blanchard, I., *The international Economy in the 'Age of Discoveries', 1470–1570: Antwerp and the English merchants' World* (Stuttgart 2009).

Blockmans, W.P., 'Autocratie ou polyarchie? La lutte pour le pouvoir politique en Flandre de 1482 à 1492', *Bulletin de la Commission royale d'Histoire*, 140 (1974), 257–368.

Blockmans, W.P., 'Financiers Italiens et Flamands aux XIII–XIVe siècle', in: S.A., *Aspetti della vita economia medievale. Atti del convegno di Studi nel X anniversario della morta Federigo Melis* (Florence 1985), 192–214.

Blockmans, W.P., 'Breuk of continuïteit? De Vlaamse privilegiën van 1477 in het licht van het staatsvormingsproces', in: Blockmans, W.P. (ed.), *Het algemene en de gewestelijke privilegiën van Maria van Bourgondië voor de Nederlanden* (Kortrijk-Heule 1985), 97–144.

Blockmans, W.P., 'De "constitutionele" betekenis van de privilegiën van Maria van Bourgondië (1477), in: Blockmans, W.P. (ed.), *Het algemene en de gewestelijke privilegiën van Maria van Bourgondië voor de Nederlanden* (Kortrijk-Heule 1985), 473–494.

Blockmans, W.P., 'Voracious States and Obstructing Cities: An aspect of State Formation in Preindustrial Europe', *Theory and Society*, 18, (1989), 733–755.

Blockmans, W.P., 'Brugge als Europees handelscentrum', in: Vermeersch, V. (ed.), *Brugge en Europa* (Antwerp 1992), 40–55.

Blockmans, W.P., 'Brugge en Frankrijk', in: Vermeersch, V. (ed.), *Brugge en Europa* (Antwerp 1992), 206–223.

Blockmans, W.P., 'The Economic Expansion of Holland and Zeeland in the Fourteenth-Sixteenth Centuries', in: Aerts, E., Henau, B., Janssens, B. & Van Uytven, R. (eds.), *Studia historica oeconomica. Liber Amicorum Herman van der Wee* (Louvain 1993), 41–58.

Blockmans, W.P., 'The Low Countries in the Middle Ages', in: Bonney, R. (ed.), *The Rise of the Fiscal State in Europe c. 1200–1815* (Oxford 1999), 281–308.

Blockmans, W.P., *Metropolen aan de Noordzee: De geschiedenis van Nederland, 1100–1650* (Amsterdam 2010).

Blockmans, W.P. & Prevenier, W., *The Promised Lands: The Low Countries under Burgundian Rule* (Pennsylvania 1999).

Blondé, B., Gelderblom, O.C. & Stabel, P., 'Foreign Merchant Communities in Bruges, Antwerp and Amsterdam', in: Calabi, D. & Christensen, S.T. (eds.), *Cultural Exchange in Early Modern Europe. Volume 2: Cities and Cultural Exchange in Europe, 1400–1700* (Cambridge 2013), 154–174.

De Boer, D., 'Joan Fogassot and 'los fets de Flandes'. A Forgotten Episode of the Catalan Mercantile Connections with Flanders in 1460–1461', in: Hoppenbrouwers, P.C.M., Janse, A. & Stein, R. (eds.), *Power and Persuasion: Essays on the Art of State Building in Honour of W.P. Blockmans* (Turnhout 2010), 243–272.

Bogojevic-Gluscevic, N., 'The Law and Practice of Average in Medieval Towns of the Eastern Adriatic', *Journal of Maritime Law & Commerce*, 36, 1 (2005), 21–60.

Bolton, J.L. & Guidi Bruscoli, F., 'When did Antwerp Replace Bruges as the Commercial and Financial Centre of North-Western Europe? The Evidence of the Borromei Ledger from 1438', *Economic History Review*, 61, 2 (2008), 360–379.

Bradford DeLong, J. & Shliefer, A., 'Princes and Merchants: European city Growth before the Industrial Revolution', *Journal of Law and Economics*, 36, 3 (1993), 671–702.

Braekevelt, J., 'Entre profit et dommage: presence et privileges de la nation Génoise à Bruges sous les Ducs de Bourgogne (1384–1477)', *Publications du Centre Européen d'Études Bourguignonnes*, 49 (2009), 117–129.

Braudel, F., *The Mediterranean and the Mediterranean world in the age of Philip II* (London 1992).

Brulez, W., *De firma Della Faille en de internationale handel van Vlaamse firma's in de zestiende eeuw* (Brussels 1959).

Brulez, W., 'De diaspora der Antwerpse kooplui op het einde van de 16e eeuw', *Bijdragen voor de Geschiedenis der Nederlanden*, 15 (1960), 279–306.

Brulez, W., 'Antwerpens bloeitijd', *Bijdragen voor de Geschiedenis der Nederlanden*, 19 (1965), 151–161.

Brulez, W., 'De handelsbalans der Nederlanden in het midden van de 16e eeuw', *Bijdragen voor de Geschiedenis der Nederlanden*, 21, 1 (1966–1967), 278–310.

Brulez, W., 'Anvers de 1585 à 1650', *Vierteljahrschrift für Sozial- und Wirtschaftgeschichte*, 54, 1 (1967), 75–99.

Brulez, W., 'Le commerce international des Pays-Bas au XVIe siècle: Essai d'appréciation quantitative', *Revue belge de philology et d'histoire*, 46, 4 (1968), 1205–1221.

Brulez, W., 'Brugge en Antwerpen in de 15e en 16e eeuw: een tegenstelling?', *Tijdschrift voor Geschiedenis*, 83 (1970), 15–37.

Brulez, W., 'Engels laken in Vlaanderen in de 14e en 15e eeuw', *Handelingen van het Genootschap voor Geschiedenis*, 108, 1–2 (1971), 5–25.

Brulez, W., 'De handel', in: Couvreur, R., *Antwerpen in de zestiende eeuw* (Antwerp 1975), 109–142.

Brulez, W., 'De scheepvaartwinst in de nieuwe tijden', *Tijdschrift voor Geschiedenis*, 92, 1 (1979), 1–19.

Brunori, L., 'History of Business Law: a European History?', *Glossae. European Journal of Legal History* 15 (2018), 62–79.

Buntinx, J., 'De Raad van Vlaanderen', in: S.A., *Consilium Magnum 1473–1973: herdenking van de 500e verjaardag van de oprichting van het Parlement en Grote Raad van Mechelen* (Brussels 1988), 187–197.

Burkhardt, M., '*Kontors* and Outposts', in: Harreld, D.J. (ed.), *A Companion to the Hanseatic League* (Leiden/Boston 2015), 127–161.

Van Caenegem, R.C., 'Ouvrages de droit Romain dans les catalogues des anciens Pays-Bas meridionaux (XIIIe–XVIe siècle), *Tijdschrift voor Rechtsgeschiedenis*, 28 (1960), 297–347.

Van Caenegem, R.C., *Le droit Romaine en Belgique* (Varese 1966).

Van Caenegem, R.C., 'Aantekeningen bij het Middeleeuwse gewoonterecht', *Tijdschrift voor Rechtsgeschiedenis*, 64 (1996), 97–111.

Callewier, H., 'Brugge, vijftiende-eeuws centrum van het notariaat in de Nederlanden', *Tijdschrift voor Rechtgeschiedenis*, 77 (2009), 73–102.

Campbell, B.M.S., *The Great Transition: Climate, Disease and Society in the Late-Medieval World* (Cambridge 2016).

Carson, P., 'Brugge en de Britse eilanden', in: Vermeersch, V. (ed.), *Brugge en Europa* (Antwerp 1992), 128–145.

Casado Alonso, H., 'La nation en le quartier des Castillians de Bruges (XVe et XVIe siècles)', *Handelingen van het Genootschap voor Geschiedenis*, 133, 1–3 (1996), 61–77.

Casado Alonso, H., 'Brugge, centrum van uitwisseling met Spanje', in: Vandewalle, A. (ed.), *Hanzekooplui en Medicibankiers: Brugge, wisselmarkt van Europese culturen* (Oostkamp 2002), 51–57.

Casado Alonso, H., 'La colonie des marchands Castilllans de Bruges au milieu du XVe siècle', *Publications du centre Europeén d'études Bourguignonnes*, 51 (2011), 233–251.

Casado Alonso, H., 'El seguro marítimo en la Carrera de Indias en la época de Felipe II', in: Iglesias Ródriguez, J.J. *et al* (eds.), *Comercio y cultura en la Edad Moderna* (Seville 2015), 1253–1270.

Casado Alonso, H., 'Juan Henriquez, un corredor de seguros de Amberes a mediados del Siglo XVI', in: Pérez Manrique, J.C. (ed.), *Palabras de archivo: homenaje a Milagros Moratinos Palomero* (Burgos 2018), 49–68.

Casado Alonso, H., 'Insuring Life, Insuring Debt: Life Insurance in Sixteenth-Century Spain', *Pedralbes*, 40, 2 (2020), 75–95.

Cauchies, J-M., *"Es plantar un mundo nuevo": Légiférer aux anciens Pays-Bas (XIIe–XVIIIe siècle)* (Brussel 2019).

Ceccarelli, G., 'Risky Business: Theological and Canonical Thought on Insurance from the Thirteenth to the Seventeenth century', *Journal of Medieval and Early Modern Studies*, 31, 3 (2001), 607–658.

Ceccarelli, G., 'The Price for Risk-Taking: Marine Insurance and Probability Calculus in the late Middle Ages', *Electronic Journal for History of Probability and Statistics*, 3, 1 (2007), 1–26.

Céspedes del Castillo, G., 'La Avería en el Comercio de Indias', *Anuario de Estudios Americanos*, 2 (1945), 515–698.

Céspedes del Castillo, G., 'El seguro marítimo en la Carrera de Indias', *Anuario de Historia del derecho Espanol*, 19 (1948–1949), 57–103.

Chaunu, P., 'Seville et la "Belgique" (1555–1648)', *Revue du Nord*, 42, 166 (1960), 259–292.

Chevreau, E., 'La lex Rhodia de iactu: un exemple de la réception d'une institution étrangère dans le droit romain', *Legal History Review*, 73 (2005), 67–80.

Clavareau, P.J.A., 'Les sources du droit maritime du Moyen Age', *Tijdschrift voor Rechtsgeschiedenis*, 18 (1950), 385–412.

De Clercq, W., Dombrecht, K., Dumolyn, J., Leloup, W. & Trachet, J., 'Monnikerede: The Rise and Decline of a Medieval Port Community in the Zwin Estuary', *Medieval Low Countries, an Annual Review*, 7 (2020), 97–130.

Le Clerq, G., 'In Brugge is er een plein ... Brugge als financiële markt in de 14e–15e eeuw', in: Le Clercq, G. (ed.) *Ter Beurze: Geschiedenis van de Aandelenhandel in België, 1300–1900* (Bruges/Antwerp 1992), 15–32.

Coase, R.H., 'The Nature of the Firm', *Economia*, 16, 4 (1937), 386–405.

Constable, O.A., 'The Problem of Jettison in Medieval Mediterranean Maritime law', *Journal of Medieval History*, 20, 3 (1994), 207–220.

Conte, E., 'Consuetudine, Coutume, Gewohnheit and Ius Commune. An Introduction', *Rechtsgeschichte*, 24 (2016), 234–243.

Coornaert, E., *Les francais et le commerce international a Anvers: fin du XV*[e]*–XVI*[e] *siècle* (2 vols.) (Paris 1961).

Cordes, A., 'The Search for a Medieval *Lex Mercatoria*', in: Piergiovanni, V. (ed.), *From Lex Mercatoria to Commercial Law* (Berlin 2005), 53–67.

Cordes, A., 'Lex Maritima? Local, Regional and Universal Maritime Law in the Middle Ages', in: Blockmans, W., Krom, M.M. & Wubs-Mrowewicz, J. (eds.), *The Routledge Handbook of Maritime Trade around Europe 1300–1600* (Abingdon/New York 2017), 69–85.

Cordes, A. & Höhn, P., 'Extra-Legal and Legal Conflict Management among Long-Distance Traders (1250–1650)', in: Pihlajamäki, H., Dubber, M.D. & Godfrey, M. (eds.), *The Oxford Handbook of European Legal History* (Oxford 2018), 509–528.

Cornah, R.H., 'The Road to Vancouver – the Development of the York-Antwerp Rules', *Journal of International Maritime Law*, 10 (2004), 155–166.

Cornah, R.H. & Reeder, J. (eds.), *Lowndes and Rudolf: The Law of General Average and the York-Antwerp Rules* (14th edition) (London 2013).

Coronas González, S.M., 'La Ordenenza de seguros maritimos del Consulado de la Nacion de España en Brujas', *Anuario de Historia del Derecho español*, 54 (1984), 385–407.

Coronas González, S.M., 'Carlos V, asegurador: una propuesta original de los comerciales de Amberes (1551)', in: Iglesia Ferreirós, A. & Sanchez-Lauro, A. (eds.), *Centralismo y autonomismo en los Siglos XVI–XVII. Hommenaje al Professore Jesús Lalinde Aladía* (Barcelona 1989), 121–130.

Cox, G.W., 'Political Institutions, Economic Liberty, and the Great Divergence', *Journal of Economic History*, 77, 3 (2017), 724–755.

Court, V., 'A Reassessment of the Great Divergence Debate: Towards a Reconciliation of Apparently Distinct Determinants', *European Review of Economic History* (2019), 1–42.

Couvreur, L., 'Recht en zeeverzekeringspraktijk in de 17e en 18e eeuwen', *Tijdschrift voor Rechtsgeschiedenis*, 16, 2 (1939), 184–214.

Craeybeckx, J., 'De organisatie en de konvooiering van de koopvaardijvloot op het einde van de regering van Karel V', *Bijdragen tot de Geschiedenis der Nederlanden* (1949), 179–208.

Crailsheim, E., *The Spanish Connection: French and Flemish Merchant Networks in Seville (1570–1650)* (Cologne 2016).

Crespo Solana, A., 'Diasporas and the Integration of "Merchant Colonies": Flemish and Dutch Networks in Early Modern Spain', *Le verger – Bouquet*, 5 (2014), 1–21.

Dauchy, S., *De processen in beroep uit Vlaanderen bij het Parlement van Parijs (1320–1521): een rechtshistorisch onderzoek naar de wording van de staat en soevereiniteit in de Bourgondisch-Habsburgse periode* (Brussels 1995).

Davids, C.A., 'Zekerheidsregelingen in de scheepvaart en het landtransport, 1500–1800', in: Van Gerwen, J. & Van Leeuwen, M.H.D. (eds.), *Studies over zekerheidsarrangementen. Risico's, risicobestrijding en verzekeringen in Nederland vanaf de Middeleeuwen* (Amsterdam/The Hague 1998), 183–202.

Davidson, J. & Gray, A., *The Scottish Staple at Veere: A Study in the Economic History of Scotland* (London/New York/Bombay/Calcutta 1909).

Davis, R., 'The Rise of Antwerp and its English Connection', in: Coleman, D.C. & John, A.J. (eds.), *Trade, Government, and Economy in Pre-Industrial England: Essays Presented to FJ Fisher* (London 1976), 2–20.

Decock, W., *Theologians and Contract Law: The Moral Transformation of the* Ius Commune *(ca. 1500–1650)* (Leiden/Boston 2012).

Decock, W., 'In Defense of Commercial Capitalism: Lessius, Partnerships and the *Contractus Trinus*', in: Van Hofstraeten, B. & Decock, W. (eds.), *Companies and Company Law in Late Medieval and Early Modern Europe* (Leuven/Paris/Bristol, CT 2016), 55–90.

De Decker, M., *Europees internationaal rivierenrecht* (Antwerp/Apeldoorn 2015).

Degryse, R., 'De admiraals en de eigen marine van de Bourgondische hertogen', *Mededelingen van de Marine Academie*, 17 (1965), 139–225.

Degryse, R., 'Brugge en de pilotage van de Spaanse vloot in het Zwin in de XVIde eeuw', *Handelingen voor het Genootschap voor Geschiedenis*, 67, 1–2 (1980), 105–178 & 67, 3–4 (1980), 227–288.

Denucé, J., *Italiaansche koopmansgeslachten te Antwerpen in de XVIe–XVIIIe eeuwen* (Mechlin/Amsterdam 1934).

Denucé, J., *Afrika in de XVIde eeuw en de handel van Antwerpen* (Antwerp 1937).

Denucé, J., *De Hanze en de Antwerpsche handelscompagnieën op de Oostzeelanden* (Antwerp/The Hague 1938).

Van Dijck, M.F., 'Towards an Economic Interpretation of Justice? Conflict Settlement, Social Control and Civil Society in Urban Brabant and Mechelen during the Late Middle Ages and the Early Modern Period', in: Van der Heijden, M., Van Nederveen Meerkerk, E. & Vermeesch, G. (eds.), *Serving the Urban Community: The Rise of Public Facilities in the Low Countries* (Amsterdam 2009), 62–88.

Dillen, K., 'A Paradox of Maritime Access. Origins and Consequences of Subaltern Relations in a Medieval Portuary System in Flanders: The Case of Hoeke', *International Journal of Maritime History*, 30, 3 (2018), 405–421.

Dixit, A., *Lawlessness and Economics: Alternative Modes of Governance* (Princeton 2007).

Doeleman, F., 'Zeggenschap op de Honte', *Tijdschrift voor Rechtsgeschiedenis*, 43 (1975), 23–43.

Doeleman, F., 'Le tonlieu Zélandais et le privilège de Zierikzee', *Revue belge de phililogie et d'histoire*, 62, 4 (1984), 682–688.

Donahue jr., C., 'Medieval and Early Modern Lex Mercatoria: An Attempt at the Probatio Diabolica', *Chicago Journal of International Law*, 139 (2004), 21–37.

Van Dongen, E.H.D., *Contributory Negligence: a Historical and Comparative Study* (Leiden/Boston 2014).

Donlan, S.P. & Heirbaut, D., '"A patchwork of Accommodations": European Legal Hybridity and Jurisdictional Complexity – an Introduction', in: Donlan, S.P. & Heirbaut, D. (eds.), *The Laws' Many Bodies: Studies in Legal Hybridity and Jurisdictional Complexity, c. 1600–1900* (Berlin 2015), 9–34.

Den Dooren de Jong, E.L.G., 'Lombard Street', *Het Verzekerings-archief*, 5 (1924–5), 11–21.

Van Doosselaere, Q., *Commercial Agreements and Social Dynamics in Medieval Genoa* (Cambridge 2009).

Dreijer, G.P., 'Maritime Averages and the Complexity of Risk Management in Sixteenth-Century Anwerp', *Tijdschrift voor Sociale en Economische Geschiedenis / Low Countries Journal of Social and Economic History*, 17, 1 (2020), 31–54.

Dreijer, G.P., 'Identity, Conflict and Commercial Law: Legal Strategies of Castilian Merchants in the Low Countries (Fifteenth-Sixteenth Centuries)', in: De ruysscher, D.,

Cordes, A., Dauchy, S., Gialdroni, S. & Pihlajamäki, H. (eds.), *Commerce, Citizenship and Identity in Legal History* (Leiden & Boston 2021), 118–138.

Dreijer, G.P. & Vervaart, O., 'Een Tractaet van Avarien – 1617', *Pro Memorie*, 21, 2 (2019), 38–41.

Drelichman, M. & Voth, H-J., *Lending to the Borrower from Hell: Debt, Taxes and Default in the Age of Philip II* (Princeton 2014).

Duerloo, L., 'The Utility of an Empty Title. The Habsburgs as Dukes of Burgundy', *Dutch Crossing*, 43, 1 (2019), 63–77.

Dumolyn, J., *De Brugse opstand van 1436–1438* (Kortrijk-Heule 1997).

Dumolyn, J., 'The Legal Repression of Revolts in Late Medieval Flanders', *Legal History Review*, 68, 4 (2000), 479–521.

Dumolyn, J., *De Raad van Vlaanderen de Rekenkamer van Rijsel: gewestelijke overheidsinstellingen als instrumenten van de centralisatie (1419–1477)* (Brussels 2002).

Dumolyn, J., *Staatsvorming en vorstelijke ambtenaren in het graafschap Vlaanderen (1419–1477)* (Antwerp / Apeldoorn 2003).

Dumolyn, J. & Haemers, J., 'Patterns of Urban Rebellion in Medieval Flanders', *Journal of Medieval History*, 31, 4 (2005), 369–393.

Dumolyn, J. & Lambert, B., 'Cities of Commerce, Cities of Constraints: International Trade, Government Institutions and the Law of Commerce in Later Medieval Bruges and the Burgundian State', *Tijdschrift voor Sociale en Economische Geschiedenis*, 11, 4 (2014), 89–102.

Dumolyn, J. & Leloup, W., 'The Zwin Estuary: A Medieval Portuary Network', in: Telechea, J.A.S., Bolumburu, B.A. & Bochaca, M. (eds.), *Las Sociedades Portuarias de la Europa Atlántica en la Edad Media* (Logroño 2016), 197–212.

Dursteler, E., *Venetians in Constantinople: Nation, Identity and Coexistence in the Early Modern Mediterranean* (Baltimore, MD 2006).

Duve, T., 'Was ist "Multinormativität"? Einführende Bemerkungen', *Rechtsgeschichte*, 25 (2017), 88–101.

Ebert, C., 'Early Modern Atlantic trade and the Development of Maritime Insurance to 1630', *Past and Present*, 213 (2011), 87–114.

Edler-De Roover, F., 'The Effects of the Financial Measures of Charles V on the Commerce of Antwerp, 1539–42', *Revue belge de philologie et d'histoire*, 16, 3–4 (1937), 665–673.

Edler-De Roover, F., 'Early Examples of Marine Insurance', *The Journal of Economic History*, 5, 2 (1945), 172–200.

Edwards, J. & Ogilvie, S., 'Contract Enforcement, Institutions, and Social Capital: the Maghribi Traders Reappraised', *The Economic History Review*, 65, 2 (2012), 421–444.

Edwards, J. & Ogilvie, S., 'What Lessons for Economic Development can we Draw from the Champagne fairs?', *Explorations in Economic History*, 49 (2012), 131–148.

Ehrenberg, R., *Das Zeitalter der Fugger: Geldkapital und Creditverkehr im 16. Jahrhunderts* (Jena 1896).

Eisenhardt, U., 'Entstehung und bedeutung der kaiserlichen privilegia de non appellando', in: S.A., *Consilium Magnum 1473–1973: herdenking van de 500e verjaardag van de oprichting van het Parlement en Grote Raad van Mechelen* (Brussels 1988), 319–341.

Elbl, I., 'Nation, Bolsa, and Factory: Three Institutions of Late-Medieval Portuguese Trade with Flanders', *International History Review*, 14, 1 (1992), 1–22.

Elliott, J.H., 'A Europe of Composite Monarchies', *Past & Present*, 137 (1992), 48–71.

Enthoven, V., *Zeeland en de opkomst van de Republiek: handel en strijd in de Scheldedelta, c. 1550–1621* (Leiden 1996).

Epstein, R.A., 'Reflections on the Historical Origins of Economic Structure of the Law Merchant', *Chicago Journal of International Law*, 139 (2004), 1–20.

Epstein, S.R., 'Regional Fairs, Institutional Innovation, and Economic Growth in Late Medieval Europe', *The Economic History Review*, 47, 3 (1994), 459–482.

Epstein, S.R., 'Constitutions, Liberties, and Growth in Pre-Modern Europe', in: Casson, M., & Godley, A. (eds.), *Cultural Factors in Economic Growth* (Heidelberg 2000), 152–181.

Epstein, S.R., *Freedom and Growth. The Rise of States and Markets in Europe, 1300–1750* (London 2001).

Everaert, J., 'A Trail of Trials: a 'Flemish' Merchant Community in Sixteenth-Century Valladolid and Medina del Campo', *Tijdschrift voor Sociale en Economische Geschiedenis*, 14, 1 (2017), 5–35.

Ewert, U.C. & Selzer, S., *Institutions of Hanseatic Trade: Studies on the Political Economy of a Medieval Network Organisation* (Frankfurt 2016).

Fagel, R.P., *De Hispano-Vlaamse wereld: de contacten tussen Spanjaarden en Nederlanders 1496–1555* (Nijmegen 1996).

Fagel, R.P., 'Spaanse kooplieden in Middelburg vóór de Opstand: succesvolle integratie met behoud van eigen identiteit', in: 't Hart, M.C., Lucassen, J. & Schmal, H. (eds.), *Nieuwe Nederlanders. Vestiging van migranten door de eeuwen heen* (Amsterdam 1996), 21–33.

Fagel, R.P., 'Spanish Merchants in the Low Countries: Stabilitas Loci or Peregrinatio?', in: Stabel, P., Blondé, B. & Greve, A. (eds.), *International Trade in the Low Countries (14th–16th centuries): Merchants, Organisation, Infrastructure* (Leuven 2000), 87–103.

Felloni, G., 'Una fonte inesplorata per la storia dell'economia marittima in età moderna: I calculi di avaria', in: Schneider, J. (ed.), *Wirtschaftkräfte un Wirtschaftswege: Festschrift für Hermann Kellenbenz. Wirtschaftskräfte in der europaischen Expansion* (Stuttgart 1980), 37–57.

Férrandiz, E.M., 'Will the Circle be Unbroken? Continuity and Change of the *Lex Rhodia*'s Jettison Principles in Roman and Medieval Mediterranean Rulings', *Al-Masaq: Journal of the Medieval Mediterranean*, 29, 1 (2017), 41–59.

Fieremans, N., '"In the Hope to have Judged a Good Sentence as Merchants": Arbitration as a Litigation Strategy in Late Medieval Bruges', *Tijdschrift voor Rechtsgeschiedenis*, 89, 3–4 (2021), 439–480.

Finot, J., *Étude historique sur les relations commerciales entre la Flandre & L'Espagne au Moyen Age* (Paris 1899).

Finot, J., *Étude historique sur les relations commerciales entre la Flandre et la Républicque de Gênes au Moyen Age* (Paris 1906).

Fleming, A., 'Legal History as Economic History', in: Pihlajamäki, H., Dubber, M.D. & Godfrey, M. (eds.), *The Oxford Handbook of European Legal History* (Oxford 2018), 207–220.

Frankot, E., 'Medieval Maritime Law from Oléron to Wisby: Jurisdictions in the Law of the Sea', in: Pan-Montojo, J. & Pedersen, F. (eds.), *Communities in European History: Representations, Jurisdictions, Conflicts* (Pisa 2007), 151–172.

Frankot, E., *"Of laws of Ships and Shipmen": Medieval Maritime Law and its Practice in Urban Northern Europe* (Edinburgh 2012).

Frankot, E., '*Die Ehrbaren Hanse-Städte See-Recht*: Diversity and Unity in Hanseatic Maritime Law', in: Wubs-Mrozewicz, J. & Jenks, S. (eds.), *The Hanse in Medieval and Early Modern Europe* (Leiden 2013), 109–128.

Frankot, E., 'De "Ordinancie van Staveren" en het Hanzeatisch zeerecht', *It beaken*, 77, 1–2 (2015), 1–23.

Friedman, L.M., *The Legal System: A Social Science Perspective* (New York 1987).

Fusaro, M., '"Migrating Seamen, Migrating Laws"? An Historiographical Genealogy of Seamen's Employment and States' Jurisdiction in the Early Modern Mediterranean', in: Gialdroni, S., Cordes, A., Dauchy, S., De ruysscher, D. & Pihlajamäki, H. (eds.), *Migrating Words, Migrating Merchants, Migrating Law: Trading Routes and the Development of Commercial Law* (Leiden/Boston 2019), 54–83.

Fusaro, M., 'Maritime History as Global History? The Methodological Challenges and a Future Research Agenda', in: Fusaro, M. & Polónia, A. (eds.), *Maritime History as Global History* (St. John's Newfoundland 2010), 267–282.

Geirnaert, N., 'Brugge en de Noordelijke Nederlanden', in: Vermeersch, V. (ed.), *Brugge en Europa* (Antwerp 1992), 72–97.

Geirnaert, N., 'Brugge en Italië', in: Vermeersch, V. (ed.), *Brugge en Europa* (Antwerp 1992), 182–205.

Van Gelder, M., *Trading Places: The Netherlandish Merchants in Early Modern Venice* (Leiden/Boston 2009).

Gelderblom, O.C., *Zuid-Nederlandse kooplieden en de opkomst van de Amsterdamse stapelmarkt (1578–1630)* (Hilversum 2000).

Gelderblom, O.C., *Cities of Commerce – The Institutional Foundations of International Trade in the Low Countries, 1250–1650* (Princeton 2013).

Gelderblom, O.C. & Jonker, J. 'The Low Countries', in: Neal, L. & Williamson, J.G. (eds.), *The Cambridge History of Capitalism* (Vol. 1) (Cambridge 2014), 314–356.

Génard, P., *Jean-Baptiste Ferrufini et les assurances maritimes à Anvers au XVIe siècle* (Antwerp 1882).

Van Gerven, J., 'Antwerpen in de veertiende eeuw. Kleine stad zonder toekomst of opkomend handelscentrum?', *Revue belge de philologie et d'histoire*, 76, 4 (1998), 907–938.

Gilissen, J., 'Phases de la codification et de l'homologation des coutumes dans les XVII provinces des Pays-Bas', *Tijdschrift voor Rechtsgeschiedenis*, 18 (1950), 36–67 & 233–290.

Gilissen, J., 'Loi et coutume – quelques aspects de l'interpenetration des sources du droit dans l'ancien droit Belge', *Tijdschrift voor Rechtsgeschiedenis*, 21 (1953), 257–296.

Gilissen, J., 'Romeins recht en inheems gewoonterecht in de Zuidelijke Nederlanden', *Tydskrif vir hedendaagse Romeins-Hollandse Reg*, 97 (1955), 97–139.

Gilissen, J., 'À propos de la réception du droit romain dans les provinces méridionales des pays de par-deçà aux XVIe et XVIIe siècle', *Revue du Nord*, 40, 158 (1958), 259–271.

Gilissen, J., 'De Grote Raad van Mechelen. Historisch overzicht', *Belgisch bulletin van de internationale unie der magistraten*, 20 (1970), 2–22.

Gilissen, J., *Introduction historique au droit* (Brussels 1979).

Glete, J., *War and the State in Early Modern Europe: Spain, the Dutch Republic and Sweden as Fiscal-Military States, 1500–1660* (London 2006).

Go, S.C.P.J., 'The Amsterdam Chamber of Insurance and Average: A New Phase in Formal Contract Enforcement (Late Sixteenth and Seventeenth Centuries)', *Enterprise & Society*, 14, 3 (2013), 511–543.

Go, S.C.P.J., 'Governance of General Average in the Netherlands in the Nineteenth Century: A Backward Development?', in: Hellwege, P. & Rossi, G. (eds.), *Maritime Risk Management: Essays on the History of Marine Insurance, General Average and Sea Loan* (Berlin 2021), 247–264.

Godding, P., 'Une justice parallèle? L'arbitrage au Conseil de Brabant (15e siècle)', in: Wijffels, A.A. (ed.), *Miscellanea Consilii Magna (III)* (Amsterdam 1988), 123–142.

Godding, P., *Le Conseil de Brabant: sous le règne de Philippe le Bon (1430–1467)* (Brussels 1999).

González Arce, J.D., 'La Universidad de mercaderes de Burgos y el consulado castellano en Brujas durante el siglo XV', *En el Espãna Medieval*, 33 (2010), 161–202.

Goldberg, J.L., 'Choosing and Enforcing Business Relationships in Eleventh-Century Mediterranean: Reassessing the Maghribi Traders', *Past & Present*, 216, 1 (2012), 3–40.

Goldschmidt, L., *Universalgeschichte des Handelsrechts: Erste Lieferung* (Stuttgart 1891).

González de Lara, Y., 'The Secret of Venetian Success: a Public-Order, Reputation-Based Institution', *European Review of Economic History*, 12 (2008), 247–285.

Goris, J.A., *Étude sur les colonies marchandes méridionales (Portugais, Espagnols, Italiens) à Anvers de 1488 à 1567* (Louvain 1925).

Gorter-Van Royen, L.V.G., *Maria van Hongarije regentes der Nederlanden. Een politieke analyse op basis van haar regenschapsordonnanties en haar correspondentie met Karel v* (Hilversum 1995).

Gottschalk, E., 'Het verval van Brugge als wereldmarkt', *Tijdschrift voor Geschiedenis*, 66 (1953), 1–26.

Gotzen, M., 'De costumiere bronnen voor de studie van het Oud-Antwerpsch burgerlijk recht', *Rechtkundig tijdschrift voor België*, 39 (1949), 3–16, 105–124 & 191–208.

Gotzen, M., 'Het Oud-Antwerps burgerlijk procesrecht volgens de Costumiere Redacties van de 16e–17e eeuw', *Rechtskundig tijdschrift voor België*, 41 (1951), 292–315 & 424–468.

Goudsmit, M.T., *Geschiedenis van het Nederlandsche zeerecht* (The Hague 1882).

Grafe, R. & Gelderblom, O.C., 'The Rise and Fall of Merchant Guilds: Re-Thinking the Comparative Study of Commercial Institutions in Premodern Europe', *Journal of Interdisciplinary History*, 40, 4 (2010), 477–511.

Grapperhaus, F.H.M., *Alva en de tiende penning* (Zutphen 1982).

Greif, A., 'Reputations and Coalitions in Medieval trade: Evidence on the Maghribi traders', *The Journal of Economic History*, 44, 4 (1989), 857–882.

Greif, A., 'Contract Enforceability and Economic Institutions in Early Trade: the Maghribi Traders' Coalition', *The American Economic Review*, 83, 2 (1993), 525–548.

Greif, A., 'Impersonal Exchange without Impartial Law: The Community Responsibility System', *Chicago Journal of International Law*, 139 (2004), 109–138.

Greif, A., *Institutions and the Path to the Modern Economy: Lessons from Medieval Trade* (Cambridge 2006).

Greif, A., 'The Maghribi Traders: A Reappraisal?', *The Economic History Review*, 65, 2 (2012), 445–469.

Greif, A. & Mokyr, J., 'Institutions and Eonomic History: A Critique of Professor McCloskey', *Journal of Institutional Economics*, 12, 1 (2016), 29–41.

Greve, A., 'Brügger Hosteliers und hansische Kaufleute: ein Netzwerk vorteilhafter Handelsbeziehungen oder programmierte Interessenkonflikte?', in: Jörn, N., Paravicini, W. & Wernicke, H (eds.), *Hansekaufleute in Brügge. Teil 4, Beitragen der Internationalen Tagung in Brügge April 1996* (Frankfurt 2000), 151–161.

Greve, A., 'Brokerage and Trade in Medieval Bruges: Regulation and Reality', in: Stabel, P., Blondé, B. & Greve, A. (eds.), *International Trade in the Low Countries (14th–16th centuries): Merchants, Organisation, Infrastructure* (Leuven 2000), 37–44.

Greve, A., 'Hoteliers en Hanzekooplieden in Brugge in de 14de en 15de eeuw', in: Vandewalle, A. (ed.), *Hanzekooplui en Medicibankiers: Brugge, wisselmarkt van Europese culturen* (Oostkamp 2002), 99–104.

Grinberg, M., *Écrire les coutumes. Les droits seigneuriaux en France XVIe–XVIIIe siècle* (Paris 2006).

De Groote, H.L.V., 'Onuitgegeven zestiende-eeuwse Antwerpse polissen', *Bijdragen tot de Geschiedenis*, 57, 3–4 (1974), 153–170.

De Groote, H.L.V. *De zeeassurantie te Antwerpen en te Brugge in de zestiende eeuw* (Antwerp 1975).

De Groote, H.L.V., 'Zeeverzekering', in: Asaert, G., Bosscher, P.M., Bruijn, J.R., Hoboken, W.J., *et al* (eds.), *Maritieme Geschiedenis der Nederlanden, deel 1* (Amsterdam 1976), 206–219.

Guiard y Laurrauri, T., *Historia del Consulado y Casa de Contractación de Bilbao y del comercio de la ville* (Vol. 1) (Bilbao 1913).

Haemers, J., *For the Common Good. State Power and Urban Revolts in the Reign of Mary of Burgundy (1477–1482)* (Turnhout 2009).

Haemers, J., 'Factionalism and State Power in the Flemish Revolt (1482–1492)', *Journal of Social History*, 42, 4 (2009), 1009–1039.

Haemers, J., *De strijd om het regentschap van Filips de Schone. Opstand, facties en geweld in Brugge, Gent en Ieper (1482–1488)* (Ghent 2014).

Haemers, J. & Stabel, P., 'From Bruges to Antwerp. International Commercial firms and Government's Credit in the Late 15th and Early 16th century', in: Ayan, C.S. & García, B.J.G. (eds.), *Banca, crédito y capital. La monarquía Hispánica y los antiguos Países Bajos (1505–1700)* (Seville 2006), 21–37.

Häpke, R., *Brügges Entwicklung zum mittelalterlichen Weltmarkt* (Berlin 1908).

Haring, C.H., *Trade and Navigation between Spain and the Indies in the Time of the Hapsburgs* (Cambridge, MA 1918).

Harreld, D.J., 'German Merchants and Their Trade in Sixteenth-Century Antwerp', in: Stabel, P., Blondé, B. & Greve, A. (eds.), *International Trade in the Low Countries (14th–16th centuries): Merchants, Organisation, Infrastructure* (Leuven 2000), 169–192.

Harreld, D.J., 'Atlantic Sugar and Antwerp's Trade with Germany in the Sixteenth Century', *Journal of Early Modern History*, 7, 1 (2003), 148–163.

Harreld, D.J., *High Germans in the Low Countries: German Merchants and Commerce in Golden Age Antwerp* (Leiden/Boston 2004).

Harreld, D.J., 'The Individual Merchant and the Trading Nation in Sixteenth-Century Antwerp', in: Parker, C. & Bentley, J.H. (eds.), *Between the Middle Ages and Modernity: Individual and Community in the Early Modern World* (Lanham 2007), 271–284.

Harris, R., 'The Encounters of Economic History and Legal History', *Law and History Review*, 21, 2 (2003), 297–346.

Harris, R., 'The Uses of History in Law and Economics', *Theoretical Inquiries in Law*, 4, 2 (2003), 659–696.

Harris, R., 'Legal Scholars, Economists, and the Interdisciplinary Study of Institutions', *Cornell Law Review*, 96 (2011), 789–810.

Harris, R., *Going the Distance: Eurasian Trade and the Rise of the Business Corporation, 1400–1700* (Princeton NJ 2020).

Heimer, C.A., *Reactive Risk and Rational Action: Managing Moral Hazard in Insurance Contracts* (Berkeley, CA 1985).

Heirbaut, D., 'Rules for Solving Conflicts of Law in the Middle Ages: Part of the Solution, Part of the Problem', in: Musson, A. (ed.), *Boundaries of the Law: Geography, Gender and Jurisdiction in Medieval and Early Modern Europe* (London 2005), 118–129.

Heirbaut, D., 'An Unknown Treasure for Historians of Early Medieval Europe: The Debate of German Legal Historians on the Nature of Medieval Law', *Rechtsgeschichte*, 17 (2010) 87–90.

Heirbaut, D., 'Exploring the Law in Medieval Minds: The Duty of the Legal Historian to Write the Books of Non-Written Law', in: Musson, A. & Stebbings, C. (eds.), *Making Legal History: Approaches and Methodology* (Cambridge 2012), 118–130.

Hermesdorf, B.H.D., 'Adriaen Verwer (1655–1717) en de Ordonnance de la Marine', *Rotterdams Jaarboekje*, 7, 5 (1967), 227–261.

Hermesdorf, B.H.D., *Römisches Recht in den Niederlanden* (Varese 1968).

Herzog, T., *A Short History of European Law: The Last Two and a Half Millennia* (Cambridge, MA 2018).

Hilaire, J., 'Reflexions sur l'heritage romain dans le droit du commerce au Moyen-Age', *Tijdschrift voor Rechtsgeschiedenis*, 70, 3 (2002), 212–228.

Hofmeister, A., 'Eine hansische Seeversicherung aus dem Jahre 1531', *Hansische Geschichtsblätter*, 5 (1886), 169–177.

Van Hofstraeten, B., *Juridisch humanisme en costumiere acculturatie: Inhouds- en vormbepalende factoren van de Antwerpse* Consuetudines Compilatae (1608) *en het* Gelderse Land- en Stadrecht (1620) *van het Roermondse Overkwartier* (Maastricht 2008).

Van Hofstraeten, B., 'Recording Customs in Early Modern Antwerp, a Commercial Metropolis', *Zeitschrift des Max-Planck-Instituts für europäische Rechtsgeschichte*, 24 (2016), 288–301.

Van Houtte, J.A., 'La genèse du grand marché international d'Anvers à la fin du Moyen-Âge', *Revue belge de philologie et d'histoire*, 19 (1940), 87–126.

Van Houtte, J.A., 'Makelaars en waarden te Brugge van de 13e tot de 16e eeuw', *Bijdragen voor de Geschiedenis der Nederlanden*, 5 (1950), 1–30 & 177–197.

Van Houtte, J.A., 'Bruges et Anvers, marchés "nationaux" ou "internationaux" du XIVe au XVIe siècle', *Revue du Nord*, 34, 134 (1952), 89–108.

Van Houtte, J.A., 'Het Nederlandse marktgebied in de vijftiende eeuw: eenheid en differenciëring', *Bijdragen en Mededelingen van het Historisch Genootschap*, 70 (1956), 11–30.

Van Houtte, J.A., 'The Rise and Decline of the Market of Bruges', *The Economic History Review*, 19, 1 (1966), 29–47.

Van Houtte, J.A, *De geschiedenis van Brugge* (Tielt/Bussum 1982).

Van Houtte, J.A., 'Portugal en de Brugse handel tijdens de middeleeuwen', in: Stols, E. & Everaert, J. (eds.), *Vlaanderen en Portugal: op de golfslag van twee culturen* (Antwerp 1991), 33–52.

Hunt, E.S. & Murray, J.M., *A History of Business in Medieval Europe, 1200–1550* (Cambridge 1999).

Iodice, A. & Piccinno, L., 'Managing Shipping Risk: General Average and Marine Insurance in Early Modern Genoa', in: Hellwege, P. & Rossi, G. (eds.), *Maritime Risk Management: Essays on the History of Marine Insurance, General Average and Sea Loan* (Berlin 2021), 83–110.

Jacobs, B., '*Ius Patrium* en *Ius Commune*: twee zijden van een medaille', *Pro Memorie*, 19, 1 (2017), 22–46.

Jahnke, C., 'Hansisches und anderes Seerecht', in: Cordes, A. (ed.), *Hansisches und hansestadtliches Recht* (Trier 2008), 41–68.

Jahnke, C., 'The Maritime Law of the Baltic Sea', in: Balard, M. (ed.), *The Sea in History. The Medieval World* (Woodbridge 2017), 574–582.

Jeannin, P., 'Anvers et la Baltique au XVIe siècle', *Revue du Nord*, 37, 146 (1955), 93–114.

De Jongh, J.M., *Tussen* societas *en* universitas*: de beursvennootschap en haar aandeelhouders in historisch perspectief* (Alphen aan de Rijn 2014).

Kadens, E., 'Order within Law, Variety within Custom: The Character of the Medieval Law Merchant', *Chicaco Journal of International Law*, 139 (2004), 39–65.

Kadens, E., 'The Myth of the Customary Law Merchant', *Texas Law Review*, 90 (2012), 1153–1206.

Kadens, E., 'Custom's Two Bodies', in: Jansen, K.L., Geltner, G. & Lester, A.E (eds.), *Center and Periphery: Studies on Power in the Medieval World in Honor of William Chester Jordan* (Leiden/Boston 2013), 239–248.

Kadens, E., 'The Medieval Law Merchant: The Tyranny of a Construct', *Journal of Legal Analysis*, 7, 2 (2015), 251–289.

Kadens, E., 'Custom's Past', in: Bradley, C.A. (ed.), *Custom's Future: International Law in a Changing World* (Cambridge 2016), 11–33.

Kadens, E., 'Convergence and the colonisation of custom in pre-modern Europe', in: Moreteau, O., Masferrer, A. & Modéer, K.A. (eds.), *Comparative Legal History* (Cheltenham/Northampton MA 2019), 167–185.

Kagan, R., *Lawsuits and Litigants in Castile, 1500–1700* (Chapel Hill, NC 1981).

Kay, A. 'A Critique of the Use of Path Dependency in Policy Studies', *Public Administration*, 83, 3 (2005), 553–571.

Khalilieh, H.S., *Islamic Maritime Law: An Introduction* (Leiden/Boston 1998).

Kingston, C., 'Governance and Institutional Change in Marine Insurance, 1350–1850', *European Review of Economic History*, 18, 1 (2013), 1–18.

Knight, F.H., *Risk, Uncertainty, and Profit* (Boston/New York 1921).

Koeningsberger, H.G., *Monarchies, States Generals and Parliaments: the Netherlands in the Fifteenth and Sixteenth centuries* (Cambridge 2001).

Kortlever, Y., 'De jaarmarkten van Bergen op Zoom', in: Van Gelder, M. & Mijers, E. (eds.), *Internationale handelsnetwerken en culturele contacten in de vroegmoderne Nederlanden* (Maastricht 2009), 9–26.

Krieger, K-F., *Ursprung und Wurzeln der Rôles d'Oléron* (Cologne/Vienna 1970).

Krieger, K-F., 'Die Entwicklung des Seerechts im Mittelmeerraum von der Antinke bis zum Consolat de Mar', *German Yearbook of International Law*, 16 (1973), 179–208.

Kruit, J.A., 'General Average – General Principle *plus* Carying Practical Application *equals* Uniformity?', *Journal of International Maritime Law*, 21 (2015), 190–202.

Kruit, J.A., *General Average, Legal Nasis and Applicable Law: The Overrated Significance of the York-Antwerp Rules* (Zutphen 2017).

Kypta, U., 'Von Brügge nach Antwerpen. Institutionen statt Organisation', in: Hammel-Kiesow, R. & Selzer, S. (eds.), *Hansischer Handel im Strukturwandel vom 15. Zum 16. Jahrhundert* (Trier 2016), 161–181.

Laenens, C., *De geschiedenis van het Antwerps gerecht* (Antwerp 1953).

Lambert, B., *The City, the Duke and their Banker: the Rapondi Family and the Formation of the Burgundian State (1384–1430)* (Turnhout 2006).

Lambert, B., '"Marchands parfois, marins plus souvent": le commerce Breton à Bruges au quinzième siècle', in: Telechia, J.A.S., Bolumburu, B.A. & Sicking, L.H.J. (eds.), *Diplomacia y comercio en la Europa atlantíca medieval* (Logroño 2015), 147–160.

Lambert, B., '"Se fist riche par draps de soye": The Intertwinement of Italian Financial Interests and Luxury Trade at the Burgundian Court (1384–1481)', in: Lambert, B. & Wilson, K.A. (eds.), *Europe's Rich Fabric: The Consumption, Commercialisation, and Production of Luxury Textiles in Italy, the Low Countries and Neighbouring Territories (Fourteenth–Sixteenth Centuries)* (Abingdon 2016), 91–106.

Lambert, B., 'Making Size matter Less: Italian Firms and Merchant Guilds in Late Medieval Bruges', in: De ruysscher, D., Cordes, A., Dauchy, S. & Pihlajamäki, H. (eds.), *The Company in Law and Practice: Did Size matter?* (Leiden/Boston 2017), 34–48.

Lambert, B., 'A legal World Market? The Exchange of Commercial Law in Fifteenth-Century Bruges', in: Gialdroni, S., Cordes, A., Dauchy, S., De ruysscher, D. & Pihlajamäki, H. (eds.), *Migrating Words, Migrating Merchants, Migrating Law: Trading Routes and the Development of Commercial Law* (Leiden/Boston 2019), 163–175.

Lambert, B., 'Steep Fall or Gradual Decline? International Trade in Sixteenth-century Bruges', in: Oberste, J. & Ehrich, S. (eds.), *Italien als Vorbild? Ökonomische und kulturelle Verflechtungen europäischer Metropolen am Vorabend der 'ersten Globalisierung' (1300–1600)* (Regensburg 2019), 167–176.

Landwehr, G., *Die haverei in den mittelalterlichten deutschen Seerechtsquellen* (Hamburg 1985).

Landwehr, G., 'Zur begriffsgeschichte der haverei vom 16. bis zum 18. Jahrhundert', in: Jayme, E. *et al* (eds.), *Festschrift für Hubert Niederländer: zum siebzigsten Geburtstag am 10. Februar 1991* (Heidelberg 1991), 57–69.

Landwehr, G., 'Prinzipien der Risikotragung beim Seefrachtvertrag. Rechtverhältnisse bei Haverei und Schiffbruch in der Nord- und Ostseeschifffahrt vom 13. Bis zum 17. Jahrhundert', in: Köbler, G. & Nehlsen, H. (eds.), *Wirkungen europäischer Rechtskultur. Festschrift für Karl Kroeschell zum 70. Geburtstag* (Munich 1997), 595–615.

Landwehr, G., 'Das Seerecht im Ostseeraum vom Mittelalter zum Ausgang des 18. Jahrhunderts', in: Eckert, J., *Geschichte und perspektiven des Rechts im Ostseeraum: erster Rechthistorikertag im Ostseeraum: 8–12 März 2000* (Berlin 2002), 275–303.

Landwehr, G., 'Seerecht im Hanseraum im 15. Jahrhundert: die Hanzerezesse, die Vonnesse von Damme und die Ordinancie der Zuidersee im Flandrischen Copiar Nr.9', in: Jahnke, C. (ed.), *Seerecht im Hanseraum des 15. Jahrhunderts. Edition und Kommentar zur Flandrischen Copiar Nr. 9* (Lübeck 2003), 95–117.

Landwehr, G., *Das Seerecht der Hanse (1365–1614): vom Schiffordungsrecht zum Seehandelsrecht* (Hamburg 2003).

Lane, F.C., *Profits from Power: Readings in Protection Costs and Violence-Controlling Enterprises* (New York 1979).

Lefebvre d'Ovidio, A., 'La contribuzione alle avarie comuni', *Rivista di Diritto della Navigazione*, 1 (1935), 36–140.

Leonard, A.P., 'London 1426–1601: Marine Insurance and the Law Merchant', in: Leonard, A.P. (ed.), *Marine Insurance: Origins and Institutions* (Basingstoke 2016), 151–178.

Leonard, A.P. (ed.), *Marine Insurance: Origins and Institutions, 1300–1850* (Basingstoke 2015).

Lesaffer, R.C.H., *European Legal History: A Cultural and Political Perspective* (Cambridge 2009).

Lesaffer, R.C.H., 'Law and History', in: Van Klink, B. & Taekema, S., *Law in Method: Interdisciplinary Research into Law* (Tübingen 2011), 133–154.

Lesger, C., *The Rise of the Amsterdam Market and Information Exchange: Merchants, Commercial Expansion and Change in the Spatial Economy of the Low Countries* (Farnham 2006).

Li, L-F., 'Information Asymmetry and the Speed of Adjustment: Debasements in the Mid-Sixteenth Century', *Economic History Review*, 68, 4 (2015), 1203–1225.

Limberger, M., '"No Town in the World Provides More Advantages": Economies of Agglomeration and the Golden Age of Antwerp', in: O'Brien, P., Keene, D., 't Hart, M. & Van der Wee, H. (eds.), *Urban Achievement in Early Modern Europe: Golden Ages in Antwerp, Amsterdam and London* (Cambridge 2001), 39–62.

Lindberg, E., 'Club Goods and Inefficient Institutions: Why Danzig and Lübeck failed in the Early Modern Period', *The Economic History Review*, 62, 3 (2009), 604–628.

Lindemann, M., *The Merchant republics: Amsterdam, Antwerp, and Hamburg, 1648–1790* (Cambridge 2017).

Lopez, R.S., *The Commercial Revolution of the Middle Ages, 950–1350* (Cambridge 1976).

Lucassen, J. & De Moor, T. (eds.), *The Return of the Guilds* (Cambridge 2008).

Lucassen, J. & Unger, R.W., 'Shipping, Productivity and Economic Growth', in: Unger, R.W. (ed.), *Shipping and Economic Growth, 1350–1850* (Leiden/Boston 2011), 3–44.

Maes, L.T., 'Twee arresten van de Grote Raad van Mechelen over de Tol van Iersekeroord', *Acta Juridica* (1977), 167–188.

Maes, L.T., *Het Parlement en de Grote Raad van Mechelen, 1473–1797* (Mechlin 2009).

Malanima, P., *Pre-Modern European Economy: One Thousand Years (10th–19th Centuries)* (Leiden/Boston 2009).

Maréchal, J., 'La colonie espagnole de Bruges du XIVe au XVIe siècle', *Revue du Nord*, 35, 137 (1953), 5–40.

Maréchal, J., 'Le depart de Bruges des marchands étrangers (XVe et XVIe siècle)', *Handelingen voor het Gemootschap 'Société d'Émulation' te Brugge*, 88 (2005), 26–74.

Marnef, G., *Antwerpen in de tijd van de Reformatie. Ondergronds protestantisme in een handelsmetropool 1550–1577* (Amsterdam/Antwerp 1996).

Marrella, F. & Mozzato, A. (eds.), *Alle origini dell'arbitrato commerciale internazionale: l'arbitrato a Venezia tra medioevo ed età moderna* (Padova 2001).

Martyn, G., 'De Portugese natie in Antwerpen: drie eeuwen kwaliteitsbewaking van privileges en gewoonterecht', in: Van Nifterik, G.P., De Vries, J. & De Wilde, M. (eds.), *De achterkant van Minerva: opstellen aangeboden aan prof. Kees Cappon ter gelegenheid van zijn afscheid aan de Universiteit van Amsterdam* (Amsterdam 2019), 74–87.

Materné, J., '"Schoon ende bequaem tot versamelinge der cooplieden". Antwerpens beurswereld tijdens de gouden zestiende eeuw', in: Le Clercq, G. (ed.) *Ter Beurze: Geschiedenis van de Aandelenhandel in België, 1300–1900* (Bruges/Antwerp 1992), 51–85.

Matthias, B., *Das Foenum Nauticum und die Geschichtliche Entwicklung der Bodmerei* (Würzburg 1881).

Mathias, P., 'Strategies for Reducing Risk by Entrepreneurs in the Early Modern Period', in: Lesger, C. & Noordegraaf, L. (eds.), *Entrepreneurs and Entrepreneurship in Early Modern Times: Merchants and Industrialists within the Orbit of the Dutch Staple Market* (The Hague 1995), 5–24.

Maucourant, J., 'New Institutional Economics and History', *Journal of Economic Issues*, 46, 1 (2012), 193–208.

Maurer, A., *Lex Maritima: Grundzüge eines transnationalen Seehandelsrechts* (Tübingen 2012).

Mauro, F., 'Merchant Communities, 1350–1750', in: Tracy, J.D. (ed.), *The Rise of Merchant Empires: Long-Distance Trade in the Early Modern World, 1350–1750* (Cambridge 1990), 255–286.

McCloskey, D.N., 'The Great Enrichment: A Humanistic and Social Scientific Account', *Scandinavian Economic History Review*, 64, 1 (2016), 6–18.

McCormick, M., *Origins of the European Economy: Communications and Commerce, A.D. 300–900* (Cambridge 2001).

Melikan, R., 'Shippers, Salvors, and Sovereigns: Competing Interests in the Medieval Law of Shipwreck', *Journal of Legal History*, 11, 2 (1990), 163–182.

Menard, R.R., 'Transport Costs and Long-Range Trade, 1300–1800: Was there a European "Transport Revolution" in the Early Modern Era?', in: Tracy, J.D. (ed.), *The Political Economy of Merchant Empires: State Power and World Trade 1350–1750* (Cambridge 1991), 228–275.

Milagres del Vas Mingo, M., *Los consulados en el tráfico indiano* (Madrid 2000).

Milgrom, P.R., North, D.C. & Weingast, B.R., 'The Role of Institutions in the Revival of Trade: the Law Merchant, Private Judges, and the Champagne fairs', *Economics and Politics*, 2, 1 (1990). 1–23.

Miranda, F., 'Commerce, conflits et justice: les marchands portugais en Flandre à la fin du Moyen Âge', *Annales de Bretagne et des Pays de l'Ouest*, 117, 1 (2010), 1–16.

Miranda, F., 'Conflict Management in Western Europe: The Case of Portuguese Merchants in England, Flanders and Normandy, 1250–1500', *Continuity and Change*, 31, 1 (2017), 11–36.

Monballyu, J., 'Van appellation ende reformatien: de ontwikkeling van het hoger beroep bij de Audientie, de Camere van den Rade en de Raad van Vlaanderen (ca. 1379–ca. 1550)', *Tijdschrift voor Rechtsgeschiedenis*, 61 (1993), 237–275.

Mukherjee, P.K., 'The Anachronism in Maritime Law that is General Average', *WMU Journal of Maritime Affairs*, 4, 2 (2005), 195–209.

Mukherjee, P.K., 'Essentials of General Average: A Synoptic Overview of an Ancient Maritime Law', *WMU Journal of Maritime Affairs*, 6, 1 (2007), 21–36.

Muldrew, C., *The Economy of Obligation: The Culture of Credit and Social Relations in Early Modern England* (Basingstoke 1998).

De Munck, B., Lourens, P. & Lucassen, J., 'The Establishment and Distribution of Craft Guilds in the Low Countries 1000–1800', in: Prak, M. *et al.* (eds), *Craft Guilds in the Early Modern Low Countries: Work, Power and Representation* (Aldershot 2006), 32–73.

Munro, J.H., 'Bruges and the Abortive Staple in English Cloth: An Incident in the Shift of Commerce from Bruges to Antwerp the Late Fifteenth Century', *Revue belge de philology et d'histoire*, 44, 4 (1966), 1137–1159.

Munro, J.H., 'Patterns of Trade, Money, and Credit', in: Brady, T.A., Oberman, H.A. & Tracy, J.D. (eds.), *Handbook of European History in the Later Middle Ages, Renaissance and Reformation, 1400–1600* (Leiden/Boston 1994), 147–195.

Munro, J.H., 'The Origin of the English 'New Draperies': The Resurrection of an Old Flemish Industry, 1270–1570', in: Harte, N.B. (ed.), *The New Draperies in the Low Countries and England, 1300–1800* (Oxford 1997), 35–128.

Munro, J.H., 'English "Backwardness" and Financial Innovations in Commerce with the Low Countries, 14th to 16th Centuries', in: Stabel, P., Blondé, B. & Greve, A. (eds.), *International Trade in the Low Countries (14th–16th Centuries): Merchants, Organisation, Infrastructure* (Leuven, 2000), 122–144.

Munro, J.H., 'Hanseatic Commerce in Textiles from the Low Countries and England during the Later Middle Ages: Changing Trends in Textiles, Markets, Prices, and Values, 1290–1570', in: Heckman, M. & Röhrkasten, J. (eds.), *Von Nowgorod bis London: studien zu Handel, Wirtschaft und Gesellschaft in mittelalterlichten Europa: Festschfit für Stuart Jenks zum 60. Geburtstag* (Berlin 2008), 97–182.

Murray, J.M., 'Failure of Corporation: Notaries Public in Medieval Bruges', *Journal of Medieval History*, 12, 2 (1986), 155–166.

Murray, J.M., 'The Profession of Notary Public in Medieval Flanders', *Tijdschrift voor Rechtsgeschiedenis*, 61 (1993), 3–31.

Murray, J.M., 'Of Nodes and Networks: Bruges and the Infrastructure of Trade in Fourteenth-Century Europe', in: Stabel, P., Blondé, B. & Greve, A. (eds.), *International Trade in the Low Countries (14th–16th Centuries): Merchants, Organisation, Infrastructure* (Leuven, 2000), 1–14.

Murray, J.M., 'Handels- en financiële technieken', in: Vandewalle, A. (ed.), *Hanzekooplui en Medicibankiers: Brugge, wisselmarkt van Europese culturen* (Oostkamp 2002), 107–111.

Murray, J.M., *Bruges, Cradle of Capitalism, 1280–1390* (Cambridge 2005).

Murray, J.M., 'The Well-Grounded Error: Bruges as *Hansestadt*', in: Wubs-Mrozewicz, J. & Jenks, S. (eds.), *The Hanse in Medieval and Early Modern Europe* (Leiden/Boston 2012), 181–190.

Nehlsen-Von Stryk, K., *Die venezianische Seeversicherung in 15. Jahrhundert* (Ebelsbach am Main 1986).

Nève, P.L., 'Ius Commune oftewel "gemeen recht": traduttore traditore?', in: Tellegen-Couperus, O.E., Nève, P.L. & Tellegen, J.W. (eds), *Tertium Datur. Drie opstellen aangeboden aan Prof. Mr. J.A. Ankum* (Tilburg 1995), 3–58.

Nève, P.L., '(Europäisches) ius commune und (nationales) gemeines Recht: Verwechslung von Begriffen?', in: Köbler, G. & Nehlsen, H. (eds.), *Wirkungen europäischer Rechtskultur. Festschrift für Karl Kroeschell zum 70. Geburtstag* (Munich 1997), 871–884.

Nève, P.L., 'Hoe "soeverein" was de Raad van Brabant?', in: Broers, E.J.M.F.C., Jacobs, B.C.M. & Lesaffer, R.C.H. (eds.), *Ius Brabanticum, Ius Commune, Ius Gentium: opstellen aangeboden aan prof. Mr. J.P.A. Coopmans ter gelegenheid van zijn tachtigste verjaardag* (Nijmegen 2006), 9–20.

Nicholas, D., 'The English Trade at Bruges in the Last Years of Edward III', *Journal of Medieval History*, 5 (1979), 23–61.

Van Niekerk, J.P., *The Development of the Principles of Insurance Law in the Netherlands from 1500 to 1800* (2 vols.) (Hilversum 1998).

North, D.C., 'Sources of Productivity Change in Ocean Shipping, 1600–1850', *Journal of Political Economy*, 76, 5 (1968), 953–970.

North, D.C., 'Transaction Costs in History', *Journal of European Economic History*, 14, 3 (1985), 557–576.

North, D.C., *Institutions, Institutional Change and Economic Performance* (Cambridge 1990).

North, D.C., 'Institutions', *The Journal of Economic Perspectives*, 5, 1 (1991), 97–112.

North, D.C., 'Institutions, Transaction Costs, and the Rise of Merchant Empires', in: Tracy, J.D. (ed.), *The Political Economy of Merchant Empires: State Power and World Trade 1350–1750* (Cambridge 1991), 22–40.

North, D.C., 'Law and Economics in Historical Perspective', in: Cafaggi, F., Nicita, A. & Pagano, U. (eds.), *Legal Orderings and Economic Institutions* (London 2007), 46–53.

North, D.C. & Thomas, R.P., *The Rise of the Western World: A New Economic History* (Cambridge 1973).

Ogilvie, S., '"Whatever is, is Right?" Economic Institutions in Pre-Industrial Europe', *Economic History Review*, 60, 4 (2007), 649–684.

Ogilvie, S., *Institutions and European trade: Merchant Guilds, 1000–1800* (Cambridge 2011).

Ogilvie, S., *The European Guilds: An Economic Analysis* (Princeton 2019).

Ogilvie, S. & Carus, A.W., 'Institutions and Economic Growth in Historical Perspective', in: Aghion, P. & Durlauf, S.N. (eds.), *Handbook of Economic Growth* (Amsterdam/Paris 2014) (Vol. 2A), 403–513.

Oosterbosch, M., '"Van groote abuysen ende ongeregelheden": overheidsbemoeiingen met het Antwerpse notariaat tijdens de XVIde eeuw', *Tijdschrift voor Rechtsgeschiedenis*, 63, 1–2 (1995), 83–101.

Osler, D.J., 'The Myth of European Legal History', *Rechtshistorisches Journal*, 16 (1997), 393–410.

Padoa-Schioppa, A., *A History of Law in Europe: From the Early Middle Ages to the Twentieth Century* (Cambridge 2007).

Paravicini, W., 'Brugge en Duitsland', in: Vermeersch, V. (ed.), *Brugge en Europa* (Antwerp 1992), 98–127.

Parker, G., *Imprudent King: A new Life of Philip II* (New Haven/London 2014).

Parker, G., *Emperor: A new Life of Charles V* (New Haven/London 2019).

Parmentier, J., 'Brugge en Scandinavië', in: Vermeersch, V. (ed.), *Brugge en Europa* (Antwerp 1992), 146–157.

Parmentier, J., 'Een maritiem-economische schets van de deltahavens, 1400–1800', in: Ebben, M. & Groenveld, S. (eds.), *De Scheldedelta als verbinding en scheiding tussen Noord en Zuid, 1500–1800* (Maastricht 2007), 11–26.

Paulsen, G.W., 'Historical Overview of the Development of Uniformity in International Maritime Law', *Tulane Law Review*, 57 (1982–2983), 1065–1091.

Paviot, J., *La politique navale des Ducs de Bourgogne 1384–1482* (Lille 1995).

Paviot, J., 'Les Portugais à Bruges', in: Stabel, P., Blondé, B. & Greve, A. (eds.), *International Trade in the Low Countries (14th–16th Centuries): Merchants, Organisation, Infrastructure* (Leuven, 2000), 55–74.

Paviot, J., 'Brugge en Frankrijk', in: Vandewalle, A. (ed.), *Hanzekooplui en Medicibankiers: Brugge, wisselmarkt van Europese culturen* (Oostkamp 2002), 43–44.

Paviot, J., 'Brugge en Portugal', in: Vandewalle, A. (ed.), *Hanzekooplui en Medicibankiers: Brugge, wisselmarkt van Europese culturen* (Oostkamp 2002), 45–50.

Petit, C., 'Handelsrecht und Rechtsgeschichte', *Zeitschrift der Savigny-Stiftung für Rechtsgeschichte: Germanistische Abteilung*, 136, 1 (2019), 306–337.

Petti Balbi, G., 'La massaria genovese di Allesandria d'Eggito nel Quattrocentro', *Studia Storici*, 38, 2 (1997), 339–353.

Petti Balbi, G., 'Brugge, haven van de Italianen', in: Vandewalle, A. (ed.), *Hanzekooplui en Medicibankiers: Brugge, wisselmarkt van Europese culturen* (Oostkamp 2002), 58–64.

Petti Balbi, G., *Mercanti e* nationes *nelle Fiandre: I genovesi in èta bassomedievale* (Pisa 1996).

Petram, L.O., *The world's First Stock Exchange* (New York 2014).

Philips, C.R., 'Spanish Merchants and the Wool Trade in the Sixteenth Century', *The Sixteenth Century Journal*, 14, 3 (1983), 259–282.

Philips jr., W.D., 'Local Integration and Long-Distance Ties: The Castilian Community in Sixteenth-Century Bruges', *The Sixteenth Century Journal*, 17, 1 (1986), 33–49.

Philips jr., W.D., 'Spain's Northern Shipping Industry in the XVIth century', *Journal of European Economic History*, 17, 2 (1988), 267–301.

Philips jr., W.D., 'Merchants of the Fleece: Castilians in Bruges and the Wool Trade', in: Stabel, P., Blondé, B. & Greve, A. (eds.), *International Trade in the Low Countries (14th–16th Centuries): Merchants, Organisation, Infrastructure* (Leuven, 2000), 75–86.

Philips jr. W.D. & Philips, C.R., 'Spanish Wool and Dutch Rebels: The Middelburg Incident of 1574', *The American Historical Review*, 82, 2 (1977), 312–330.

Pirenne, H., *Historique de Belgique* (seven volumes, vol. 3) (Brussels 1902–1932).

Pirenne, H., 'The formation and constitution of the Burgundian state (fifteenth and sixteenth centuries)', *The American Historical Review*, 14, 3 (1909), 477–502.

Pirenne, *Les villes du Moyen Âge: essai d'histoire économique et sociale* (Brussels 1927).

De Pleijt, A.M. & Van Zanden, J.L., 'Accounting for the "Little Divergence": What drove Economic Growth in Pre-Industrial Europe, 1300–1800', *European Review of Economic History*, 20 (2016), 387–409.

Pohl, H., *Die Portugiesen in Antwerp (1567–1648): zur Geschichte einer minderheit* (Wiesbaden 1977).

Pohl, H., 'De Portugezen in Antwerpen', in: Stols, E. & Everaert, J. (eds.), *Vlaanderen en Portugal: op de golfslag van twee culturen* (Antwerp 1991), 53–80.

Posner, R.A., *Economic Analysis of Law* (New York 2007).

Puts, E., 'Raad van Brabant', in: Van Uytven, R., Bruneel, C., Coppens, H. & Augustyn, B. (eds.), *De gewestelijke en lokale overheidsinstellingen in Brabant en Mechelen tot 1795* (Brussels 2000), 147–171.

Puttevils, J., *Merchants and Trading in the Sixteenth Century: The Golden Age of Antwerp* (London 2015).

Puttevils, J., '"Eating the Bread out of their Mouth": Antwerp's Export Trade and Generalized Institutions, 1544–5', *The Economic History Review*, 68, 4 (2015), 1339–1364.

Puttevils, J., 'Waarom deden sommige handelssteden het zo goed? Een overzicht van het historisch onderzoek naar handel en instituties in Nederlandse en Europese steden, 1300–1800', *Stadsgeschiedenis*, 10, 1 (2015), 74–95.

Puttevils, J. & Deloof, M., 'Marketing and Pricing Risk in Marine Insurance in Sixteenth-Century Antwerp', *The Journal of Economic History*, 77, 3 (2017) 796–837.

Puttevils, J., Stabel, P. & Verbist, B., 'Een eenduidig pad van modernisering van het handelsverkeer: van het liberale Brugge naar het gereguleerde Antwerpen?', in: Blondé, B. (ed.), *Overheid en economie: geschiedenissen van een spanningsveld* (Antwerp 2014), 39–54.

Reatz, C.F., *Geschichte des Europäischen Seeversicherungsrecht* (Leipzig 1870).

Reatz, C.F., 'Ordonnances du duc d'Albe sur les assurances maritimes de 1569, 1570, 1571, avec un précis de l'histoire du droit d'assurance maritime dans les Pays-Bas', *Compte-rendu des séances de la commission royale d'histoire*, Deuxième Série, 5 (1878), 41–118.

Reid, A., 'The Hybrid Maritime actors of Southeast Asia', in: Buchet, C. & Le Bouëdec, G. (eds.), *The Sea in History – the Early Modern World* (London 2017), 112–122.

Reinert, S.A. & Fredona, R., 'Merchants and the Origins of Capitalism', in: Da Silva Lopes, T., Lubinski, C. & Tworek, H. (eds.), *The Routledge Companion to Makers of Global Business* (London 2020), 171–188.

Van Rhee, C.H., *Litigation and Legislation: Civil Procedure at First Instance in the Great Council for the Netherlands in Malines (1522–1559)* (Brussels 1997).

Van Rhee, C.H., 'Continental European Superior Courts and Procedure in Civil Actions (11th–19th centuries)', in: Moreteau, O., Masferrer, A. & Modéer, K.A. (eds.), *Comparative Legal History* (Cheltenham/Northampton MA 2019), 318–340.

De Ridder-Symoens, H., 'De universitaire vorming van de Brabantse stadsmagistraat en stadsfunktionarissen – Leuven en Antwerpen, 1430–1580', *Studia Historica Gandensia*, 208 (1977), 21–125.

De Rock, J., Puttevils, J. & Stabel, P., 'Handelsnetwerken, stedelijke ruimte en culturele omgeving in het 16e-eeuwse Antwerpen', in: Van Gelder, M. & Mijers, E.

(eds.), *Internationale handelsnetwerken en culturele contacten in de vroegmoderne Nederlanden* (Maastricht 2009), 27–42.

Rodger, N.A.M., 'The Law and Language of Private Naval Warfare', *Mariner's Mirror*, 100, 1 (2014), 5–16.

Roelofsen, C.G., 'L'amirauté à Veere, considérée dans ses attributions judiciaires (XVe–XVIe siècles)', *Publications du Centre Européen d'Etudes Bourguignonnes*, 24 (1984), 67–80.

Van Rompaey, J., 'Het onstaan van de Grote Raad onder Filips de Goede', *Koninklijke Zuidnederlandse Maatschappij voor Taal- en Letterkunde en Geschiedenis. Handelingen*, 25 (1971), 297–310.

Van Rompaey, J., *De Grote Raad van de hertogen van Boergondië en het Parlement van Mechelen* (Brussels 1973).

Van Rompaey, J., 'Hofraad en Grote Raad in de hofordonnantie van 1 januari 1469', in: Asaert, G. *et al* (eds.), *Recht en instellingen in de oude Nederlanden tijdens de Middeleeuwen en de nieuwe tijd: Liber Amicorum Jan Buntinx* (Leuven 1981), 303–324.

Van Rompaey, J., 'De procedure in beroep bij het Parlement van Mechelen', in: S.A., *Consilium Magnum 1473–1973: herdenking van de 500e verjaardag van de oprichting van het Parlement en Grote Raad van Mechelen* (Brussels 1988), 371–381.

Rooseboom, M.P., *The Scottish Staple in the Netherlands: An Account of the Trade Relations between Scotland and the Low Countries from 1292 till 1676, with a Calendar of Illustrative Documents* (The Hague 1910).

De Roover, R., *Money, Banking and Credit in Mediaeval Bruges* (Cambridge MA 1948).

De Roover, R., 'La communauté des marchands Lucquois à Bruges de 1377 à 1404', *Handelingen van het Genootschap voor Geschiedenis*, 86, 1 (1949), 23–89.

De Roover, R., 'La balance commerciale entre les Pays-Bas et l'Italie au quinzième siècle', *Revue belge de philologie et d'histoire*, 37, 2 (1959), 374–386.

Rossi, G., *Insurance in Elizabethan England: the London Code* (Cambridge 2016).

Rossi, G., 'The Liability of the Shipmaster in Early Modern Law: Comparative (and Practice-Oriented) Remarks', *Historia et Ius*, 12 (2017), paper 12, 1–47.

Rossi, G., 'The Abandonment to the Insurers in Sixteenth-Century Insurance Practice: Comparative Remarks and (a Few) Methodological Notes', in: Pihlajamäki, H., Cordes, A., Dauchy, S. & De ruysscher, D. (eds.), *Understanding the Sources of Early Modern and Modern Commercial Law: Courts, Statutes, Contracts, and Legal Scholarship* (Leiden/Boston 2018), 87–118.

Rossi, G., 'The Barratry of the Shipmaster in Early Modern Law: Polysemy and *mos Italicus*', *Tijdschrift voor Rechtsgeschiedenis*, 87, 1–2 (2019), 65–85.

Rossi, G., 'The Barratry of the Shipmaster in Early Modern Law: The Approach of Italian and English Law Courts', *Tijdschrift voor Rechtsgeschiedenis*, 87, 3–4 (2019), 504–574.

Rossi, G. & Spagano, S., 'From Custom to Law, an Economic Rationale behind the Black Lettering', *Journal of Economic Issues*, 52, 4 (2018), 1109–1124.

Rüfner, T., 'Substance of Medieval Roman Law: The Development of Private Law', in: Pihlajamäki, H., Dubber, M.D. & Godfrey, M. (eds.), *The Oxford Handbook of European Legal History* (Oxford 2018), 309–333.

Runyan, T.J., 'The Rolls of Oleron and the Admiralty Court in Fourteenth-Century England', *American Journal of Legal History*, 19 (1975), 95–111.

De ruysscher, D., 'Law Merchant in the Mould. The Transfer and Transformation of Commercial Practices into Antwerp Customary Law (16th–17th centuries)', in: Duss, V., Linder, N., Kastl, K., Börner, C., Hirt, F. & Züsli, F. (eds.), *Rechtstransfer in der Geschichte – Legal Transfer in History* (Munich 2006), 433–445.

De ruysscher, D., *"Naer het Romeinsch recht alsmede den stiel mercantiel". Handel en recht in de Antwerpse rechtbank (16e–17e eeuw)* (Kortrijk 2009).

De ruysscher, D., 'Antwerp Commercial Legislation in Amsterdam in the 17th Century: Legal Transplant or Jumping Board?', *Tijdschrift voor Rechtgeschiedenis*, 77 (2009), 459–479.

De ruysscher, D., 'L'acculturation juridique des coutumes commerciales à Anvers. L'exemple de la letter de change (XVIe–XVIIe siècle)', in: Coppein, B., Stevens, F. & Waelkens, L. (eds.), *Modernisme, tradition et acculturation juridique* (Brussels 2011), 151–160.

De ruysscher, D., 'La *Lex Mercatoria* contexualisée: tracer son parcours intellectuel', *Revue histoire de droit*, 90, 4 (2012), 499–515.

De ruysscher, D., 'Van kade naar stadhuis: informatieuitwisseling, fraudebestrijding en gereglementeerde innovatie in Antwerpse zeeverzekeringen (ca. 1550–ca. 1700)', *Tijdschrift voor Geschiedenis*, 125, 3 (2012), 366–383.

De ruysscher, D., *Gedisciplineerde vrijheid: een geschiedenis van het handels- en economisch recht* (Antwerp/Apeldoorn 2014).

De ruysscher, D., 'Antwerp 1490–1590: Insurance and Speculation', in: Leonard, A.P. (ed.), *Marine Insurance: Origins and Institutions* (Basingstoke 2016), 79–105.

De ruysscher, D., 'Pieter Peck, Ad rem nauticam', in: Dauchy, S., Martyn, G., Musson, A., Pihlajamäki, H. & Wijffels, A.A. (eds.), *The Formation and Transmission of Western Legal Culture. 150 Books that made the Law in the Age of Printing* (Heidelberg 2016), 110–113.

De ruysscher, D., 'Belgium: Marine Insurance', in: Hellwege, P. (ed.), *Comparative History of Insurance Law in Europe. A Research Agenda* (Berlin 2018), 110–132.

De ruysscher, D., 'Customs and Municipal Law: The Symbolic Authority of the Past (Low Countries, 16th–17th century)', *Dutch crossing*, Published/Early View.

De ruysscher, D., 'Conceptualising *lex mercatoria*: Malynes, Schmitthoff and Goldman Compared', *Maastricht Journal for European and Comparative Law*, 27, 4 (2020), 465–483.

De ruysscher, D., 'Maxims, Principles and Legal Change: Maritime Law in Merchant and Legal Culture (Low Countries, 16th Century)', *Zeitschrift der Savigny-Stiftung für Rechtsgeschichte. Germanistische Abteilung*, 138, 1 (2021), 260–275.

De ruysscher, D. & Puttevils, J., 'The Art of Compromise: Legislative Deliberations on Marine Insurance Institutions in Antwerp (c. 1550–c. 1570), *BMGN-Low Countries Historical Review* 130, 3 (2015), 25–49.

Ryckaert, M., 'Brugge als Europese haven', in: Vermeersch, V. (ed.), *Brugge en Europa* (Antwerp 1992), 26–39.

S.A., *The University of Louvain 1425–1975* (Louvain 1975).

Sachs, S.E., 'Conflict Resolution at a Medieval English Fair', in: Cordes, A. & Dauchy, S. (eds.), *Eine Grenze in Bewegung. Öffentliche und private Justiz im Handels- und Seerecht* (Munich 2013), 19–38.

De Schepper, H., 'De Grote Raad van Mechelen, hoogste rechtscollege in de Nederlanden?', *Bijdragen en Mededelingen voor de Geschiedenis der Nederlanden*, 93, 3 (1978), 389–411.

De Schepper, H., 'The Burgundian-Habsburg Netherlands', in: Brady, T.A., Oberman, H.A. & Tracy, J.D. (eds.), *Handbook of European History in the Later Middle Ages, Renaissance and Reformation, 1400–1600* (Leiden/Boston 1994), 499–533.

De Schepper, H., 'Geheime Raad', in: Aerts, E. *et al* (eds.), *De Centrale Overheidsinstellingen van de Habsburgse Nederlanden* (Brussels 1994), 295–324.

De Schepper, H., 'Staatsgezag en macht in de Nederlanden: verworvenheden en beperkingen in het Bourgondisch-Habsburgse systeem', in: Geurts, J. & De Schepper, H. (eds.), *Staatsvorming onder Bourgondiërs en Habsburgers: theorie en praktijk* (Maastricht 2006), 13–49.

De Schepper, H. & Cauchies, J-M., 'Legal Tools of the Public Power in the Netherlands, 1200–1600', in: Padoa-Schioppa, A. (ed.), *Legislation and Justice* (Oxford 1997), 229–268.

Scheltjens, W., 'Het ontstaan van een geïntegreerde maritieme transportruimte in de Lage Landen, ca. 1300–1800', *Revue belge de philologie et d'histoire*, 92, 2 (2014), 293–363.

Scheltjens, W., *Dutch Deltas. Emergence, Functions and Transport of the Low Countries' Maritime Transport System, ca. 1300–1850* (Leiden/Boston 2015).

Schweitzer, J., *Schiffer und Schiffsmann in den Rôles d'Oléron und im Llibre del Consolat de Mar: ein Vergleich zweier mittelalterlicher Seerechtsquellen* (Frankfurt am Main/New York 2007).

Seinecke, R., 'Rechtspluralismus in der Rechtsgeschichte', *Rechtsgeschichte*, 25 (2017), 215–228.

Selmer, K.S., *The Survival of General Average: A Necessity or an Anachronism?* (Oslo 1958).

Senior, W., 'The History of Maritime Law', *The Mariner's Mirror*, 38, 4 (1952), 260–275.

Shephard, J.W., 'The *Rôles d'Oléron*: A *Lex Mercatoria* of the Sea?', in: Piergiovanni, V. (ed.), *From Lex Mercatoria to Commercial Law* (Berlin 2005), 207–253.

Sicking, L.H.J., 'Prijsrechtspraak in de Nederlanden: de Admiraliteiten van Veere, Duinkerke en Gent, 1488–1568', in: Heirbaut, D. & Lambrecht, D. (eds.), *Van oud en nieuw recht: handelingen van het XVde Belgisch-Nederlandse rechtshistorisch congres, Universiteit Gent, 16 en 17 april 1998* (Antwerp 1999), 69–84.

Sicking, L.H.J., *Neptune and the Netherlands: State, Economy, and War at Sea in the Renaissance* (Leiden/Boston 2004).

Sicking, L.H.J., 'Le paradoxe de l'accès: le rôle des avant-ports dans les anciens Pays-Bas à la fin du Moyen Âge et au début de l'époque moderne (approche comparative générale)', in: Bochaca, M. & Sarrazin, J-L. (eds.), *Ports et littoraux de l'Europe atlantique: transformations naturelles et aménagements humains (XIVe–XVIe siècles)* (Rennes 2007), 227–255.

Sicking, L.H.J., 'State and Non-State Violence at Sea: Privateering in the Habsburg Netherlands', in: Starkey, D.J. & Hahn-Pedersen, M. (eds.), *Bridging Troubled Waters. Conflict and Co-Operation in the North Sea Region since 1550* (Esbjerg 2005), 31–43.

Sicking, L.H.J., 'Stratégies de réduction de risque dans le transport maritime des Pays-Bas au XVIe siècle', in: Cavaciocchio, S. (ed.), *Ricchezza del mare – ricchezza dal mare, secc. XIII–XVIII: atti della Trentasettesima settimana di studi, 11–15 Aprile 2005* (2 vol.) (Florence 2006), 795–808.

Sicking, L.H.J., 'A Wider Spread of Risk: A Key to Understanding Holland's Domination of Eastward and Westward Seafaring from the Low Countries in the Sixteenth Century', in: Brand, H. & Müller, L. (eds.), *The Dynamics of Economic Culture in the North Sea- and Baltic region* (Hilversum 2007), 122–135.

Sicking, L.H.J., 'Les marchands espagnols et portugais aux Pays-Bas et la navigation à l'époque de Charles Quint: gestion des risques et législation', *Publications du Centre Européen d'Etudes Bourguignonnes*, 51 (2011), 253–274.

Sicking, L.H.J., 'Los grupos de intereses marítimos de la Península Ibérica en la ciudad de Amberes: la gestión de riesgos y la navigación en el siglo XVI', in: Telechea, J.A.S., Bochacha, M. & Andrade, A.A. (eds.), *Gentes de mar en la ciudad Atlántica medieval* (Logroño 2012), 167–199.

Sicking, L.H.J., 'De zaak Draeck: Antwerp tegenover Zierikzee. Een interstedelijk conflict tijdens de Vlaamse opstand', in: Delsalle, P., Docquier, G., Marchandisse, A. & Schnerb, B. (eds.), *Pour la singuliere affection qu'avons a luy. Etudes bourguignonnes offertes à Jean-Marie Cauchies* (Turnhout 2017), 406–417.

Sicking, L.H.J., 'The Pirate and the Admiral: Europeanisation and Globalisation of Maritime Conflict Management', *Journal of the History of International Law*, 20 (2018), 429–470.

Sicking, L.H.J., 'The Medieval Origin of the Factory or the Institutional Foundations of Overseas Trade: Toward a Model for Global Comparison', *Journal of World History*, 31, 2 (2020), 295–326.

Sicking, L.H.J. & Van Rhee, C.H., 'Procedure en proceskosten. De afhandeling van een prijszaak volgens de Romano-Canonieke procedure voor de Admiraliteit en de Grote Raad van Mechelen tijdens de Engels-Schotse Oorlog van 1547', *Tijdschrift voor Rechtsgeschiedenis*, 71 (2003), 337–357.

Sicking, L.H.J. & Van Rhee, C.H., 'Prize Law, Procedure and Politics. The Settlement of a Prize Case before the Admiralty Court and the Great Council of the Netherlands (1554–1555)', in: Dondorp, H., Schermaier, M. & Sirks, B. (eds.), *De rebus divinis et humanis. Essays in Honour of Jan Hallebeek* (Göttingen 2019), 302–322.

Siems, M.M., *Comparative ;aw* (Cambridge 2018).

Signori, U., 'Reti consolari veneziane nell'Impero ottomano del Seicento', in: Gallia, A., Pinzarrone, L. & Scaglione, G. (eds.), *Isole e frontiere nel Mediterraneo moderno e contemporaneo* (Palermo 2017), 19–34.

De Smedt, O.C., *De Engelse natie te Antwerpen (1496–1582)* (2 vols.) (Antwerp 1951–1954).

De Smidt, J.T. & Huussen jr., A.H., 'De Grote Raad van Mechelen als hoogste rechtscollege in de Nederlanden', *Tijdschrift Holland*, 2, 4/5 (1970), 89–107.

Smith, R.S., *The Spanish Guild Merchant: a History of the Consulado, 1250–1700* (Durham, NC 1940).

Sneller, Z.W., *Walcheren in de vijftiende eeuw* (Utrecht 1916).

Soly, H., 'De aluinhandel in de Nederlanden in de 16e eeuw', *Revue belge de philologie et d'histoire* 52, 4 (1974), 800–857.

Spooner, F.C., *Risk at Sea: Amsterdam Insurance and Maritime Europe, 1766–1780* (Cambridge 1983).

Spufford, P., *Profit and Power: The Merchant in Medieval Europe* (London 2006).

Spufford, P., 'From Genoa to London: The Places of Insurance in Europe', in: Leonard, A.P. (ed.), *Marine Insurance: Origins and Institutions* (Basingstoke 2016), 271–297.

Stabel, P., *Dwarfs among Giants: The Flemish Urban Network in the Later Middle Ages* (Leuven 1997).

Stabel, P., 'Economic Development, Urbanization and Political Organisation in the Late Medieval Low Countries', in: Bernholz, P., Streit, M.E. & Vaubel, R. (eds.), *Political Competition, Innovation and Growth: A Historical Analysis* (Berlin/Heidelberg 1998), 183–204.

Stabel, P., 'Venice and the Low Countries: Commercial Contacts and Intellectual Inspirations', in: Aikema, B. & Brown, B.L. (eds.), *Renaissance Venice and the North: Crosscurrents in the Time of Bellini, Dürer and Titian* (New York 2000), 30–43.

Stabel, P., 'Marketing Cloth in the Low Countries: Manufacturers, Brokers and Merchants (14th–16th centuries)', in: Stabel, P., Blondé, B. & Greve, A. (eds.), *International Trade in the Low Countries (14th–16th Centuries): Merchants, Organisation, Infrastructure* (Leuven, 2000), 15–36.

Stabel, P., 'De gewenste vreemdeling', *Jaarboek voor Middeleeuwse geschiedenis*, 4 (2001), 189–221.

Stabel, P., 'Bruges and the German Hanse: brokering European commerce', in: François, L. & Isaacs, A.K. (eds.), *The Sea in European history* (Pisa 2001), 35–56.

Stabel, P., 'Kooplieden in de stad', in: Vandewalle, A. (ed.), *Hanzekooplui en Medicibankiers: Brugge, wisselmarkt van Europese culturen* (Oostkamp 2002), 85–96.

Stabel, P., 'Italian Merchants and the Fairs in the Low Countries (12th–16th centuries)', in: Lanaro, P. (ed.), *La pratica dello scambio: Sistemi di fiere, Mercanti e città in Europa (1400–1700)* (Venice 2003), 131–159.

Stabel, P., Puttevils, J. & Dumolyn, J., 'Production, Markets and Socio-Economic Structures I: c. 1100–c. 1320', in: Brown, A. & Dumolyn, J. (eds.), *Medieval Bruges, c. 850–c. 1550* (Cambridge 2018), 86–123.

Stabel, P., Puttevils, J., Dumolyn, J., Lambert, B., Murray, J.M. & Dupont, G., 'Production Markets and Socio-Economic Structures II: c. 1320–c. 1500', in: Brown, A. & Dumolyn, J. (eds.), *Medieval Bruges, c. 850–c. 1550* (Cambridge 2018), 196–267.

Steensgaard, N., 'The Dutch East India Company as an Institutional Innovation', in: Aymard, M. (ed.), *Dutch Capitalism and World Capitalism* (Cambridge 1982), 235–257.

Stols, E., 'Les marchands flamands dans la Péninsule Ibérique à la fin du seizième siècle et pendant la première moitié du dix-septième siècle', in: Kellenbenz, H. (ed.), *Fremde Kaufleute auf der Iberischen halbinsel* (Cologne 1970), 226–238.

Stols, E., *De Spaanse Brabanders, of de handelsbetrekkingen der Zuidelijke Nederlanden met de Iberische wereld, 1598–1648* (Brussels 1971).

Stein, R., *Magnanimous Dukes and Rising States: The Unification of the Burgundian Netherlands, 1380–1480* (Oxford 2017).

Subacchi, P., 'Italians in Antwerp in the Second Half of the Sixteenth Century', in: Soly, H. & Thijs, K.L. (eds.), *Minderheden in Westeuropese steden (16e–20e eeuw)* (Brussels 1995), 73–90.

Subacchi, P., 'The Italian Community in 16th-century Antwerp', in: Veeckman, J., Jennings, S., Dumortier, C., Whitehouse, D. & Verhaeghe, F. (eds.), *Majolica and Glass. From Italy to Antwerp and Beyond. The Transfer of Technology in the 16th–early 17th Century* (Antwerp 2002), 23–38.

Talavan, M.L., 'La avería en el tráfico marítimo-mercantil indiano: notas para su studio (siglos XVI–XVIII)', *Revista Complutense de Historia de América*, 24 (1998), 113–145.

Tenenti, A., *Naufrages, corsairs et assurances maritimes à Venise: 1592–1609* (Paris 1959).

Tetley, W., 'The General Maritime Law – the Lex Maritima', *Syracuse Journal of International Law & Commerce*, 20 (1994), 105–146.

Tilly, C., *Coercion, Capital, and European States: AD 990–1992* (Cambridge, MA 1992).

Van Tielhof, M., *De Hollandse graanhandel, 1470–1570: koren op de Amsterdamse molen* (The Hague 1995).

Trakman, L.E., 'The Evolution of the Law Merchant: Our Commercial Heritage', *Journal of Maritime Law & Commerce*, 12 (1980), 1–24 & 153–182.

Trivellato, F., *The Familiarity of Strangers: The Sephardic Diaspora, Livorno, and Cross-Cultural Trade in the Early Modern Period* (New Haven 2014).

Trivellato, F., '"Amphibious Power": The Law of Wreck, Maritime Customs, and Sovereignty in Richelieu's France', *Law and History Review*, 33, 4 (2015), 915–944.

Trivellato, F., 'Usages and Customs of the Sea: Ettiene Cleirac and the Making of Maritime Law in Seventeenth-Century France', *Tijdschrift voor Rechtsgeschiedenis*, 84, 1–2 (2016), 193–224.

Trivellato, F., 'Economic and Business History as Cultural History: Pitfalls and Possibilities', *I Tatti Studies in the Italian Renaissance*, 22, 2 (2019), 403–410.

Twining, W., 'Normative and Legal Pluralism: A Global Perspective', *Duke Journal of Comparative and International Law*, 20 (2010), 473–517.

Unger, R.W., 'Scheepsbouw en scheepsbouwers', in: Asaert, G., Bosscher, P.M., Bruijn, J.R., Hoboken, W.J., *et al* (eds.), *Maritieme Geschiedenis der Nederlanden, deel 1* (Amsterdam 1976), 155–179.

Unger, R.W., 'Ships and Shipping Technology', in: Jowitt, C., Lambert, C. & Mentz, S. (eds.), *The Routledge Companion to Marine and Maritime Worlds, 1400–1800* (London/New York 2020), 221–241.

Unger, W.S., 'Middelburg als handelsstad (XIIIe tot XVIe eeuw)', *Archief van het Zeeuws Genootschap*, 1, 3 (1935), 1–176.

Van Uytven, R., '1477 in Brabant', in: Blockmans, W.P. (ed.), *Het algemene en de gewestelijke privilegiën van Maria van Bourgondië voor de Nederlanden* (Kortrijk-Heule 1985), 253–372.

Vandamme, L., Stabel, P., Dumolyn, J., Brown, A., Martens, M.P.J., Gabriëls, N. & Oosterman, J., 'Bruges in the Sixteenth Century: A "Return to Normalcy"', in: Brown, A. & Dumolyn, J. (eds.), *Medieval Bruges, c. 850-c. 1550* (Cambridge 2018), 445–484.

Vandewalle, A., 'Brugge en het Iberisch schiereiland', in: Vermeersch, V. (ed.), *Brugge en Europa* (Antwerp 1992), 158–181.

Vandewalle, A., 'El Consulado de Burgos en los Países Bajos', *Actas del v Centenario del Consulado de Burgos* (Vol. 1) (Burgos 1994), 283–300.

Vandewalle, A., 'De vreemde naties in Brugge', in: Vandewalle, A. (ed.), *Hanzekooplui en Medicibankiers: Brugge, wisselmarkt van Europese culturen* (Oostkamp 2002), 27–42.

Vergouwen, J.P., *De geschiedenis der makelaardij in assurantiën hier te lande tot 1813* (The Hague 1945).

Verhaest, H., 'De gedwongen tenuitvoerlegging van vonnissen en acten in de rechtspraak van de Raad van Vlaanderen (1430–1520)', in: Wijffels, A.A. (ed.), *Miscellanea Consilii Magna (III)* (Amsterdam 1988), 295–324.

Verhulst, A., 'An Aspect of the Question of Continuity between Antiquity and Middle Ages: The Origin of the Flemish cities between the North Sea and the Scheldt', *Journal of Medieval History*, 3 (1977), 175–206.

Verhulst, A., *The Rise of Cities in North-West Europe* (Cambridge 1999).

Verkerk, C.L., 'Evocatie in de Landen van Herwaarts-over tussen 1470 en 1540 (avec résumé)', in: S.A., *Consilium Magnum 1473–1973: herdenking van de 500e verjaardag van de oprichting van het Parlement en Grote Raad van Mechelen* (Brussels 1988), 419–447.

Verlinden, C., 'De zeeverzekeringen der Spaanse kooplui in de Nederlanden gedurende de XVIe eeuw', *Bijdragen voor de Geschiedenis der Nederlanden*, 2 (1946), 191–216.

Vanderlinden, J., 'Here, There and Everywhere ... or Nowhere? Some Comparative and Historical Afterthoughts about Custom as a Source of Law', in: Moreteau, O., Masferrer, A. & Modéer, K.A. (eds.), *Comparative Legal History* (Cheltenham/Northampton MA 2019), 140–166.

Vila Vilar, E., 'Algunas consideraciones sobre la creación del Consulado de Sevilla', in: S.A. (ed.), *Congreso de Historia del Descrubrimiento (1492–1556): Actas* (Vol. 4) (Madrid 1992), 53–66.

Vila Vilar, E., *El Consulado de Sevilla de Mercaderes a Indias. Un Órgano de Poder* (Seville 2016).

Volckart, O. & Mangels, A., 'Are the Roots of the Modern Lex Mercatoria really Medieval?', *Southern Economic Journal*, 65, 3 (1999), 427–450.

Vries, P.H.H., *Escaping Poverty: The Origins of Modern Economic Growth* (Vienna 2013).

Waelkens, L., 'Origine de l'enquete par turbe', *Tijdschrift voor Rechtsgeschiedenis*, 53, 3–4 (1985) 337–346.

Ward, R., *The World of the Medieval Shipmaster: Law, Business and the Sea c. 1350–c. 1450* (Cambridge 2009).

Wasserstein Fassberg, C., 'Lex Mercatoria – Hoist with its own Petard', *Chicago Journal of International Law*, 139 (2004), 67–82.

Watson, W.B., 'The Structure of the Florentine Galley Trade with Flanders and England in the Fifteenth Century', *Revue belge de philologie et d'histoire*, 39, 4 (1961), 1073–1091 & 40, 2 (1962), 317–347.

Van der Wee, H., 'Sporen van disconto te Antwerpen tijdens de 16e eeuw', *Bijdragen voor de Geschiedenis der Nederlanden*, 10 (1956), 68–128.

Van der Wee, H., *The Growth of the Antwerp Market and the European Economy, Fourteenth-Sixteenth centuries* (3 vols.) (The Hague 1963).

Van der Wee, H., 'De handelsbetrekkingen tussen Antwerpen en de noordelijke Nederlanden tijdens de 14e, 15e en 16e eeuw', *Bijdragen voor de Geschiedenis der Nederlanden*, 20 (1966), 267–285.

Van der Wee, H., 'De economie als factor bij het begin van de opstand in de Zuidelijke Nederlanden', *Bijdragen en Mededelingen van het Historisch Genootschap*, 83 (1969), 15–32.

Van Werveke, H., *Brugge en Antwerpen, acht eeuwen Vlaamse handel* (Ghent 1941).

Van Werveke, H., '"Hansa" in Vlaanderen en aangrenzende gebieden', *Handelingen van het Genootschap voor Geschiedenis*, 90, 1–2 (1953), 5–42.

Wijffels, A.A., '*Mos Italicus* in der Antwaltspraxis des Grossen Rates zu Mecheln und des Hofes von Holland (ca. 1460–1580)', in: De Schepper, H. (ed.), *Höchste Gerichtsbarkeit im spätmittelalter und der frühen Neuzeit* (Amsterdam 1985), 105–123.

Wijffels, A.A., 'Grote Raad voor de Nederlanden te Mechelen', in: Aerts, E. *et al* (eds.), *De Centrale Overheidsinstellingen van de Habsburgse Nederlanden* (Brussels 1994), 448–461.

Wijffels, A.A., 'Flanders and the Scheldt Question: A Mirror of the Law of International Relations and its Actors', *Sartoniana*, 15 (2002), 213–280.

Wijffels, A.A., 'Zeeuwse steden voor de Grote Raad', *Pro Memorie*, 4, 2 (2002), 266–293.

Wijffels, A.A., 'Ius Commune and International Wine Trade – a Revision', *Tijdschrift voor Rechtsgeschiedenis*, 71, 3 (2003), 289–317.

Wijffels, A.A., 'Taxation and Litigation: Dutch Cities as Litigants in Late Fifteenth-Century Tax-Cases', in: Ascheri, M. *et al* (eds.), *"Ins Wasser geworfen und Ozeane durchquert": Festschrift für Knut Wolfgang Nörr* (Cologne 2003), 1075–1097.

Wijffels, A.A., 'Business Relations between Merchants in Sixteenth-Century Belgian Practice-Orientated Civil Law Literature', in: Piergiovanni, V. (ed.), *From Lex Mercatoria to Commercial Law* (Berlin 2005), 255–290.

Wijffels, A.A., 'Justitia in Commerciis: Public Governance and Commercial Litigation before the Great Council of Mechlin in the Late Fifteenth and Early Sixteenth Century', in: Pihlajamäki, H., Cordes, A., Dauchy, S. & De ruysscher, D. (eds.), *Understanding the Sources of Early Modern and Modern Commercial Law: Courts, Statutes, Contracts, and Legal Scholarship* (Leiden/Boston 2018), 32–54.

Wijffels, C., 'Een Antwerpse zeeverzekeringspolis uit het jaar 1557', *Handelingen van de Koninklijke Commissie voor Geschiedenis*, 63, 1–2 (1948), 95–103.

Wijffels, C., 'De Vlaamse Hanze van Londen op het einde van de XIIIe eeuw', *Handelingen van het Genootschap voor Geschiedenis*, 97, 1 (1960), 5–30.

Williams, A.C. & Heins, R.M., *Risk Management and Insurance* (New York 1964).

Williamson, O.E., 'Transaction-Cost Economics: The Governance of Contractual Relations', *Journal of Law and Economics*, 22 (1979), 233–262.

Williamson, O.E., 'The Economics of Organization: The Transaction Costs Approach', *American Journal of Sociology*, 87, 3 (1981), 548–577.

Wouters, K., 'Een open oligarchie? De machtstructuur in de Antwerpse magistraat tijdens de periode 1520–1555', *Revue belge de philologie et d'histoire*, 82, 4 (2004), 905–934.

Wubs-Mrozewicz, J.J., 'Conflict Management and Interdisciplinary History', *Tijdschrift voor Sociale en Economische Geschiedenis*, 15, 1 (2018), 89–107.

Wubs-Mrozewicz, J.J. & Wijffels, A.A., 'Diplomacy and Advocacy: The Aase of the *King of Denmark v. Dutch Skippers* before the Danzig City Council (1564–1567)', *Tijdschrift voor Rechtsgeschiedenis*, 84 (2016), 1–53.

Yante, J-M., 'Commerce et marchands italiens dans les Pays-Bas (XIVe–XVIe siècles)', *Publications du Centre Européen d'Etudes Bourguignonnes*, 49 (2009), 87–99.

Yante, J-M., 'Le commerce espagnol dans les Pays-Bas (XVe–XVIe siècles)', *Publications du Centre Européen d'Etudes Bourguignonnes*, 51 (2011), 217–232.

Yun-Casalilla, B., *Iberian World Empires and the Globalization of Europe 1415–1668* (Singapore 2019).

Van Zanden, J.L., 'Holland en de Zuidelijke Nederlanden in de periode 1500–1570: divergerende ontwikkelingen of voortgaande economische integratie', in: Aerts, E., Henau, B., Janssens, B. & Van Uytven, R. (eds.), *Studia historica oeconomica. Liber Amicorum Herman van der Wee* (Louvain 1993), 357–368.

Van Zanden, J.L., 'The "Revolt of the Early Modernists" and the "First Modern Economy": An Assessment', *The Economic History Review*, 55, 4 (2002), 619–641.

Van Zanden, J.L., *The Long Road to the Industrial Revolution: The European economy in a Global Perspective, 1000–1800* (Leiden/Boston 2009).

Van Zanden, J.L. & Van Tielhof, M., 'Roots of Growth and Productivity Change in Dutch Shipping Industry, 1500–1800', *Explorations in Economic History*, 46 (2009), 389–403.

Zijlmans, R.F.G.M., *Troebele betrekkingen. Grens, scheepvaart- en waterstaatskwesties in de Nederlanden tot 1800* (Hilversum 2017).

Published Lectures

Koeningsberger, H.G., '*"Dominium Regale"* or *"Dominium Politicum et Regale"*: Monarchies and Parliaments in Early Modern Europe', Inaugural lecture, University of London King's College, 25th February 1975.

North, D.C., *Transaction Costs, Institutions, and Economic Performance*, International Center for Economic Growth Occasional Paper Series, nr. 30 (San Francisco 1992).

Spufford, P., *From Antwerp to London. The Decline of Financial Centres in Europe.* Ortelius Lecture NIAS 4 (Wassenaar 2005).

Internet Sources

Cordes, A., 'Conflicts in 13th-century Maritime Law: A Comparison between five European Ports', *Oxford University Comparative Law Forum* 2 (2020), https://ouclf.law.ox.ac.uk/conflicts-in-13th-century-maritime-law-a-comparison-between-five-european-ports/ {Retrieved 19/10/2020}.

Foster, N., 'Foundation Myth as Legal Formant: The Medieval Law Merchant and the New Lex Mercatoria, Forum Historiae Iuris, https://forhistiur.de/legacy/zitat/0503foster.htm {Retrieved 14/05/2020}.

'Suez Canal: Fresh Efforts to Refloat Wedged Container Ship', *BBC*, available at https://www.bbc.com/news/world-middle-east-56550350 {Retrieved 20/12/2021}.

'Ever Given, vrachtship dat wereldhandel ontregelde, arriveert in Rotterdam', *NRC*, available at https://www.nrc.nl/nieuws/2021/07/29/ever-given-vrachtschip-dat-wereldhandel-ontregelde-arriveert-in-rotterdam-a4052826 {Retrieved 20/12/2021}.

'General Average Declared for Stricken Maersk Honam Vessel', *Lloyd's Loading List*, available at https://www.lloydsloadinglist.com/freight-directory/news/General-average-declared-for-stricken-Maersk-Honam-vessel/71536.htm {Retrieved 18/03/2020}.

'More Holistic, Industry Wide Approach to Containers would be Welcomed: AP Muller-Maersk CTO', *Insurance Marine News*, available at https://insurancemarinenews.com/insurance-marine-news/more-holistic-industry-wide-approach-to-containers-would-be-welcomed-ap-moller-maersk-cto/ {Retrieved 30/10/2020}.

'High Costs expected after Maersk Honam Fire', *World Maritime News*, available at https://worldmaritimenews.com/archives/247260/high-costs-expected-after-maersk-honam-fire/ {Retrieved 25/03/2020}.

https://humanities.exeter.ac.uk/history/research/centres/maritime/research/avetransrisk/team/ {Retrieved 14/04/2020}.

https://humanities.exeter.ac.uk/history/research/centres/maritime/research/avetransrisk/summary/ {Retrieved 05/05/2020}.

https://humanities.exeter.ac.uk/history/research/centres/maritime/research/avetransrisk/glossary/ {Retrieved 30/06/2020}.

http://humanities-research.exeter.ac.uk/avetransrisk/average/example/ {Retrieved 20/07/2020}. http://humanities.exeter.ac.uk/history/research/centres/maritime/research/avetransrisk/ {Retrieved 31/08/2020}.

http://humanities.exeter.ac.uk/history/research/centres/maritime/research/avetransrisk/datasets/ {Retrieved 31/08/2020}.

http://humanities.exeter.ac.uk/media/level1/academicserviceswebsite/it/documents/avetransrisk/RolesOnBoardSpanishShips.pdf {Retrieved 21/01/2021}.

http://humanities.exeter.ac.uk/history/research/centres/maritime/research/modernity/roles/ {Retrieved 21/01/2021}.

http://riskybusinessdb.nl/ {Retrieved 24/04/2020}.

https://www.oed.com/view/Entry/71946?redirectedFrom=flotsam#eid {Retrieved 25/06/2020}.

https://www.oed.com/view/Entry/101177#eid40368110 {Retrieved 25/06/2020}.

https://www.oed.com/view/Entry/210212#eid17064071 {Retrieved 05/02/2021}.

https://www.oed.com/view/Entry/166306?rskey=t5t3bY&result=1&isAdvanced=false#eid {Retrieved 05/02/2021}.

https://www.oed.com/view/Entry/42302?isAdvanced=false&result=3&rskey=R2ev64& {Retrieved 05/02/2021}.

https://www.oed.com/view/Entry/122086?redirectedFrom=moral+hazard#eid36035063 {Retrieved 21/01/2021}.

https://www.oed.com/view/Entry/147370?redirectedFrom=polysemy#eid {Retrieved 21/01/2021}.

https://www.oed.com/view/Entry/38477?redirectedFrom=condemnation#eid {Retrieved 19/01/2021}.

https://www.oed.com/view/Entry/47005?rskey=RZs3zv&result=1#eid {Retrieved 08/03/2021}.

https://en.oxforddictionaries.com/definition/average {retrieved 13/06/2018}.

http://www.duhaime.org/LegalDictionary/Y/YorkAntwerpRules.aspx {retrieved 15/11/2017}.

http://www.duhaime.org/LawMuseum/LawArticle-383/Lex-Rhodia-The-Ancient-Ancestor-of-Maritime-Law-800-BC.aspx {Retrieved 03/10/2019}.

https://www.britannica.com/topic/efficiency-economics-and-organizational-analysis {Retrieved 22/01/2021}.

https://comitemaritime.org/work/york-antwerp-rules-yar/ {Retrieved 30/06/2020}.

https://thelawdictionary.org/act-of-god/ {Retrieved 17/07/2020}.

https://en.wiktionary.org/wiki/club_good {Retrieved 27/01/2020}.

https://www.debinnenvaart.nl/binnenvaarttaal/index.php?woord=ver#verbodemen {Retrieved 27/04/2020}.

Unpublished Secondary Literature

Addobbati, A., 'Principles and Inferences of General Average: Statutory and Contractual Loss Allowances from the *Lex Rhodia* to the Early Modern Mediterranean', in: Fusaro, M., Addobbati, A. & Piccinno, L. (eds.), *General Average and Risk Management in Medieval and Early Modern Europe* (forthcoming).

Asaert, G., 'Onder de vlag met de hand' (Unpublished book, Antwerp, 2019) (2 Vols.).

Braekevelt, J., *Une prince de justice. Vorstelijke wetgeving, soevereiniteit en staatsvorming in het graafschap Vlaanderen tijdens de regering van Filips de Goede (1419–1467)* (Unpublished PhD thesis, Ghent University 2013).

Cassiers, M., *Bijdrage tot de geschiedenis van de Antwerpse scheepvaart en scheepvaartbeweging in het midden van de 16e eeuw (1555–1558)* (Unpublished MA thesis, Ghent University, 1978).

Dreijer, G.P., 'Castilian Normative Practice and the Development of General Average in the Southern Low Countries (Sixteenth Century)', in: Fusaro, M., Addobbati, A. & Piccinno, L. (eds.), *General Average and Risk Management in Medieval and Early Modern Europe* (forthcoming).

Everaert, J., *Macht in de metropool: politieke elitevorming tijdens de demografische en economische bloeifase van Antwerpen (ca. 1400–1550)* (Unpublished PhD thesis, Vrije Universiteit Brussel & University of Antwerp 2020).

Fusaro, M., 'Sharing Risks, on Averages and Why They Matter', in: Fusaro, M., Addobbati, A. & Piccinno, L. (eds.), *General Average and Risk Management in Medieval and Early Modern Europe* (forthcoming).

García Garralón, M., 'The Nautical Republic of the *Carrera de Indias*: Commerce, Navigation, Fortuitous Mishaps, and *avería gruesa* in the Sixteenth Century', in: Fusaro, M., Addobbati, A. & Piccinno, L. (eds.), *General Average and Risk Management in Medieval and Early Modern Europe* (forthcoming).

Go, S.C.P.J., 'GA Adjustments in Amsterdam: Reinforcing Authority through Transparency and Accountability (Late Sixteenth–Early Seventeenth Century)', in: Fusaro, M., Addobbati, A. & Piccinno, L. (eds.), *General Average and Risk Management in Medieval and Early Modern Europe* (forthcoming).

Khalilieh, H.S., 'Rules and Practices of General Average in the Islamic Mediterranean on the Eve of the Emergence of the Italian Communes', in: Fusaro, M., Addobbati, A. & Piccinno, L. (eds.), *General Average and Risk Management in Medieval and Early Modern Europe* (forthcoming).

Kohn, M., 'Risk Instruments in the Medieval and Early Modern Economy', Dartmouth College Department of Economics Working Paper No 99–07, available at https://papers.ssrn.com/sol3/papers.cfm?abstract_id=151871.

Maggiore, L., *De Italiaanse kolonie te Antwerpen (1598–1648)* (Unpublished MA thesis, Leuven University 1998).

Schaffer, S., 'Newtonian Calculations', Unpublished paper presented Genoa 18-05-2019.

Signori, U., *Venezia e Smirne tra sei e settecento. Istituzioni, commerci e communitá mercantile* (Unpublished PhD thesis, University of Padova 2014).

Verbist, B., *Traditie of innovatie? Wouter Ameyde, een makelaar in het laatmiddeleeuwse Brugge* (Unpublished PhD thesis, University of Antwerp 2014).

Wade, L., *Privilege at a Premium: Insurance, Maritime Law and Political Economy in Early Modern France, 1664–c. 1710* (Unpublished PhD thesis, University of Exeter 2021).

Wastiels, A., *Juan Henriquez, makelaar in zeeverzekeringen te Antwerpen (1562–1563)* (Unpublished MA thesis, Ghent University 1967).

Wells, G.E., *Antwerp and the Government of Philip II: 1555–1567* (Unpublished PhD thesis, Cornell University 1982).

Index